with love,   Christmas 2016
Gela

CLASSIC YELLOWSTONE

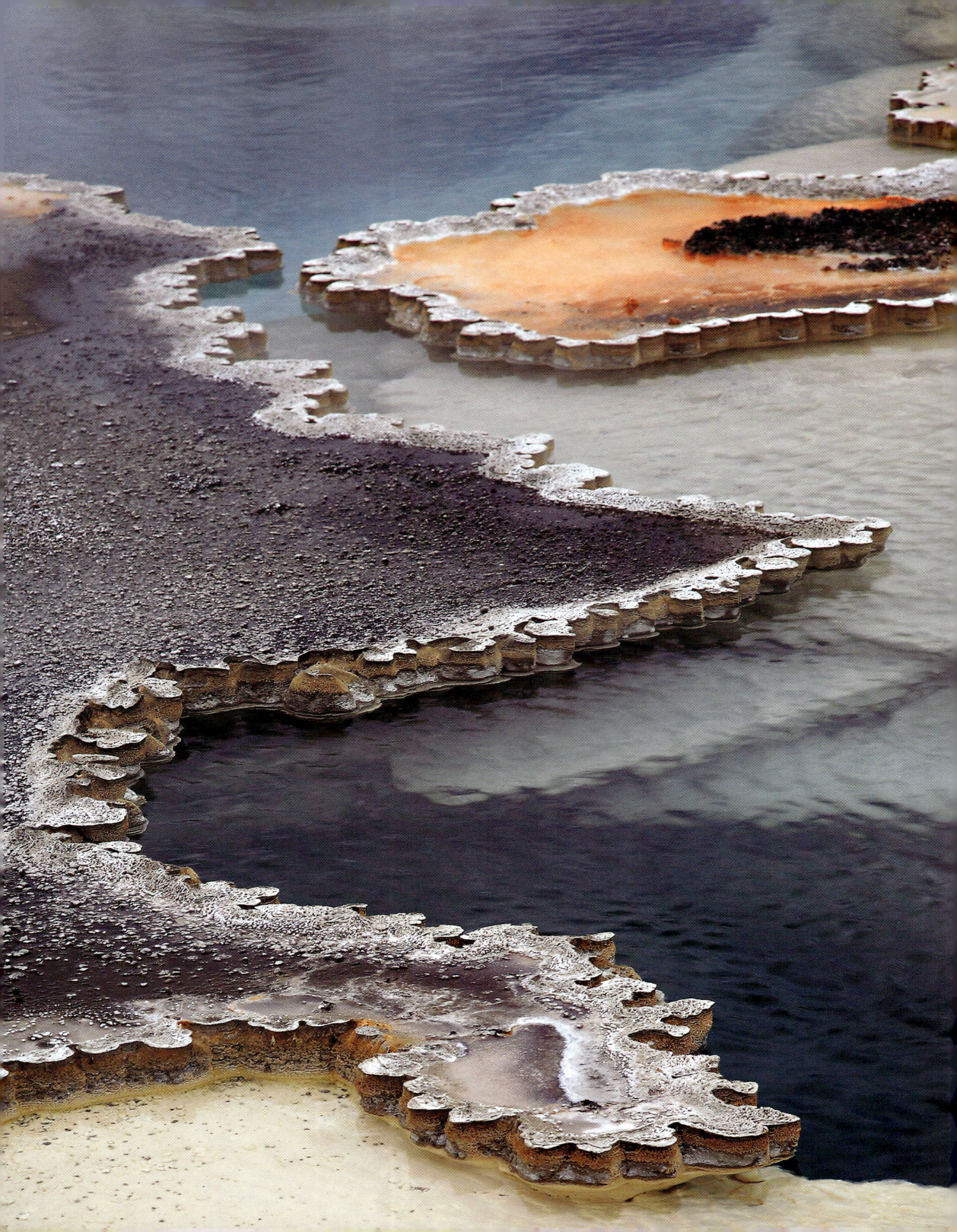

CLASSIC YELLOWSTONE

THE BEST OF THE WORLD'S FIRST NATIONAL PARK

SUSAN M. NEIDER

RAINSTONE PRESS

OTHER TITLES BY THE AUTHOR

Color Country: Touring the Colorado Plateau

High Country: Touring the Colorado Rockies

Golden Country: Touring Scenic California

Wild Yosemite: Personal Accounts of Adventure,
Discovery, and Nature

Some Like It Hot! Yellowstone's Favorite Geysers,
Hot Springs, and Fumaroles

www.susanmneider.com

Classic Yellowstone
Copyright 2015 by Susan M. Neider
Published by Rainstone Press

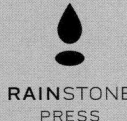

RAINSTONE
PRESS

Cover: Midway Geyser Basin
Title page: Doublet Pool

ISBN-10: 0985778318

ISBN-13: 978-0-9857783-1-6

Photographs by Susan M. Neider except for pages 46 (top), 131, and 250
by Anne N. Ferry; p. 220 (top) by James M. Ferry; and p. 240 by Ernest J.
DeLaCruz, M.D.

Design by Jeff Wincapaw, Tintype Studio

Printed and bound in the Unites States of America by QuadGraphics
Distributed by Mountain Press Publishing Company
800-234-5308 www.mountain-press.com

The author and the publisher assume no liability for accidents happening
to, or injuries sustained by, readers who engage in the activities described
in this book.

Some animals were photographed in captivity or outside the boundaries
of Yellowstone National Park. All are representative of the species found
within.

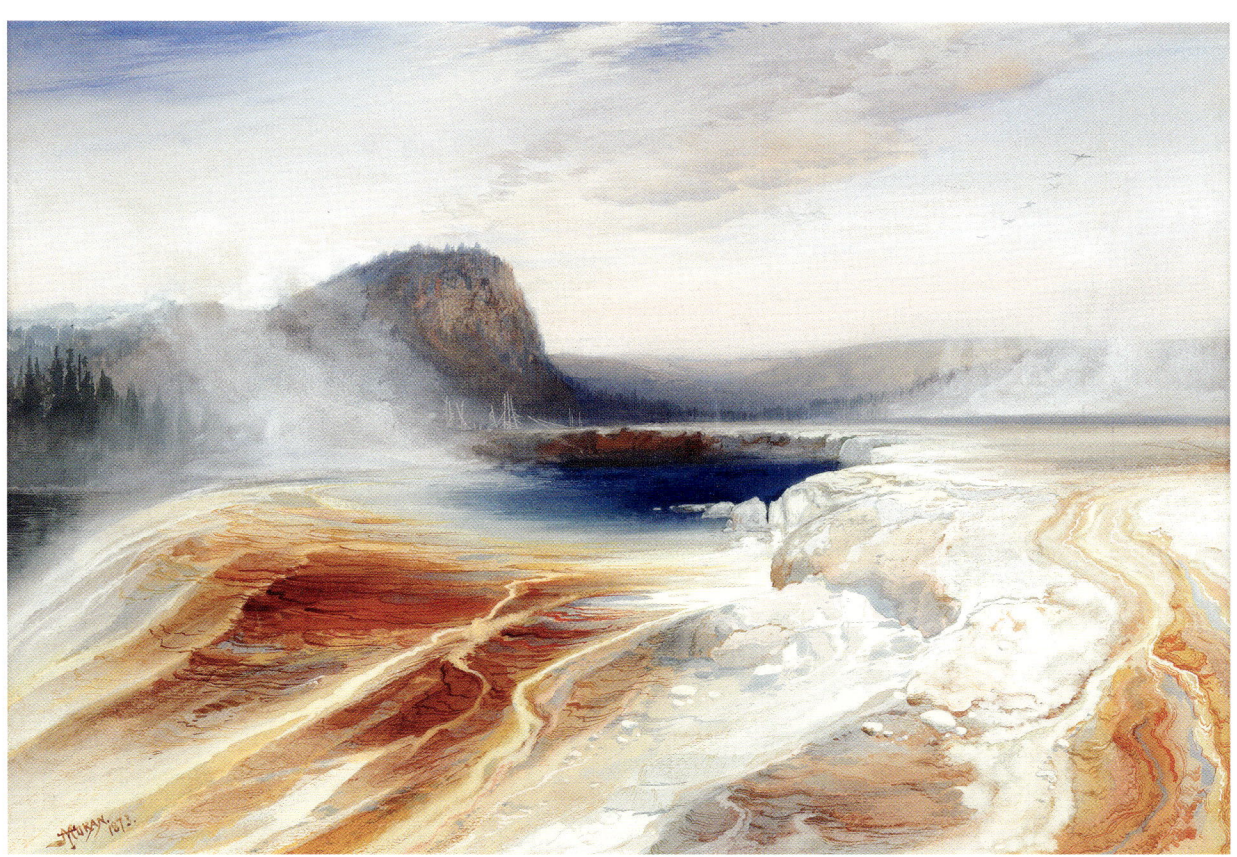

Lower Geyser Basin
Thomas Moran, 1873
Gilcrease Museum, Tulsa, OK
0226.1365

"Every artist of genius experiences during his life a great spiritual revelation and upheaval. This revelation came to Thomas Moran as he journeyed on horseback through an almost unbelievable wilderness. To him it was all grandeur, beauty, color, and light—nothing of man at all, but nature, virgin, unspoiled and lovely. In the Yellowstone country he found fairy-like color and form that his dreams could not rival."

THOMAS MORAN'S DAUGHTER

"Yellowstone retains its hold upon my imagination with a vividness of yesterday.... The impression then made upon me by the stupendous and remarkable manifestations of nature's forces will remain with me as long as memory lasts."

THOMAS MORAN (1837-1926)

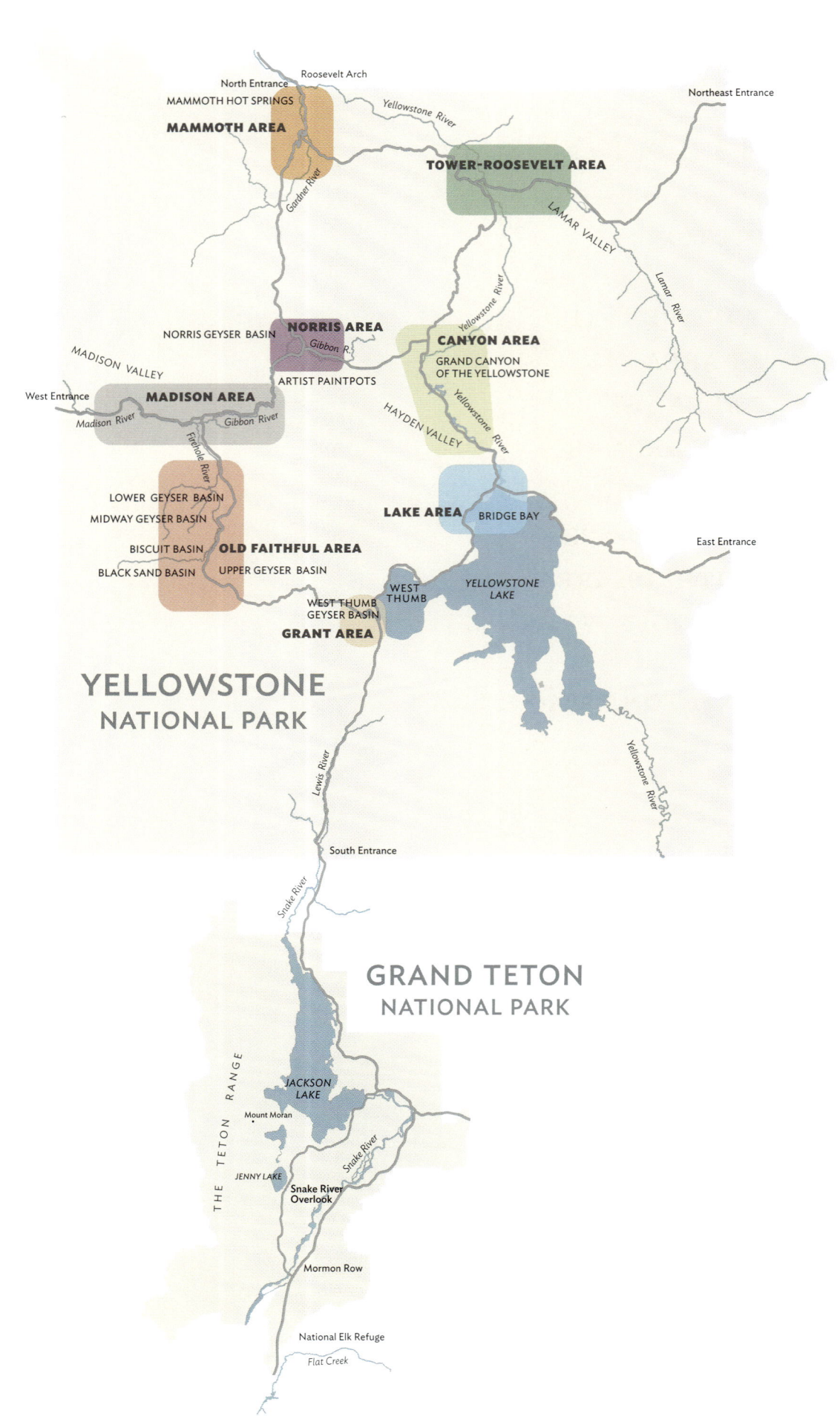

Roosevelt Arch

North Entrance

MAMMOTH HOT SPRINGS

MAMMOTH AREA

Northeast Entrance

Yellowstone River

TOWER-ROOSEVELT AREA

Gardner River

LAMAR VALLEY

Lamar River

NORRIS GEYSER BASIN

NORRIS AREA

Gibbon R.

CANYON AREA

GRAND CANYON
OF THE YELLOWSTONE

Yellowstone River

MADISON VALLEY

ARTIST PAINTPOTS

West Entrance

MADISON AREA

Madison River   *Gibbon River*

HAYDEN VALLEY

Yellowstone River

Firehole River

LOWER GEYSER BASIN

MIDWAY GEYSER BASIN

LAKE AREA   BRIDGE BAY

East Entrance

BISCUIT BASIN   **OLD FAITHFUL AREA**

BLACK SAND BASIN   UPPER GEYSER BASIN

**WEST
THUMB**

*YELLOWSTONE
LAKE*

WEST THUMB
GEYSER BASIN

GRANT AREA

YELLOWSTONE
NATIONAL PARK

Yellowstone River

Lewis River

South Entrance

Snake River

GRAND TETON
NATIONAL PARK

*JACKSON
LAKE*

Mount Moran

THE TETON RANGE

Snake River

JENNY LAKE

**Snake River
Overlook**

Mormon Row

National Elk Refuge

Flat Creek

CONTENTS

"Mr. [Cornelius] Hedges then said that he did not approve of any of these plans—that there ought to be no private ownership of any portion of that region, but that the whole of it ought to be set apart as a great National Park, and that each one of us ought to make an effort to have this accomplished."

Sapphire Pool in Biscuit Basin

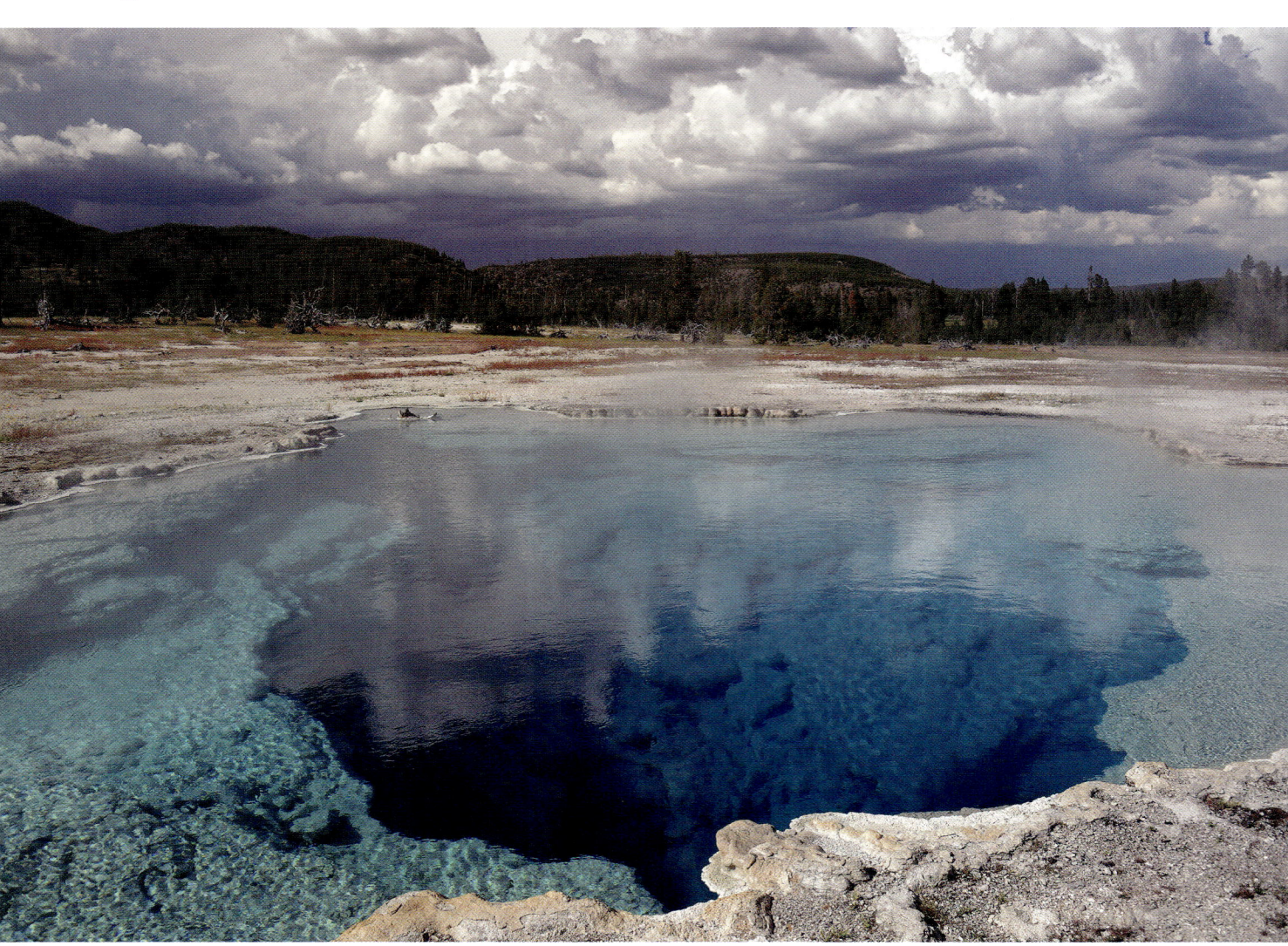

INTRODUCTION

"Tuesday, September 20, 1870.—Last night, and also this morning in camp, the entire party had a rather unusual discussion. The proposition was made by some member that we utilize the result of our exploration by taking up quarter sections of land at the most prominent points of interest, and a general discussion followed. One member of our party suggested that if there could be secured by pre-emption a good title to two or three quarter sections of land opposite the lower fall of the Yellowstone and extending down the river along the canyon, they would eventually become a source of great profit to the owners. Another member of the party thought that it would be more desirable to take up a quarter section of land at the Upper Geyser Basin, for the reason that that locality could be more easily reached by tourists and pleasure seekers. A third suggestion was that each member of the party pre-empt a claim, and in order that no one should have an advantage over the others, the whole should be thrown into a common pool for the benefit of the entire party.

"Mr. [Cornelius] Hedges then said that he did not approve of any of these plans—that there ought to be no private ownership of any portion of that region, but that the whole of it ought to be set apart as a great National Park, and that each one of us ought to make an effort to have this accomplished. His suggestion met with an instantaneous and favorable response from all—except one—of the members of our party, and each hour since the matter was first broached, our enthusiasm has increased. It has been the main theme of our conversation today as we journeyed. I lay awake half of last night thinking about it;—and if my wakefulness deprived my bed-fellow (Hedges) of any sleep, he has only himself and his disturbing National Park proposition to answer for it.

"Our purpose to create a park can only be accomplished by untiring work and concerted action in a warfare against the incredulity and unbelief of our National legislators when our proposal shall be presented for their approval. Nevertheless, I believe we can win the battle.

"I do not know of any portion of our country where a national park can be established furnishing to visitors more wonderful attractions than here. These wonders are so different from anything we have ever seen—they are so various, so extensive—that the feeling in my mind from the moment they began to appear until we left them has been one of intense surprise and of incredulity. Every day spent in surveying them has revealed to me some new beauty, and now that I have left them, I begin to feel a skepticism which clothes them in a memory clouded by doubt."

NATHANIEL PITT LANGFORD
The Discovery of Yellowstone Park:
Journal of the Washburn Expedition
to the Yellowstone and Firehole Rivers
in the Year 1870, 1905

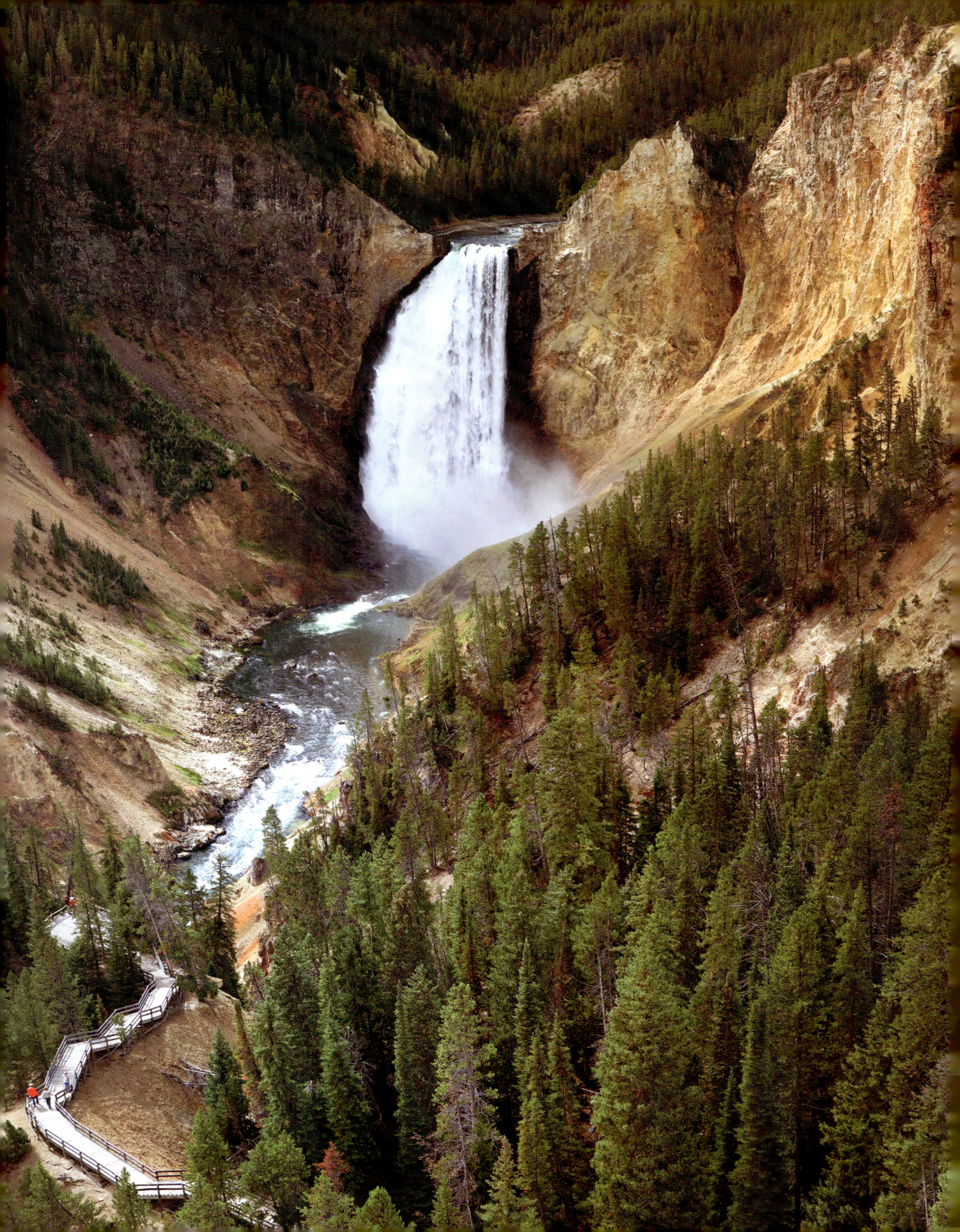

CANYON AREA

GRAND CANYON OF THE YELLOWSTONE
> ARTIST POINT

> BRINK OF THE LOWER FALLS

> LOOKOUT POINT

> POINT SUBLIME AND INSPIRATION POINT

HAYDEN VALLEY
> YELLOWSTONE RIVER

MUD VOLCANO AREA
> DRAGON'S MOUTH SPRING

> MUD CALDRON

> MUD VOLCANO

Lower Falls

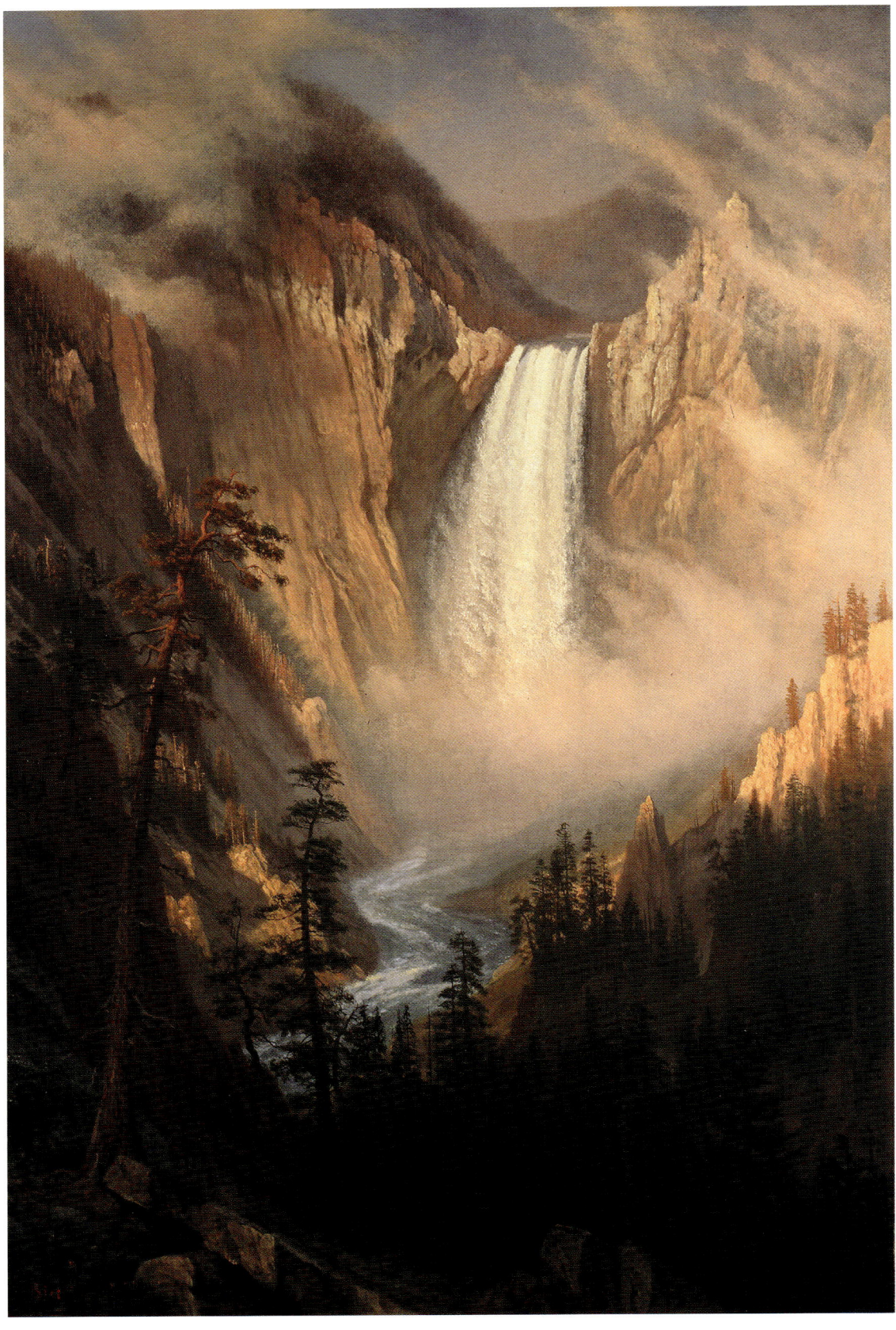

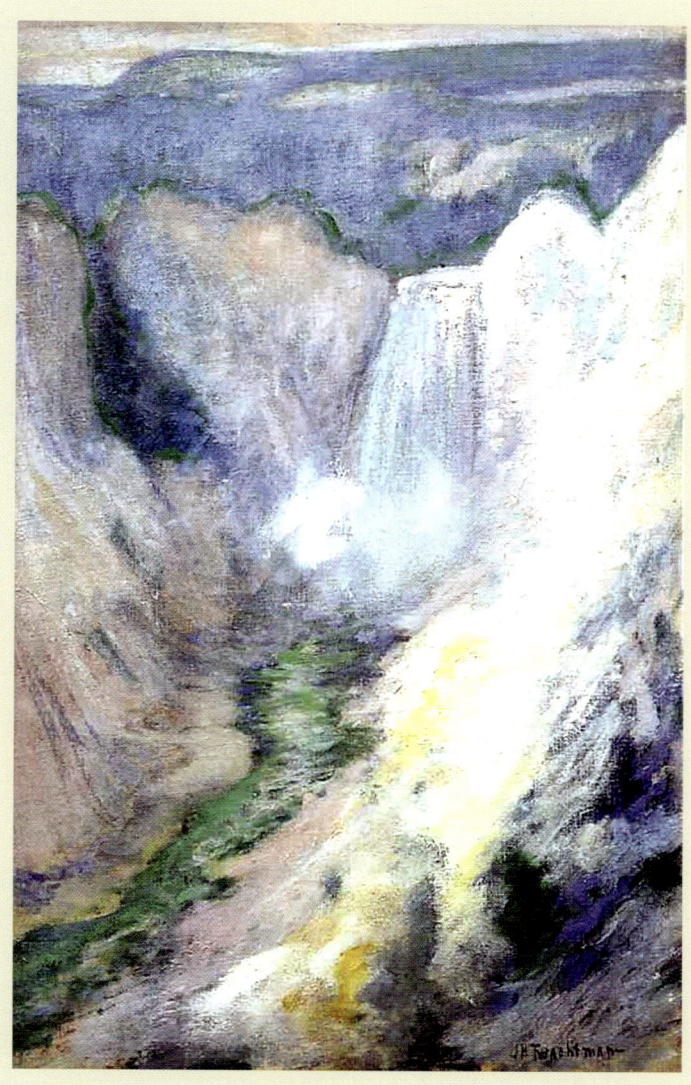

Waterfall in Yellowstone
John Henry Twachtman, 1895

<

Yellowstone Falls
Albert Bierstadt, 1881

"Every great cascade has a language and an idea peculiarly it own, embodied, as it were, in the flow of its waters. Thus the impression on the mind conveyed by Niagara may be summed up as 'Overwhelming power;' of the Yosemite, as 'Altitude;' of the Shoshone fall, in the midst of a desert, as 'Going to waste.' So the upper fall of the Yellowstone may be said to embody the idea of 'Momentum,' and the lower fall of 'Gravitation.'"

LIEUTENANT GUSTAVUS C. DOANE
Yellowstone Expedition of 1870

GRAND CANYON
OF THE
YELLOWSTONE

"This has been a 'red-letter' day with me, and one which I shall not soon forget, for my mind is clogged and my memory confused by what I have today seen. General Washburn and Mr. [Cornelius] Hedges are sitting near me, writing, and we have an understanding that we will compare our notes when finished. We are all overwhelmed with astonishment and wonder at what we have seen, and we feel that we have been near the very presence of the Almighty. General Washburn has just quoted from the psalm:

'When I behold the work of Thy hands, what is man
    that Thou art mindful of him!'

"My own mind is so confused that I hardly know where to commence in making a clear record of what is at this moment floating past my mental vision. I cannot confine myself to a bare description of the falls of the Yellowstone alone, for these two great cataracts are but one feature in a scene composed of so many of the elements of grandeur and sublimity, that I almost despair of giving to those who on our return home will listen to a recital of our adventures, the faintest conception of it. The immense canyon or gorge of rocks through which the river descends, perhaps more than the falls, is calculated to fill the observer with feelings of mingled awe and terror.

"The stillness is horrible, and the solemn grandeur of the scene surpasses conception. You feel the absence of sound—the oppression of absolute silence. Down, down, down, you see the river attenuated to a thread. If you could only hear that gurgling river, lashing with puny strength the massive walls that imprison it and hold it in their dismal shadow, if you could but see a living thing in the depth beneath you, if a bird would but fly past you, if the wind would move any object in that awful chasm, to break for a moment the solemn silence which reigns there, it would relieve that tension of the nerves which the scene has excited, and with a grateful heart you would thank God that he had permitted you to gaze unharmed upon this majestic display of his handiwork. But as it is, the spirit of man sympathizes with the deep gloom of the scene, and the brain reels as you gaze into this profound and solemn solitude.

"The place where I obtained the best and most terrible view of the canyon was a narrow projecting point [Inspiration Point] situated two or three miles below the lower fall. Standing there or rather lying there for greater safety, I thought how utterly impossible it would be to describe to another the sensations inspired by such a presence. As I took in this scene, I realized my own littleness, my helplessness, my dread exposure to destruction, my inability to cope with or even comprehend the mighty architecture of nature. More than all this I felt as never before my entire dependence upon that Almighty Power who had wrought these wonders. A sense of danger, lest the rock should crumble away, almost overpowered me. My knees trembled, and I experienced the terror which causes men to turn pale and their countenances to blanch with fear, and I recoiled from the vision I had seen, glad to feel the solid earth beneath me and to realize the assurance of returning safety.

"The two grand falls of the Yellowstone form a fitting completion to this stupendous climax of wonders. They impart life, power, light and majesty to an assemblage of elements, which without them would be the most gloomy and horrible solitude in nature. Their eternal anthem, echoing from canyon, mountain, rock and woodland, thrills you with delight, and you gaze with rapture at the iris-crowned curtains of fleecy foam as they plunge into gulfs enveloped in mist and spray. The stillness which held your senses spellbound, as you peered into the dismal depths of the canyon below, is now broken by the uproar of waters; the terror it inspired is superseded by admiration and astonishment, and the scene, late so painful from its silence and gloom, is now animate with joy and revelry.

"Very beautiful as is this [upper] fall, it is greatly excelled in grandeur and magnificence by the cataract half a mile below it, where the river takes another perpendicular plunge of three hundred and twenty feet into the most gloomy cavern that ever received so majestic a visitant. Between the two falls, the river, though bordered by lofty precipices, expands in width and flows gently over a nearly level surface until its near approach to the verge. Here a sudden convergence in the rocks compresses its channel, and with a gurgling, choking struggle, it leaps with a single bound, sheer from an even level shelf, into the tremendous chasm. The sheet could not be more perfect if wrought by art. The Almighty has vouchsafed no grander scene to human eyes. Every object that meets the vision increases its sublimity. There is a majestic harmony in the whole, which I have never seen before in nature's grandest works. The fall itself takes its leap between the jaws of rocks whose vertical height above it is more than six hundred feet, and more than nine hundred feet above the chasm into which it falls. Long before it reaches the base it is enveloped in spray, which is woven by the sun's rays into bows radiant with all the colors of the prism, and arching the face of the cataract with their glories. Five hundred feet below the edge of the canyon, and one hundred and sixty feet above the verge of the cataract, and overlooking the deep gorge beneath, on the flattened summit of a projecting crag, I lay with my face turned into the boiling chasm, and with a stone suspended by a large cord measured its profoundest depths. Three times in its descent the cord was parted by abrasion, but at last, securing the weight with a leather band, I was enabled to ascertain by a measurement which I think quite exact, the height of the fall. It is a little more than three hundred and twenty feet; while the perpendicular wall down which I suspended the weight was five hundred and ten feet.

"Mr. Hedges and I sat on the table-rock to which I have referred, opposite the upper fall, as long as our limited time would permit; and as we reluctantly left it and climbed to the top, I expressed my regret at leaving so fascinating a spot, quoting the familiar line:

'A thing of beauty is a joy forever.'

"Mr. Hedges asked me who was the author of the line, but I could not tell. I will look it up on my return. [John Keats]

"Yes! This stupendous display of nature's handiwork will be to me 'a joy forever.' It lingers in my memory like the faintly defined outlines of a dream. I can scarcely realize that in the unbroken solitude of this majestic range of rocks, away from civilization and almost inaccessible to human approach, the Almighty has placed so many of the most wonderful and magnificent objects of His creation, and that I am to be one of the few first to bring them to the notice of the world. Truly has it been said, that we live to learn how little may be known, and of what we see, how much surpasses comprehension."

NATHANIEL PITT LANGFORD
The Discovery of Yellowstone Park: Journal of the Washburn Expedition to the Yellowstone and Firehole Rivers in the Year 1870, 1905

"A hundred feet higher than Niagara, [the Lower Fall of the Yellowstone] is far more beautiful than Niagara, in spite of the loss of breadth, because of its magnificent setting in the noblest mountain scenery. It adds to the impressiveness, too, that you can see hardly anything of the river before it makes the plunge. It makes an abrupt turn just before its leap, so that what you see is not a long, prosaic stream dropping suddenly over a rock; but only what looks like a small and quiet pool, sending this splendid messenger to the river below.

"The milk-white walls drop suddenly from the very edge of the dark pine forests, down, down, down, down, carved into most splendid grottoes holding, perhaps, snow in their deep recesses, rising again in slender pinnacles on which the eagles build their nests, and may be seen fluttering around them, looking like sparrows in the distance; down, down, to the river, clasped, but not held, in this splendid embrace, not lying as the guide-books say 'like a green ribbon' or 'a silver thread,' at their base, but writhing, gleaming, hurrying from these strong arms like a great, glittering, splendid serpent, alive, determined, terrible, but too far away to be dangerous, its emerald scales glorious in the sunlight.

"Yet it is not the height of the cliffs alone, nor their wonderful sculpture, that makes the Yellowstone Canyon what it is. The cliffs in Colorado are often higher and steeper, or quite as beautifully carved. As one of the guides put it, 'There's canyons most anywhere; but they ain't painted.' Here, if anywhere, is the place to recall Sir Thomas Brown's definition of Nature, as 'the art of God.' The splendor of color at the Yellowstone—the gorgeous streaks of crimson, orange, violet, and green—are even more wonderful than the snowy walls themselves. It is less the color, than the purity of the color, that makes the scene such a wealth of glowing loveliness. These are not merely alternate layers of dull red and pale yellow, curious but faint, like those which are thought so remarkable at Gay Head [Martha's Vineyard]; nor does 'snowy' mean here, as it is apt to be when applied to nature, merely a soiled and grimy gray. What is snowy is milk-white; what is red is blood-red; what is pink is the loveliest rose-color. . . .

"Perhaps the best word to describe it, to distinguish it from other noble canyons, is *fascinating*. It is not less awful, less beautiful, less sublime, than other higher canyons; but it has the added quality of fascination. It holds you. It is a scene of which it is no exaggeration to say that it brings tears to the eyes. It is the one place where it seems as if nature might have a soul. There she seems, not only beautiful, but conscious that she is beautiful. She smiles back at you with a splendid smile, like a glorious woman whom you may both adore and love. . . . That the geysers were too exactly like the pictures of them expresses in a negative way what the canyon is in a positive way. You have a complete and perfect idea of what a geyser is from any good photograph of one. You know exactly how the Royal Gorge of the Arkansas looks from the best pictures of it. But no picture, not even an oil

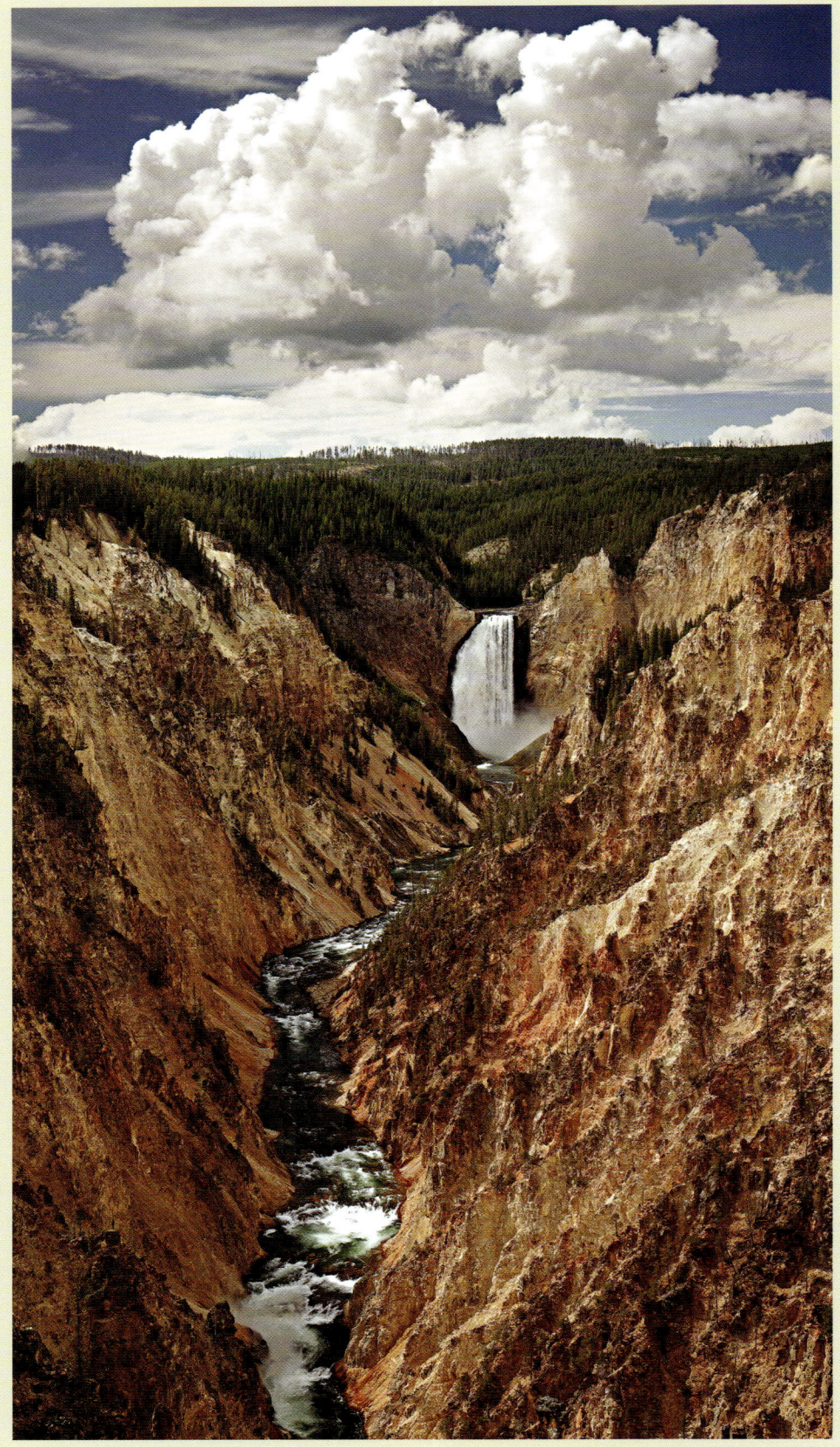

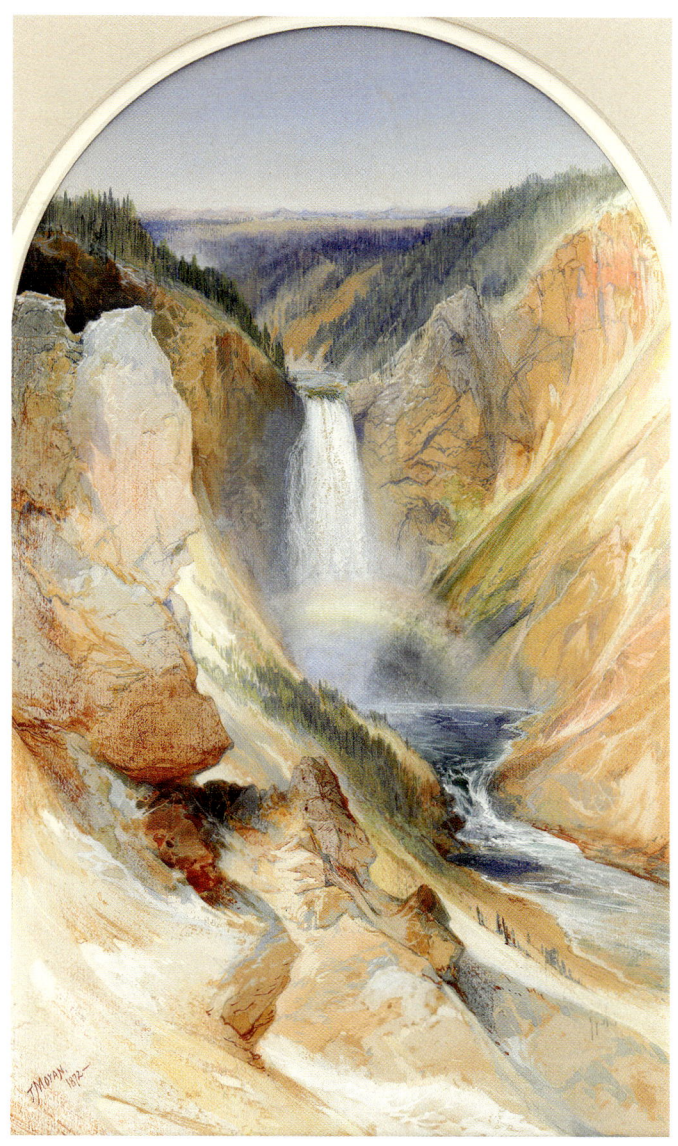

Wyoming Falls, Yellowstone River
Thomas Moran, 1872
Gilcrease Museum, Tulsa, OK
0226.1452

‹

Lower Falls and the Yellowstone River
from Artist Point

painting that attempts to reproduce the colors, can give you the faintest conception of what it will mean to you if ever it should be your glorious privilege to gaze into the canyon of the Yellowstone.

"And this is another test. As awed as you are by the Royal Gorge, much as you admire the Black Canyon, picturesque as Clear Creek Canyon is to you, you never think of lingering, or wanting to linger, in any of them. Though you whirl through them all in a railway car, you are satisfied. They have been enchanting, stupendous, marvelous; you say to yourself that sometime you will certainly come and see them again. But at the Yellowstone you say that you will never go away!"

ALICE WELLINGTON ROLLINS
The Three Tetons, 1887

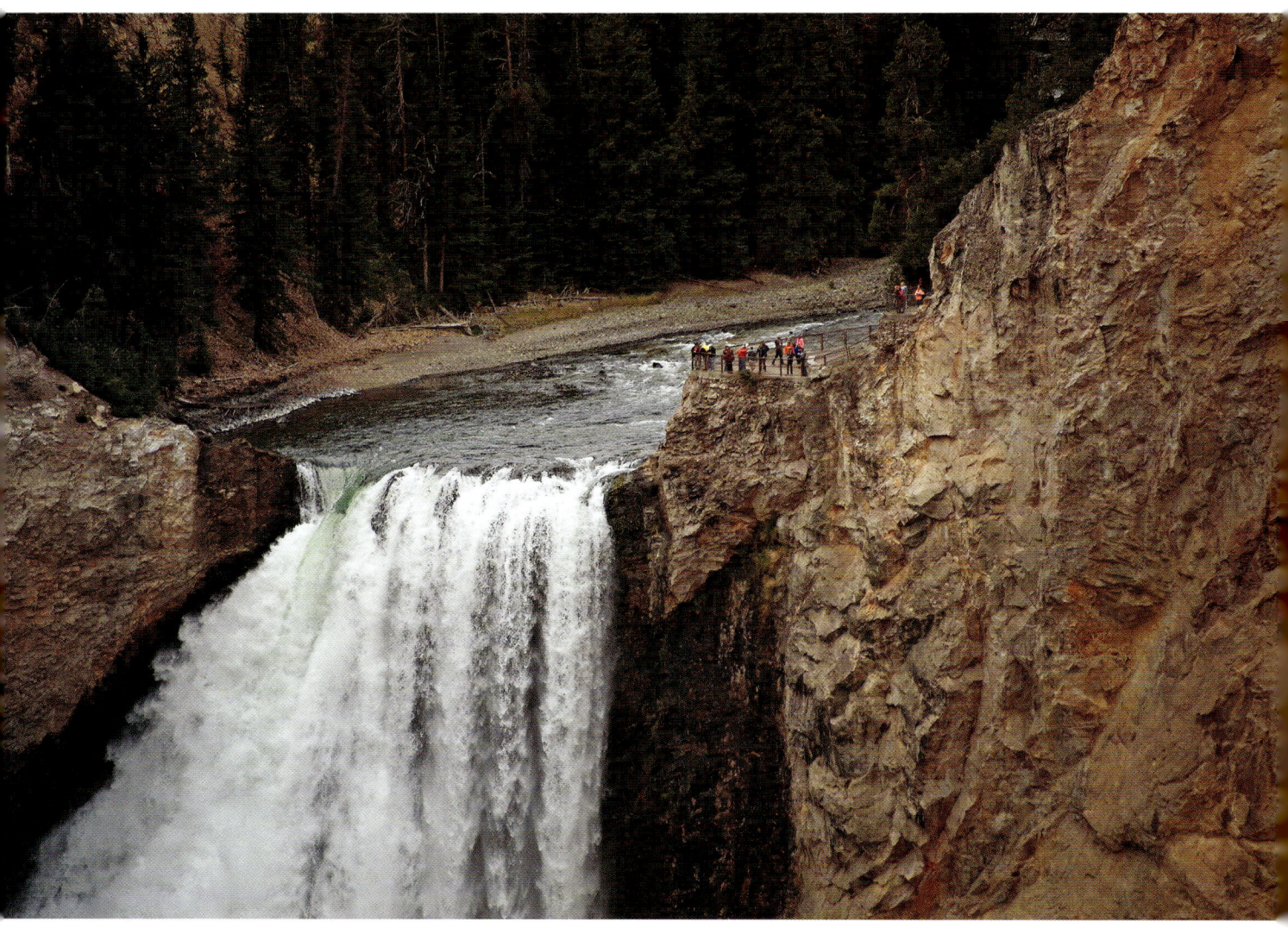

"The scene was wild and savage in the extreme. On both sides of us rugged mountains towered almost perpendicularly three thousand feet above. Through the narrow pass between them, the Yellowstone, swollen by the melting snow from the mountains, tore and plunged like a mad thing."

GEORGE WOOD WINGATE
Through the Yellowstone Park on Horseback, 1886

"Standing on the brink of the chasm the heavy roaring of the imprisoned river comes to the ear only in a sort of hollow, hungry growl, scarcely audible from the depths, and strongly suggestive of demons in torment below. Lofty pines on the bank of the stream 'dwindle to shrubs in dizziness of distance.' Everything beneath has a weird and deceptive appearance. The water does not look like water, but like oil. Numerous fish-hawks are seen busily plying their vocation, sailing high above the waters, and yet a thousand feet below the spectator. In the clefts of the rocks down, hundreds of feet down, bald eagles have their eyries, from which we can see them swooping still further into the depths to rob the ospreys of their hard-earned trout. It is grand, gloomy, and terrible; a solitude peopled with fantastic ideas; an empire of shadows and of turmoil."

LIEUTENANT GUSTAVUS C. DOANE
Yellowstone Expedition of 1870

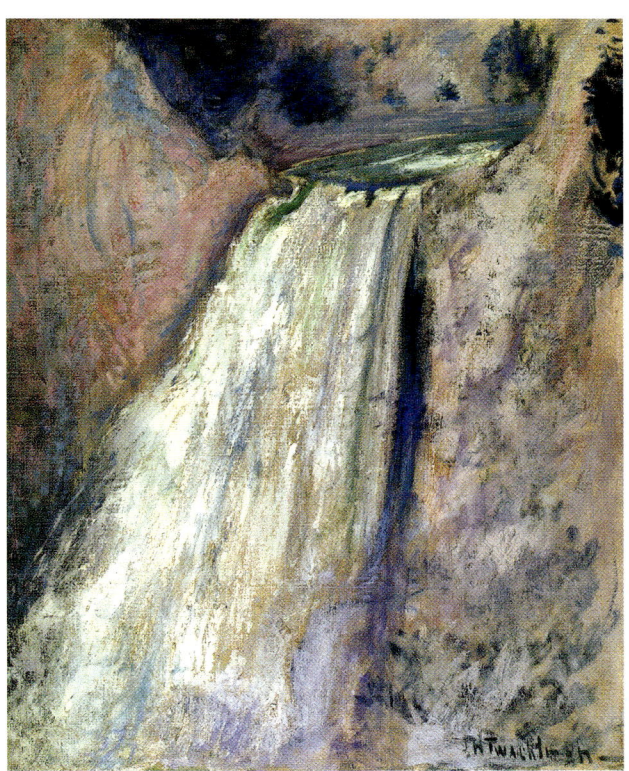

<
Brink of the Lower Falls

Waterfall, Yellowstone
John Henry Twachtman, 1895
private collection

LOOKOUT POINT

"One seems suspended 'tween heaven and earth."

ROBERT EDMUND STRAHORN, JOURNALIST, 1881

"Continuing along the trail and close to the dizzy depths of the canyon, I finally reached my party, who were gathered on a projecting cliff known as Lookout Point, and which is two miles below the hotel.

"Here, for the first time, I enjoyed a good view of one of the grandest sights in the world, the Great Canyon of the Yellowstone. No one who has ever seen this majestic creation of nature can forget it, but to adequately describe the scene is beyond the power of language.

"For a mile or so from the place where we had camped, the cliffs increased in height and hem in the river more closely, forcing the water into more and more turbulent rapids and cascades, until at the Upper Fall the water is confined into a chasm of eighty feet in width, with banks from two to three hundred feet high. The torrent rushes over this Fall with an impetuous sweep, and drops with a sheer descent of one hundred and twelve feet in an unbroken sheet upon a huge rock below, with a shock which throws up great clouds of spray, nearly to the summit of the Fall

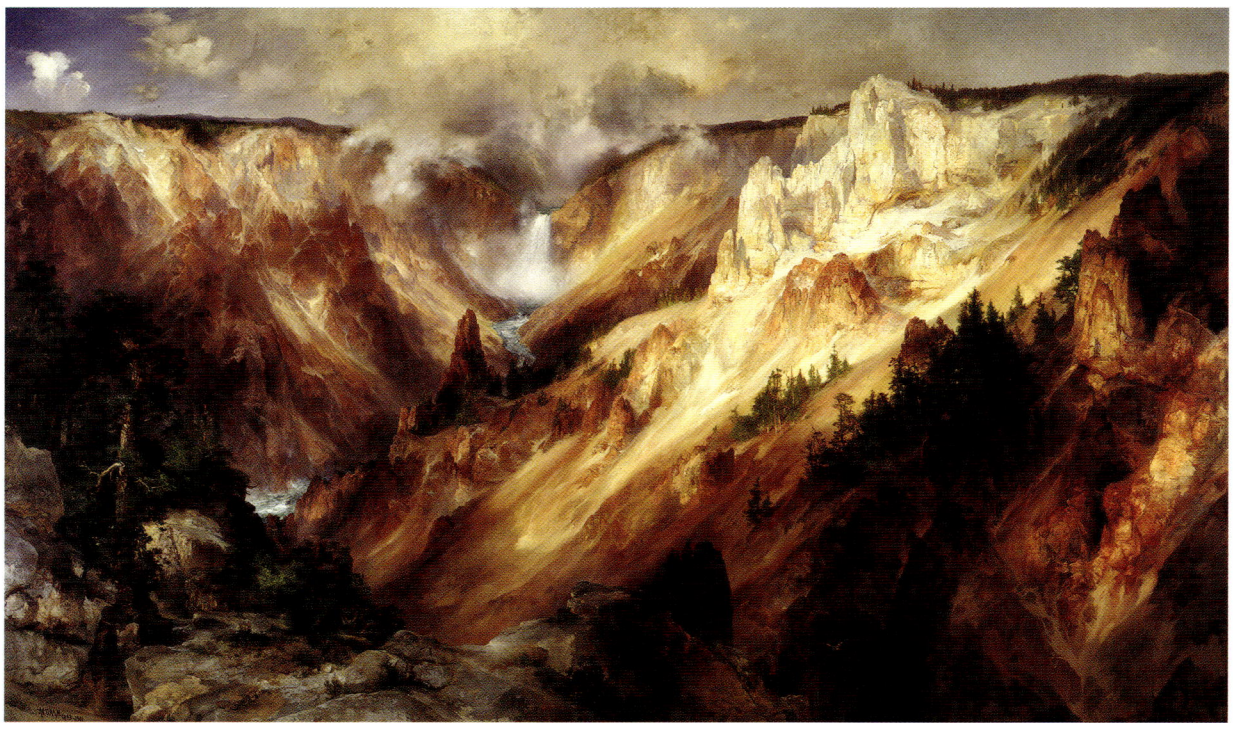

above the water, forming an immense whirlpool, which slowly circles at the foot of the Fall. Emerging from this, the river tears like a mad thing, breaking into rapids and cascades, for half a mile further, between rocky cliffs, which grow constantly higher and higher, until it hurls itself over the Great Fall, in an appalling leap of three hundred feet, and then plunges in a succession of cascade after cascade, into the dark abyss of the Great Canyon.

"The point where we stood afforded a magnificent view of both the Great Fall and the Canyon, although it required some nerve to enjoy the prospect, and most of the party showed a decided inclination to keep a firm grip upon something solid while looking at it.

"On the right was the Great or Lower Fall, the water dark blue on the surface of the river above, and changing into a huge snow-white curve as it made its vast plunge of three hundred feet (higher than the piers of the Brooklyn Bridge and double the height of Niagara), and terminating in an enormous fountain of spray, from which huge clouds of mist rolled far up the canyon, and through which a beautiful rainbow could at times be seen.

"But the Canyon itself was so stupendous that the Fall, grand as it was, formed but an incident to it.

"Far beneath, and to each side of us, extended a vast gorge or cleft in the mountains more than a thousand feet deep, a thousand yards wide at the top, and narrowing at the bottom to almost nothing; so deep that the river below seemed like a green ribbon, flecked here and there with patches of

<

The Grand Canyon of the Yellowstone
Thomas Moran, 1893-1901
Smithsonian Museum

Lower Falls from Lookout Point

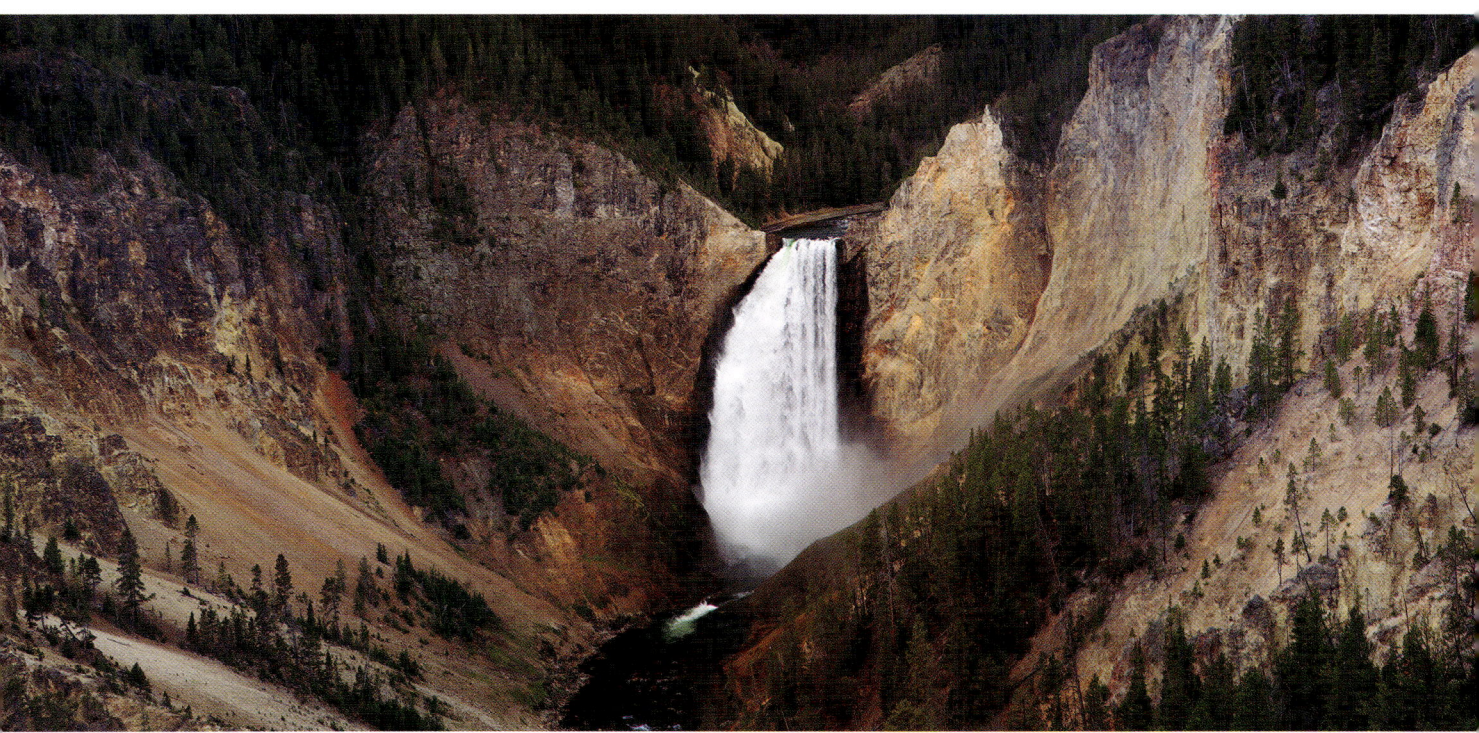

white; and great trees below appeared no larger than one's finger. The sides were perpendicular cliffs, like five rows of the Palisades of the Hudson, set one above another. These were not simply naked stone, such as is seen in other canyons, but were of the most variegated and startling hues, partly caused by the natural colors of the rocks, partly from the different mosses and algae, which are nourished by the mists of the falls, and partly from the action of hot springs, which had formed different colored deposits through the ages that had been occupied by the water in wearing out this huge passage through the rocks. On one side would be a vast cliff of a pale pink; adjoining it, another of buff, and opposite, a promontory of purple. Red, yellow, orange and brown were all visible at once, and beneath all ran the river, changing from blue to green, and flecked with white cascades. On the right side, just below the falls, was a great bank of snow, the size of a house. The sun was shining brightly, but the snow lay far below where its rays could penetrate. At each change in the sunlight these colors would change almost like a kaleidoscope, making it almost impossible to sketch them.

"Here and there along the sides of the Canyon projected huge rocks, forming pinnacles of great height, which had been molded by the elements into grotesque shapes, some resembling steeples, and one like a minaret. Yet, tall as they are, they were dwarfed by the vast abyss in which they ware situated.

"The Canyon extends for some twenty-four miles, winding and turning so that but a short portion of it could be seen from any point. At each turn the scene changed. At one place the walls of the Canyon were perpendicular, at another they extended with an even slope from the brink above to the edge of the river, and at a third they were broken into projecting crags and peaks, which rose one above the other to the level of the plateau above.

"At all times several eagles were slowly circling through this dizzy gorge, but looking like sparrows in the immensity around them. One of them had built its nest on a knob which surmounted a pinnacle just below us.

"The silence, the depth, and the vastness of the scene were overpowering.

"We sat and gazed in silence, for words could not do justice to our feelings. The impressiveness of the scene may be judged from its effect upon one of our soldiers, as narrated by himself. 'When I first saw the Canyon,' said he, 'I just sat still for a straight hour and looked at it without saying a word,' and then after a pause he added with great emphasis, 'and it was dinner time, too!'

"Few not familiar with army life will appreciate the full force of this tribute to the wonders of the scene."

GEORGE WOOD WINGATE
Through the Yellowstone Park on Horseback, 1886

POINT SUBLIME
AND INSPIRATION POINT

"No language can do justice to the wonderful grandeur and beauty of the canyon below the Lower Falls; the very nearly vertical walls, slightly sloping down to the water's edge on either side, so that from the summit the river appears like a thread of silver foaming over its rocky bottom, the variegated colors of the sides, yellow, red, brown, white, all intermixed and shading into each other; the Gothic columns of every form standing out from the sides of the walls with greater variety and more striking colors than ever adorned a work of human art. The margins of the canyon on either side are beautifully fringed with pines. In some places the walls of the canyon are composed of massive basalt, so separated by the jointage as to look like irregular mason-work going to decay....

"Standing near the margin of the Lower Falls, and looking down the canyon, which looks like an immense chasm or cleft in the basalt, with its sides twelve hundred to fifteen hundred feet high, and decorated with the most brilliant colors that the human eye ever saw, with the rocks weathered into an almost unlimited variety of forms, with here and there a pine sending its roots into the clefts on the sides as if struggling with a sort of uncertain success to maintain an existence—the whole presents a picture that it would be difficult to surpass in nature. Mr. Thomas Moran, a celebrated artist, and noted for his skill as a colorist, exclaimed with a kind of regretful enthusiasm that these beautiful tints were beyond the reach of human art."

FERDINAND VANDEVEER HAYDEN
Preliminary Report of the United States Geological Survey of Montana and Portions of Adjacent Territories, 1872

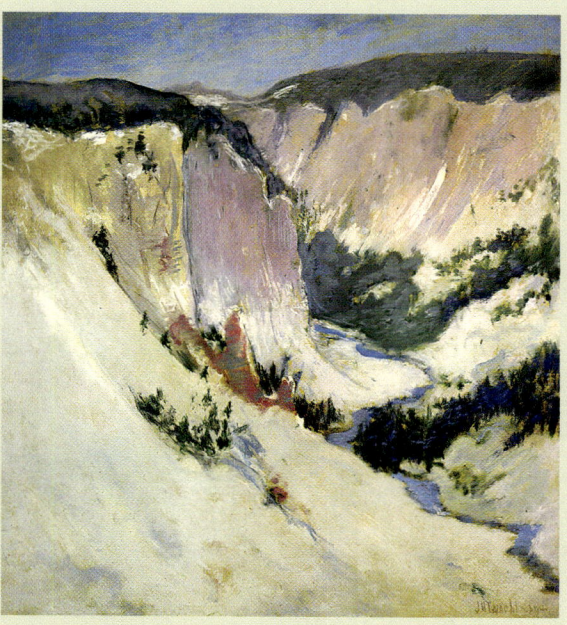

Yellowstone Park
John Henry Twachtman, 1895
private collection

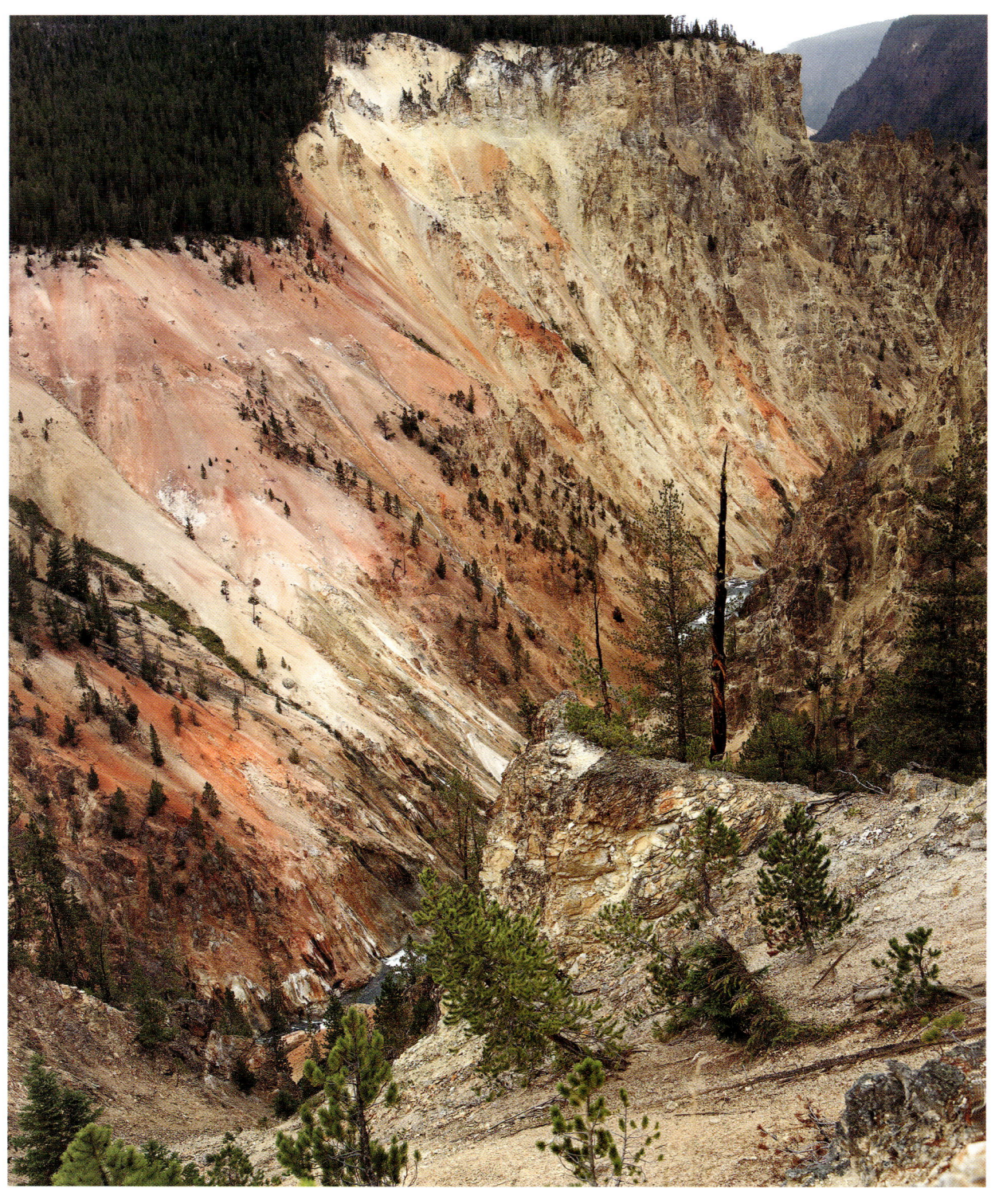

"Pretty, beautiful, picturesque, magnificent, grand, sublime, awful, terrible"

DAVID FOLSOM OF THE FOLSOM-COOK-PETERSON EXPEDITION, 1869

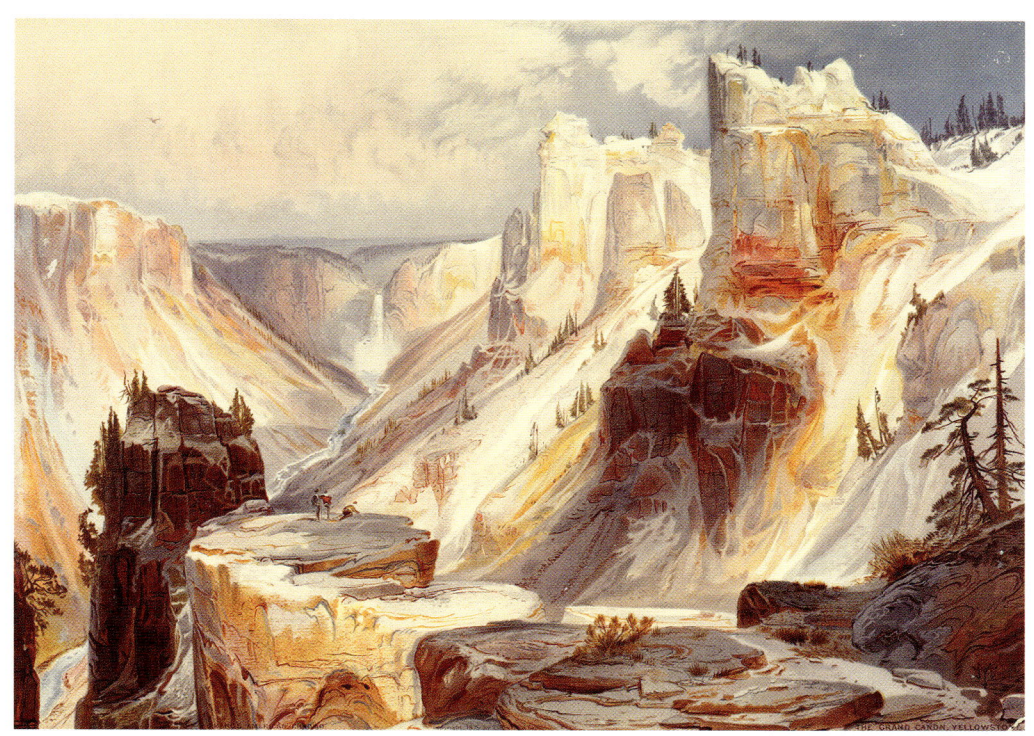

"The canyon is so tremendously wild and impressive that even these great falls cannot hold your attention. It is about twenty miles long and a thousand feet deep,—a weird, unearthly-looking gorge of jagged, fantastic architecture, and most brilliantly colored. Here the Washburn range, forming the northern rim of the Yellowstone basin, made up mostly of beds of rhyolite decomposed by the action of thermal waters, has been cut through and laid open to view by the river; and a famous section it has made. It is not the depth or the shape of the canyon, nor the waterfall, nor the green and gray river chanting its brave song as it goes foaming on its way, that most impresses the observer, but the colors of the decomposed volcanic rocks. With few exceptions, the traveler in strange lands finds that, however much the scenery and vegetation in different countries may change, Mother Earth is ever familiar and the same. But here the very ground is changed, as if belonging to some other world. The walls of the canyon from top to bottom burn in a perfect glory of color, confounding and dazzling when the sun is shining,—white, yellow, green, blue, vermilion, and various other shades of red indefinitely blending. All the earth hereabouts seems to be paint. Millions of tons of it lie in sight, exposed to wind and weather as if of no account, yet marvelously fresh and bright, fast colors not to be washed out or bleached out by either sunshine or storms."

JOHN MUIR
"The Yellowstone National Park," The Atlantic Monthly, April 1898

The Grand Canyon, Yellowstone
Thomas Moran, 1875
Gilcrease Museum, Tulsa, OK
2426.47.8

‹

Grand Canyon of the Yellowstone between Point Sublime and Inspiration Point

"'This evening we shall do the Grand Canyon of the Yellowstone,' said the maiden.

"'Together?' said I; and she said, 'Yes.'

"The sun was beginning to sink when we heard the roar of falling waters and came to a broad river along whose banks we ran. . . . The Yellowstone River has occasion to run through a gorge about eight miles long. To get to the bottom of the gorge it makes two leaps, one of about one hundred and twenty and the other of three hundred feet. I investigated the upper or lesser fall, which is close to the hotel.

"Up to that time nothing particular happens to the Yellowstone—its banks being only rocky, rather steep, and plentifully adorned with pines.

"At the falls it comes round a corner, green, solid, ribbed with a little foam, and not more than thirty yards wide. Then it goes over, still green, and rather more solid than before. After a minute or two, you, sitting upon a rock directly above the drop, begin to understand that something has occurred; that the river has jumped between solid cliff walls, and that the gentle froth of water lapping the sides of the gorge below is really the outcome of great waves.

"And the river yells aloud; but the cliffs do not allow the yells to escape.

"That inspection began with curiosity and finished in terror, for it seemed that the whole world was sliding in chrysolite from under my feet. I followed with the others round the corner to arrive at the brink of the canyon. We had to climb up a nearly perpendicular ascent to begin with, for the ground rises more than the river drops. Stately pine woods fringe either lip of the gorge, which is the gorge of the Yellowstone. You'll find all about it in the guidebooks.

"All that I can say is that without warning or preparation I looked into a gulf seventeen hundred feet deep, with eagles and fish-hawks circling far below. And the sides of that gulf were one wild welter of color—crimson, emerald, cobalt, ochre, amber, honey splashed with port wine, snow white, vermilion, lemon, and silver gray in wide washes. The sides did not fall sheer, but were graven by time, and water, and air into monstrous heads of kings, dead chiefs—men and women of the old time. So far below that no sound of its strife could reach us, the Yellowstone River ran a finger-wide strip of jade green.

"The sunlight took those wondrous walls and gave fresh hues to those that nature had already laid there.

"Evening crept through the pines that shadowed us, but the full glory of the day flamed in that canyon as we went out very cautiously to a jutting piece of rock—blood-red or pink it was—that overhung the deepest deeps of all.

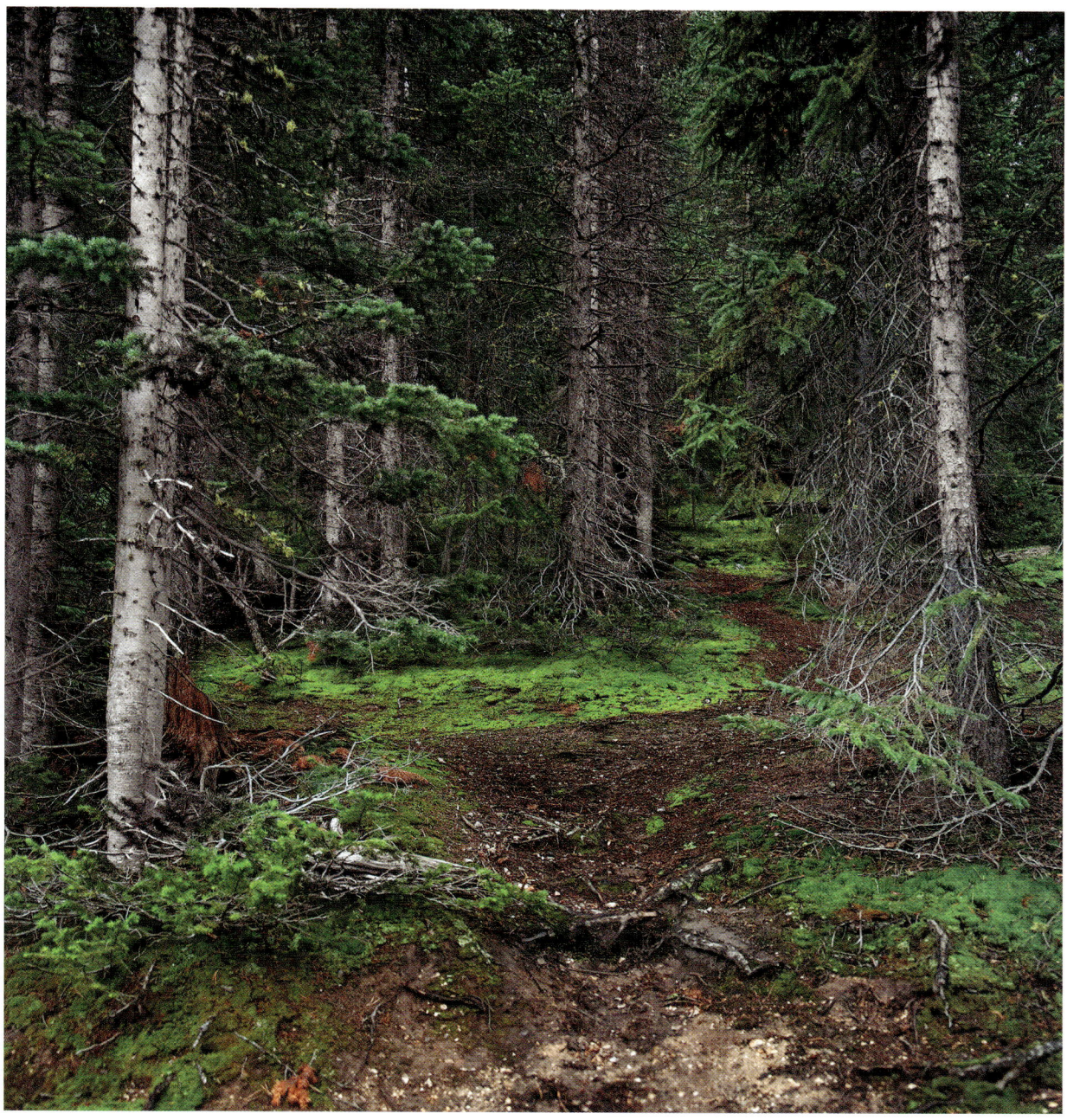

Near Ribbon Lake Trail

"Now I know what it is to sit enthroned amid the clouds of sunset as the spirits sit in Blake's pictures. Giddiness took away all sensation of touch or form, but the sense of blinding color remained.

"When I reached the mainland again I had sworn that I had been floating."

RUDYARD KIPLING
American Notes, 1891

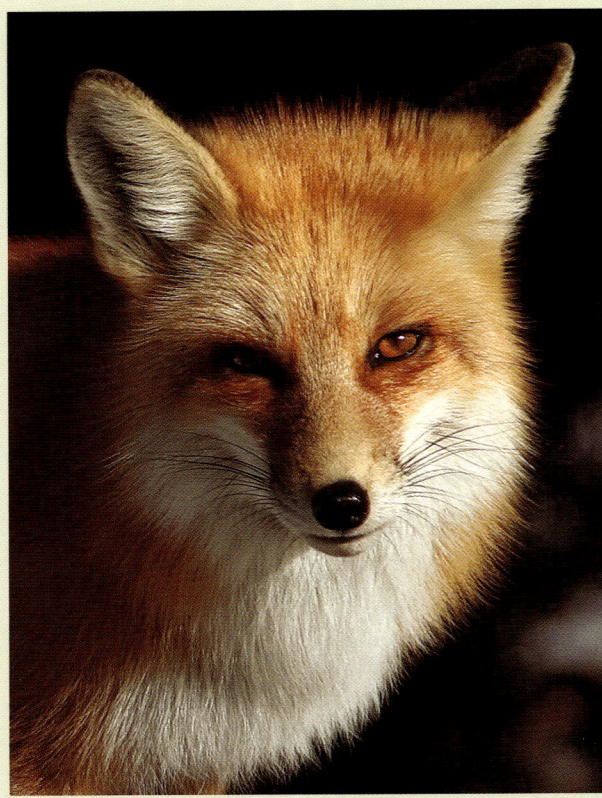

Red fox

"When, however, by means of the Northern Pacific Railroad, the falls of the Yellowstone and the geyser basin are rendered easy of access, probably no portion of America will be more popular as a watering place or summer resort than that which we had the pleasure of viewing, in all the glory and grandeur of its primeval solitude."

WALTER TRUMBALL
Overland Monthly, June 1871

Rough-legged hawk

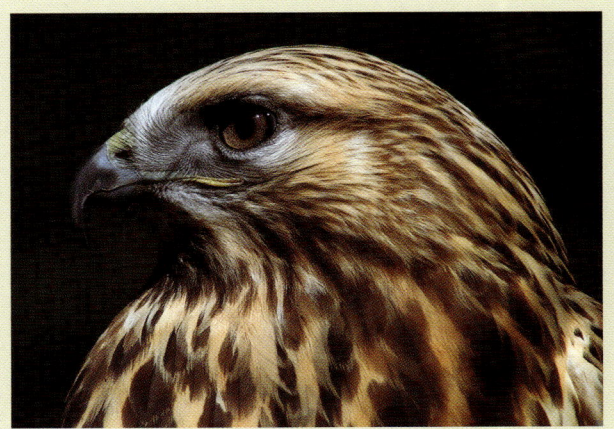

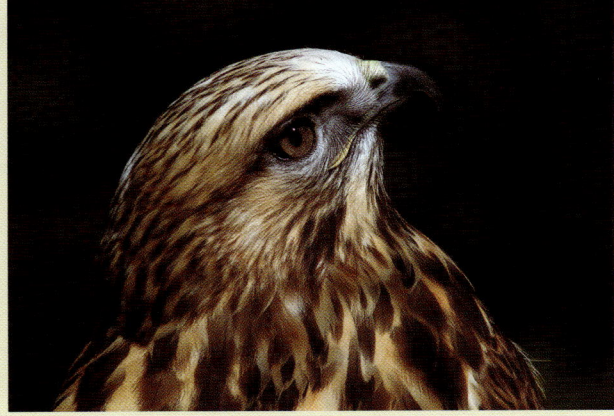

HAYDEN VALLEY

"These magnificent changes in mountain scenery occasioned by light and shade during one of these terrific tempests, with all the incidental accompaniments of thunder, lightning, rain, snow and hail, afford the most awe-inspiring exhibition in nature."

NATHANIEL PITT LANGFORD
The Discovery of Yellowstone Park: Journal of the Washburn Expedition to the Yellowstone and Firehole Rivers in the Year 1870, 1905

Hayden Valley and the
Yellowstone River

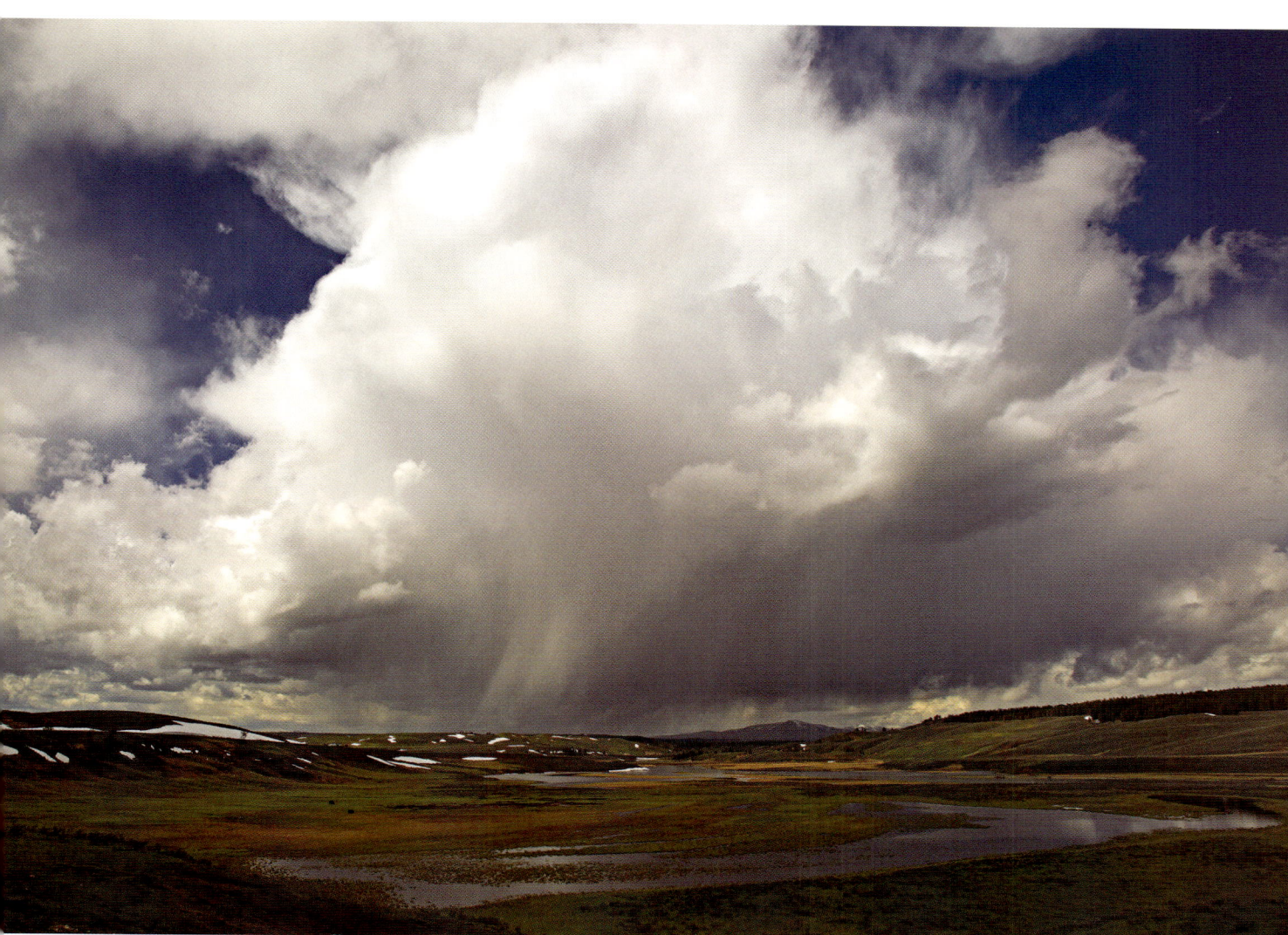

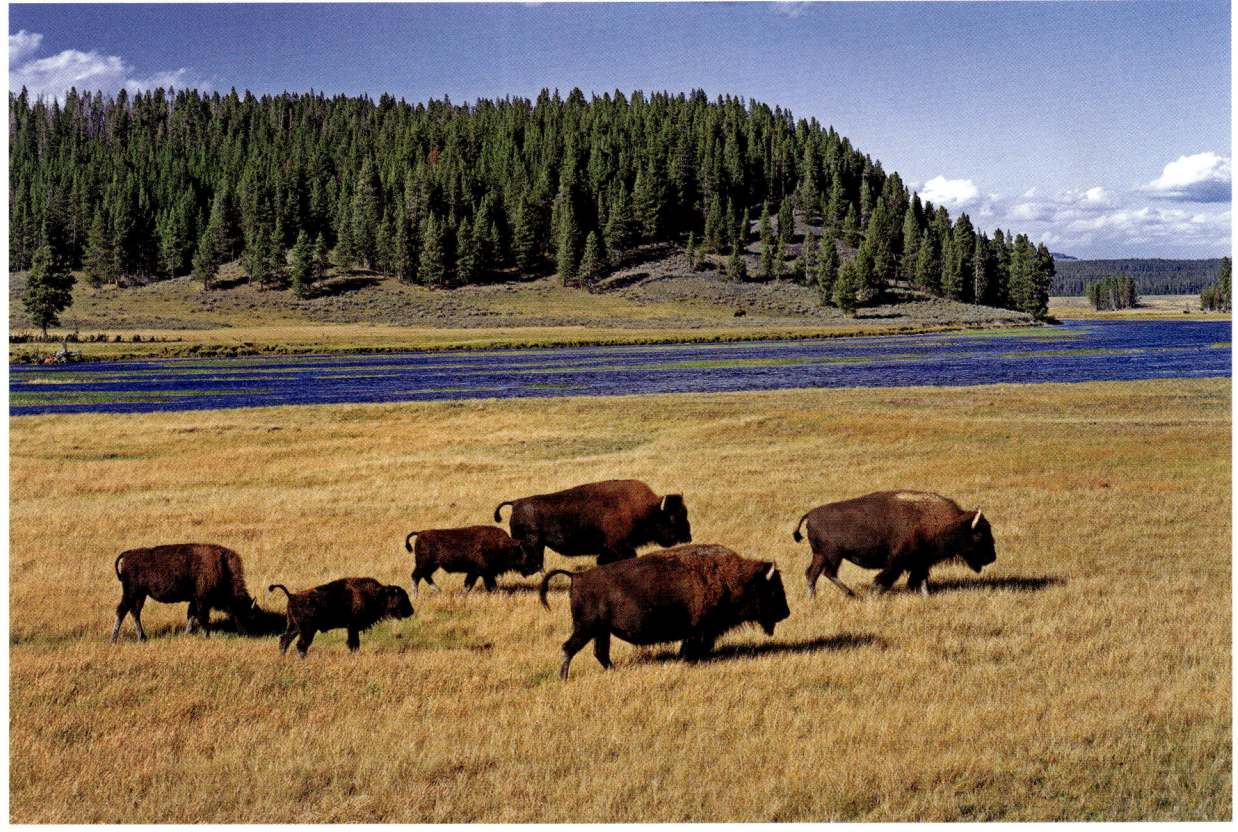

Bison along the Yellowstone River

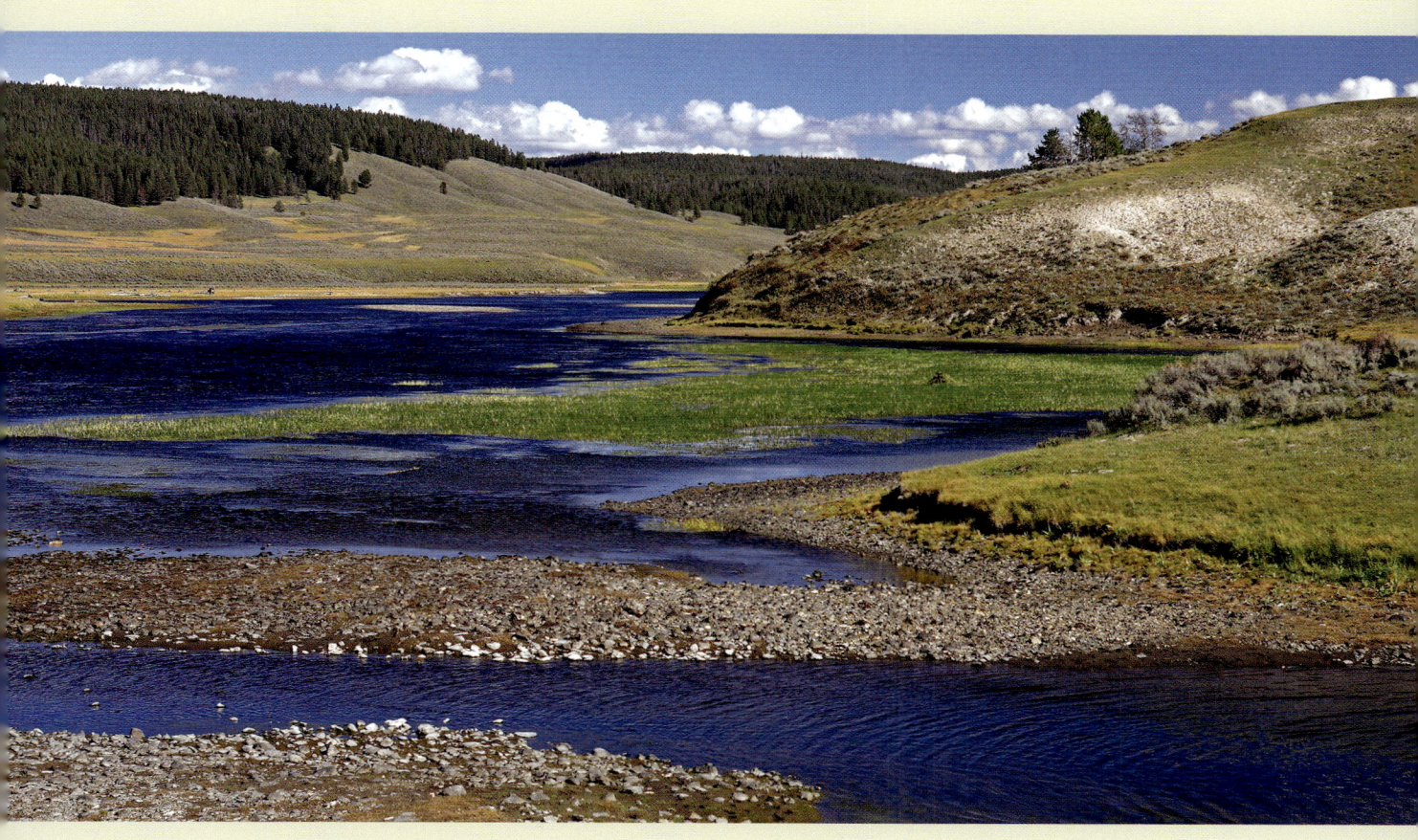

Yellowstone River at Elk Antler Creek

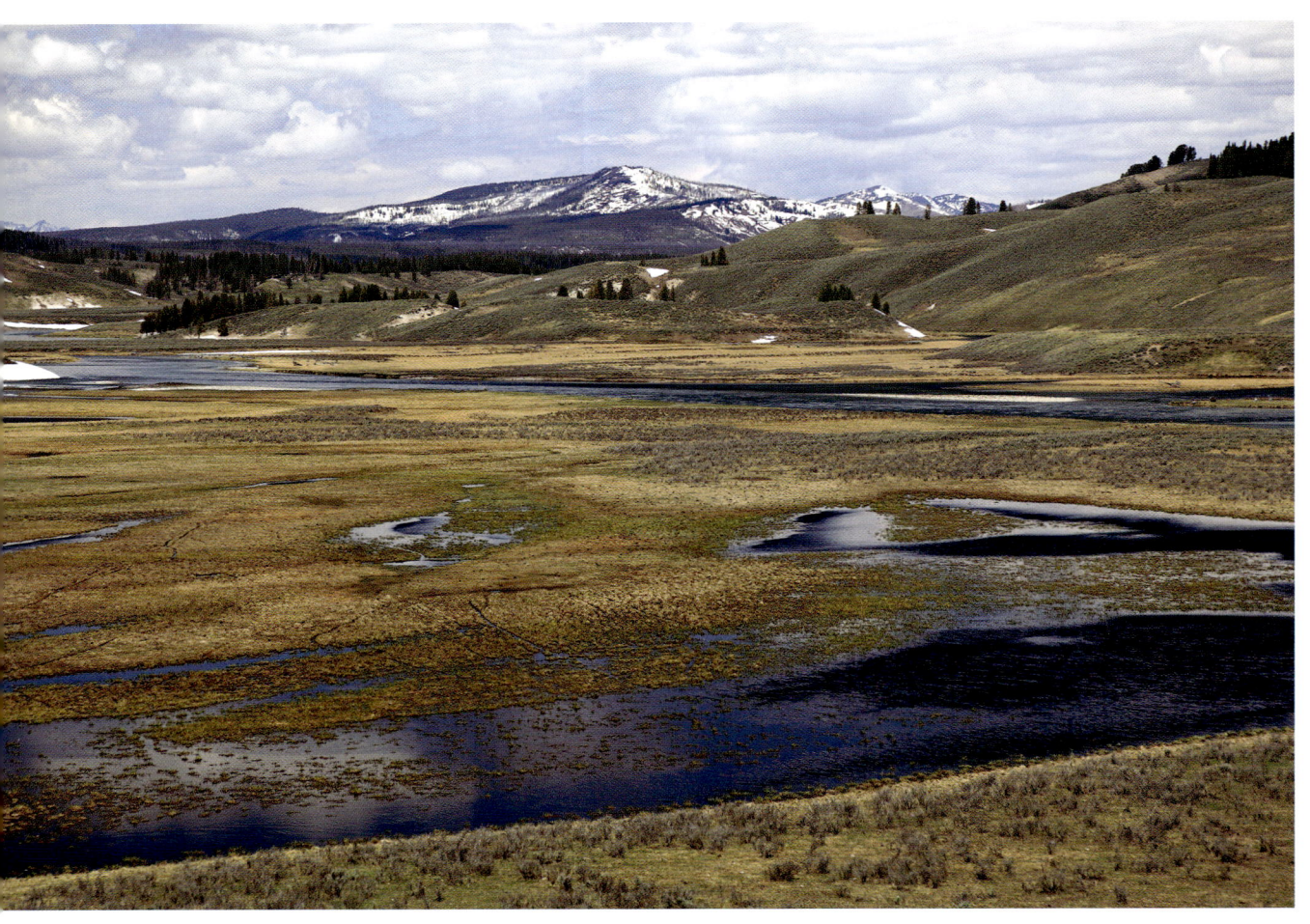

Yellowstone River and Pelican Peak in May

>

Yellowstone River and Pelican Peak in June

"A grassy valley, branching between low ridges, running from the river toward the center of the basin. A small stream rose in this valley, breaking through the ridges to the west in a deep canyon, and falling into the channel of the Yellowstone, which here bears in a northeast course, flowing in view as far as the confluence of the small stream, thence plunged into the Grand Canyon, and hidden from sight."

LIEUTENANT GUSTAVUS C. DOANE
Yellowstone Expedition of 1870

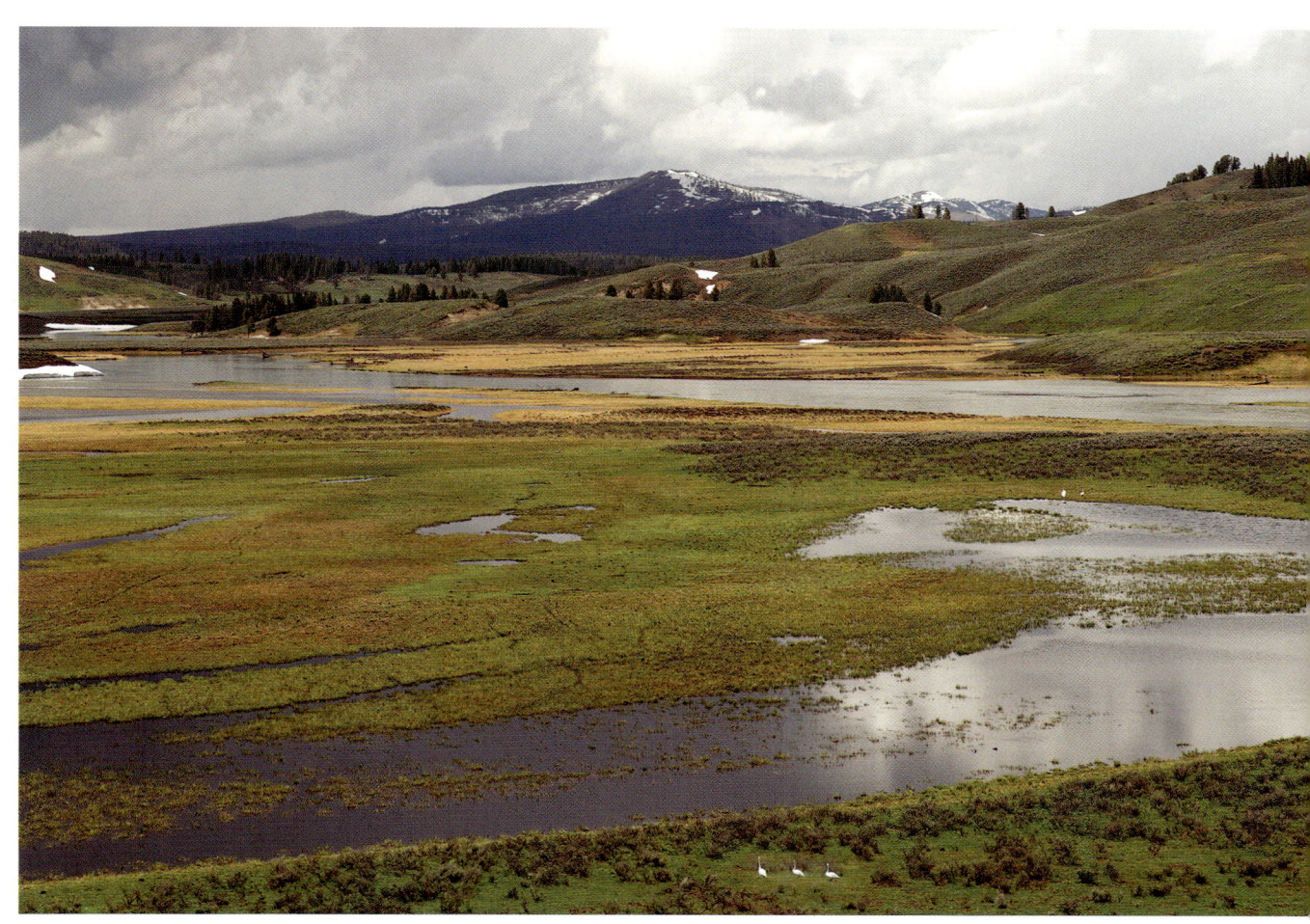

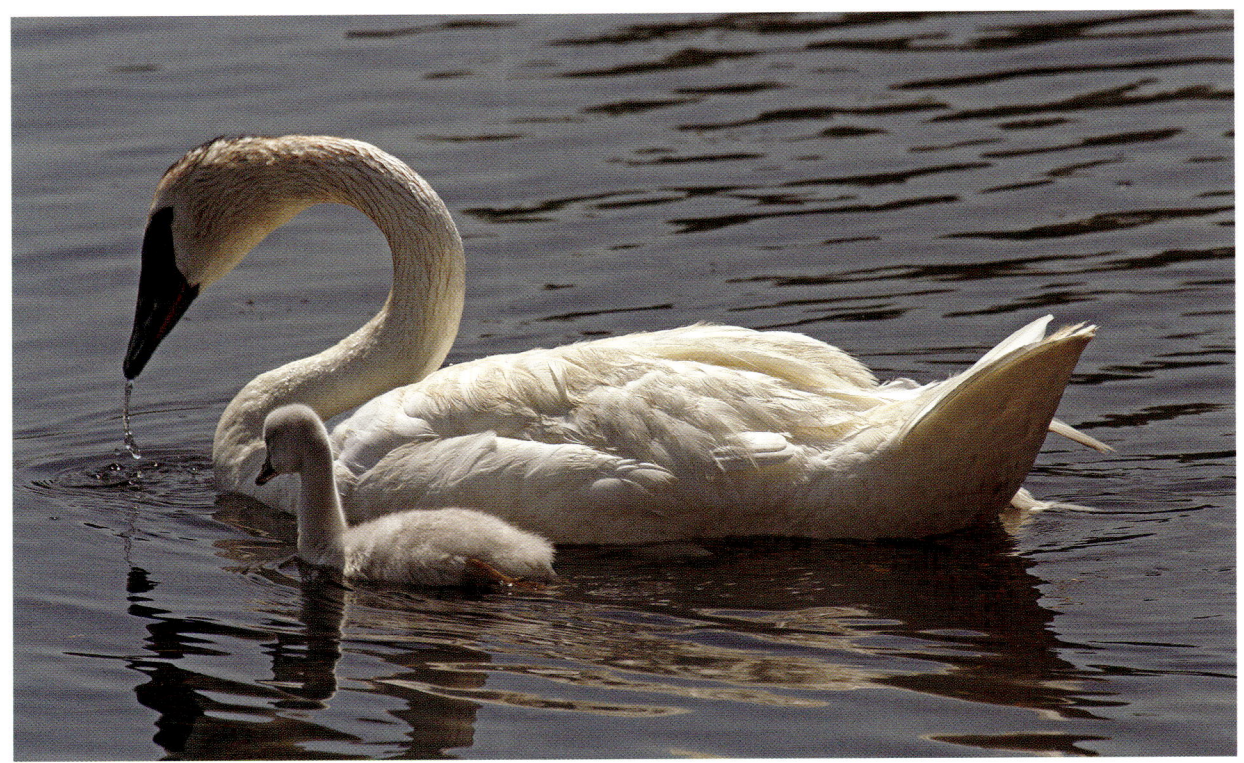

Trumpeter swan and cygnet

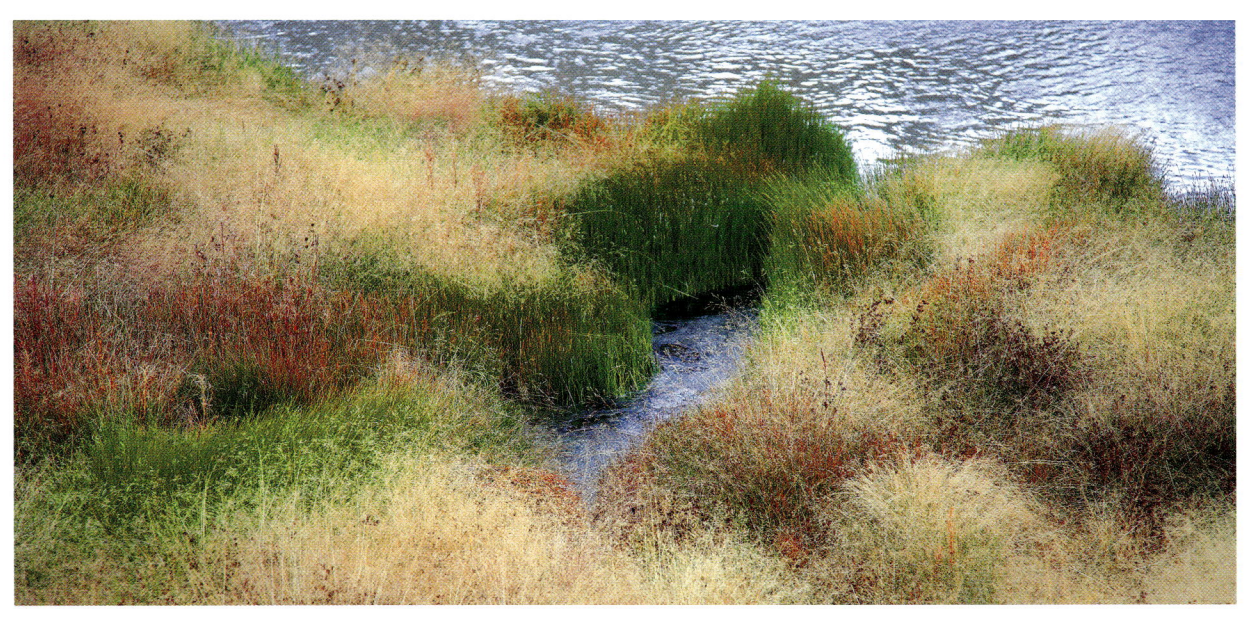

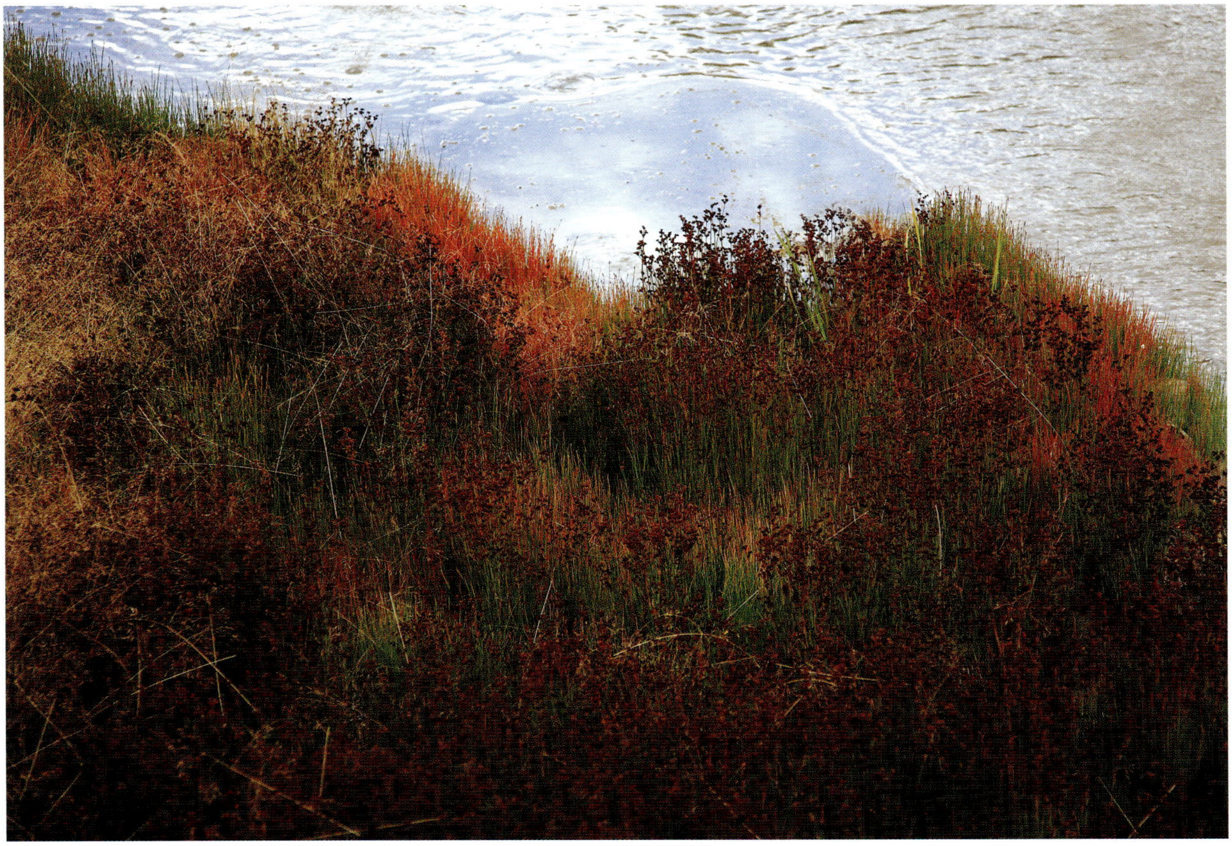

MUD VOLCANO AREA

DRAGON'S MOUTH SPRING

"Passing over the plain we camped on the riverbank, near a series of mud springs [Mud Volcano Area]. Three of the largest were about ten feet over the top and had built up ten or twelve feet high. In the bottom of the crater thus [mud was] sputtering and splashing, as we have often seen in a pot of hasty pudding when nearly cooked."

GENERAL HENRY D. WASHBURN
Explorations in a New and Wonderful Country, 1870

"As you look into the cave, it has the appearance of an opening to a subterranean lake. A small, hot stream flows from it. The water is continually washing its ten or twelve feet of shore, like an agitated lake. The bright pebbles in the bottom, the clean sand, and the smooth, white, flat stones left in regular ripples on its margin, together with the green, mossy sides of the cave, and the musical monotones of the rippling waters, almost lead one to think it the entrance to an enchanted lake."

WALTER TRUMBALL
Overland Monthly, June 1871

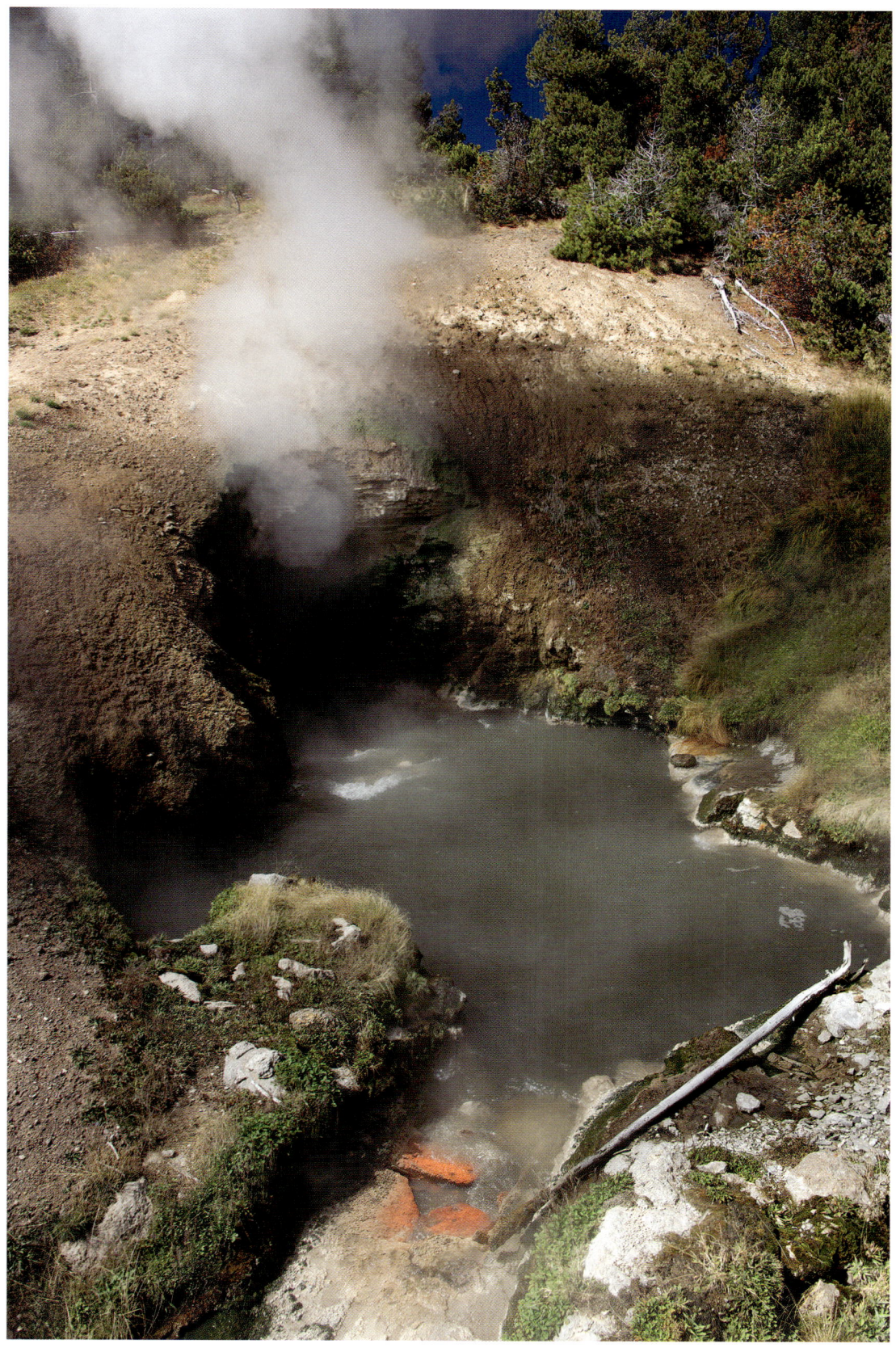

Dragon's Mouth Spring

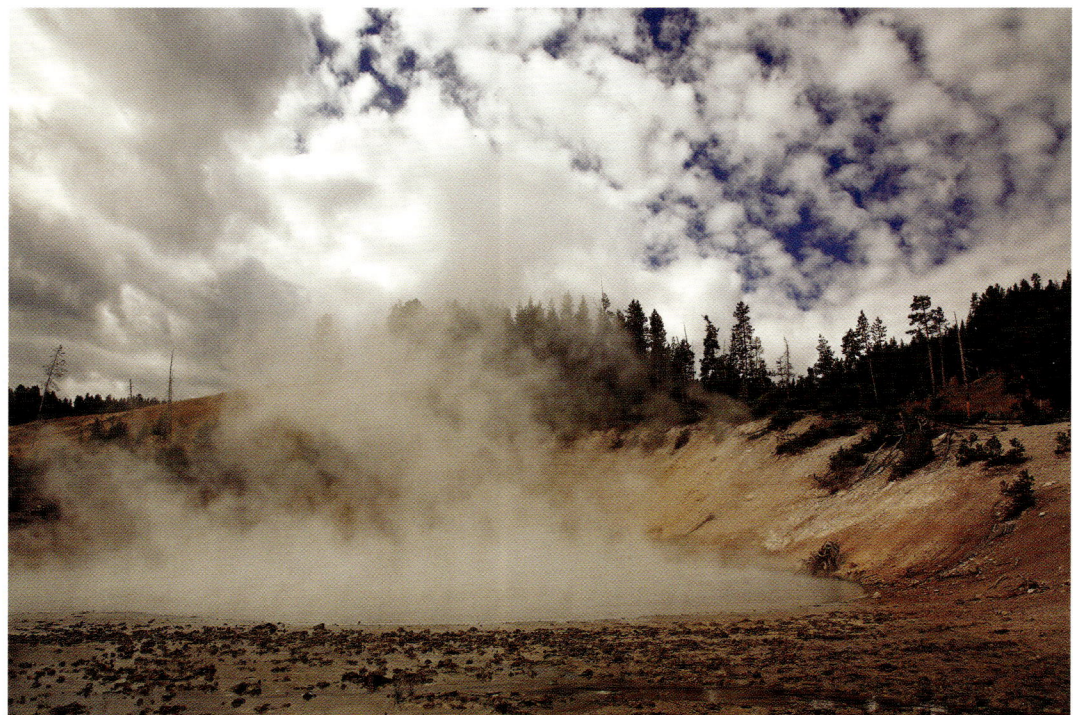

"The spring, more diabolical in appearance, filled with a hot brownish substance of the consistency of mucilage, is in constant noisy ebullition, emitting fumes of villainous odor. Its surface is covered with bubbles, which are constantly rising and bursting, and emitting sulphurous gases from various parts of its surface. Its appearance has suggested the name, which Hedges has given, of Hell-Broth Springs; for, as we gazed upon the infernal mixture and inhaled the pungent sickening vapors, we were impressed with the idea that this was a most perfect realization of Shakespeare's image in Macbeth. It needed but the presence of Hecate and her weird band to realize that horrible creation of poetic fancy, and I fancied the 'black and midnight hags' concocting a charm around this horrible cauldron. . . .

"The mud in these springs is in most cases a little thinner than mortar prepared for plastering, and, as it is thrown up from one to two feet, I can liken its appearance to nothing so much as Indian meal hasty pudding when the process of boiling is nearly completed, except that the puffing, bloated bubbles are greatly magnified, being from a few inches to two feet in diameter. In some of the springs the mud is of dark brown color, in others nearly pink, and in one it was almost yellow. . . . This mud having been worked over and over for many years is as soft as the finest pigments."

Mud Caldron

NATHANIEL PITT LANGFORD
The Discovery of Yellowstone Park: Journal of the Washburn Expedition to the Yellowstone and Firehole Rivers in the Year 1870, 1905

"While surveying these wonders, our ears were constantly saluted by dull, thundering, booming sounds, resembling the reports of distant artillery. As we approached the spot whence they proceeded, the ground beneath us shook and trembled as from successive shocks of an earthquake. Ascending a small hillock, the cause of the uproar was found to be a mud volcano—the greatest marvel we have yet met with. . . .

"Some of these pulsations are much more violent than others, but each one is accompanied by the discharge of an immense volume of steam, which at once shuts off all view of the inside of the crater; but sometimes, during the few seconds intervening between the pulsations, or when a breeze for a moment carries the steam to one side of the crater, we can see to the depth of thirty feet into the volcano, but cannot often discover the boiling mud; though occasionally, when there occurs an unusually violent spasm or concussion, a mass of mud as large in bulk as a hogshead is thrown up as high as our heads, emitting blinding clouds of steam in all directions, and crowding all observers back from the edge of the crater. . . .

"Everything around us—air, earth, water—is impregnated with sulphur. We feel it in every drop of water we drink, and in every breath of air we inhale. Our silver watches have turned to the color of poor brass, tarnished.

"General Washburn and I again visited the mud volcano today. I especially desired to see it again for the one especial purpose, among others of a general nature, of assuring myself that the notes made in my diary a few days ago are not exaggerated. No! they are not! The sensations inspired in me today, on again witnessing its convulsions, and the dense clouds of vapor expelled in rapid succession from its crater, amid the jarring of the earth, and the ominous intonations from beneath, were those of mingled dread and wonder. At war with all former experience it was so novel, so unnaturally natural, that I feel while now writing and thinking of it, as if my own senses might have deceived me with a mere figment of the imagination. But it is not so. The wonder, than which this continent, teeming with nature's grandest exhibitions, contains nothing more marvelous, still stands amid the solitary fastnesses of the Yellowstone, to excite the astonishment of the thousands who in coming years shall visit that remarkable locality."

NATHANIEL PITT LANGFORD
The Discovery of Yellowstone Park: Journal of the Washburn Expedition to the Yellowstone and Firehole Rivers in the Year 1870, 1905

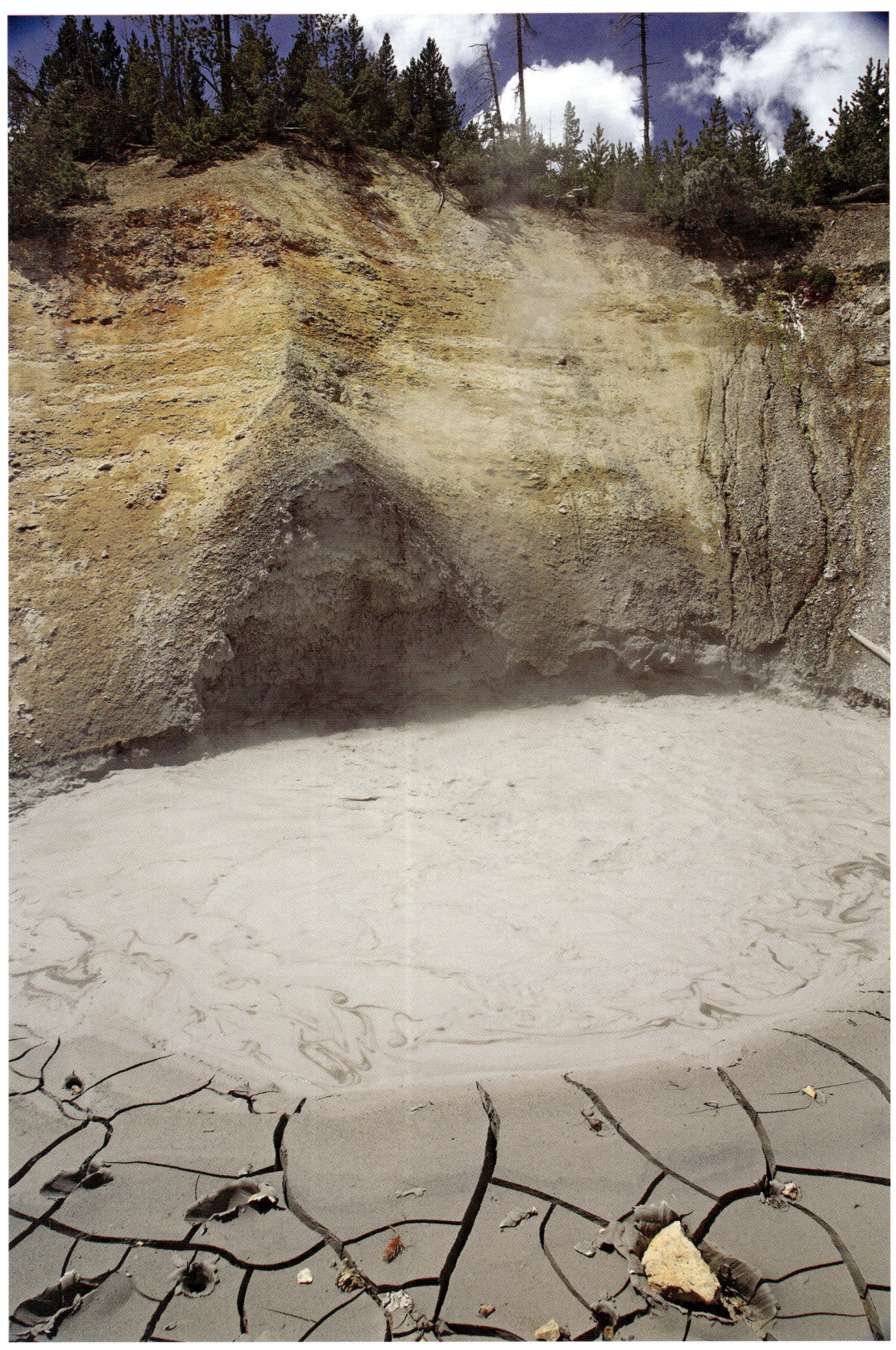

MUD VOLCANO

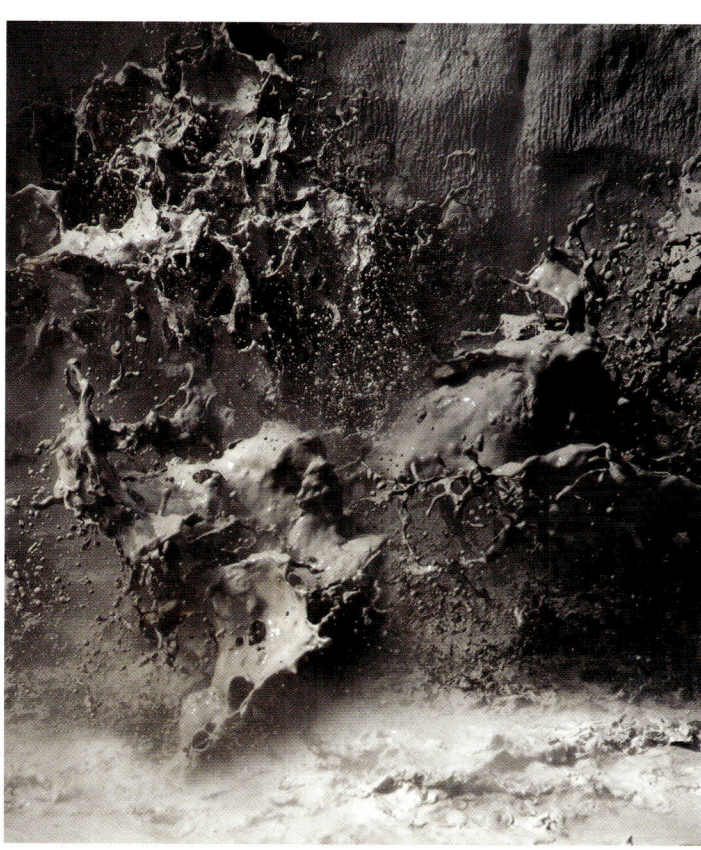

<

Mud Volcano

Mud Volcano mud

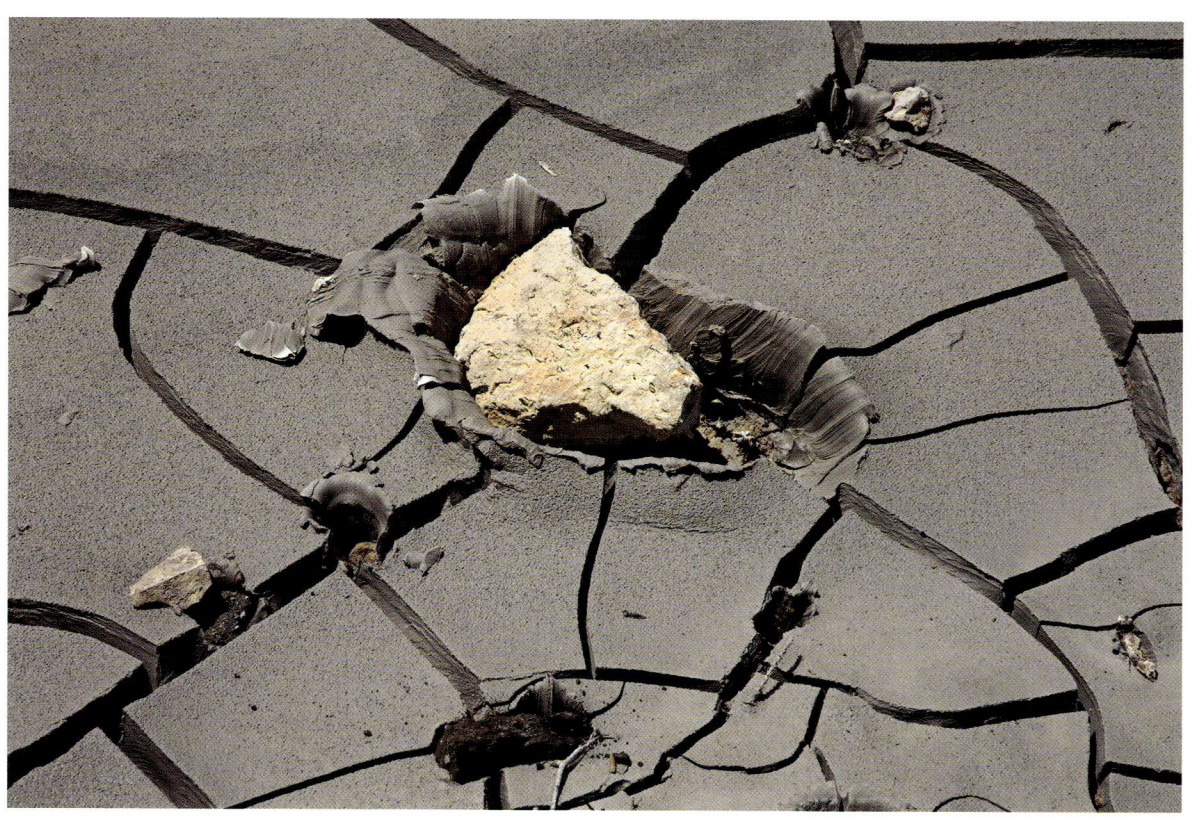

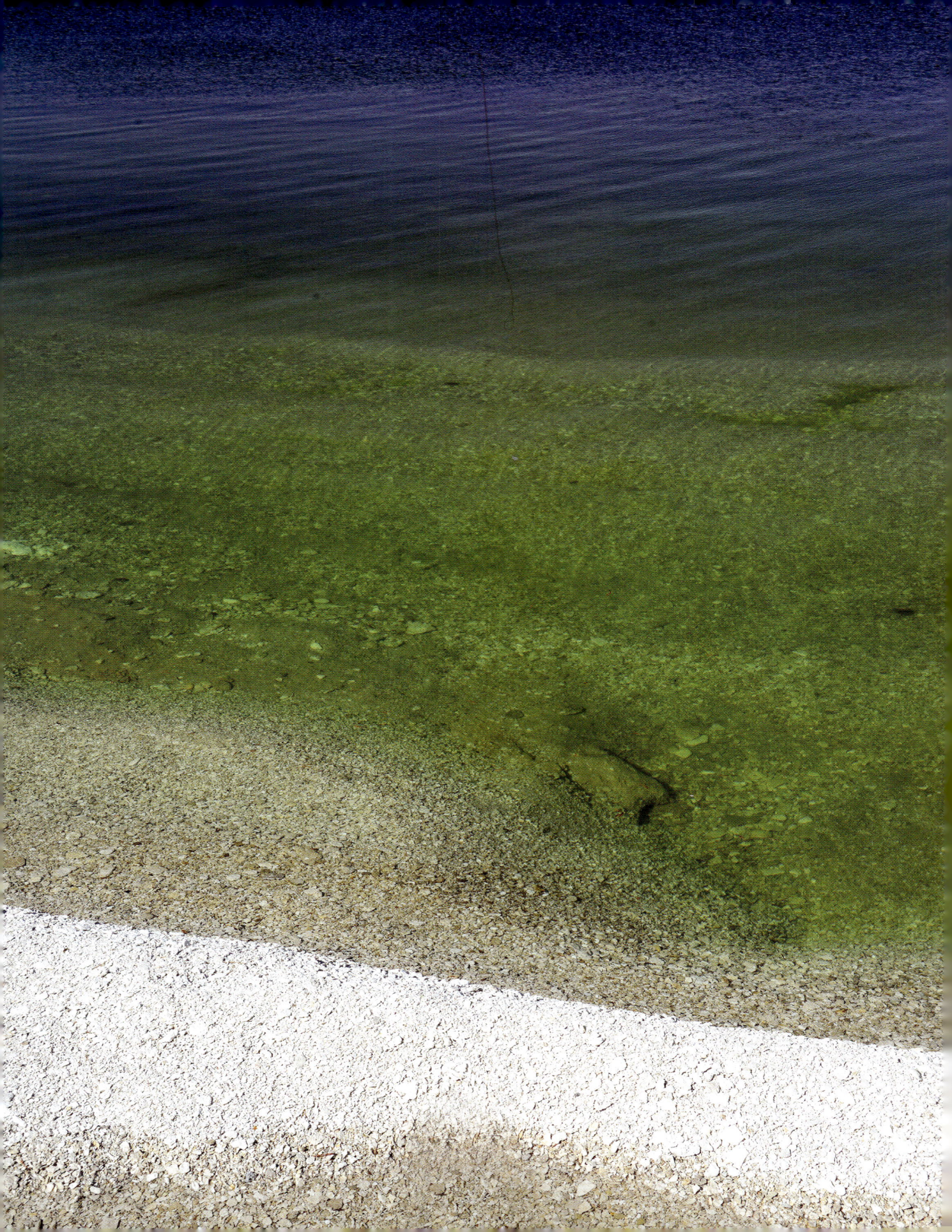

GRANT AREA

CRAIG PASS

> ISA LAKE

LEWIS RIVER

> LEWIS FALLS

WEST THUMB GEYSER BASIN

> ABYSS POOL

> BIG CONE

> BLACK POOL

> FISHING CONE

> SEISMOGRAPH AND BLUEBELL POOLS

> THUMB PAINT POTS

> YELLOWSTONE LAKE

Yellowstone Lake

CRAIG PASS

ISA LAKE

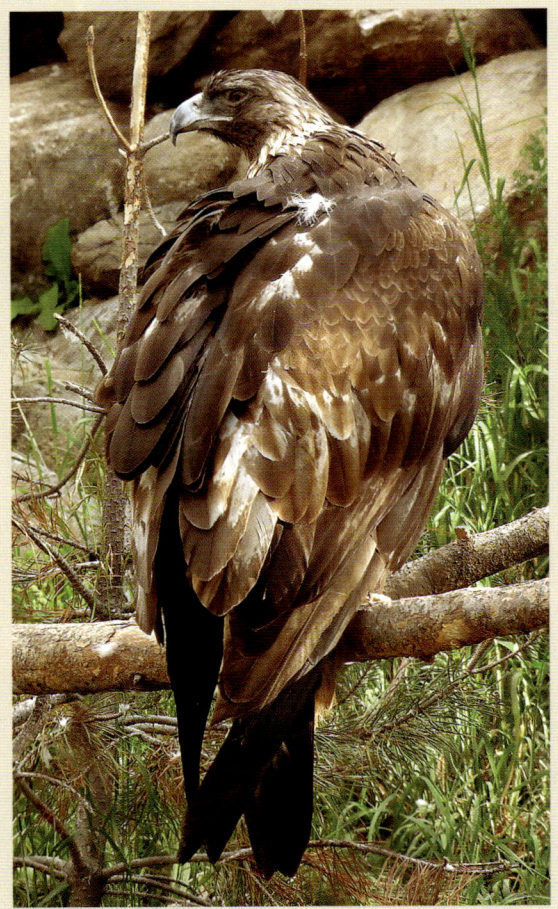

Golden eagle

Isa Lake on Craig Pass

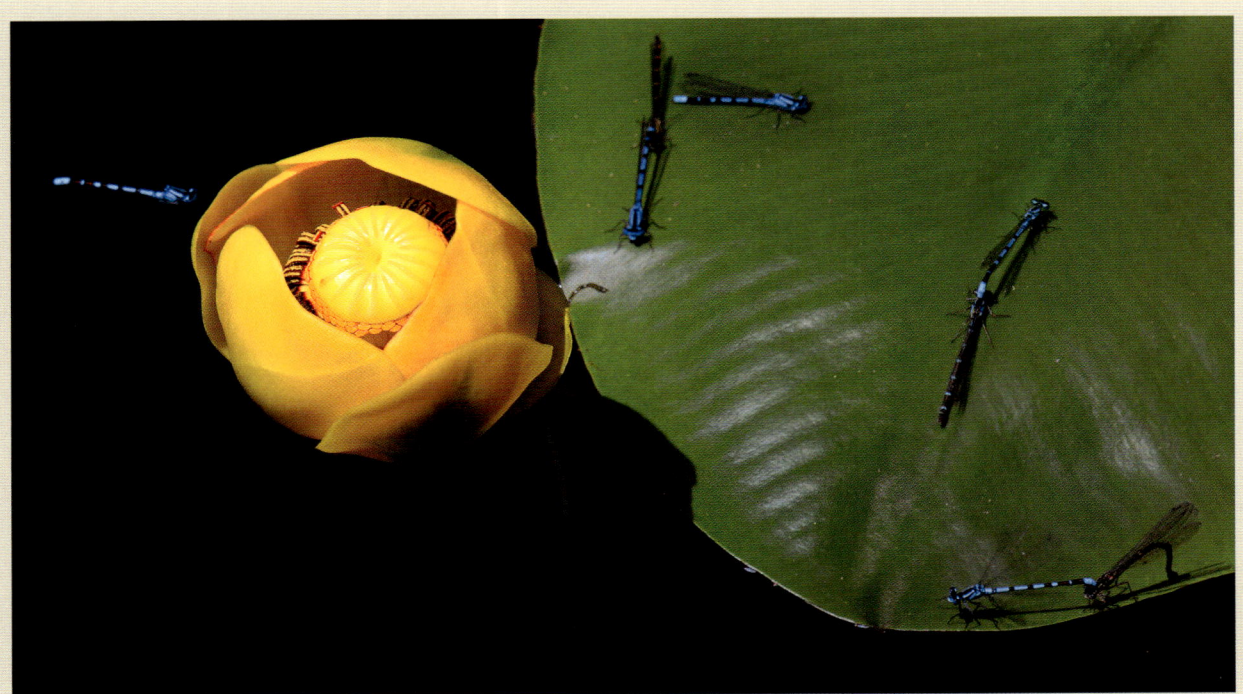

LEWIS RIVER

LEWIS FALLS

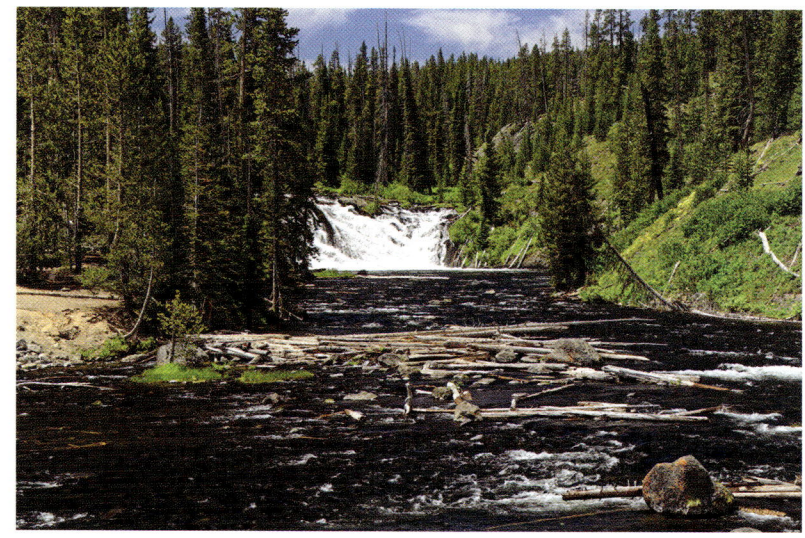

Lewis Falls

Lewis River

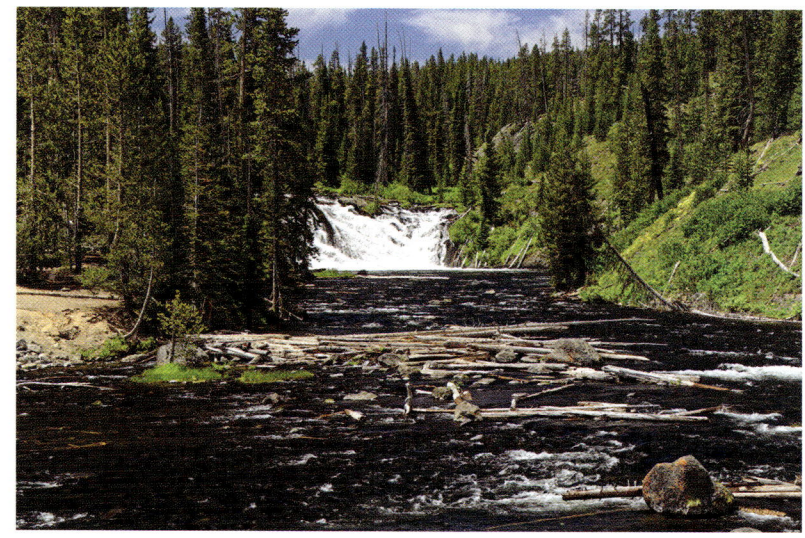

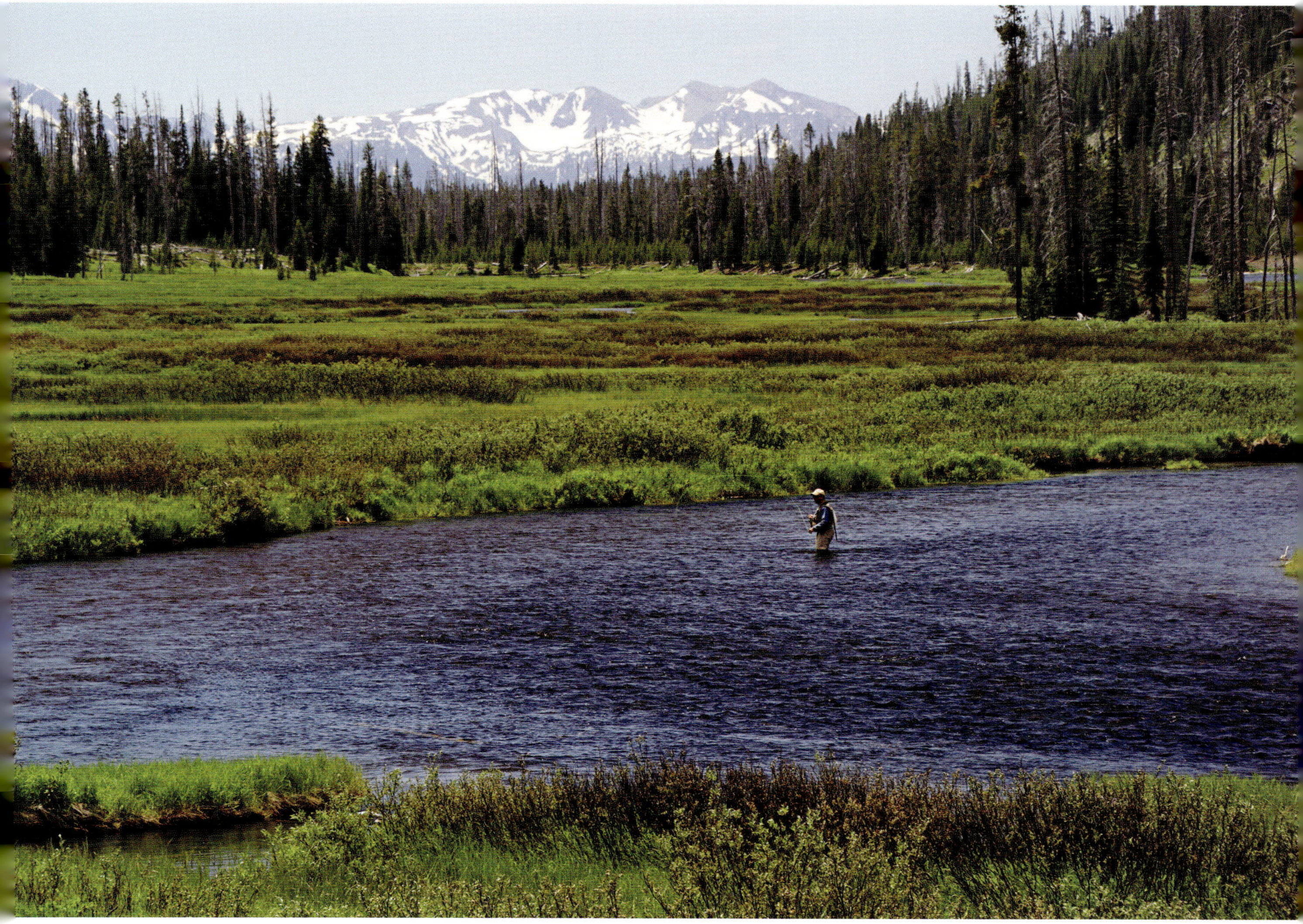

WEST THUMB GEYSER BASIN

"I rode around the head of [Yellowstone] lake to the steam jets visible from camp; this was the largest system we had yet seen, located at the extreme point of the most westerly arm of the lake, and on a gentle slope, reaching along the shore for a mile, and extending back into the woods for the same distance; this system embraced every variety of hot water and mud springs seen thus far on the route, with many other heretofore unseen. Four hundred yards from the lakeshore is a basin of mud having a bright pink color; this is a system of itself, being seventy feet in diameter, and projecting thick mud through small craters of a conical shape around the edge of the basin, while the center is one seething mass. The deposit speedily hardens into a firm, laminated clay stone, of beautiful texture, though the brilliant pink color fades to a chalky white. Near and around this basin are a dozen springs, from six to twenty-five feet across, boiling muddy water of paint-like consistency, in colors varying from a pure white to a dark yellow; then come several flowing springs, from ten to fifty feet in diameter, of clear, hot water, the basins and channels of which were lined with deposits of red, green, yellow, and black, giving them an appearance of gorgeous splendor; these deposits were too friable to preserve, crumbling at the touch. The bright colors were on the surface of the rock only, not extending to its interior. Below these were several large craters of bluish water impregnated with sulphate of copper; these boiled to the height of two feet in the center and flowed large streams of water; their rims were raised a few inches, in a delicate rocky margin of a fringe-like appearance, deposited from the water. . . . No figure of imagination, no description of enchantment, can equal in imagery the vista of these great basins."

LIEUTENANT GUSTAVUS C. DOANE
Yellowstone Expedition of 1870

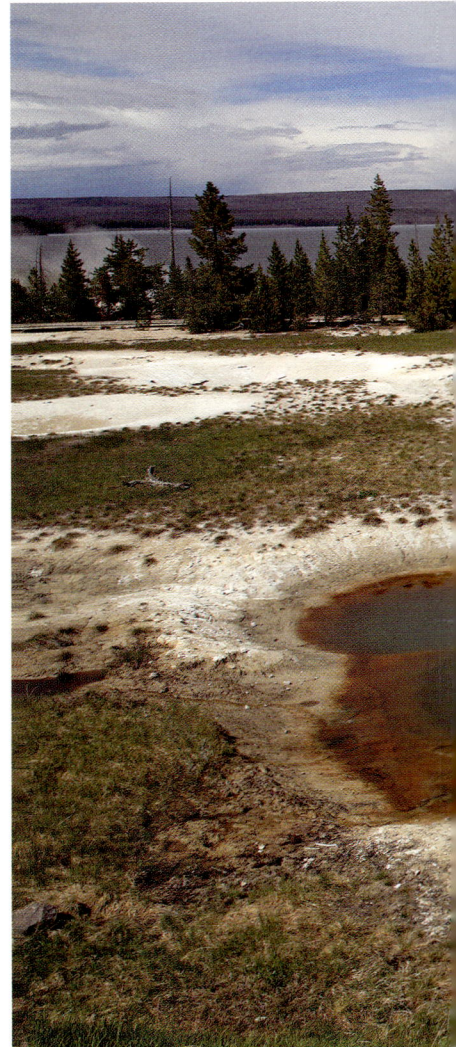

Central Basin

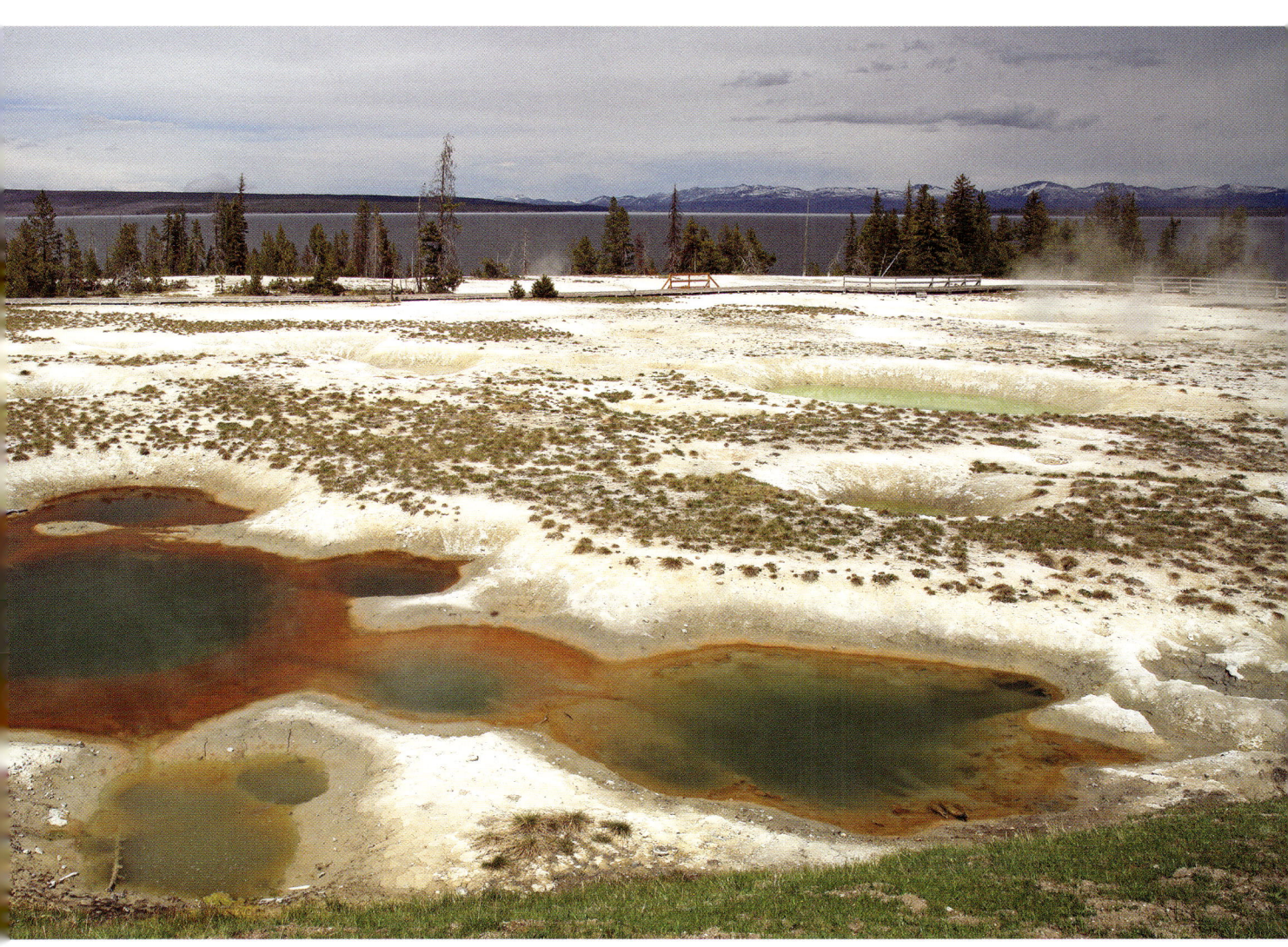

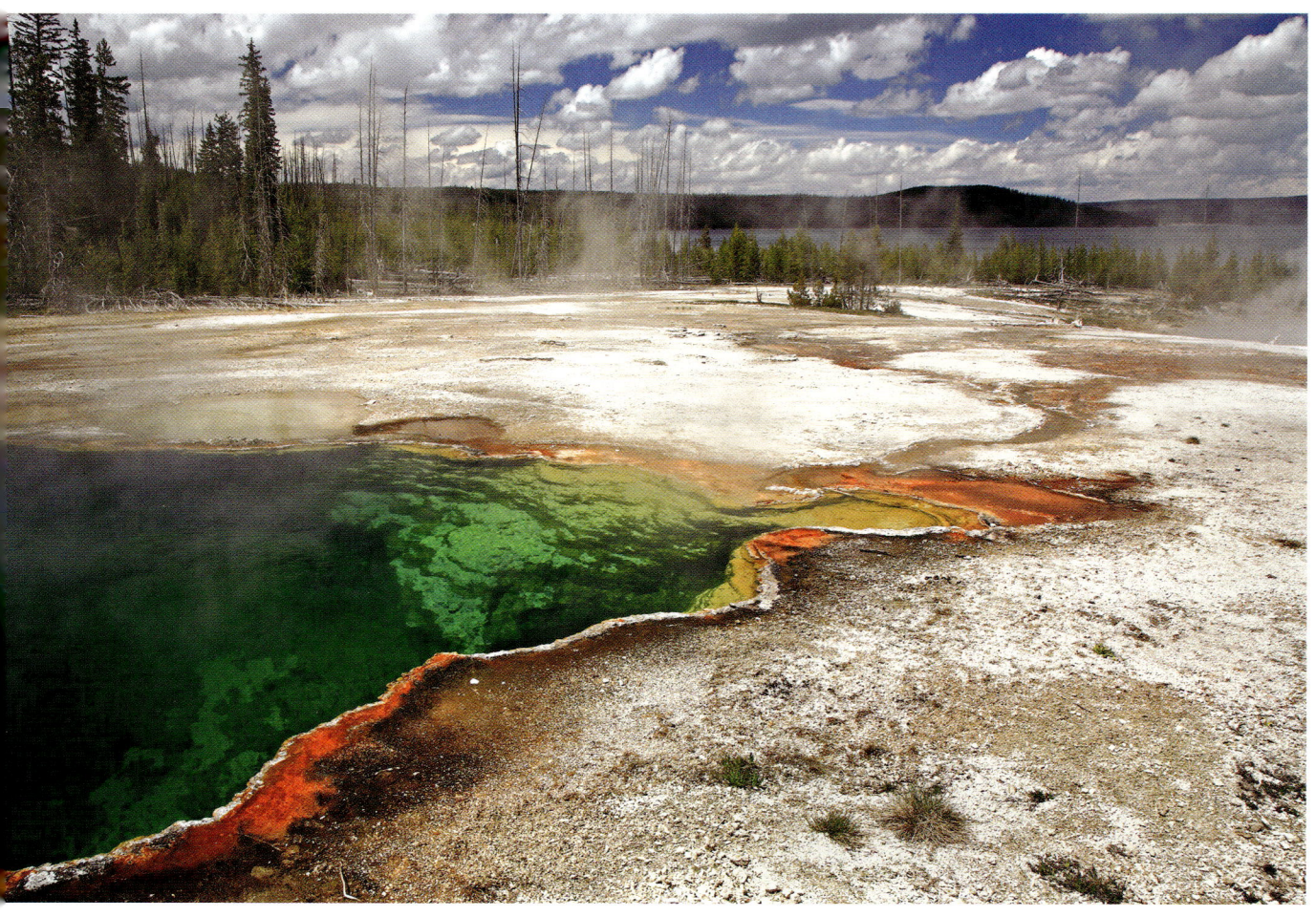

Abyss Pool

ABYSS POOL

Abyss Pool's "ultramarine hue of the transparent depth in the bright sunlight was the most dazzlingly beautiful sight I have ever beheld."

FERDINAND VANDEVEER HAYDEN
Preliminary Reports, 1871

Abyss Pool's walls, "coral-like in formation and singular in shape, tinted by the water's color, are surely good representations of fairy palaces."

W.W. WYLIE
Yellowstone, 1882

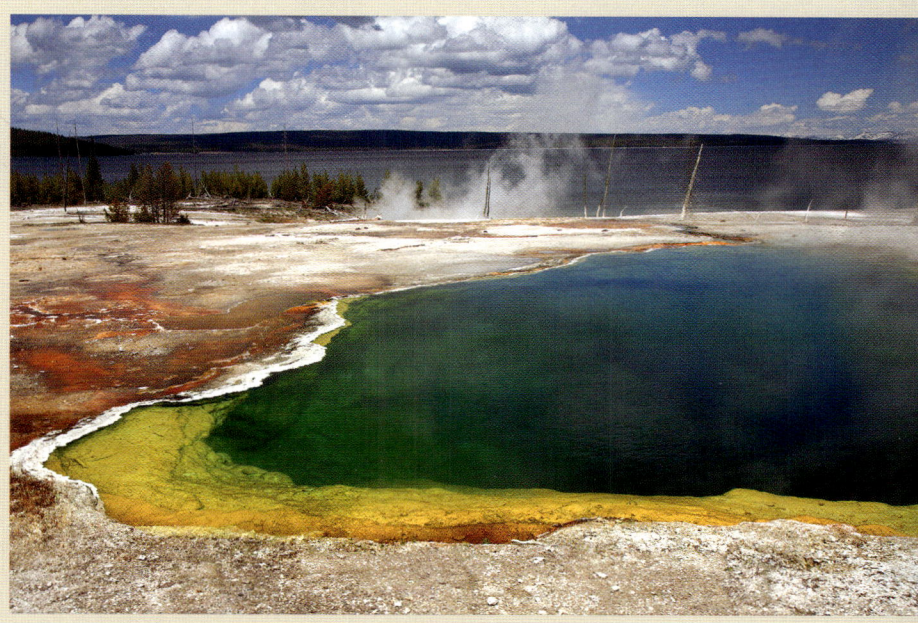

Abyss Pool

Bacterial mats

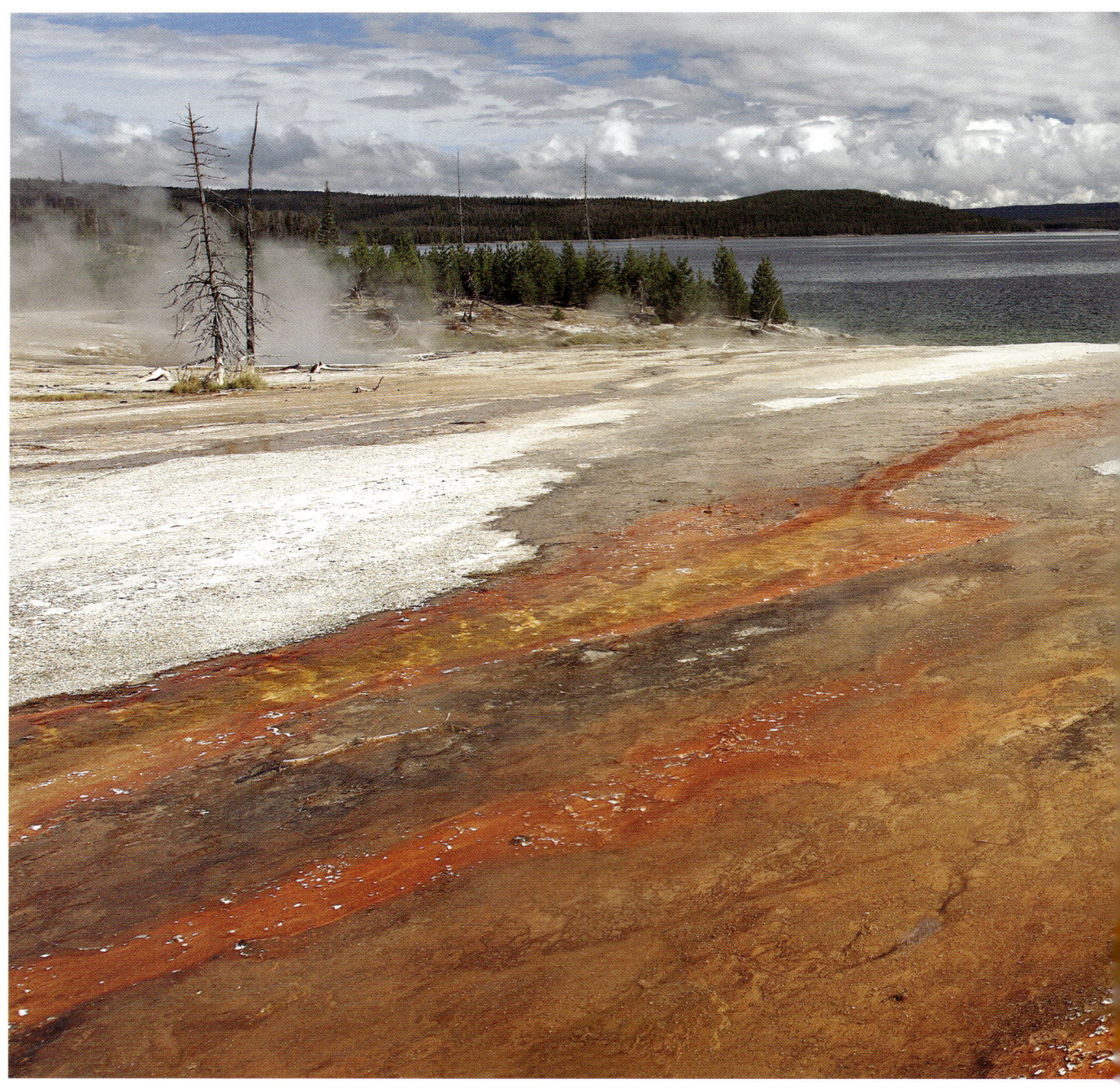

"Around the larger [springs] the ground was marshy, and largely composed of a reddish earth, which looked like wet brickdust. A number of hot streams flowed from these springs into the lake."

WALTER TRUMBALL
Overland Monthly, June 1871

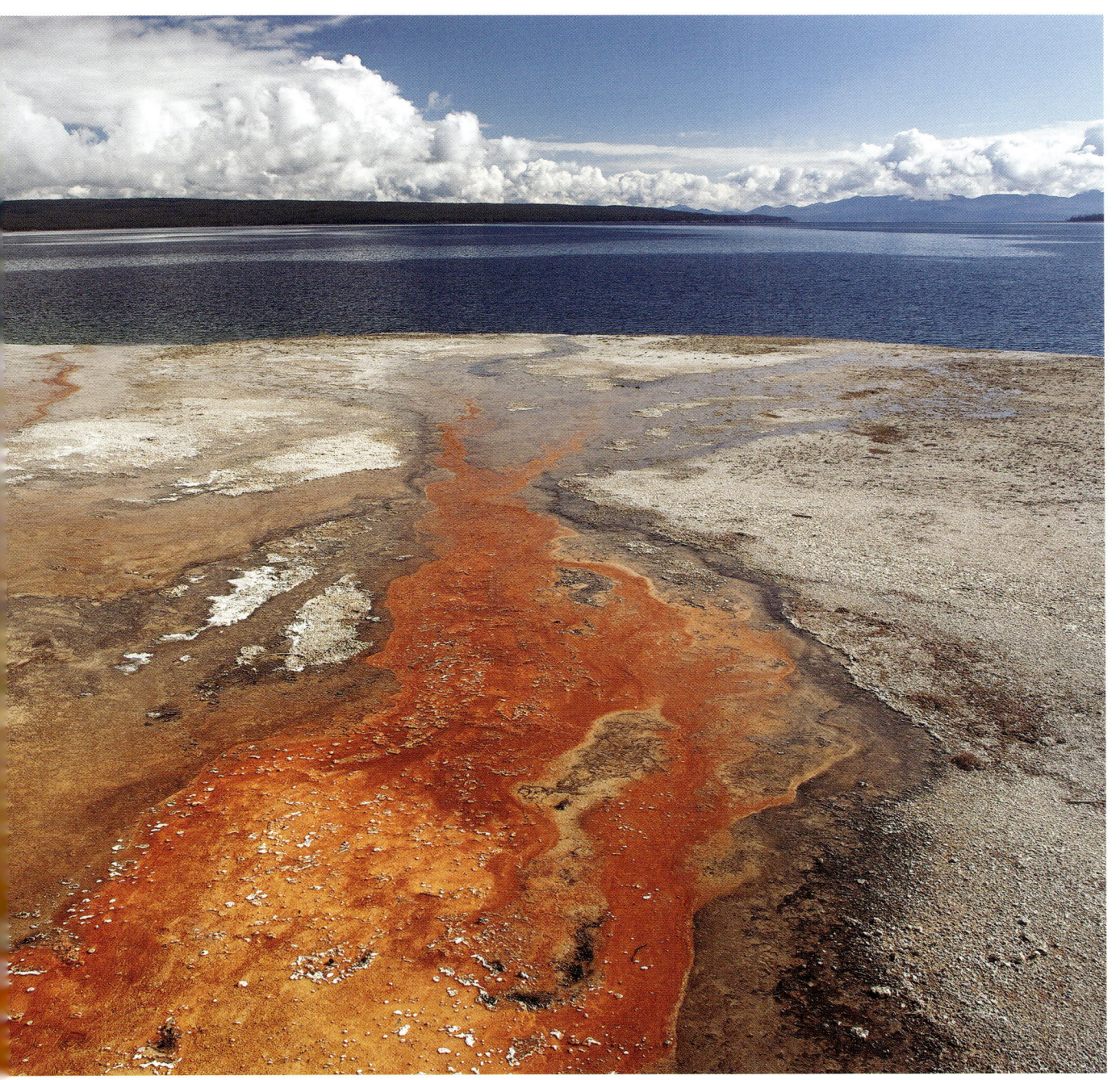

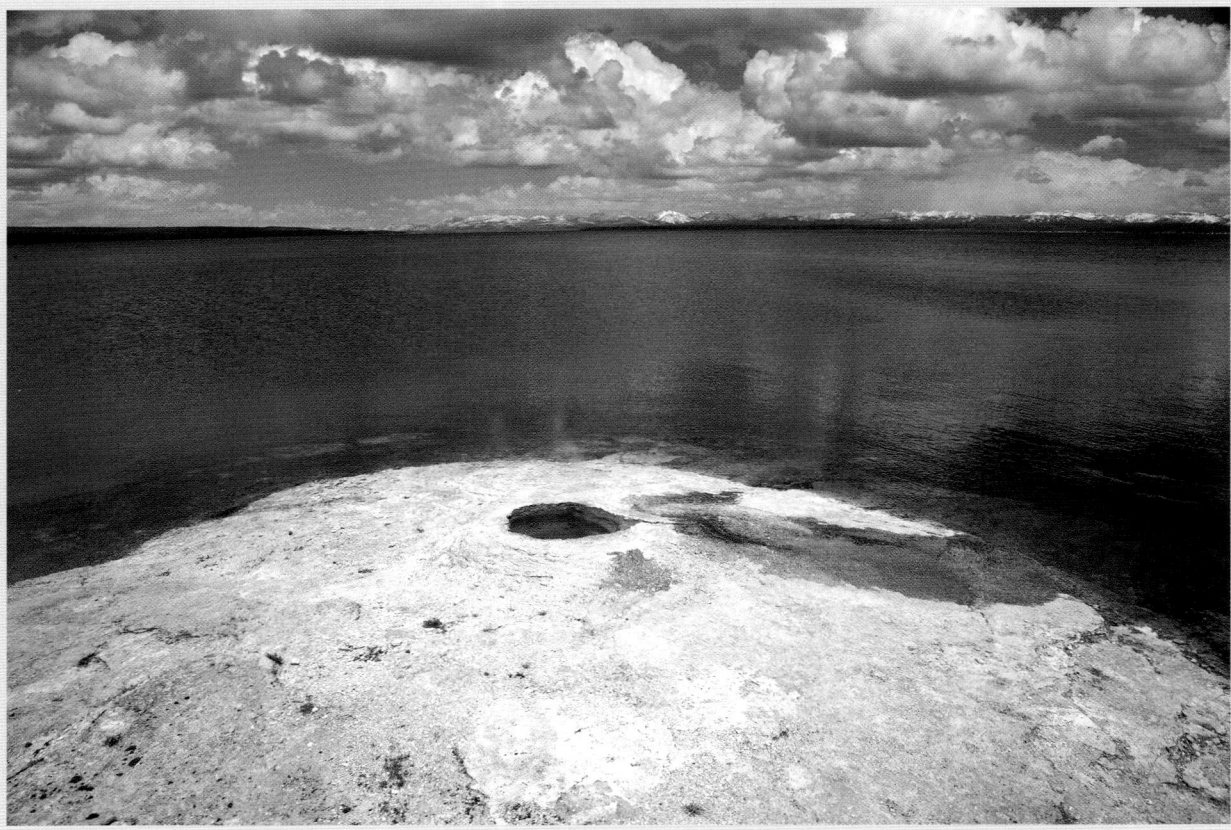

Big Cone

"At the water's edge, along the lakeshore, there were several mounds of solid stone, on the top of each of which was a small basin with a perforated bottom; these also overflowed at times, and the hot water trickled down on every side. Thus, by the slow process of precipitation, through the countless lapse of ages, these stone monuments have been formed."

DAVID FOLSOM OF THE FOLSOM-COOK-PETERSON EXPEDITION, 1869

BLACK POOL

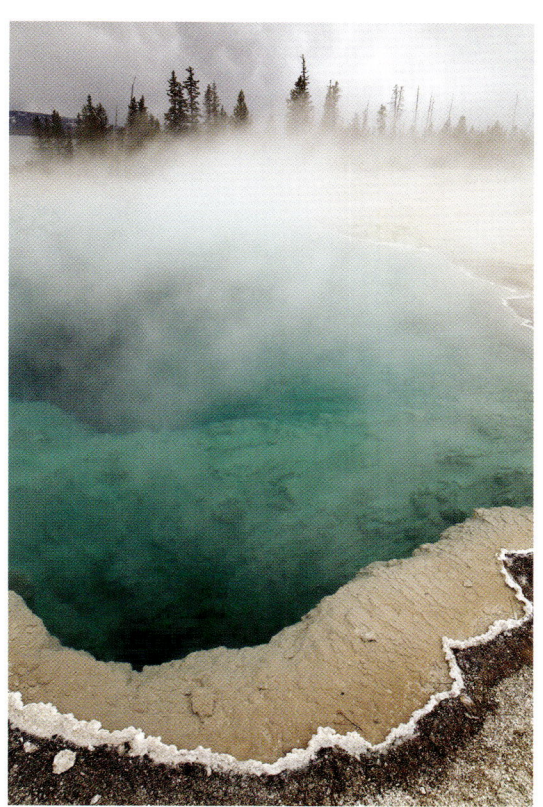

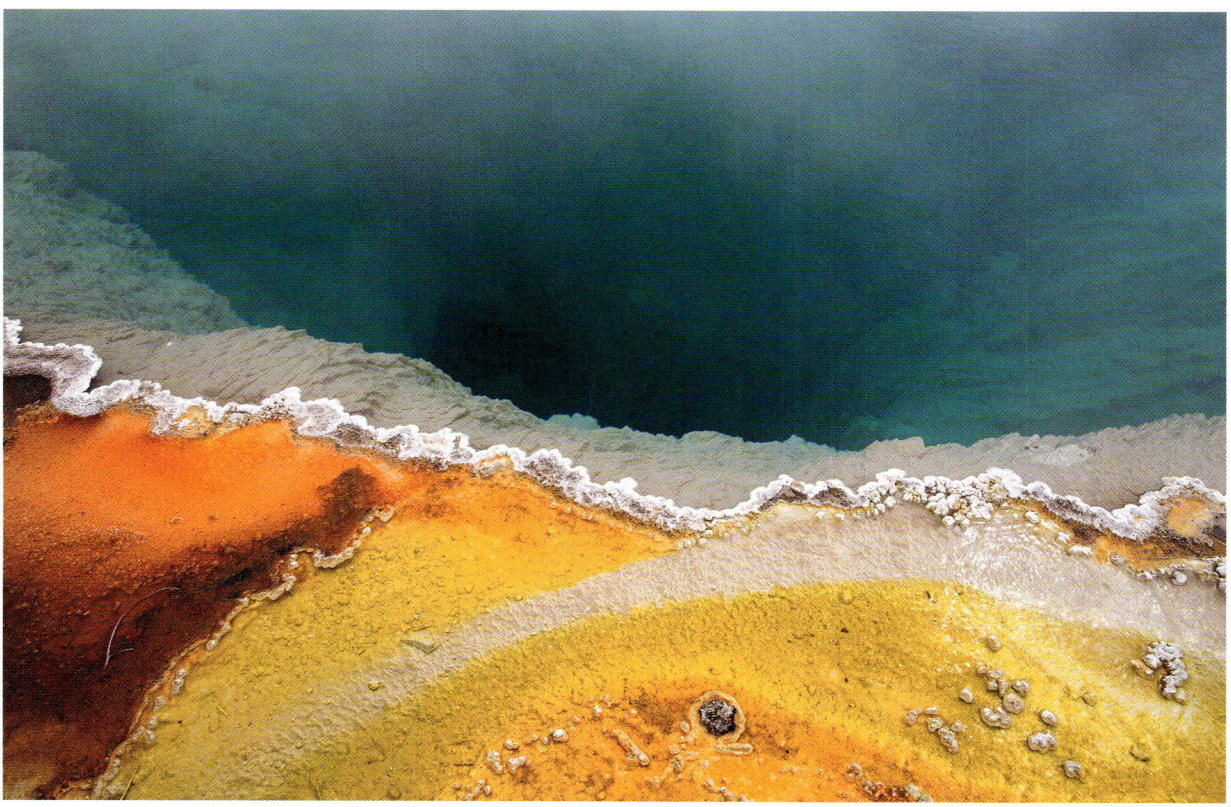

Black Pool

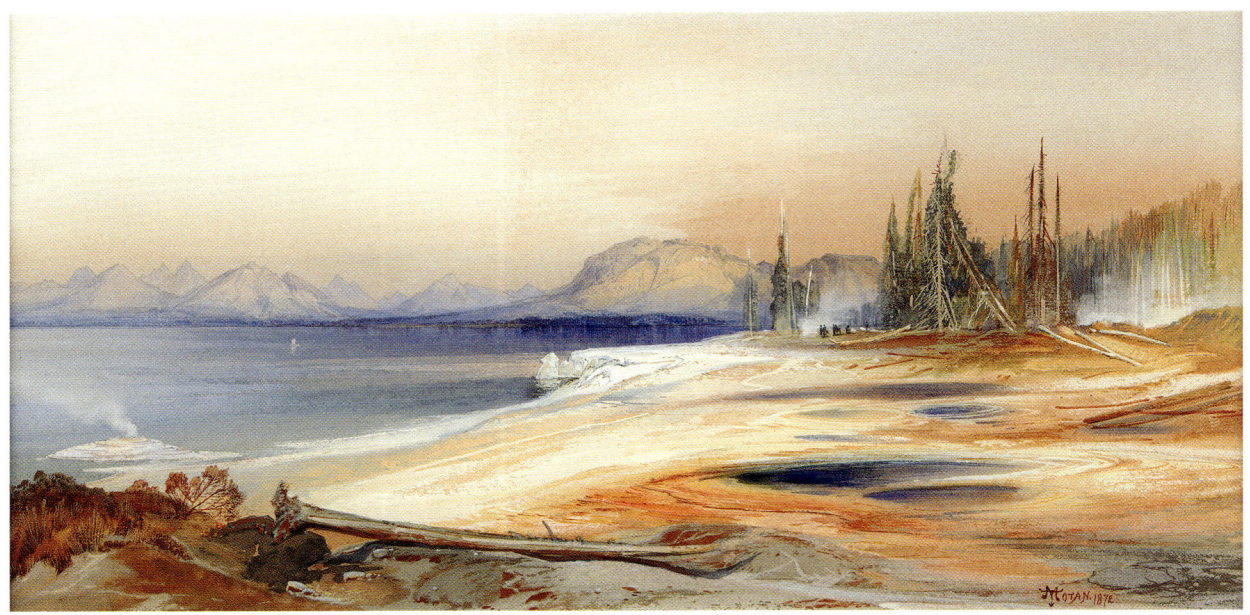

The Yellowstone Lake with Hot Springs
Thomas Moran, 1872
Gilcrease Museum, Tulsa, OK
0226.1362

"There were several hundred springs here, varying in size from miniature fountains to pools or wells seventy-five feet in diameter and of great depth. The water had a pale violet tinge, and was very clear, enabling us to discern small objects fifty or sixty feet below the surface. In some of these, vast openings led off at the side; and as the slanting rays of the sun lit up these deep caverns, we could see the rocks hanging from their roofs, their water-worn sides and rocky floors, almost as plainly as if we had been traversing their silent chambers."

DAVID FOLSOM OF THE FOLSOM-COOK-PETERSON EXPEDITION, 1869

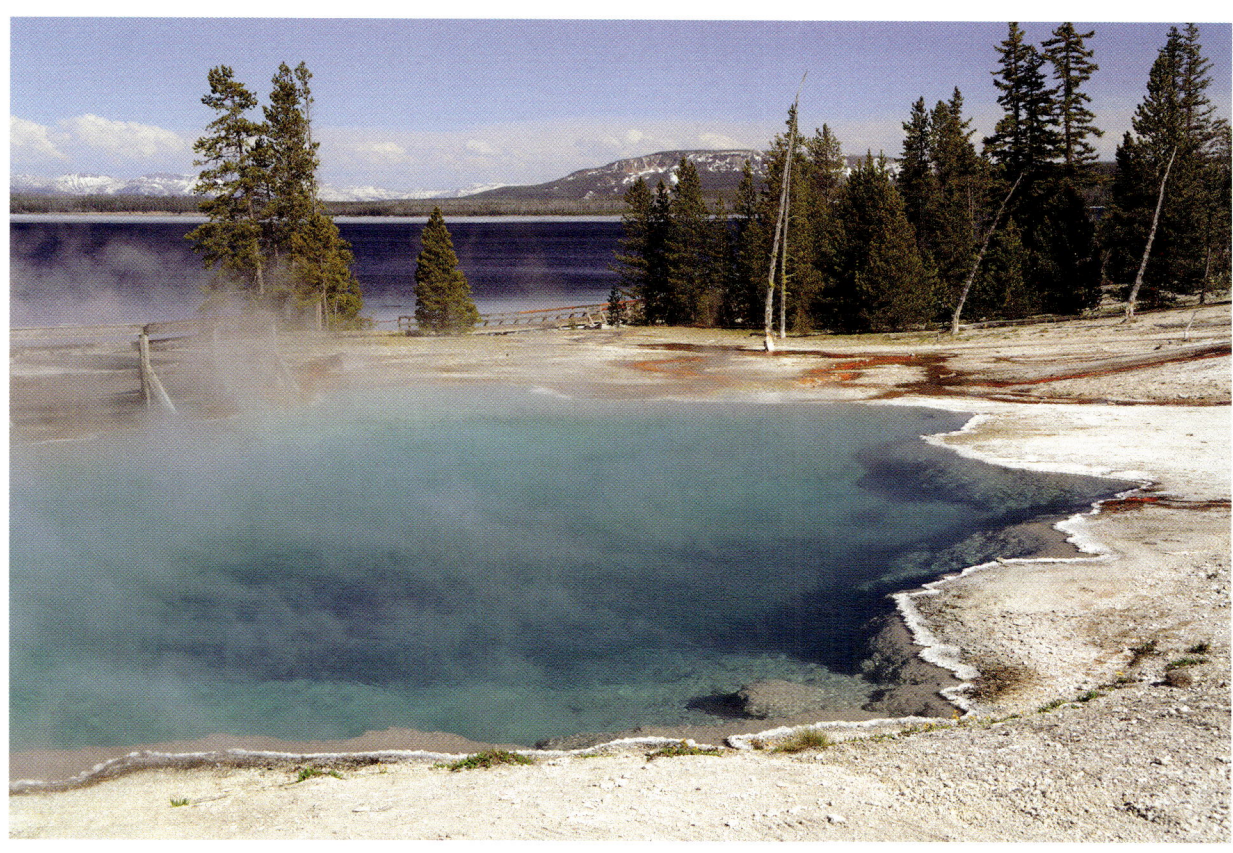

Black Pool and Yellowstone Lake

FISHING CONE

"A gentleman [Cornelius Hedges] was fishing from one of the narrow isthmuses, or shelves of rock, which divided one of these hot springs from [Yellowstone] lake, when, swinging a trout ashore, it accidentally got off the hook and fell into the spring. For a moment it darted about with wonderful rapidity, as if seeking an outlet. Then it came to the top, dead, and literally boiled."

WALTER TRUMBALL
Overland Monthly, June 1871

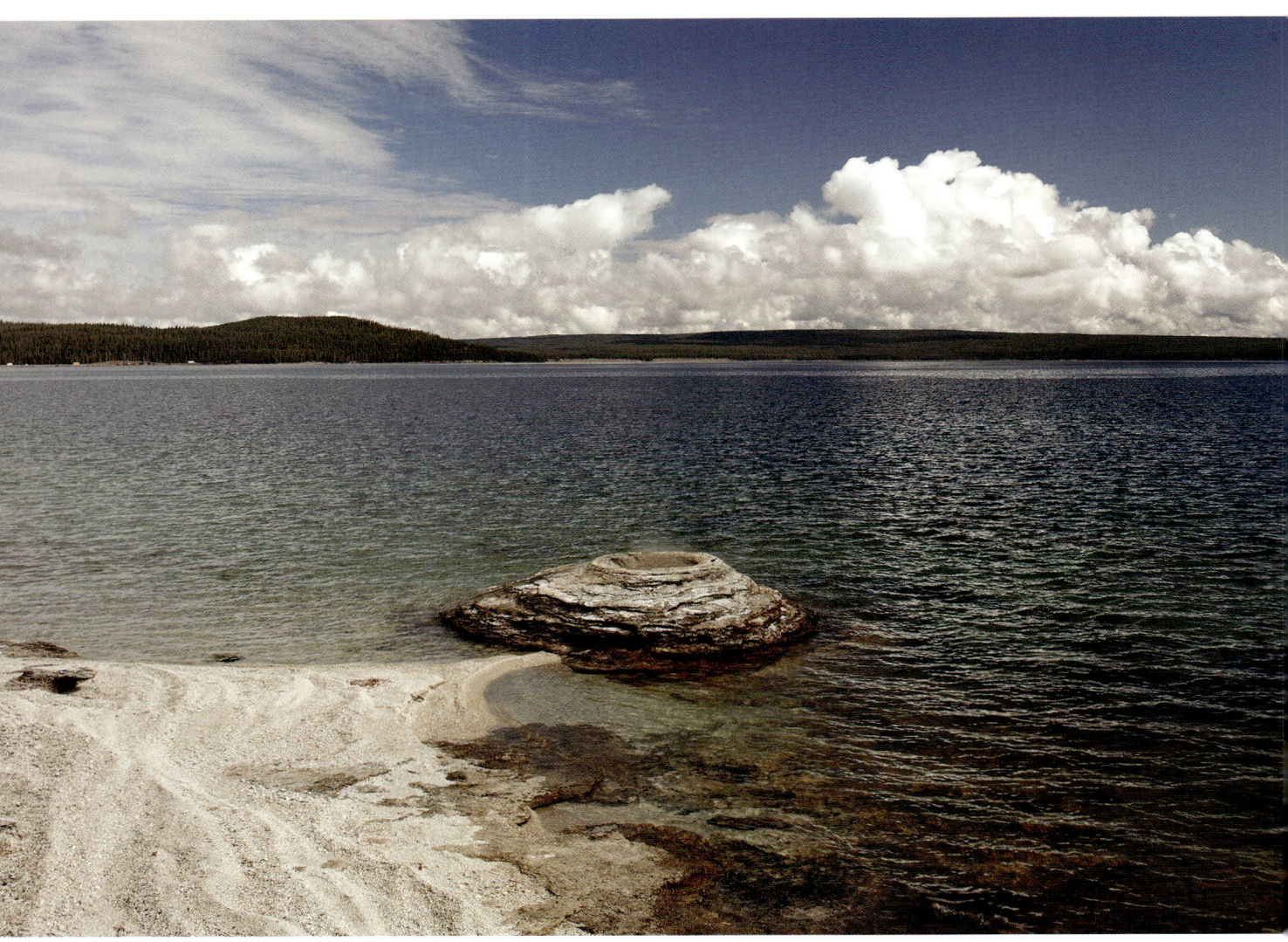

‹

Fishing Cone

Fishing Cone is submerged when lake
water level is high

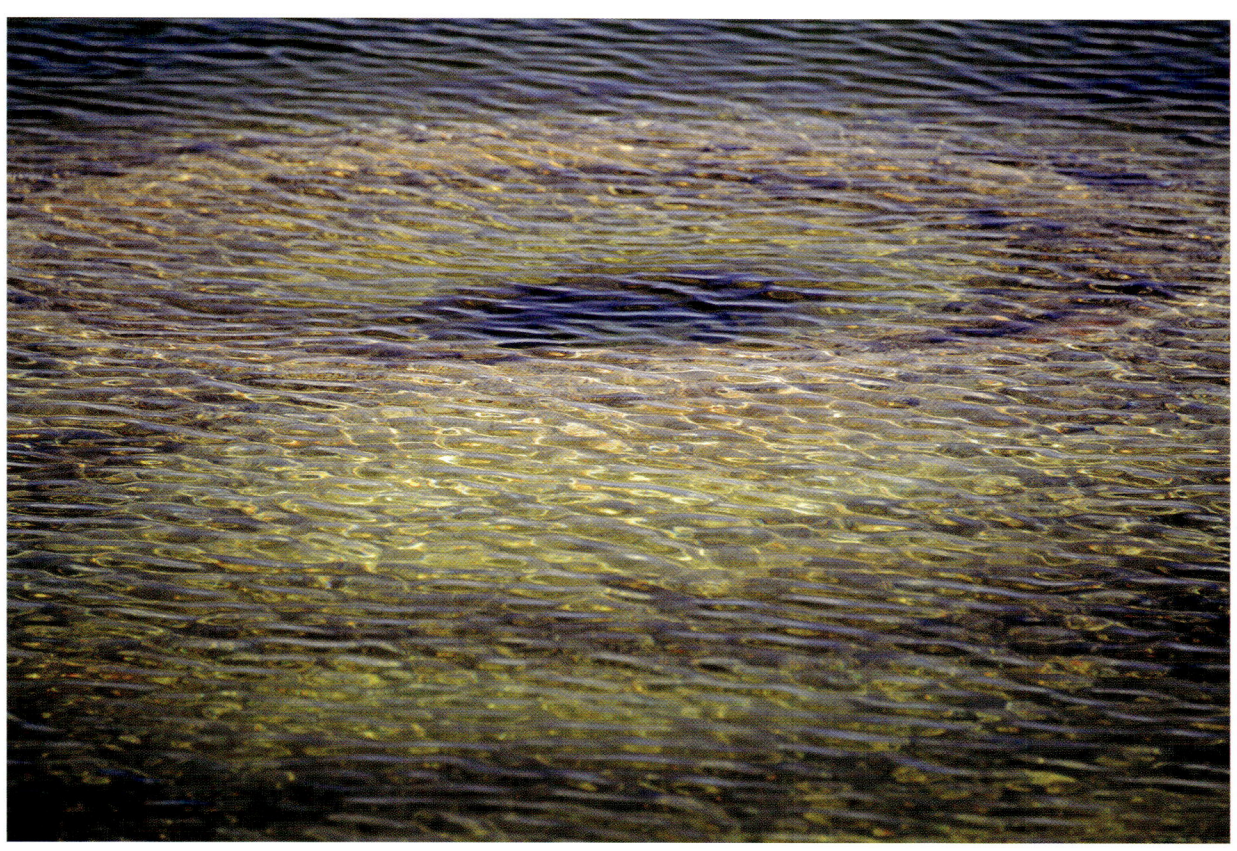

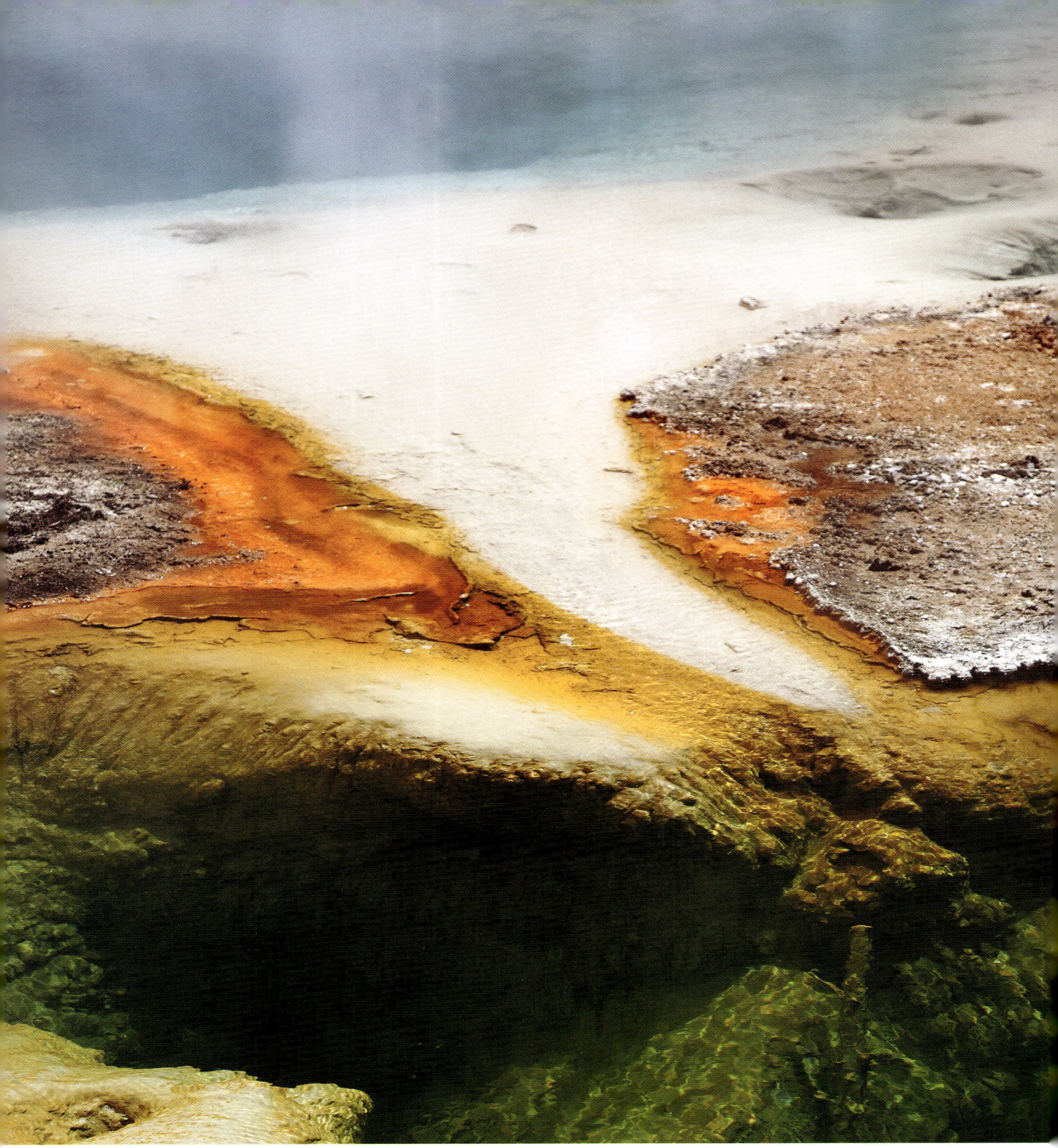

Seismograph and Bluebell Pools

SEISMOGRAPH AND BLUEBELL POOLS

"These are basins of different sizes and unknown depths, in which float what appear to be raw bullock-hides as they look in a tanner's vat, waving sluggishly about with every undulation of the water; the resemblance is complete. On examination the leathery substance proves to be a fragile texture, something like the vegetable scum in stagnant pools, (and yet it is not vegetable) with brilliant colors of red, yellow, green, and black, on the shaded side. It is easily torn and could not be preserved, unless indeed by pressure, like rose leaves; it has the thickness and flabbiness of rawhide, and is quite heavy when wet. Digging down into the basins, I found that this singular substance filled the whole depth, layer upon layer being deposited; and stranger than all, the lower strata were solidified, turning to pure, finely-grained sheets of alabaster, specimens of which I brought in."

LIEUTENANT GUSTAVUS C. DOANE
Yellowstone Expedition of 1870

"Farthest from the beach are the springs of boiling mud, in some of which the mud is very thin, in others of such a consistency that it is heaped up as it boils over, gradually spreading under its own weight until it covers quite a large surface. The mud or clay is of different colors. That in some of the springs is nearly as white as white marble; in others it is of a lavender color; in others it is of a rich pink, of different shades. . . . The hard incrustations around the edges of the springs are of various colors, in some cases being dark red, in others scarlet, in others yellow, and in still others green."

NATHANIEL PITT LANGFORD
The Discovery of Yellowstone Park: Journal of the Washburn Expedition to the Yellowstone and Firehole Rivers in the Year 1870, 1905

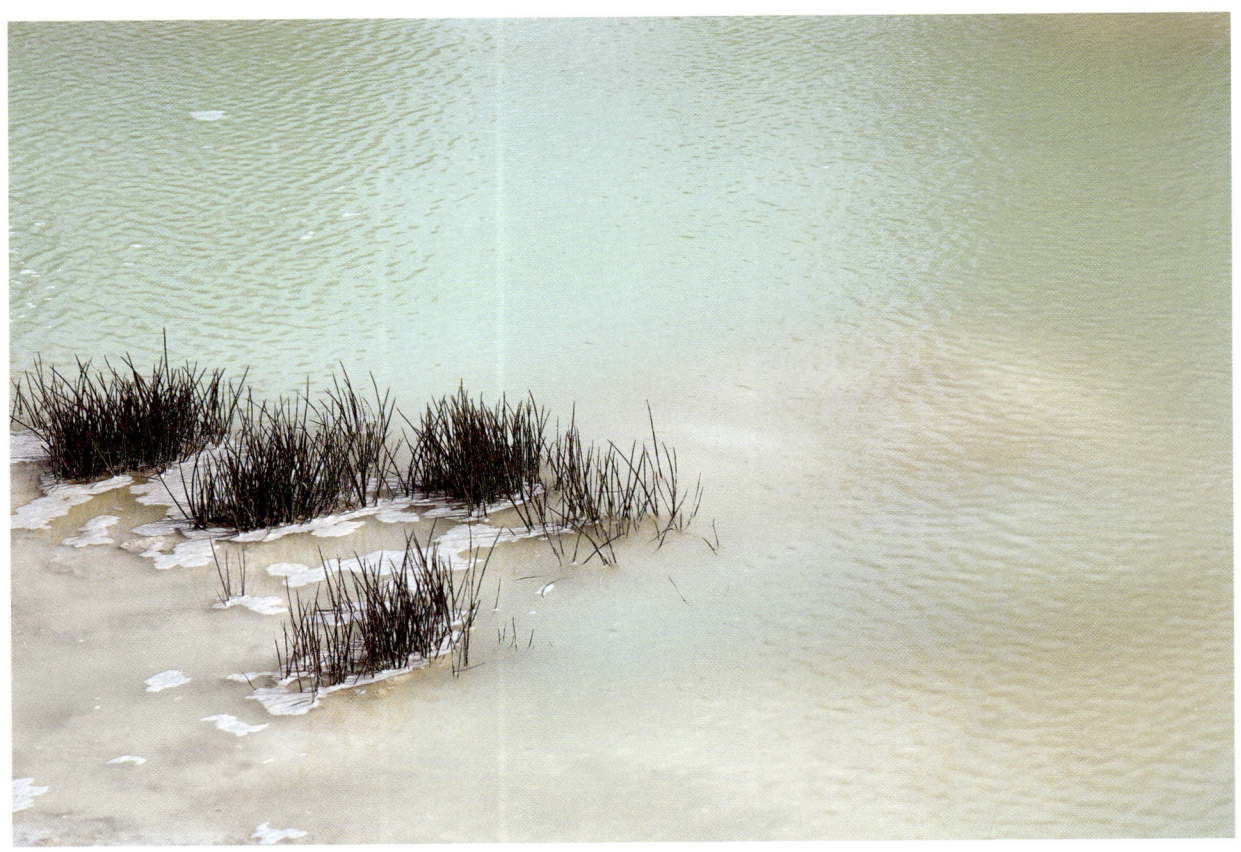

Thumb Paint Pots

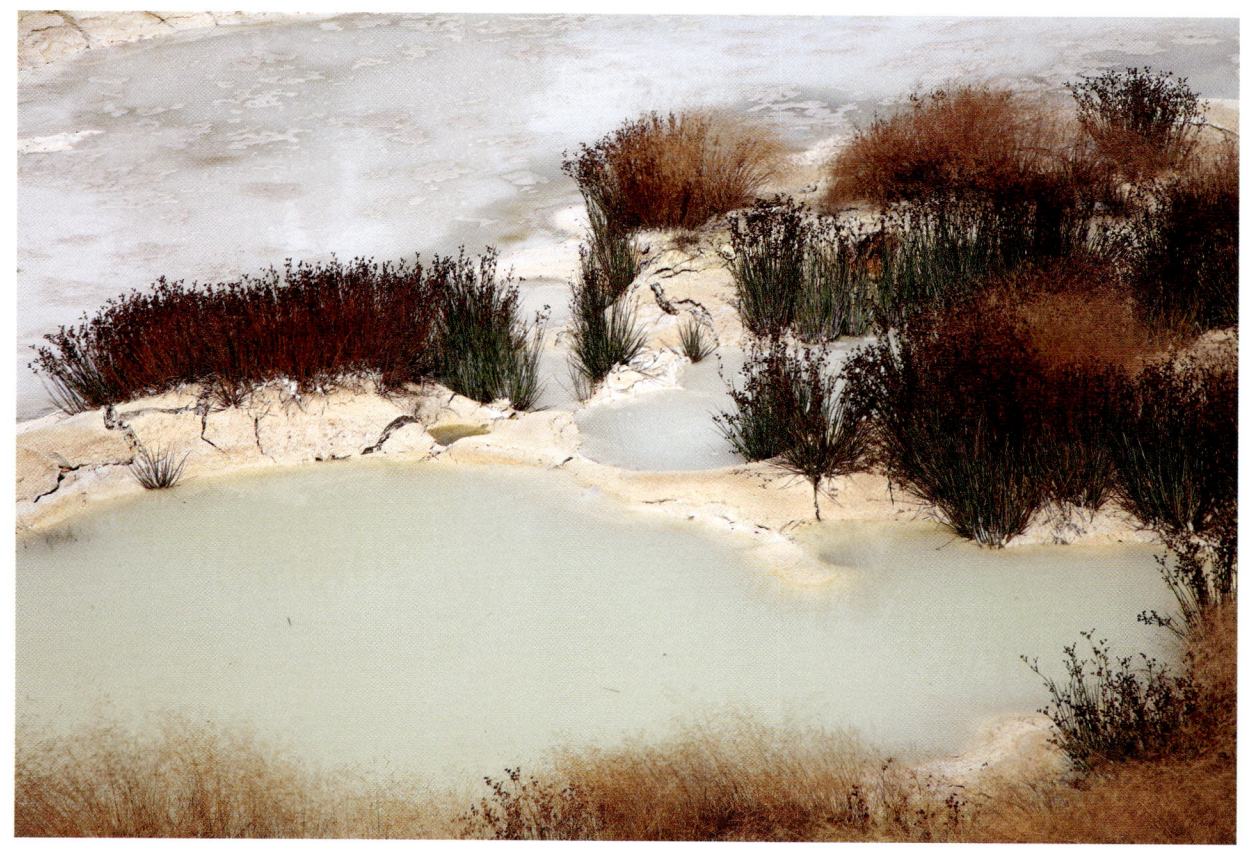

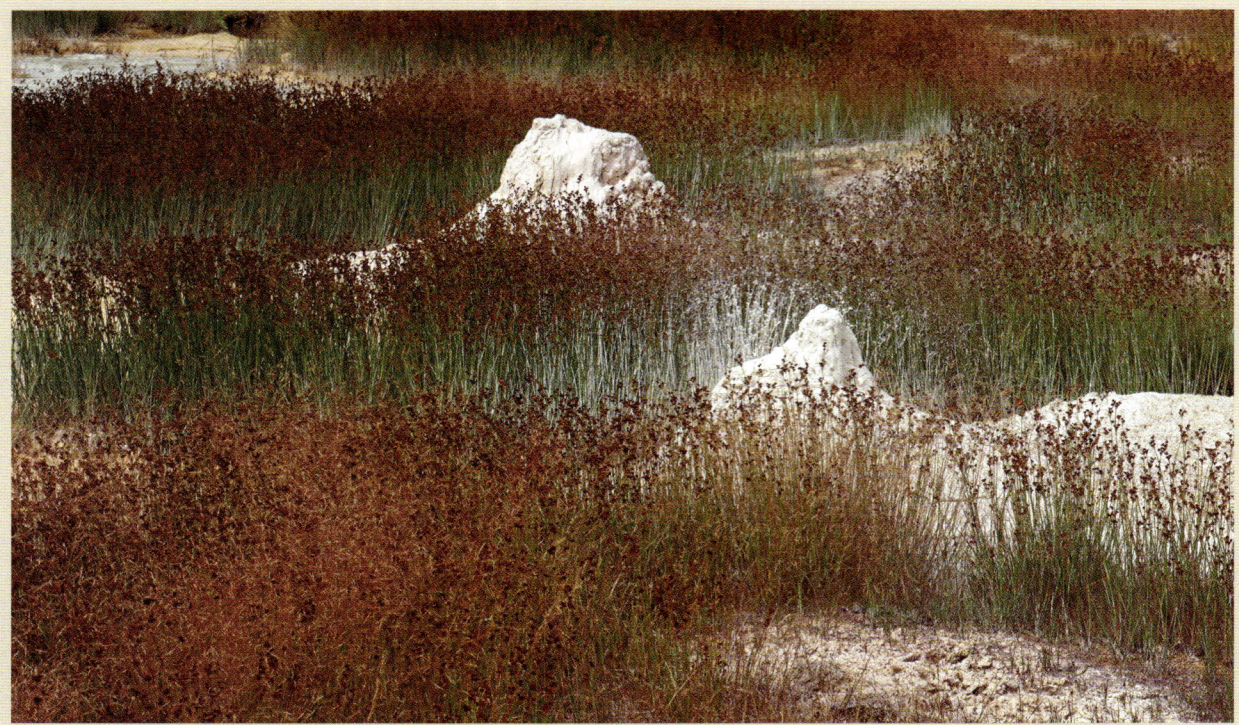

Thumb Paint Pots

"A small cluster of mud springs nearby claimed our attention. They were like hollow truncated cones and oblong mounds, three or four feet in height. These were filled with mud, resembling thick paint of the finest quality, differing in color, from pure white to the various shades of yellow, pink, red and violet."

DAVID FOLSOM OF THE FOLSOM-COOK-PETERSON EXPEDITION, 1869

"Yellowstone Lake, as seen from our camp tonight, seems to me to be the most beautiful body of water in the world. In front of our camp it has a wide sandy beach like that of the ocean, which extends for miles and as far as the eye can reach, save that occasionally there is to be found a sharp projection of rocks. . . . Fire and water have been at work here together—fire to throw out the deposit in a rough shape, and water to polish it."

NATHANIEL PITT LANGFORD
The Discovery of Yellowstone Park: Journal of the Washburn Expedition to the Yellowstone and Firehole Rivers in the Year 1870, 1905

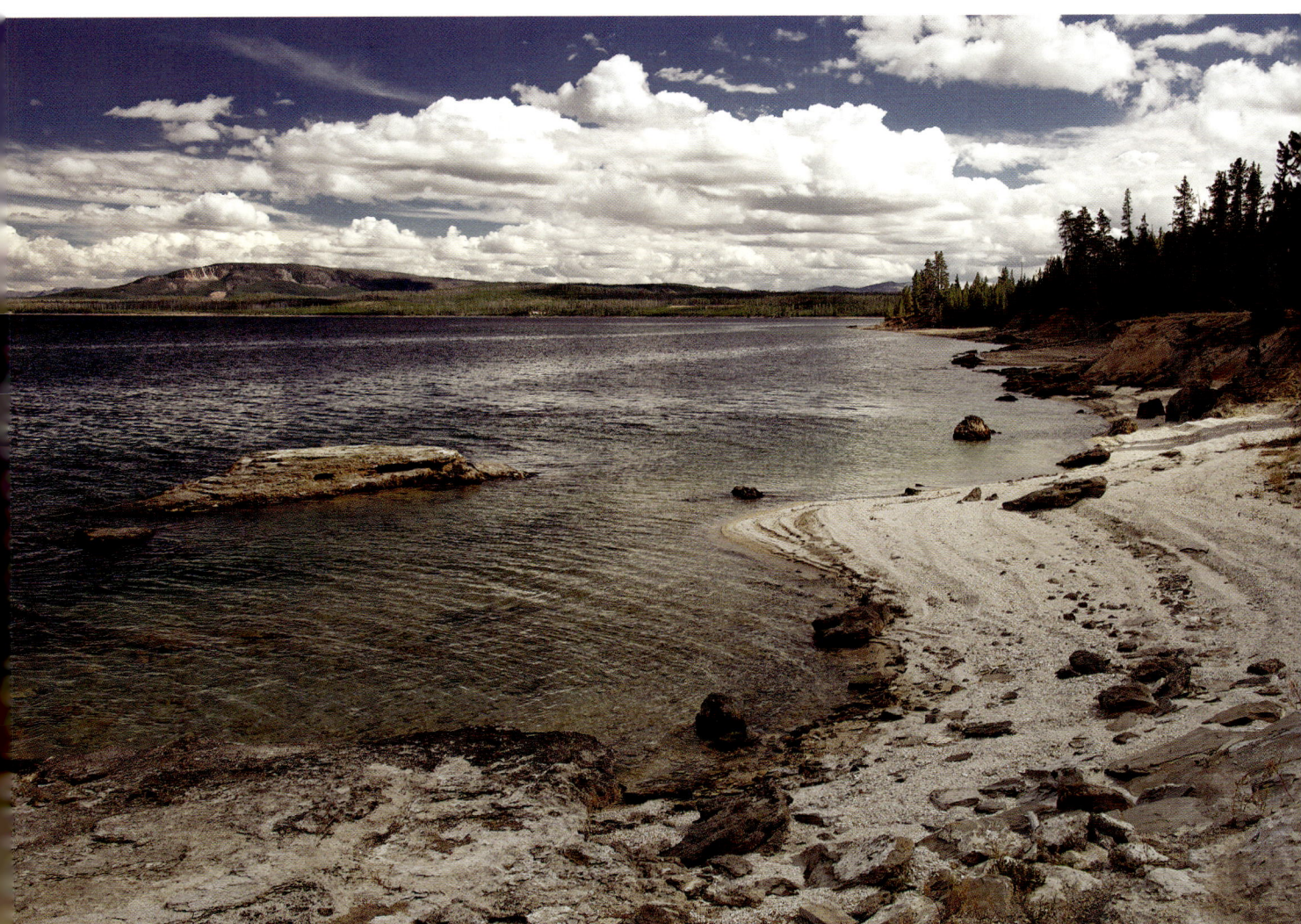

Yellowstone Lake at West Thumb

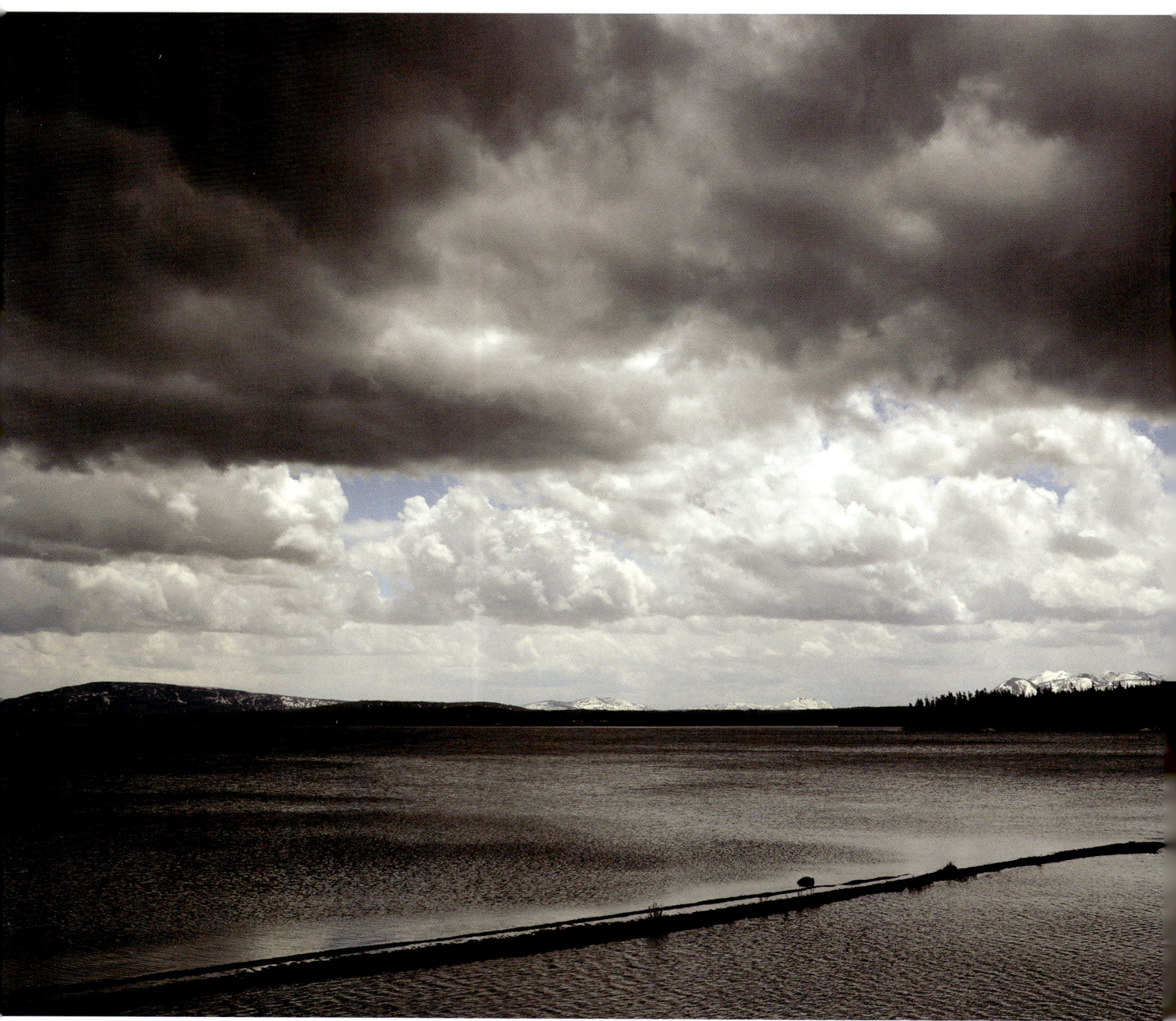

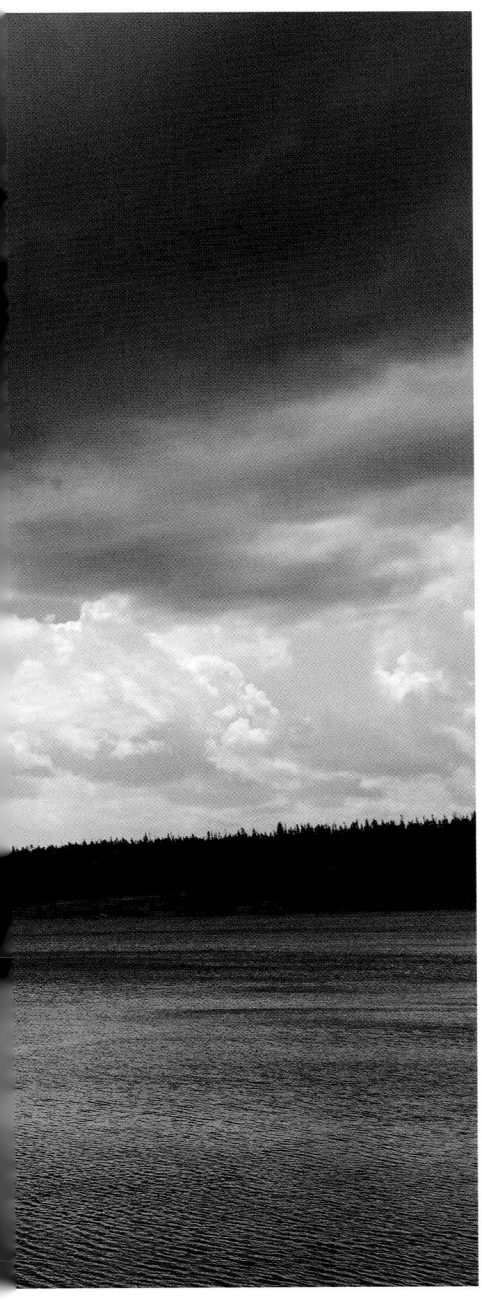

"The overlooking bench rises from the water's edge about eight feet, forming a bank of sand or natural levee, which serves to prevent the overflow of the land adjoining, which, when the lake is receiving the water from the mountain streams that empty into it while the snows are melting, is several feet below the surface of the lake."

NATHANIEL PITT LANGFORD
The Discovery of Yellowstone Park: Journal of the Washburn Expedition to the Yellowstone and Firehole Rivers in the Year 1870, 1905

Yellowstone Lake at Little Thumb Creek

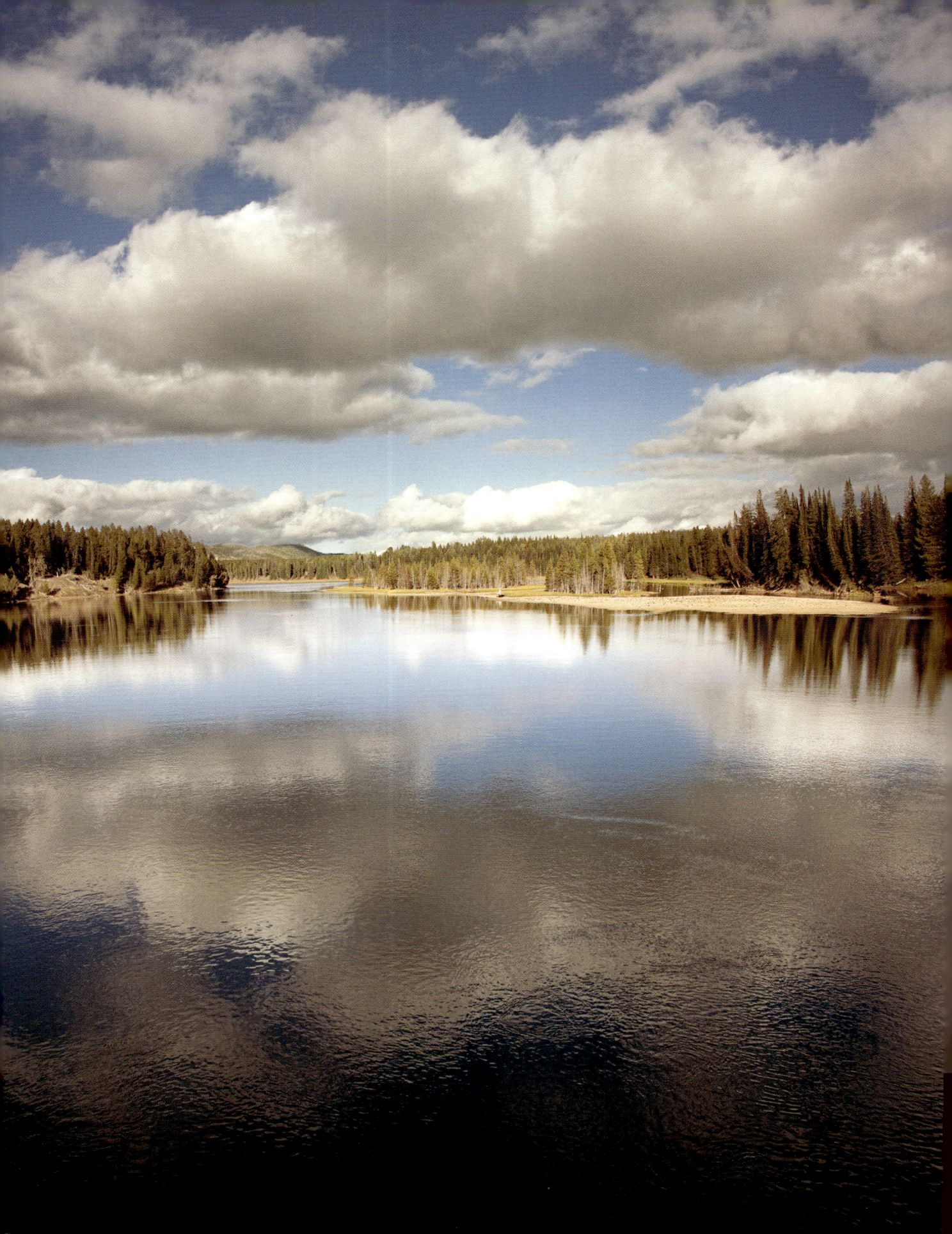

LAKE AREA

BRIDGE BAY FROM GULL POINT DRIVE

FISHING BRIDGE

HEAD OF THE YELLOWSTONE RIVER

LAKE LODGE

LAKE YELLOWSTONE HOTEL

YELLOWSTONE LAKE

Yellowstone River

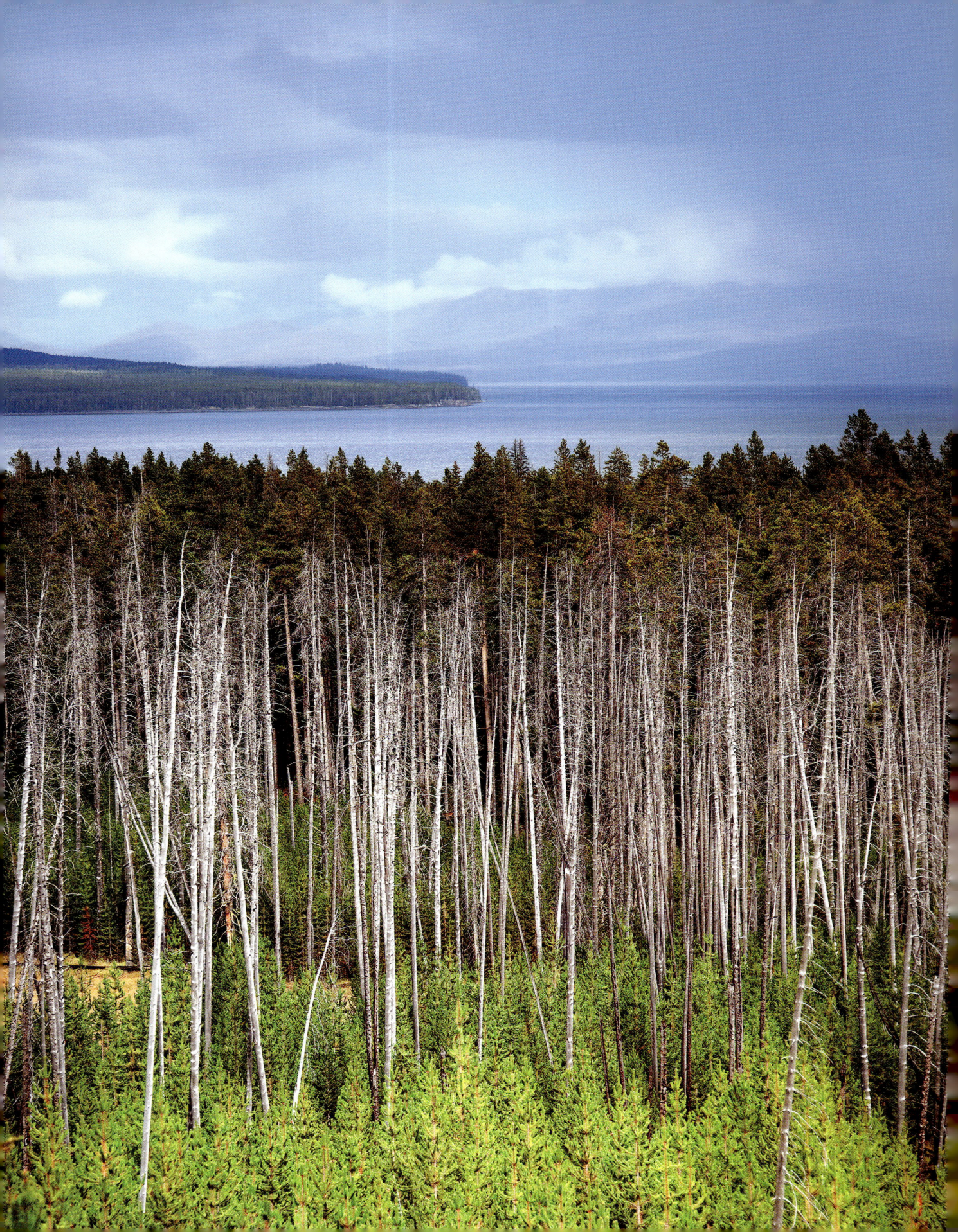

"Lake Yellowstone is a lonely, but lovely inland sea, everywhere surrounded by 'forests primeval,' and nestled in the bosom of the Rocky Mountains. Its shape resembles the broad hand. . . . The palm of the hand represents the main body, or north part, of the lake. The fingers and thumb, spread to their utmost extent—the thumb and little finger being much the longest—represent inlets indenting the south shore, and stretching inland, as if to wash away the Rocky Mountains. Between these inlets project high, rocky promontories, covered with dense timber."

WALTER TRUMBALL
Overland Monthly, June 1871

"The lakeshore was covered with subsilica, broken into small pieces, and washed smooth by the action of the waves. Many of these pieces were pure and white as alabaster."

WALTER TRUMBALL
Overland Monthly, June 1871

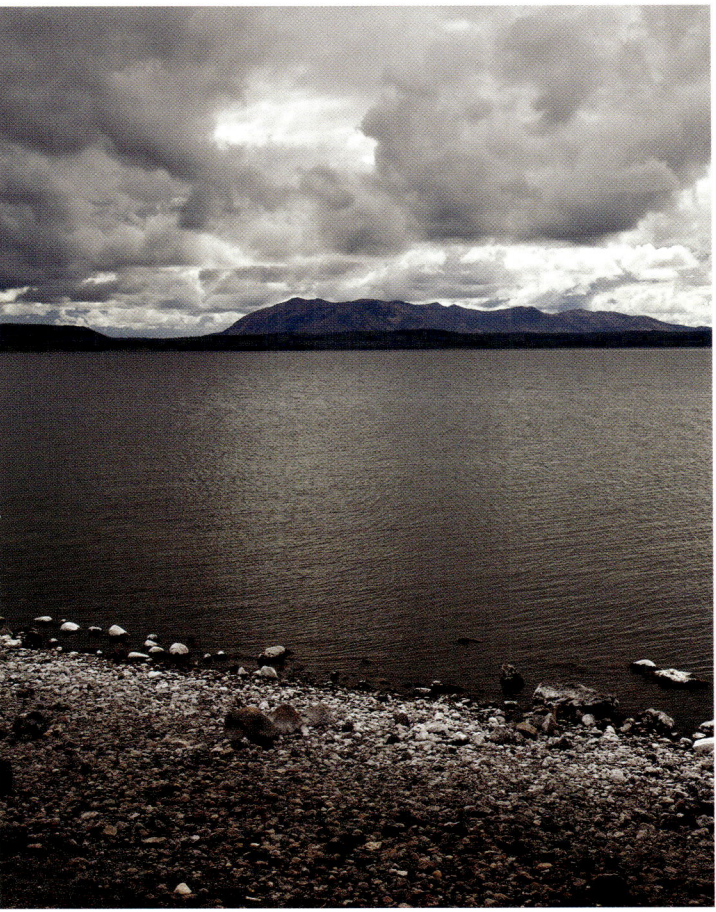

Pumice Point

<

Yellowstone Lake

BRIDGE BAY FROM GULL POINT DRIVE

"We came to a small grassy opening upon the opposite side of which was a beautiful little lake, separated from the main lake by only a sandbar, which the surf had thrown up across the narrow neck which formerly connected them. . . . Large flocks of geese and ducks were feeding near the shore or floating gracefully on its smooth surface. Beyond the lake the timber was tall and straight and to appearances as thick as cane in a southern swamp. This was one of the beautiful places we had found fashioned by the practiced hand of nature, that man had not desecrated."

DAVID FOLSOM OF THE FOLSOM-COOK-PETERSON EXPEDITION, 1869

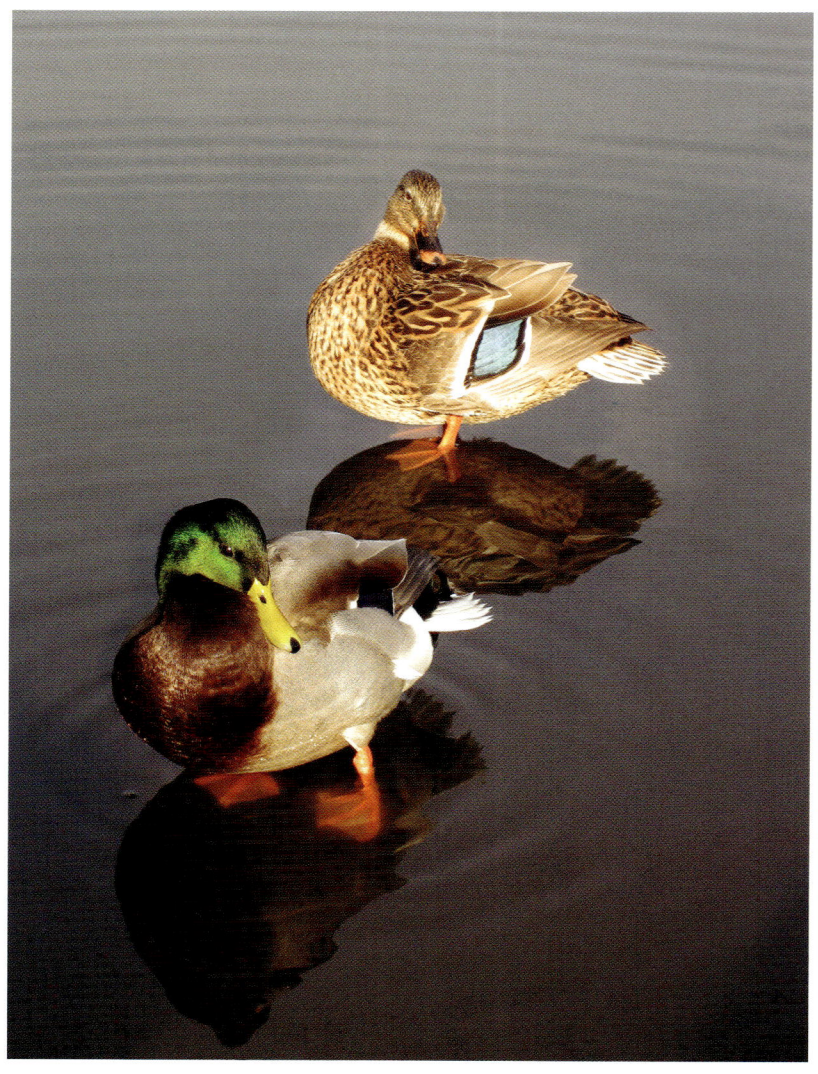

Mallards

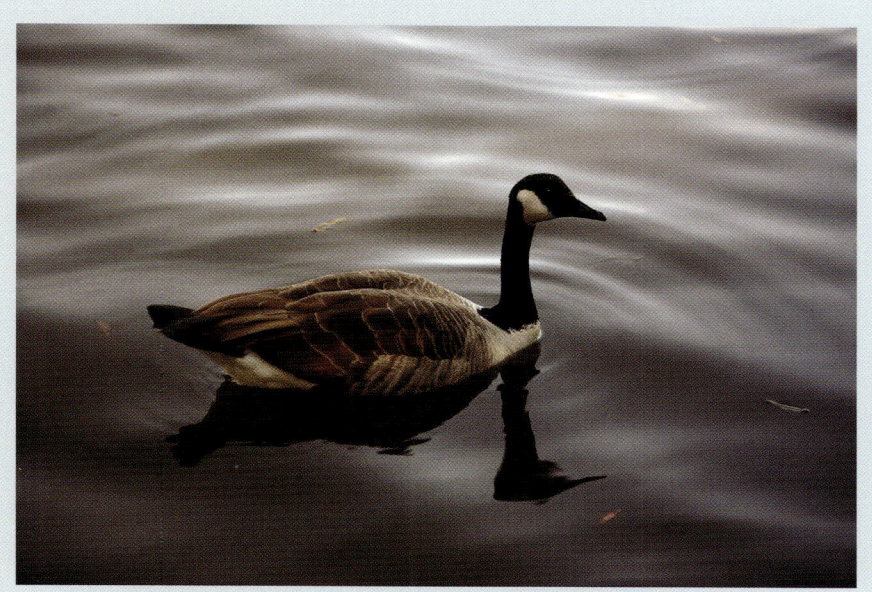

Canada goose

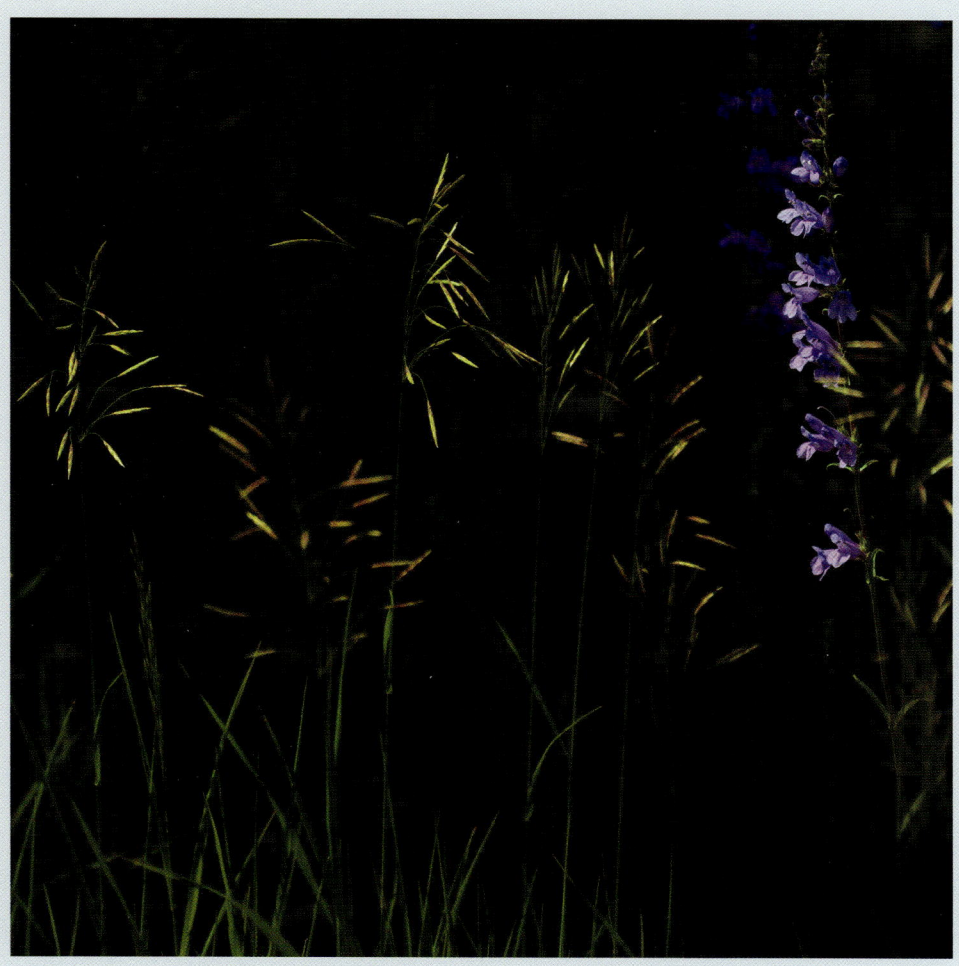

"The mood of the lake is ever changing; the character of its shore is ever varying. At one moment, it is placid and glassy as a calm summer's sea; at the next, 'it breaks into dimples, and laughs in the sun.' Half an hour later, beneath a stormy sky, its waters may be broken and lashed into an angry and dangerous sea . . .."

WALTER TRUMBALL
Overland Monthly, June 1871

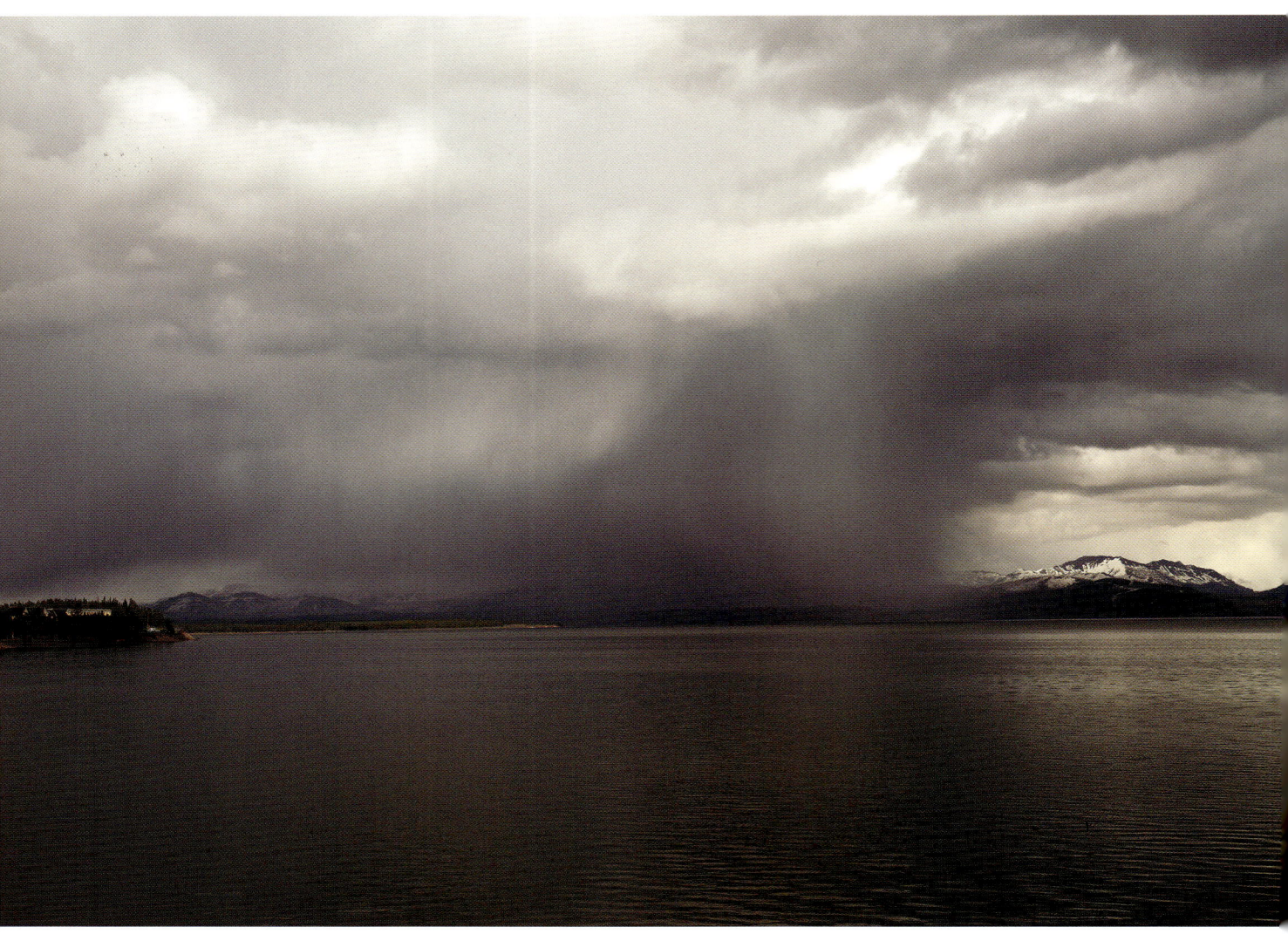

FISHING BRIDGE

<

Bridge Bay with Lake Yellowstone
Hotel on the promontory

Fishing Bridge and the Yellowstone
River

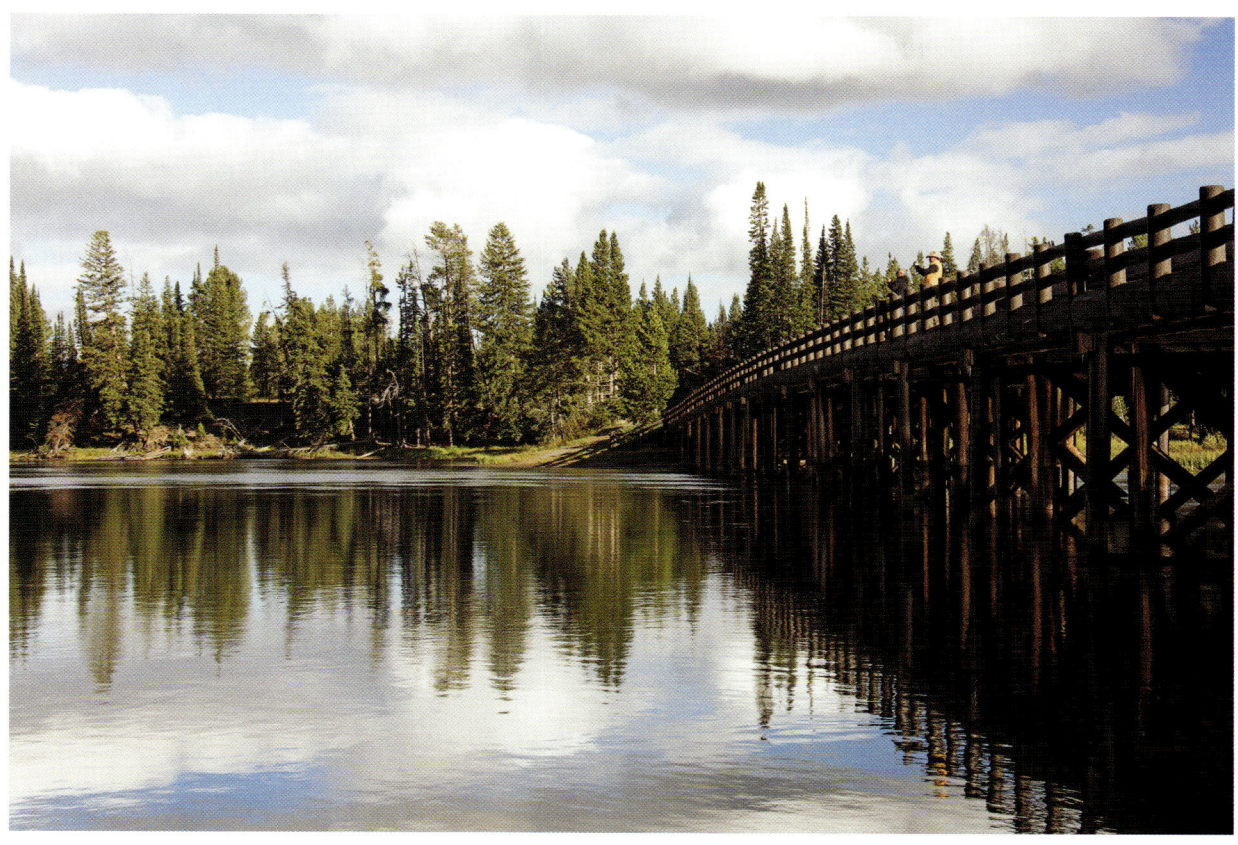

HEAD OF THE
YELLOWSTONE RIVER

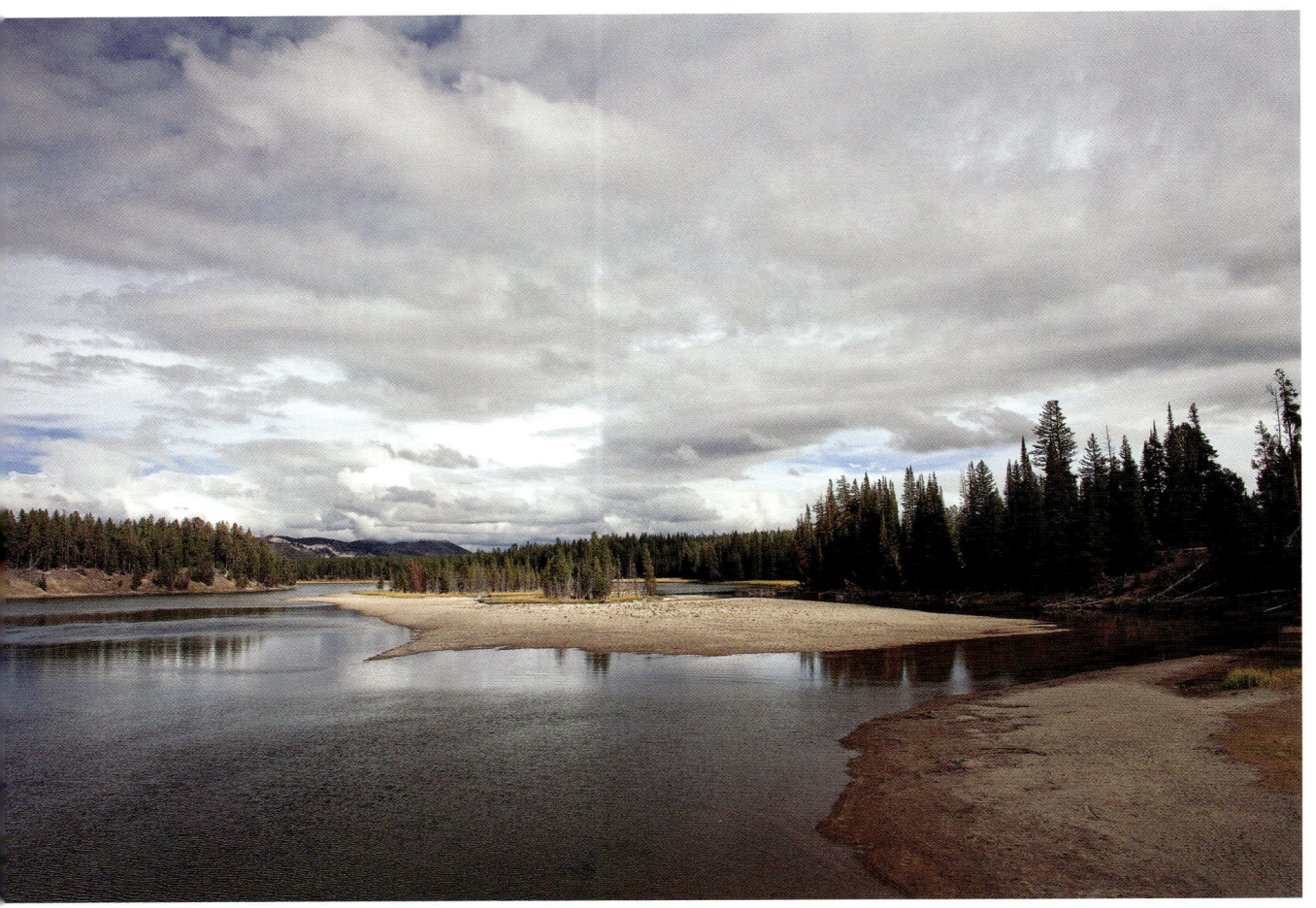

Head of the Yellowstone River
from Fishing Bridge

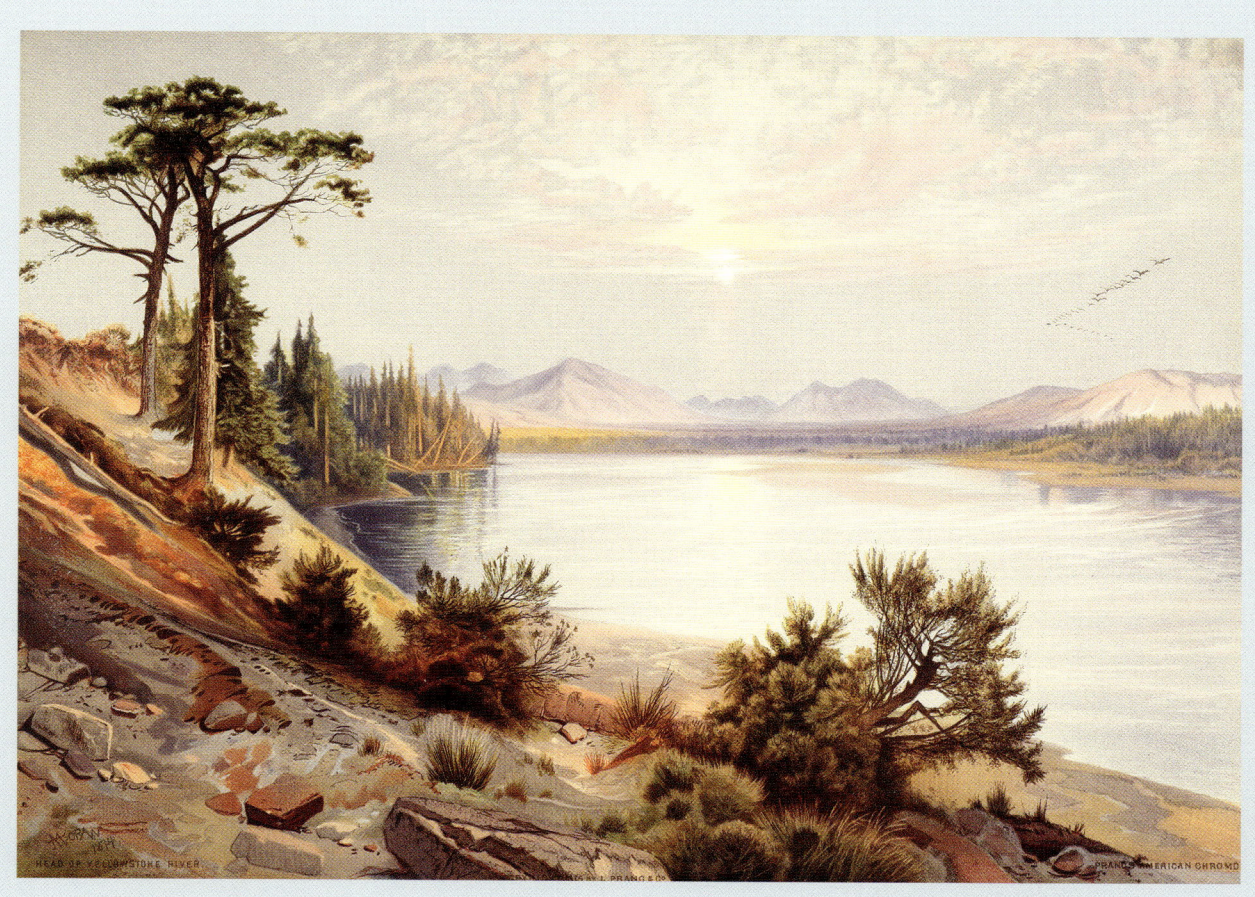

Head of Yellowstone River
Thomas Moran, 1874
Gilcrease Museum, Tulsa, OK
2426.47.7

LAKE LODGE

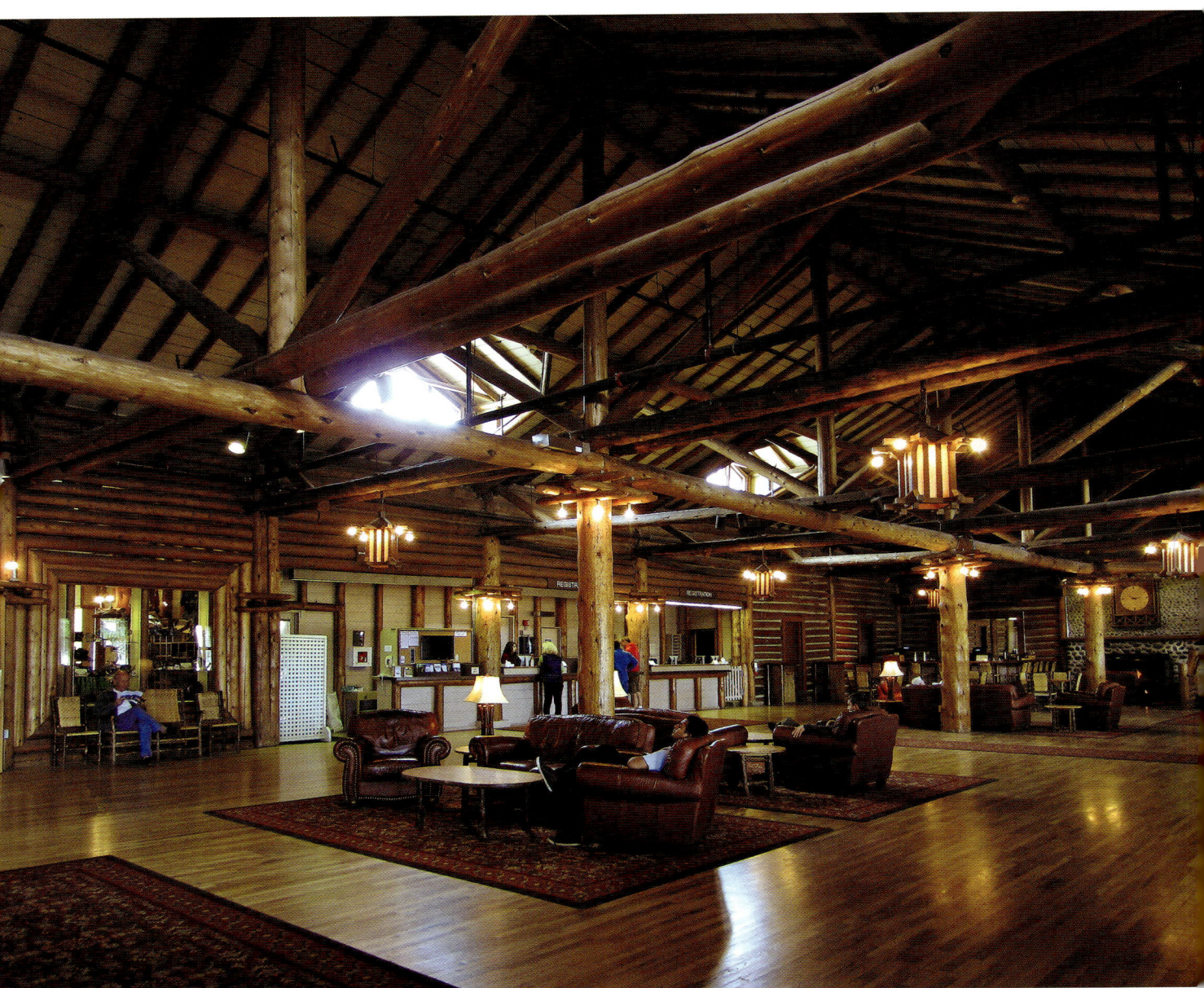

LAKE YELLOWSTONE
HOTEL

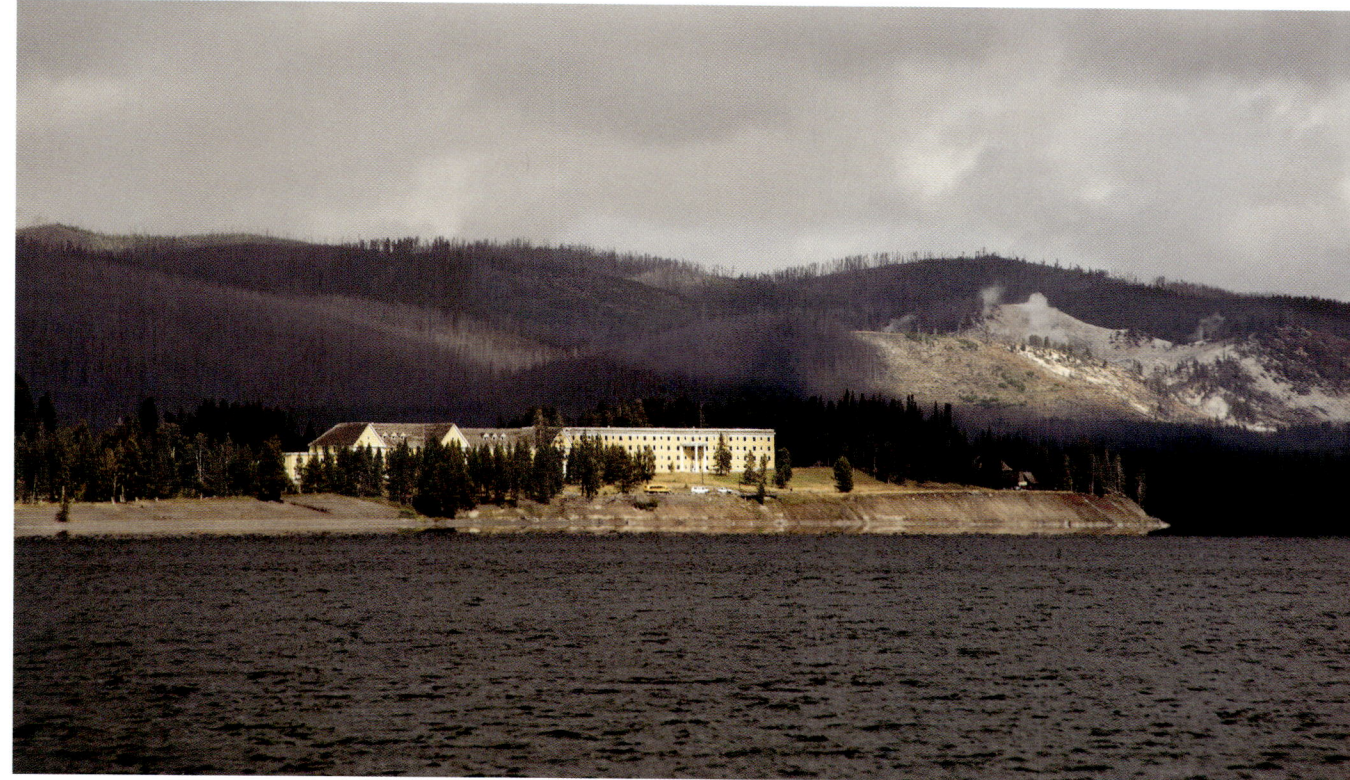

Lake Yellowstone Hotel
from Bridge Bay

<
Lake Lodge

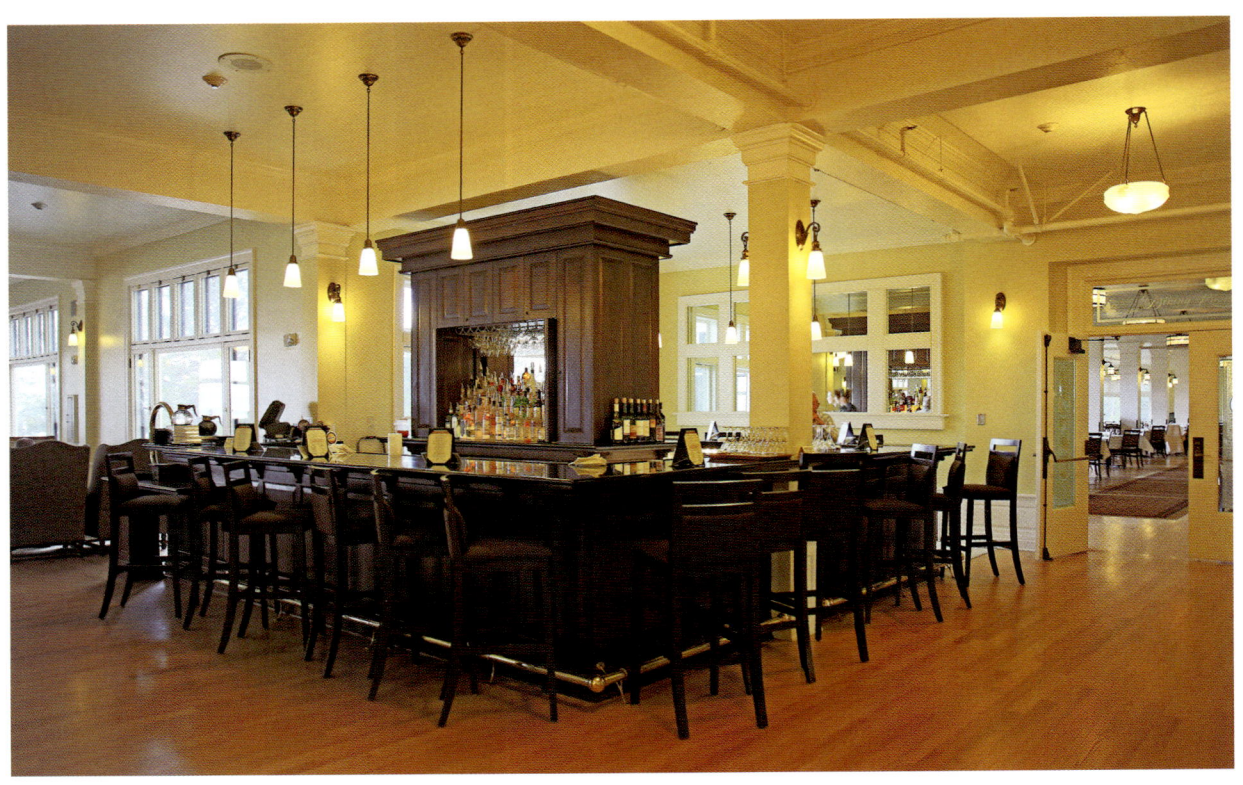

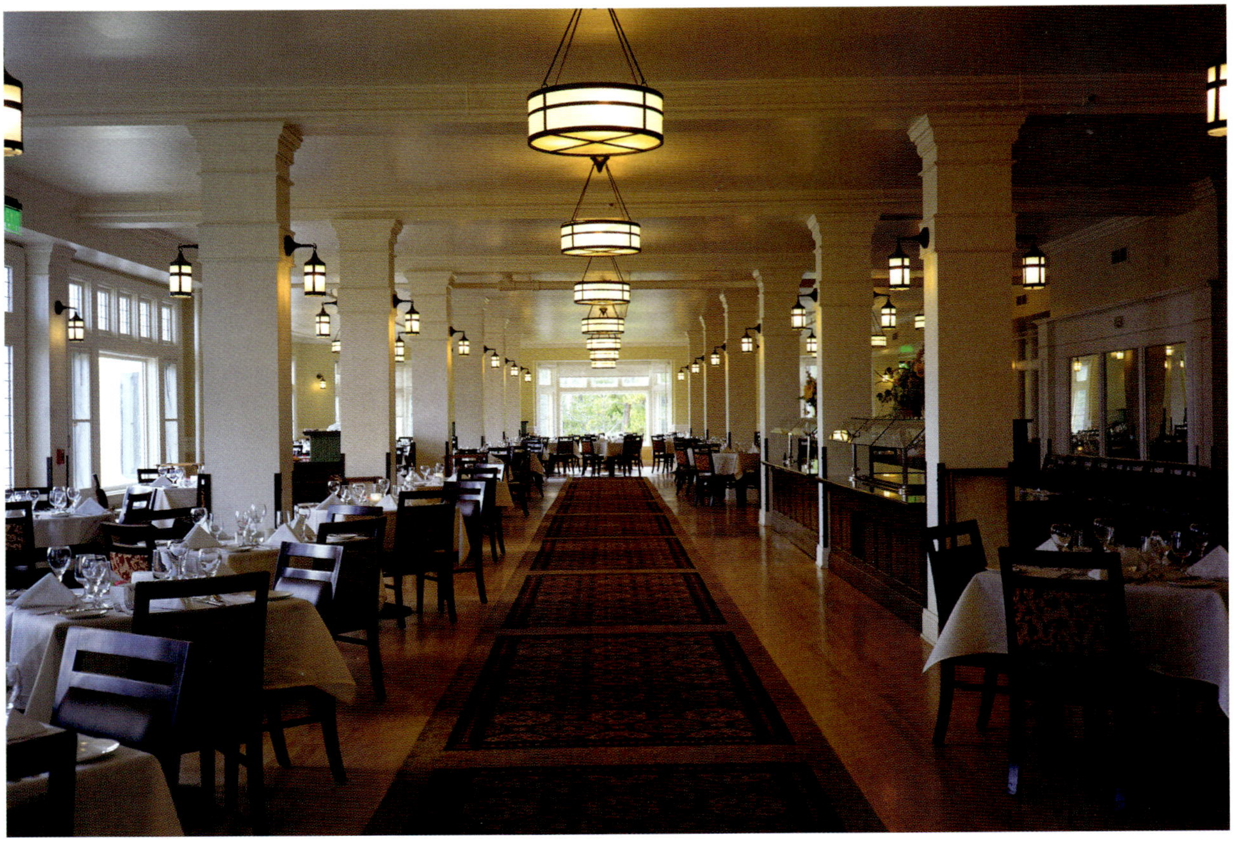

Lake Yellowstone Hotel

Yellowstone National Park bus

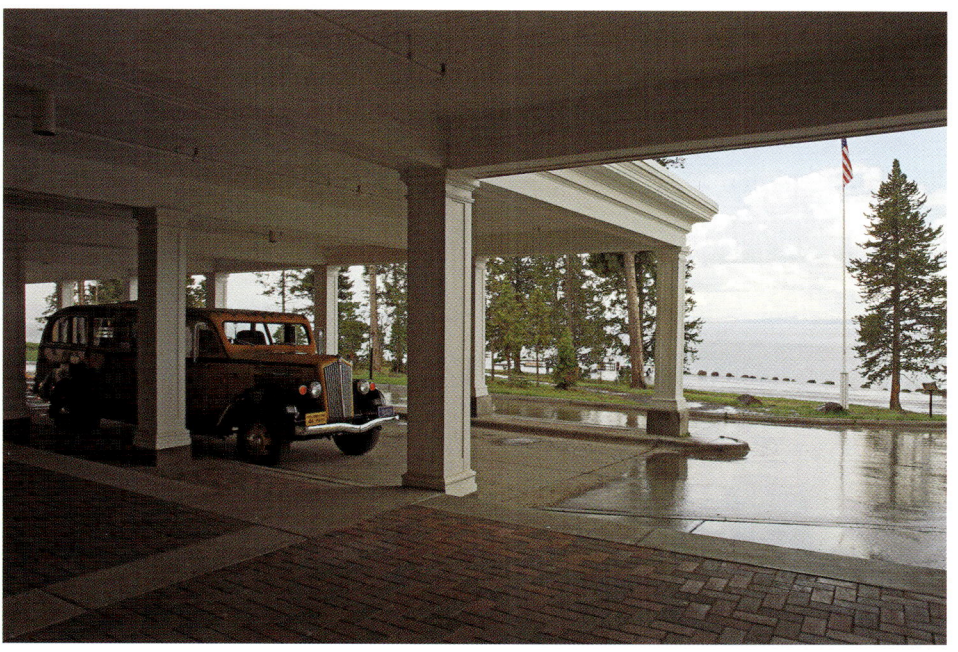

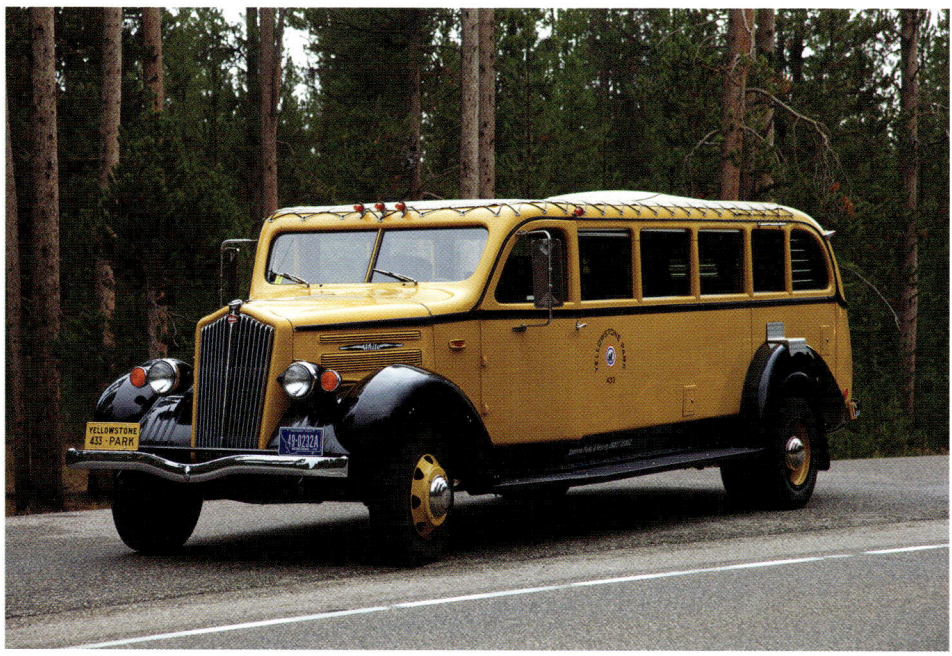

YELLOWSTONE LAKE

"Passing through many a mile of pine and spruce woods, toward the centre of the park you come to the famous Yellowstone Lake. It is about twenty miles long and fifteen wide, and lies at a height of nearly eight thousand feet above the level of the sea, amid dense black forests and snowy mountains. Around its winding, wavering shores, closely forested and picturesquely varied with promontories and bays, the distance is more than one hundred miles. It is not very deep, only from two hundred to three hundred feet, and contains less water than the celebrated Lake Tahoe of the California Sierra, which is nearly the same size, lies at a height of sixty-four hundred feet, and is over sixteen hundred feet deep. But no other lake in North America of equal area lies so high as the Yellowstone, or gives birth to so noble a river. The terraces around its shores show that at the close of the glacial period its surface was about one hundred sixty feet higher than it is now, and its area nearly twice as great.

"In calm weather it is a magnificent mirror for the woods and mountains and sky, now pattered with hail and rain, now roughened with sudden storms that send waves to fringe the shores and wash its border of gravel and sand. The Absaroka Mountains and the Wind River Plateau on the east and south pour their gathered waters into it, and the river issues from the north side in a broad, smooth, stately current, silently gliding with such serene majesty that one fancies it knows the vast journey of four thousand miles that lies before it, and the work it has to do."

JOHN MUIR
"The Yellowstone National Park," The Atlantic Monthly, April 1898

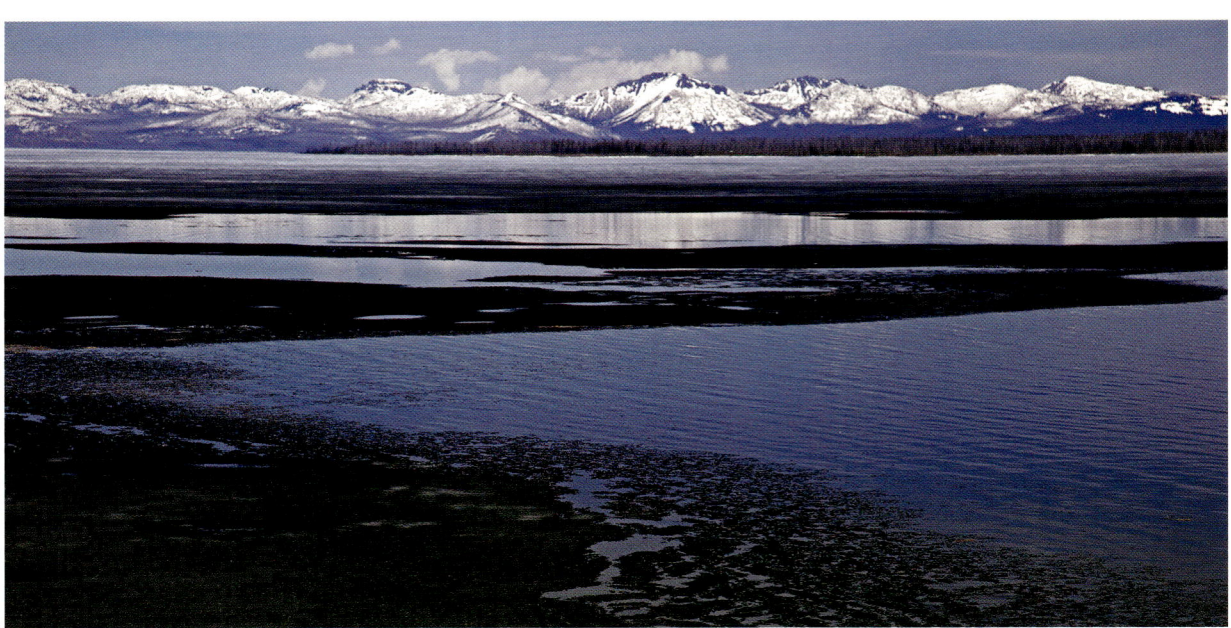

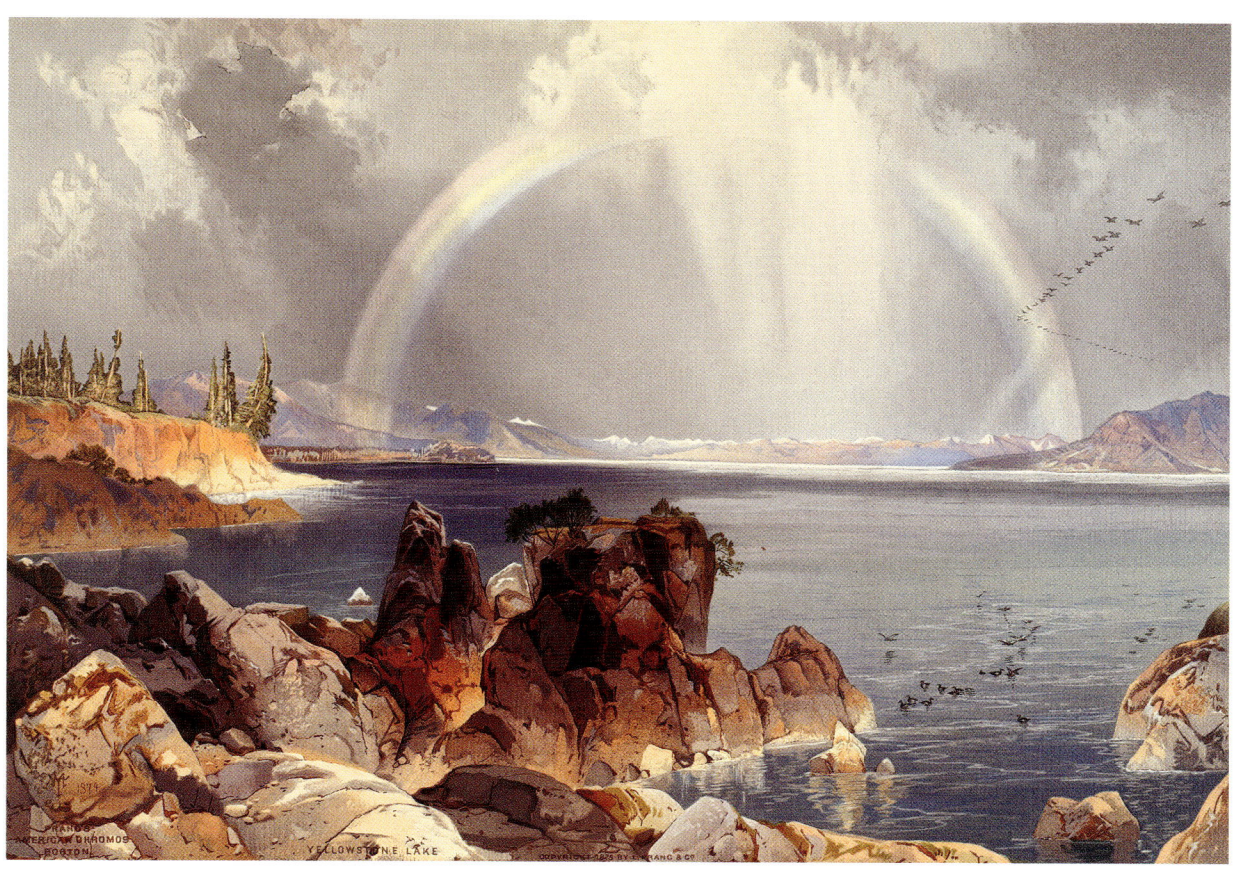

Yellowstone Lake
Thomas Moran, 1874
Gilcrease Museum, Tulsa, OK
2426.47.5

<
Yellowstone Lake and the Absaroka Range

Yellowstone Lake's "surpassing loveliness is due to the fact that it is not one great prairie of water, stretched out before you so that you see the whole of it at once. It curves, and bends, and narrows, and widens into beautiful rivers and noble bays; over it, across it and through it, float myriads of white swans, ducks, geese, pelicans and sea-gulls; at times it stretches out in a long line of pounding surf, breaking white upon a pebbly beach; it is dotted with lovely islands; and it is all held in place by mountains ten thousand or twelve thousand feet high, clad all the year round with snow."

ALICE WELLINGTON ROLLINS
The Three Tetons, 1887

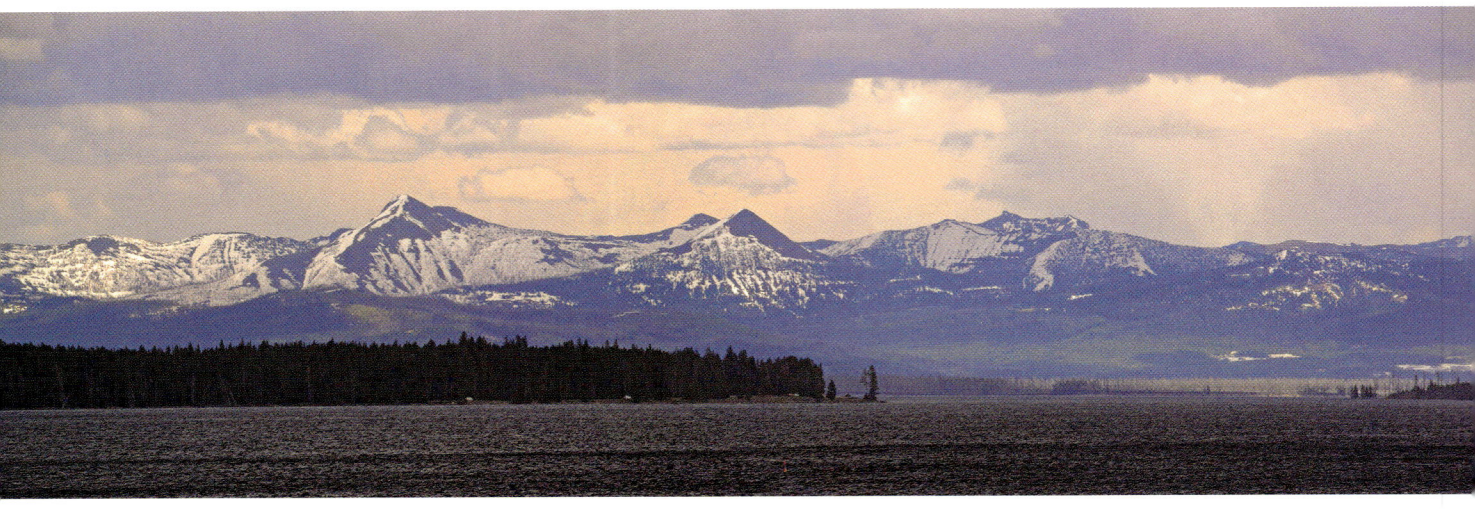

Yellowstone Lake and the Absaroka Range

>
Yellowstone Lake at Mary Bay

"Nestled among the forest-crowned hills which bounded our vision, lay this inland sea, its crystal waves dancing and sparkling in the sunlight as if laughing with joy for their wild freedom. It is a scene of transcendent beauty."

DAVID FOLSOM OF THE FOLSOM-COOK-PETERSON EXPEDITION, 1869

"a matchless mountain lake"

JOHN COLTER, EXPLORER

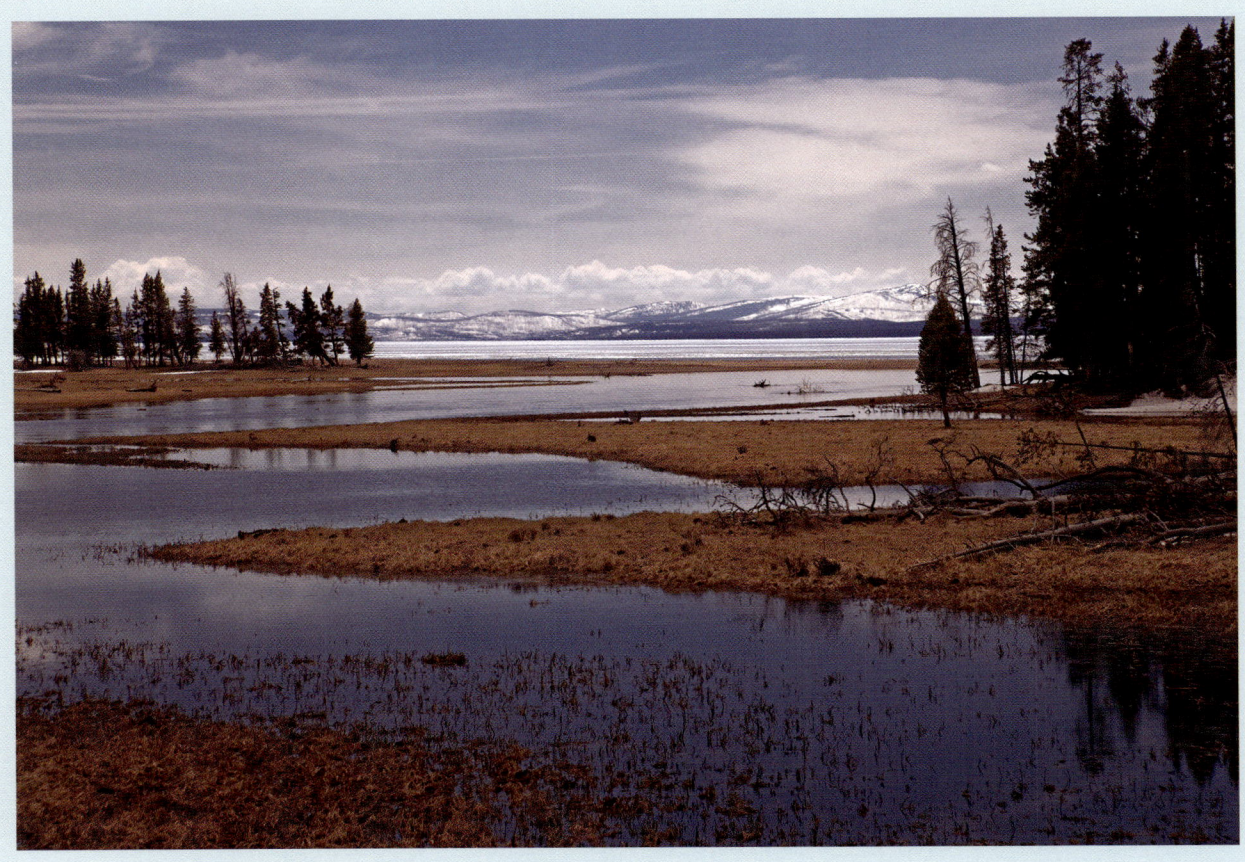

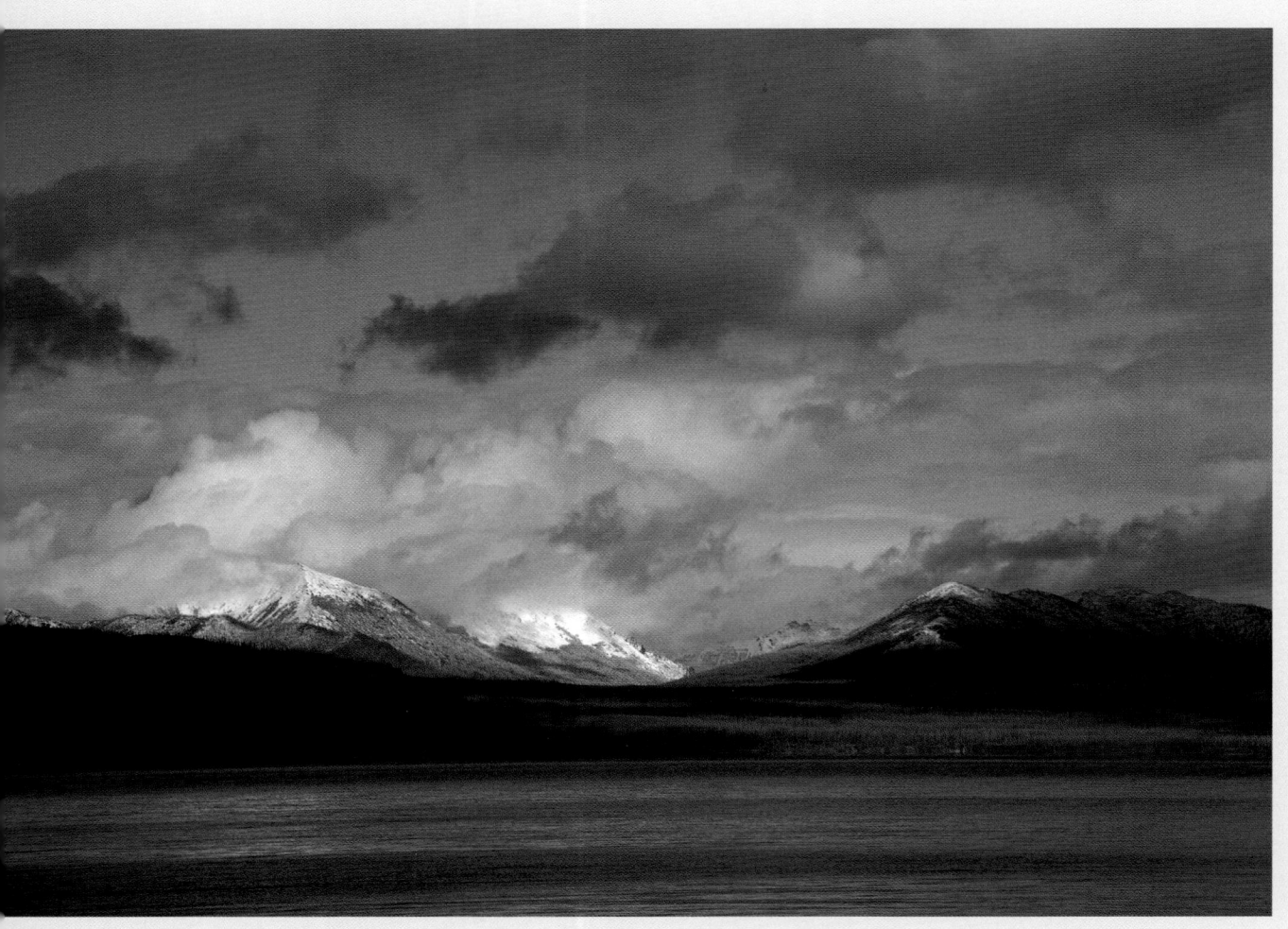

Yellowstone Lake and the Absaroka Range

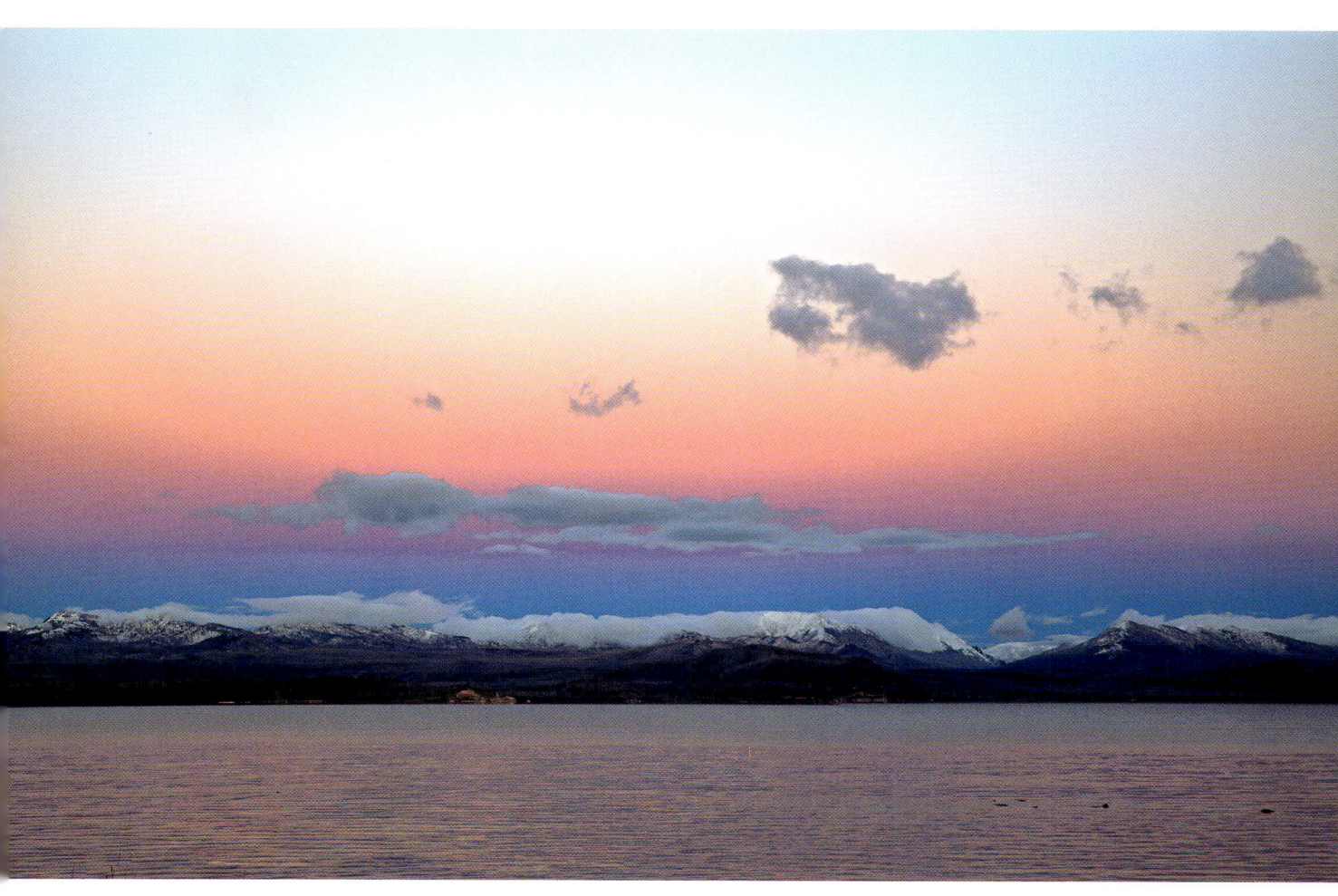

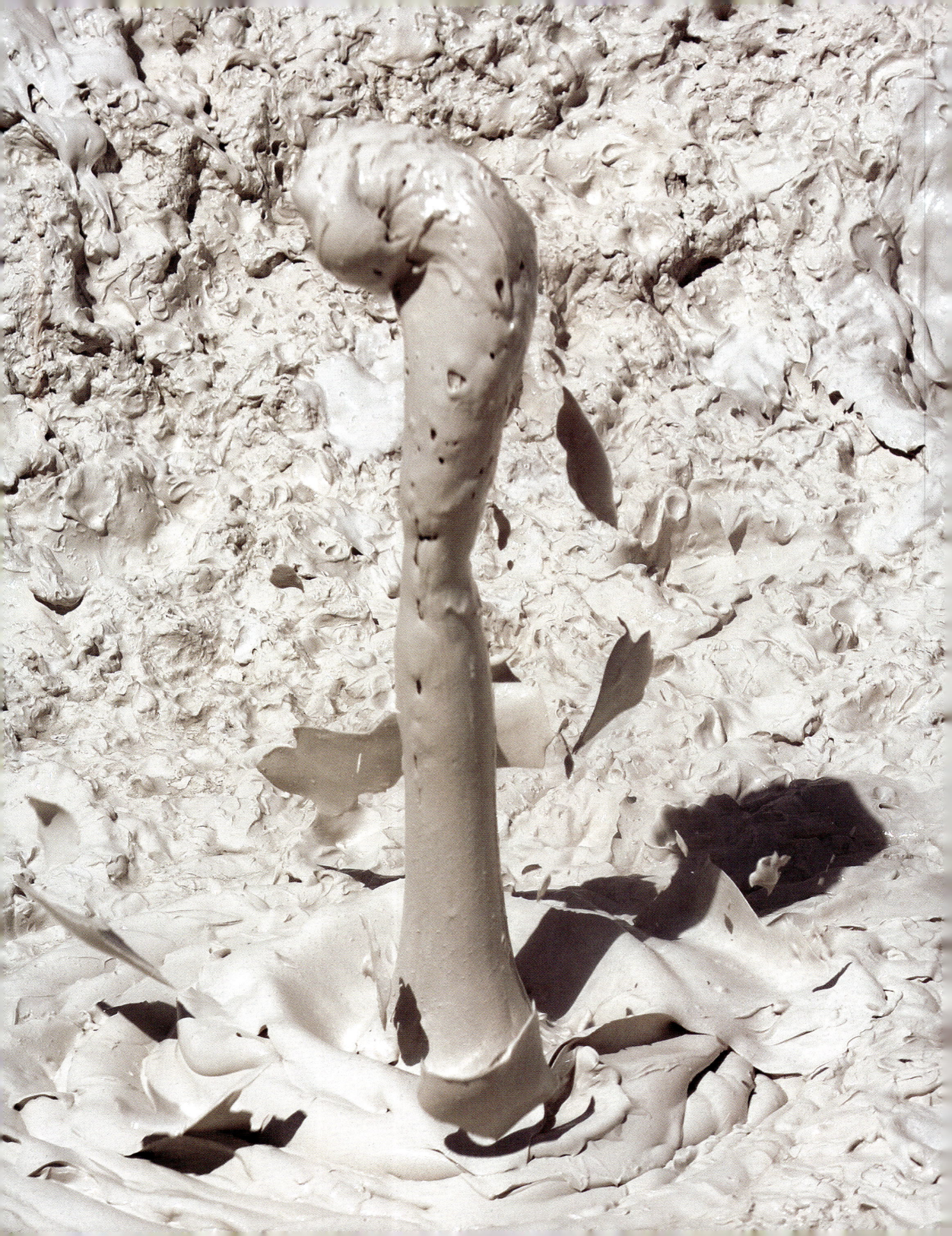

MADISON AREA

ARTISTS PAINTPOTS

FIREHOLE FALLS

GIBBON FALLS

GIBBON RIVER

MADISON RIVER

Bubbling mud at Artists Paintpots

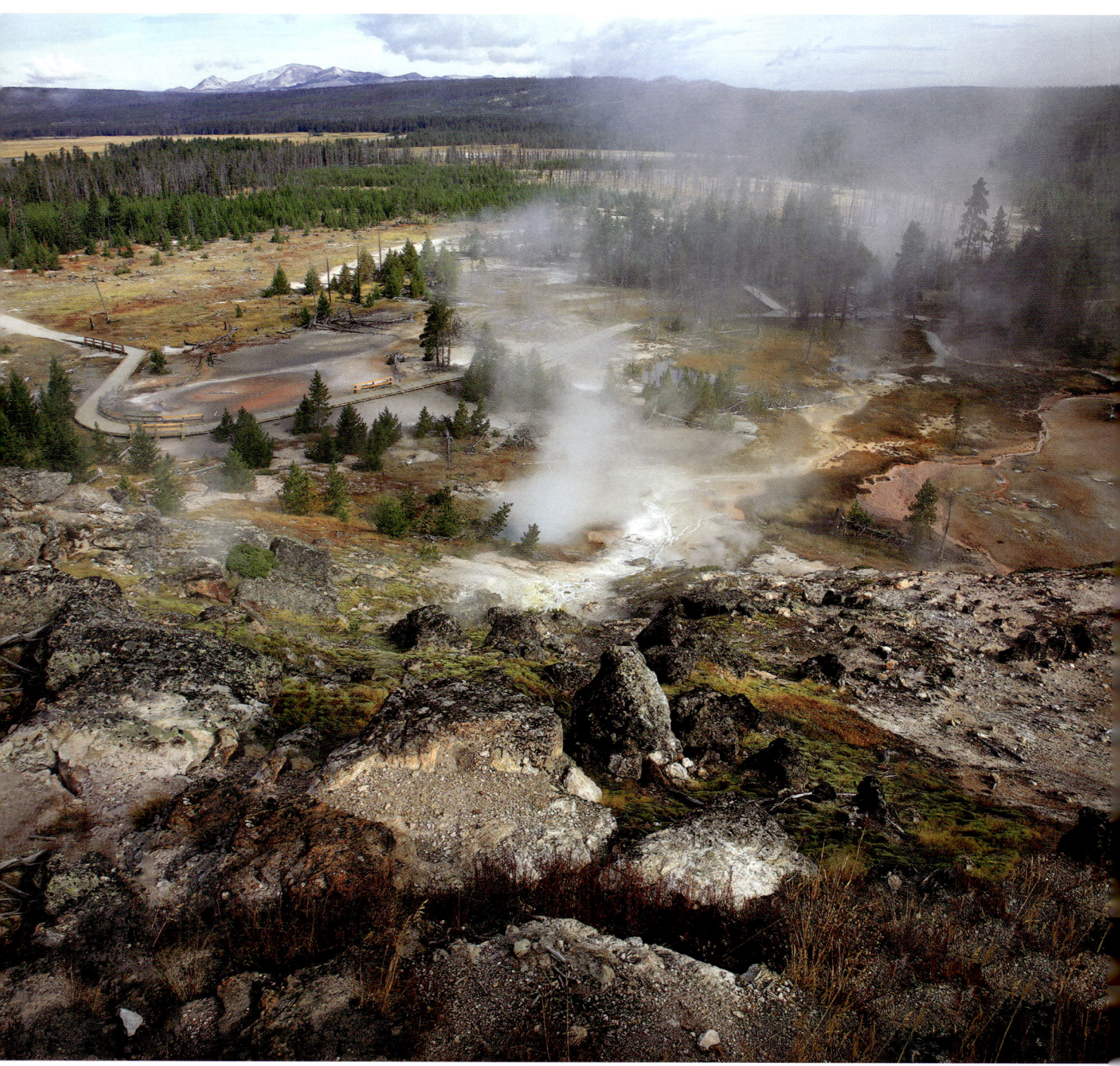

At Foot of Paint Pot Hill
John Henry Renshawe, 1883

<

Artists Paintpots and Gibbon Meadows

Paintpot

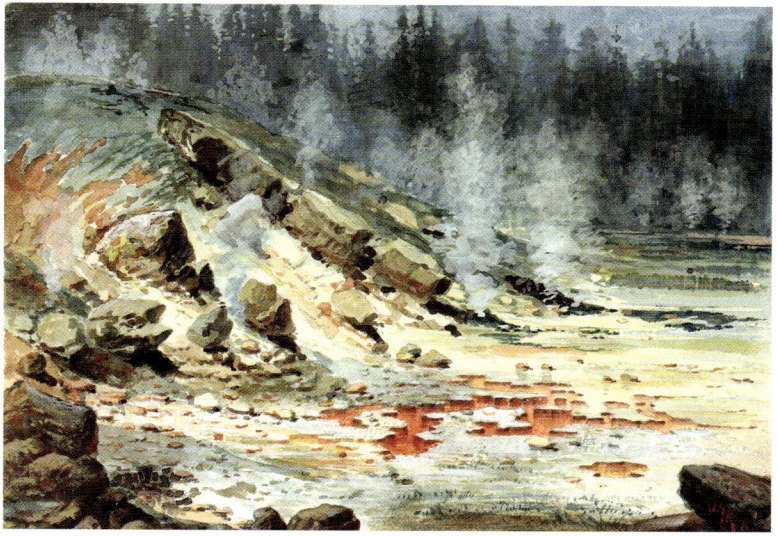

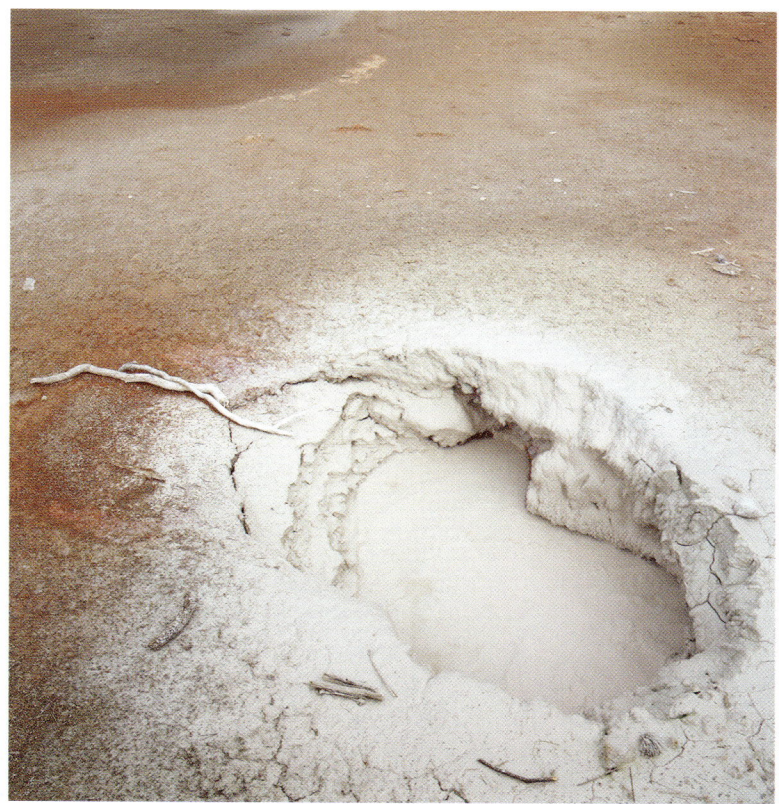

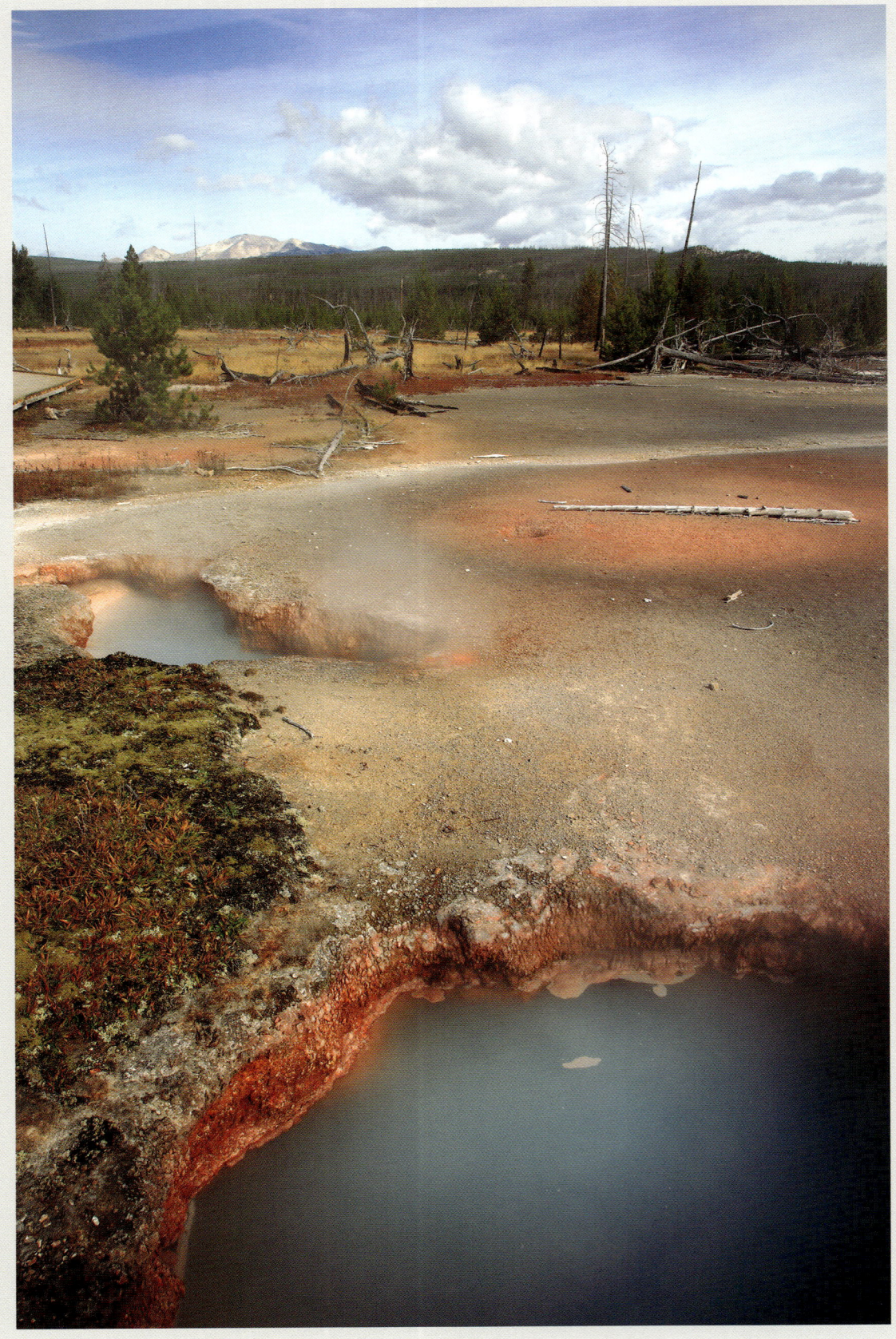

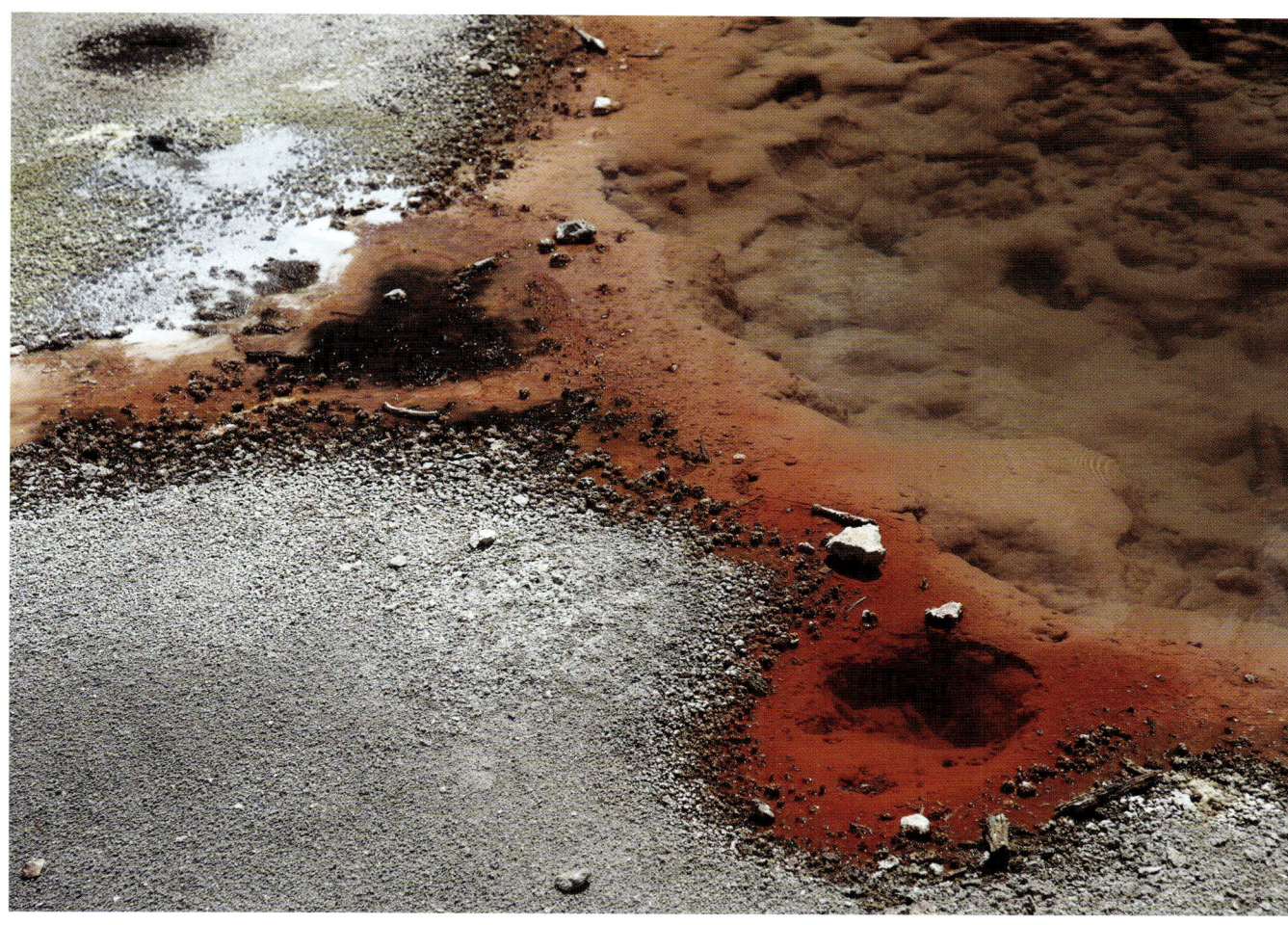

Paintpots

"On the east side of the main road are several curious 'paint pots.' One of these is like a pool of white lead twenty feet across. Others are interesting from their brilliant hues. Pink, salmon, red and yellow; almost every tinge of color is represented."

GEORGE WOOD WINGATE
Through the Yellowstone Park on Horseback, 1886

"The little pools are nothing so much as great paint pots, and the bubbling, boiling, gurgling mass seething within them is nothing so much as paint. It is soft, smooth, and satiny to the touch, though it turns hard later in lovely coral work around the basins . . . . But the wonder of these hot paint-pots is the coloring. . . . Within two or three feet of each other, were pools some of which were blood-red, some sulphur-orange, some delicate rose-color, and some looking as if filled with hot cream.

"But there is one paint pot at Yellowstone that is a genuine joke.

"It is a great pool, apparently full of white paint. The effort of this thick white paint to be a geyser, resulting in a sputter, sputter, sputter,—gurgle, gurgle, gurgle,—blob, blob, blob—and then for a moment silence—is something so ludicrous that no one can stand beside it and not laugh aloud in sympathy. It is not the seething of the hot spring, not the bubbling of the boiling pool, not the hiss of steam rushing from subterranean caverns, nor the roar of the geyser; it is sputter, sputter, sputter,—gurgle, gurgle, gurgle,—blob, blob, blob—till the spectator is convulsed with merriment. . . . All over the surface of this sticky, smooth white paint, besides the convulsive efforts in the middle, . . . thick white bubbles opaque and fat, leap up and down exactly like great white frogs, in their motions and their croaking."

ALICE WELLINGTON ROLLINS
The Three Tetons, 1887

Bubbling mud

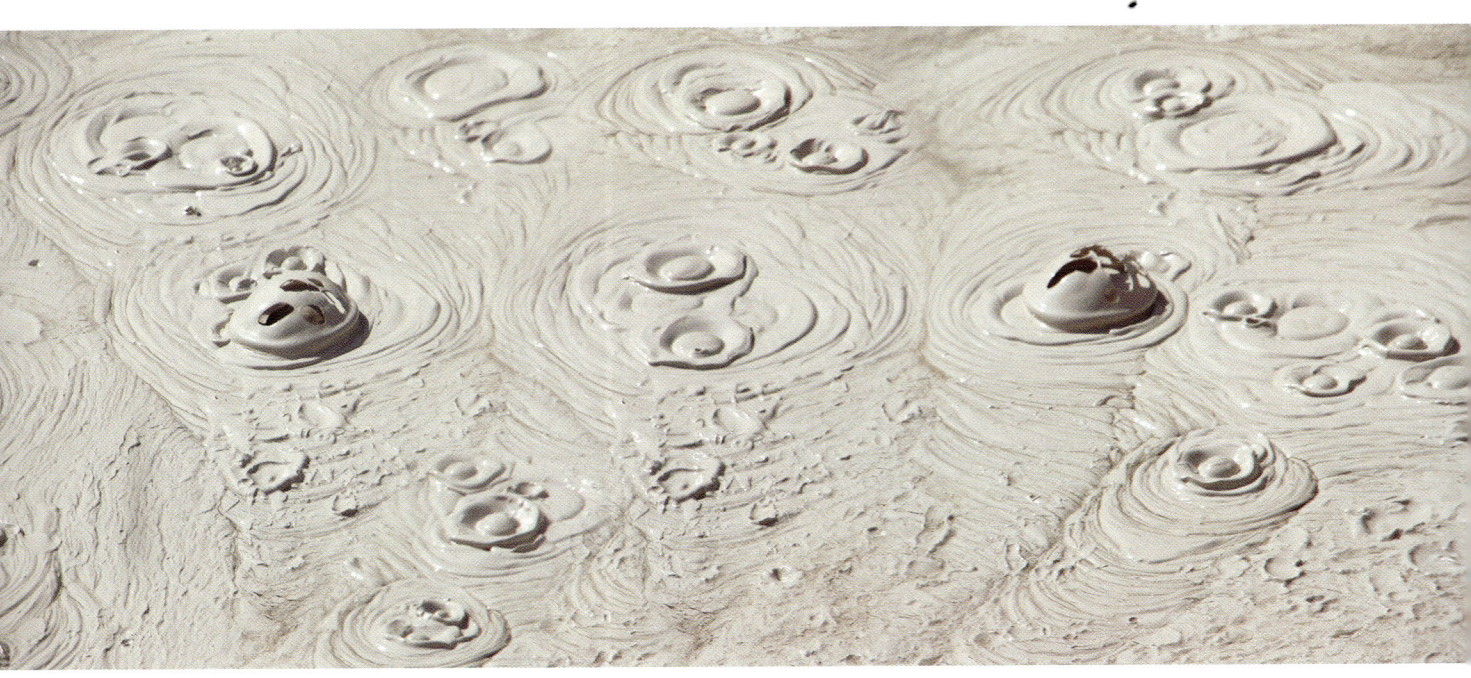

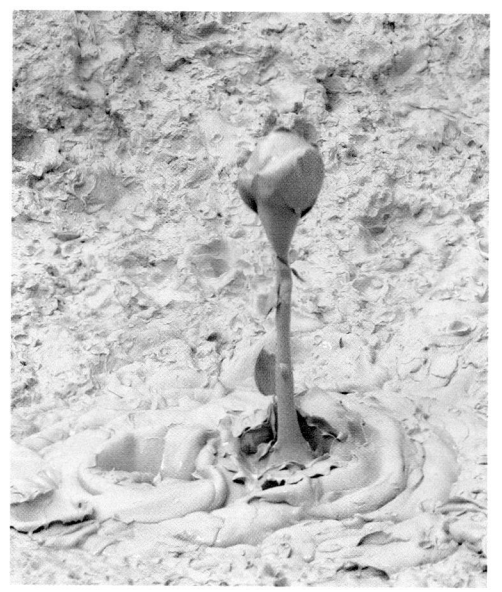
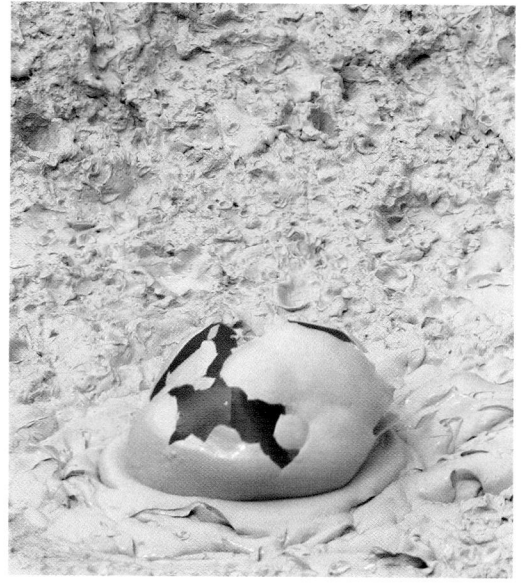

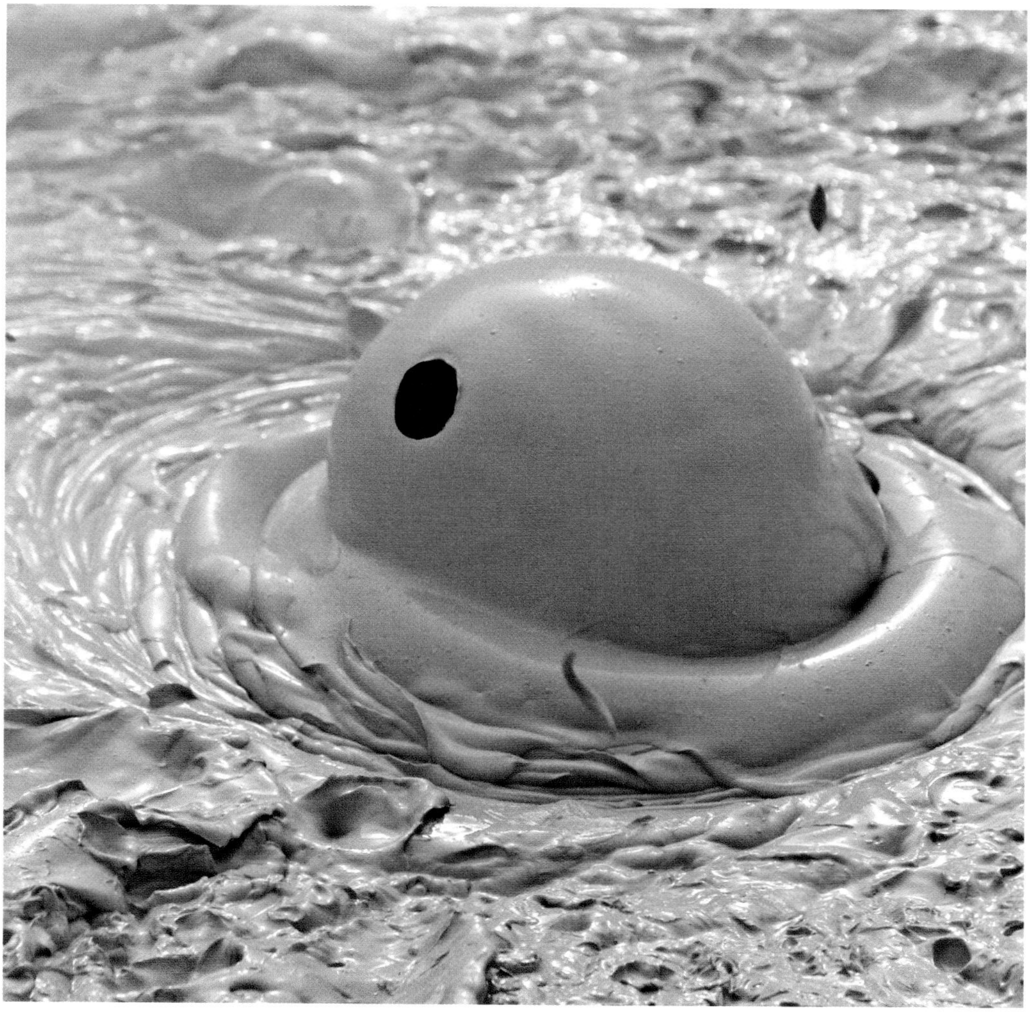

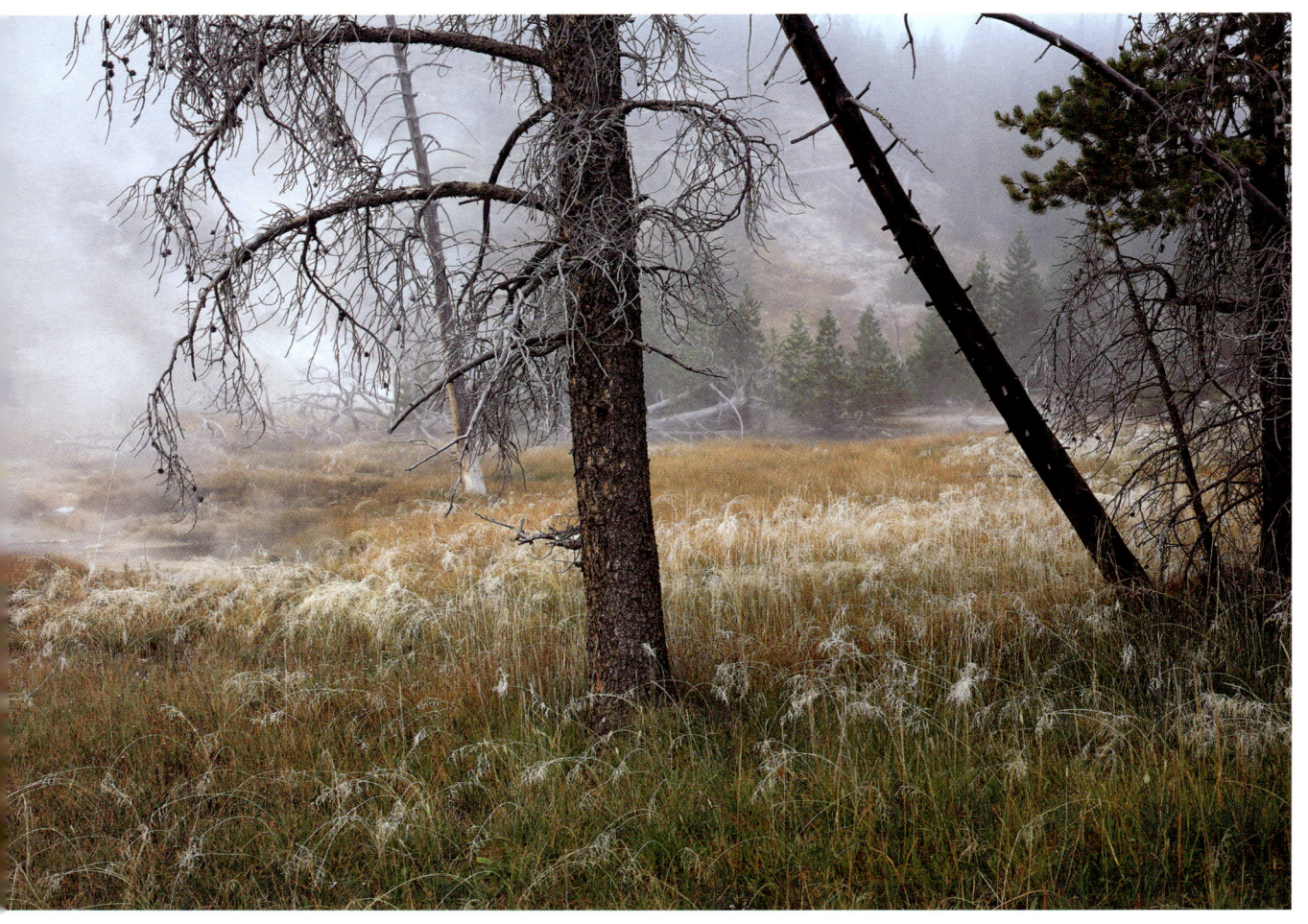

Artists Paintpots

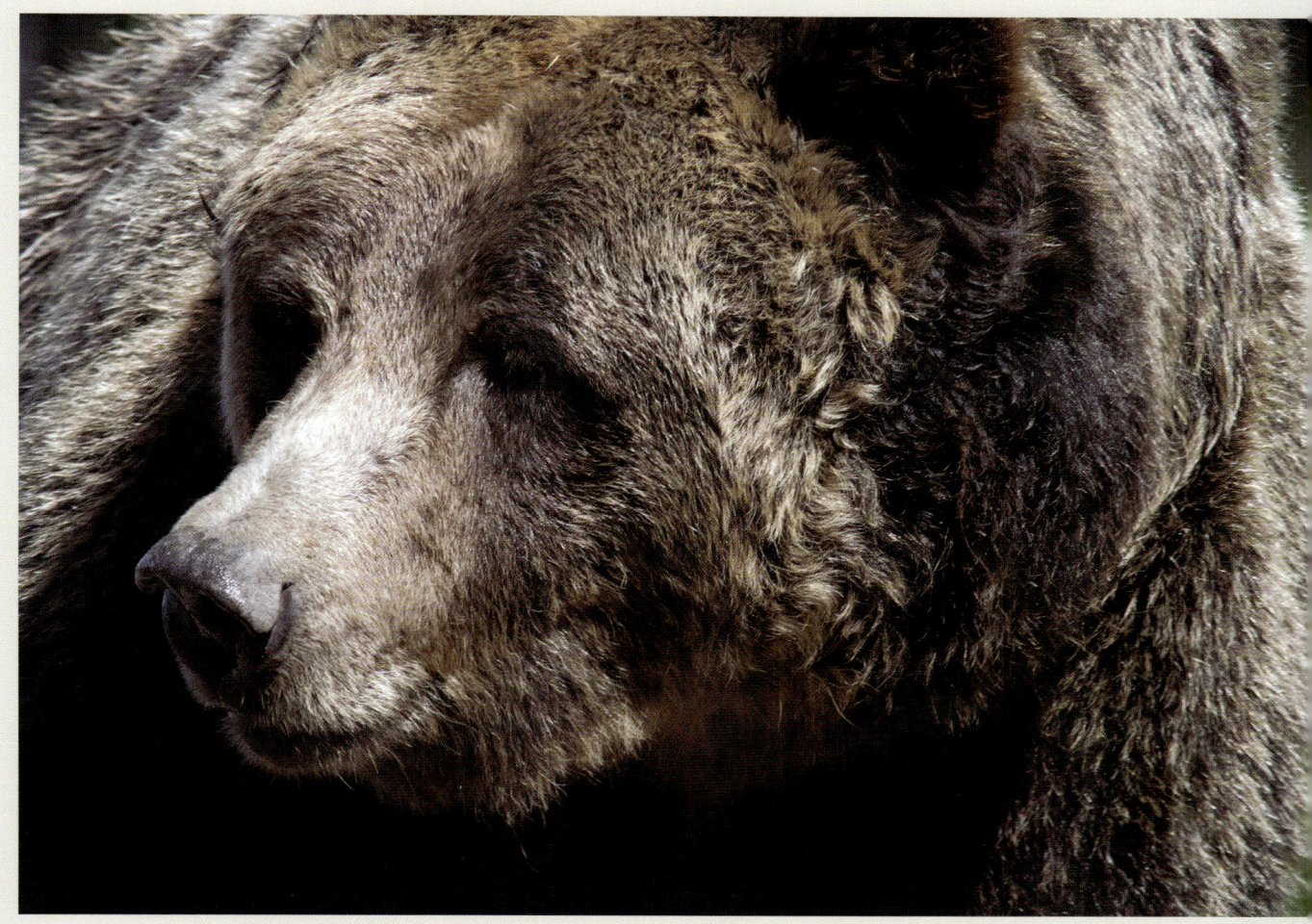

Grizzly bear

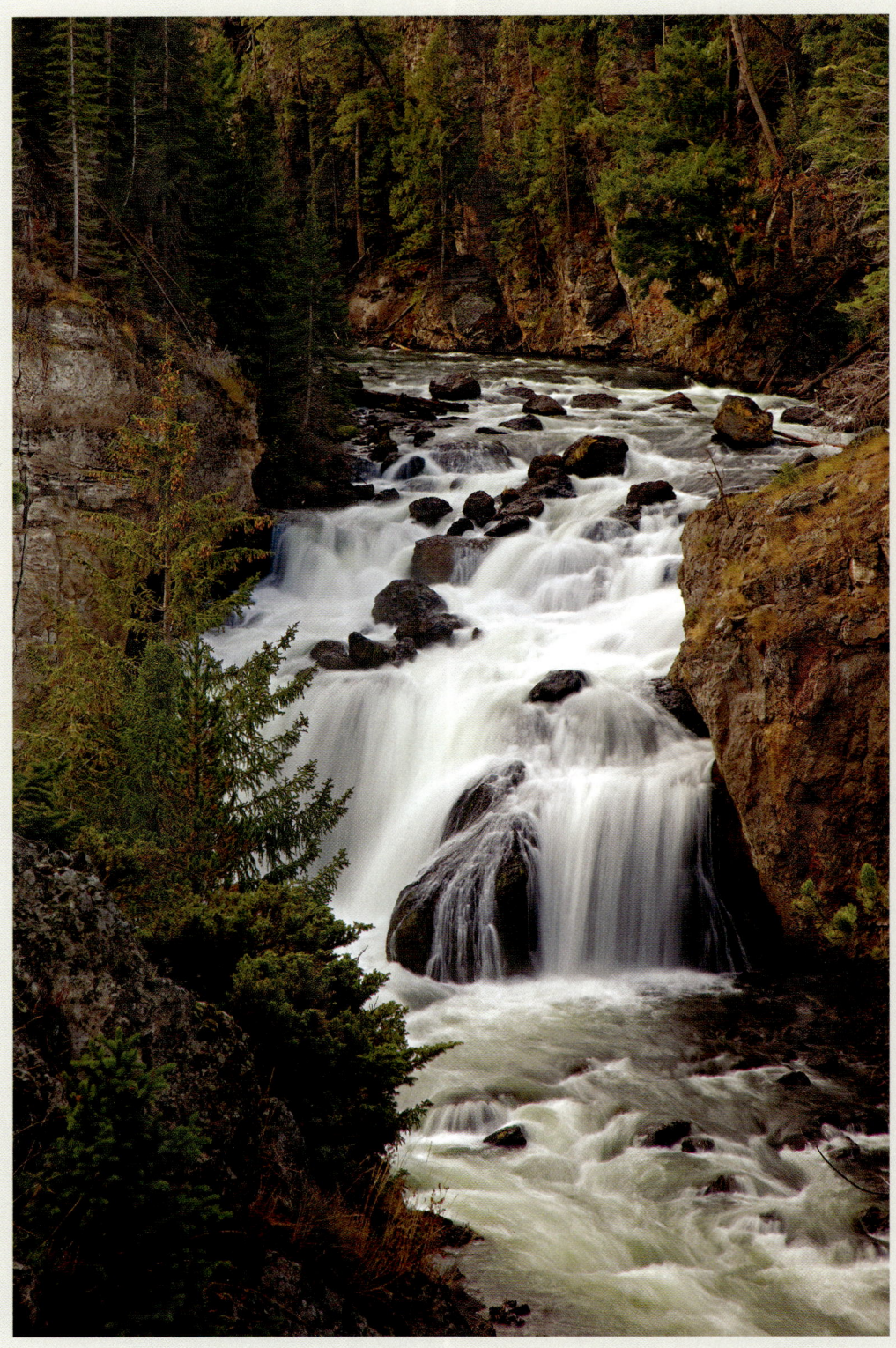

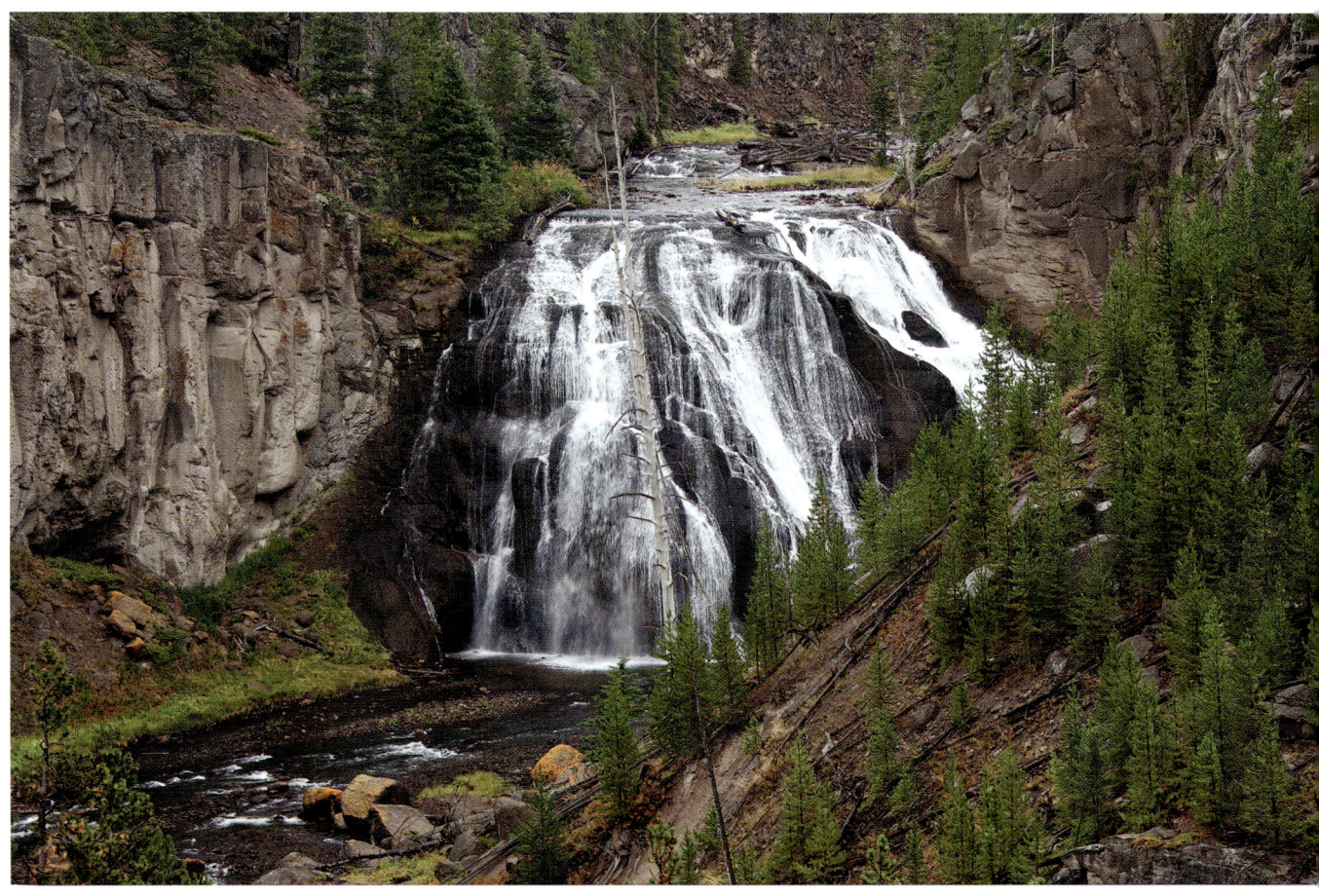

Gibbon Falls

<

Firehole Falls on Firehole Canyon
Drive

The Falls of the Gibbon "are situated four miles from the entrance to the canyon, and are reached by a trail on the right of the road. The descent is quite steep, but the stalwart tourist will not regret the strain upon his muscles after a sight of the magnificent falls. The water tumbles over them in a foamy sheet, full eighty feet in depth, making a charming picture, full of life and vigor, which is in striking contrast to its setting or grim rocks and dusky pines."

HENRY J. WINSER
The Yellowstone National Park-A Manual for Tourists, 1883

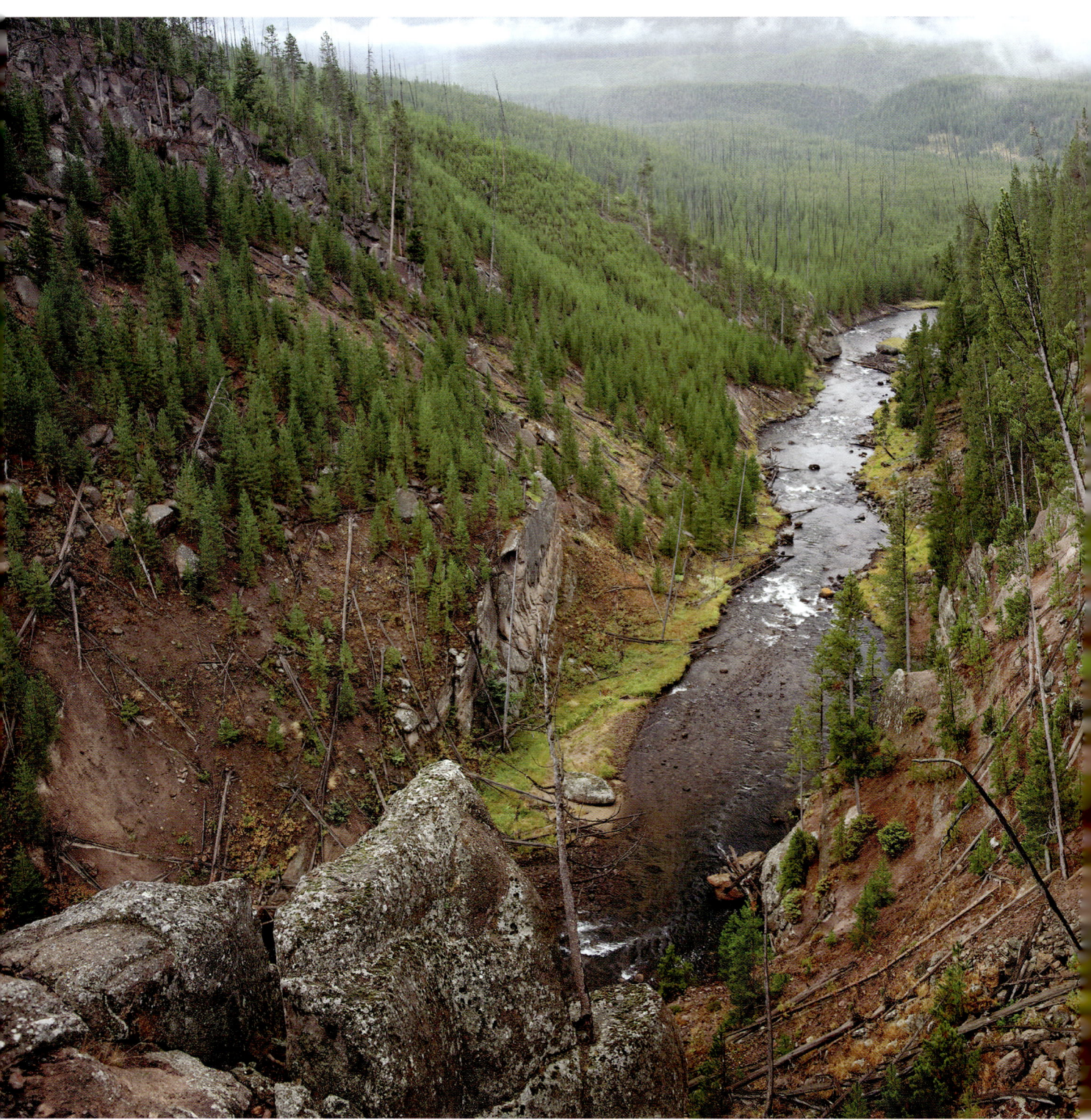

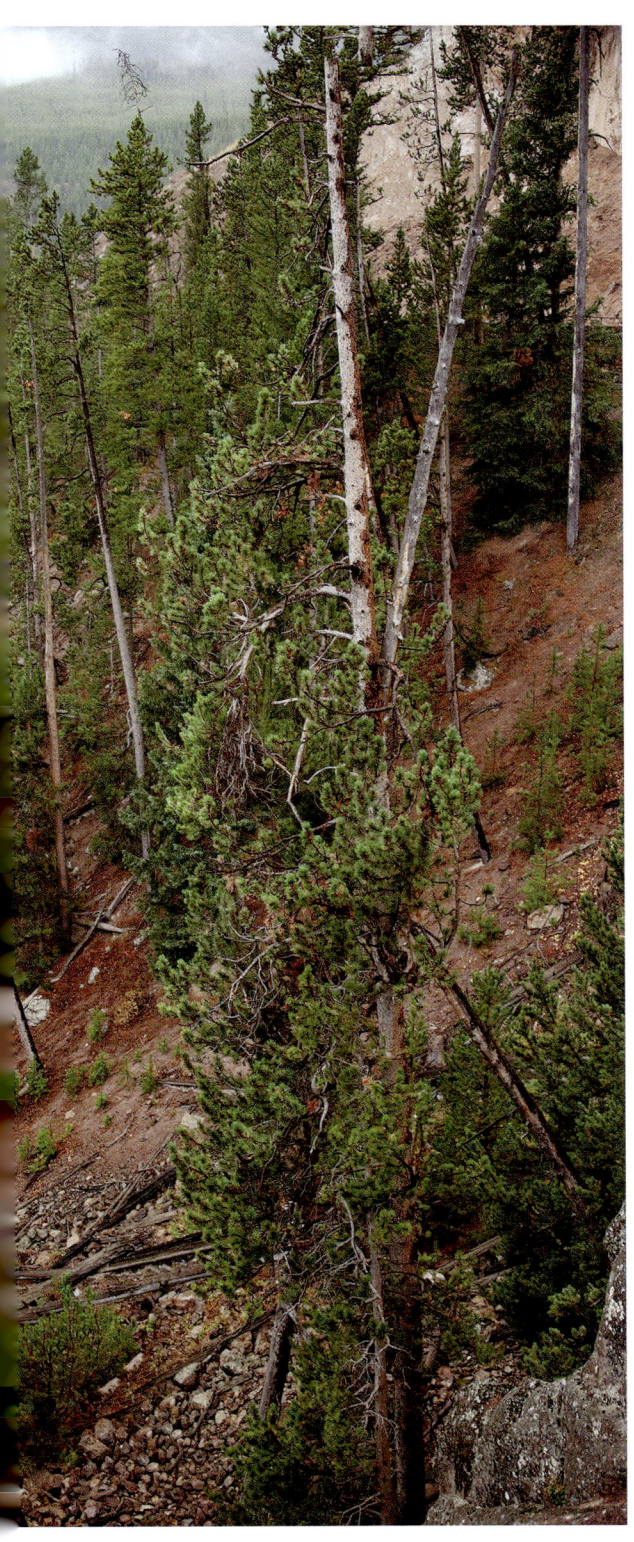

"The [Gibbon] river glides over a rocky shelf and falls in a plunge of full eighty feet, dividing into two sheets, one being an unbroken torrent, and the other a thin sheet resembling a huge veil of delicate lace, constantly broken and reproduced."

GEORGE WOOD WINGATE
Through the Yellowstone Park on Horseback, 1886

Gibbon River below Gibbon Falls

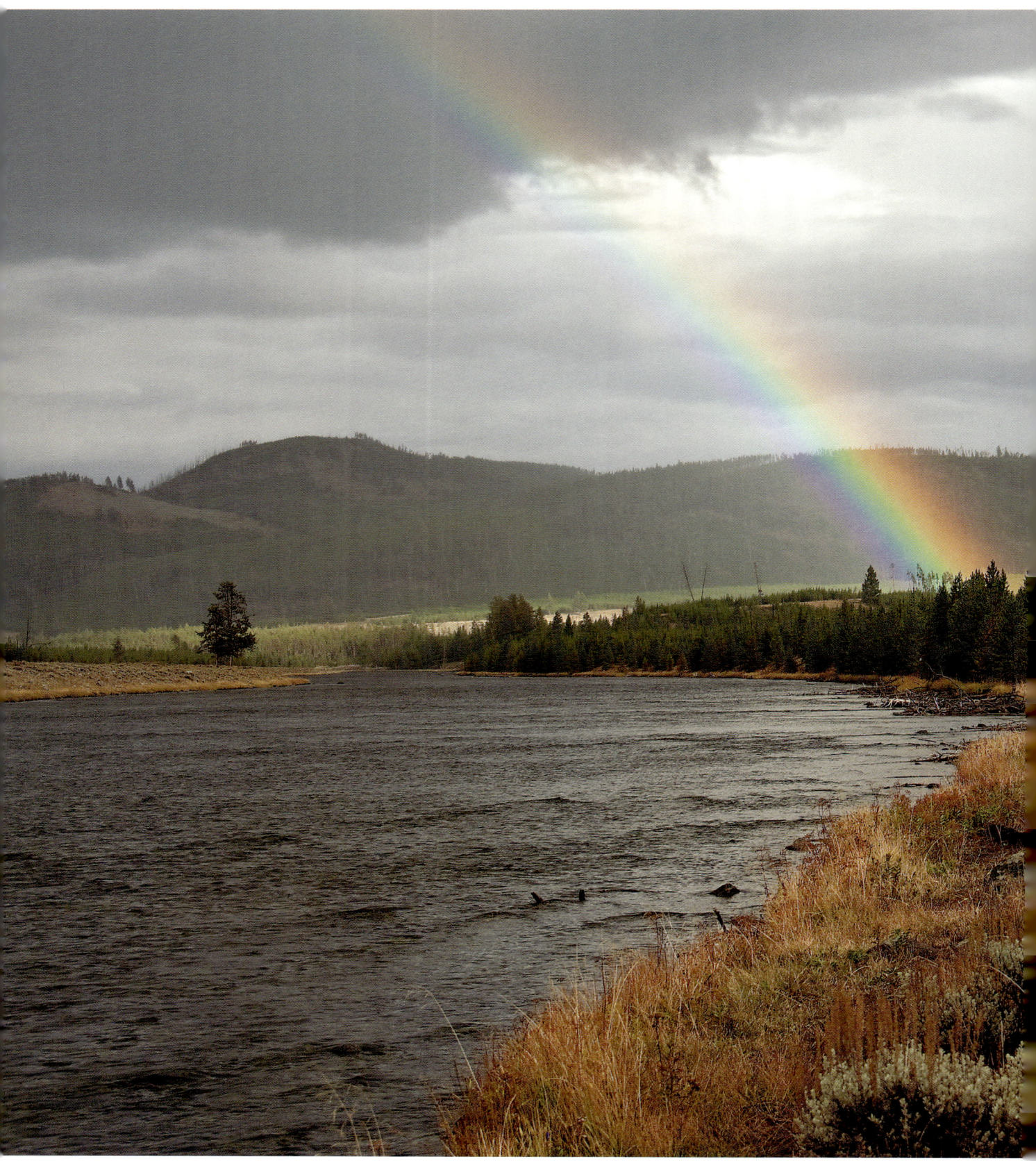

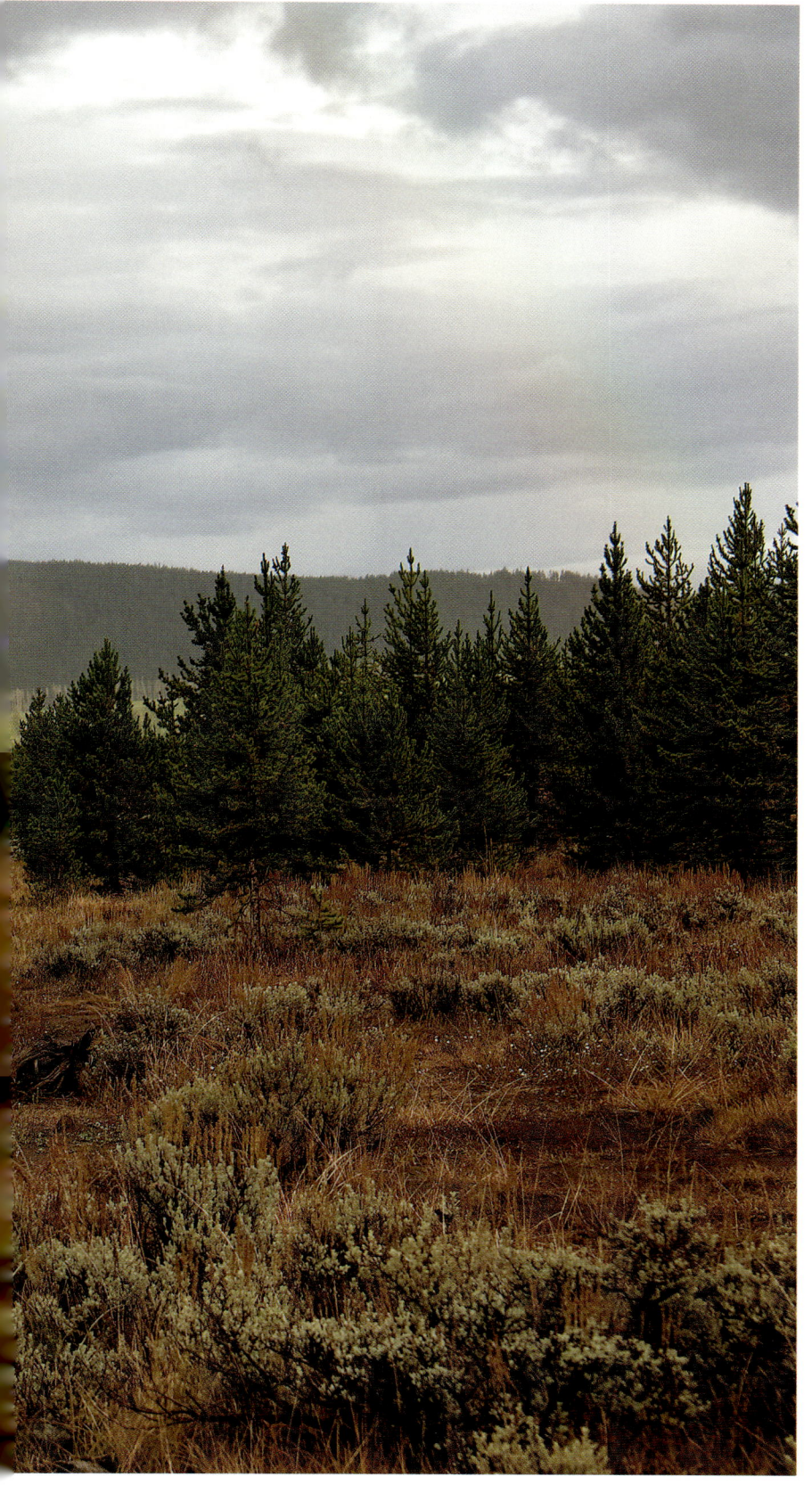

Madison River

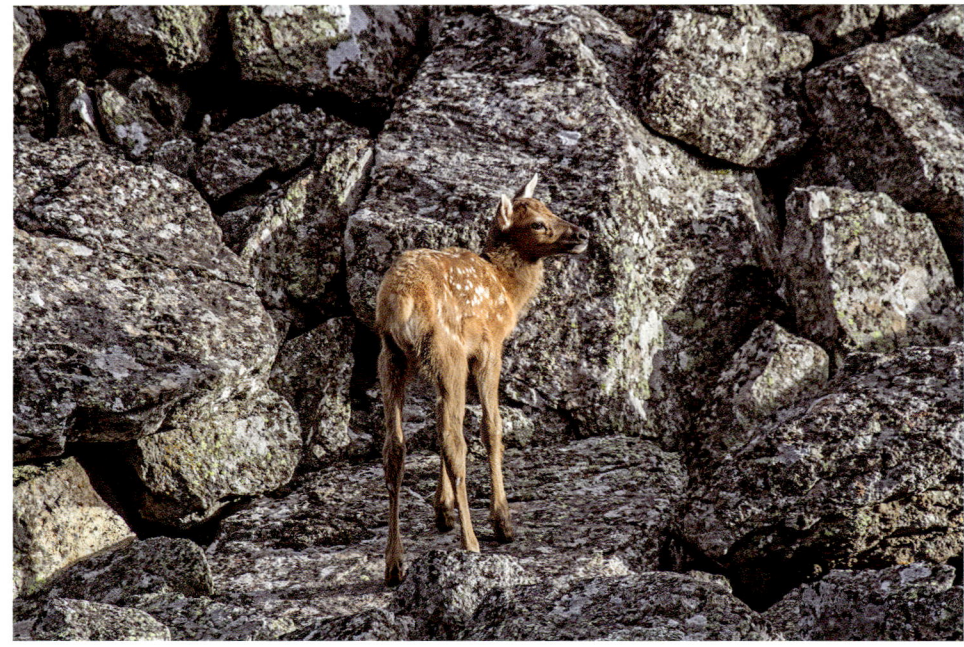

Elk calf

Bull elk

Bald eagle

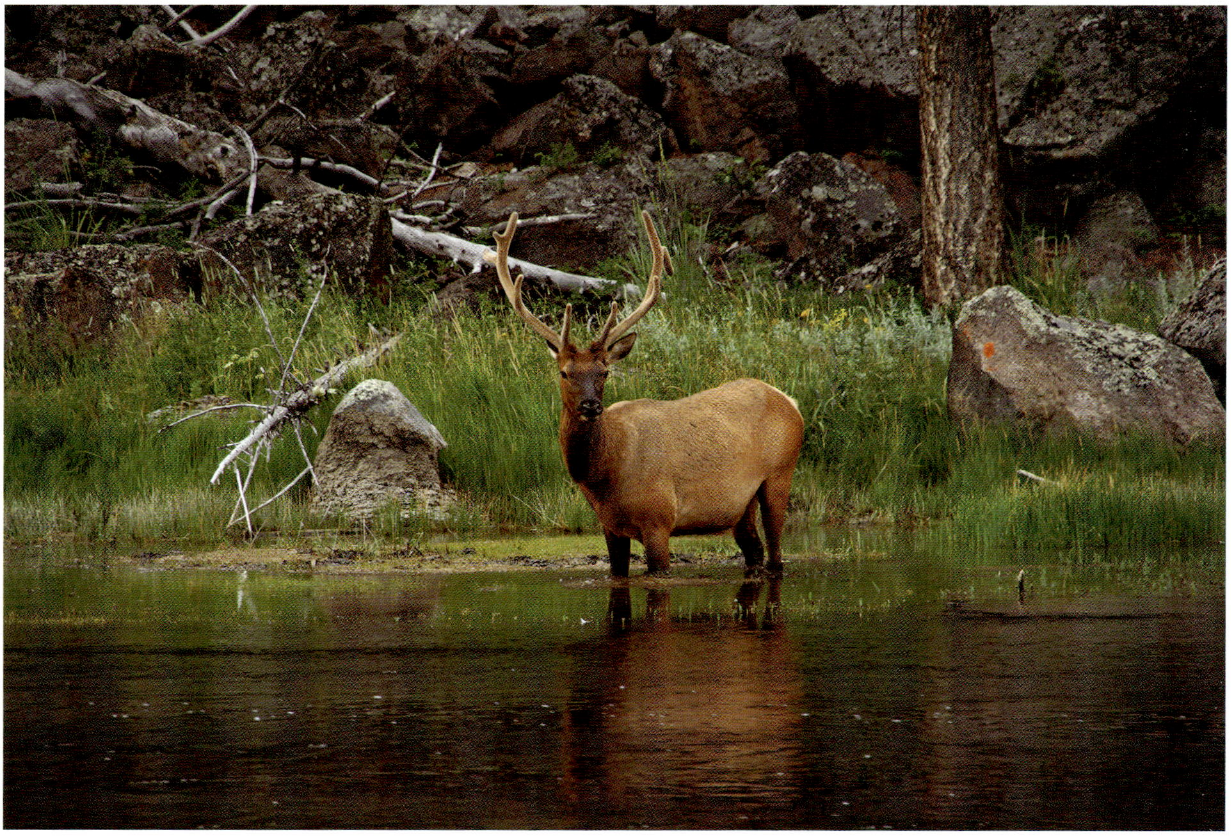

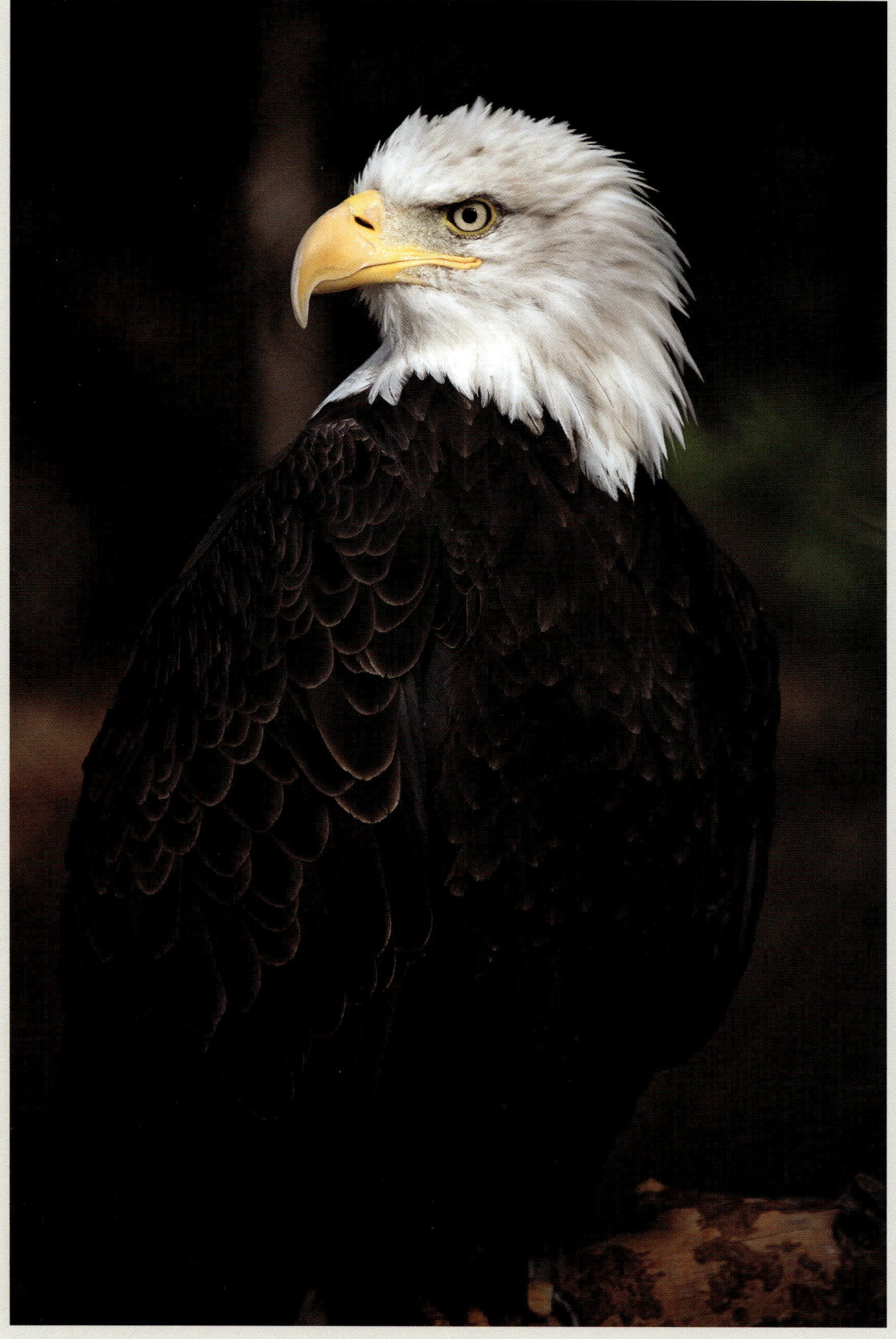

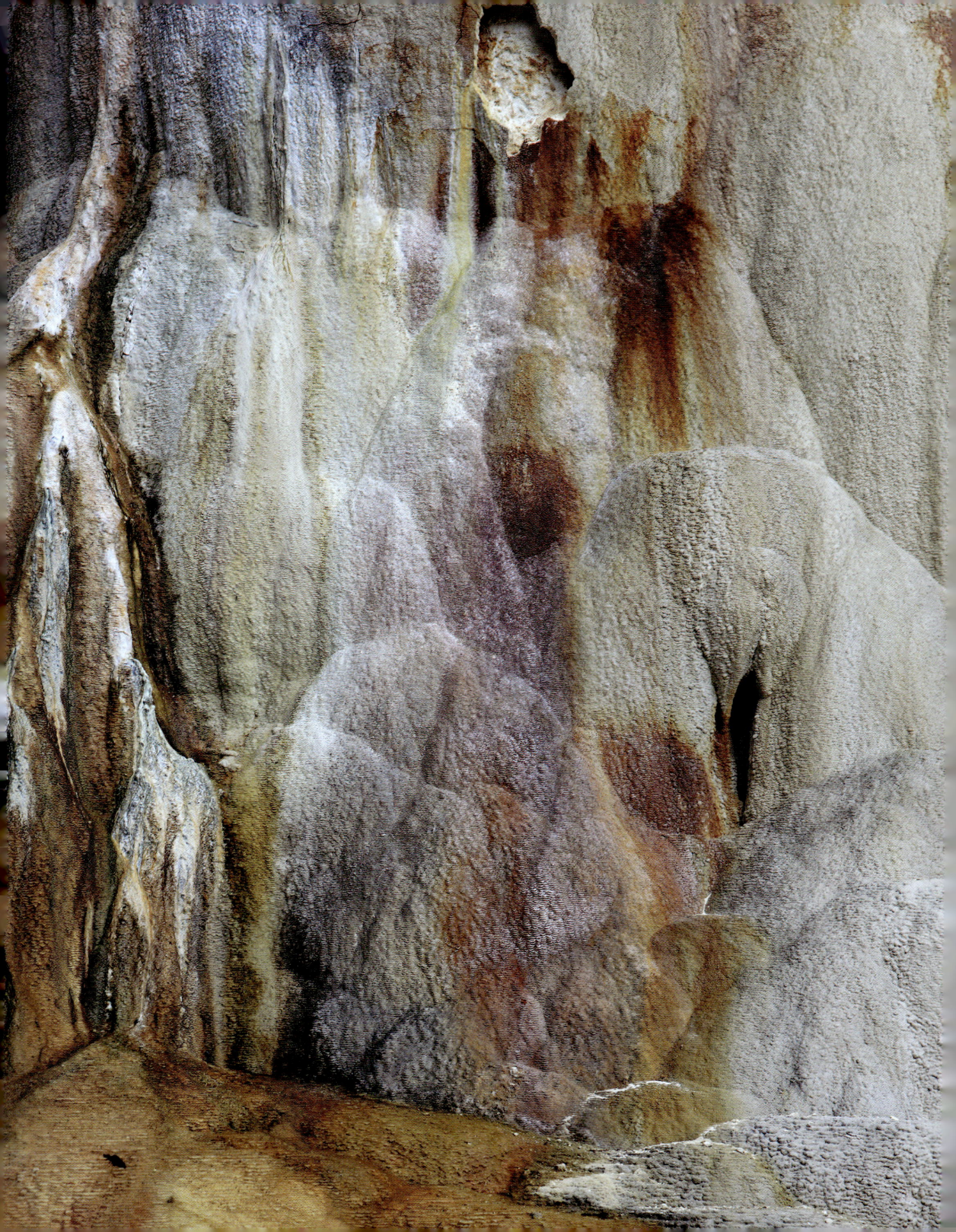

MAMMOTH AREA

GARDNER RIVER

MAMMOTH HOT SPRINGS

> CANARY SPRING

> DEVIL'S THUMB

> LIBERTY CAP

> MINERVA TERRACE

> PALETTE SPRING

> UPPER TERRACE

ROOSEVELT ARCH

SWAN LAKE FLAT AND ELECTRIC PEAK

UNDINE FALLS

Orange Spring Mound

GARDNER RIVER

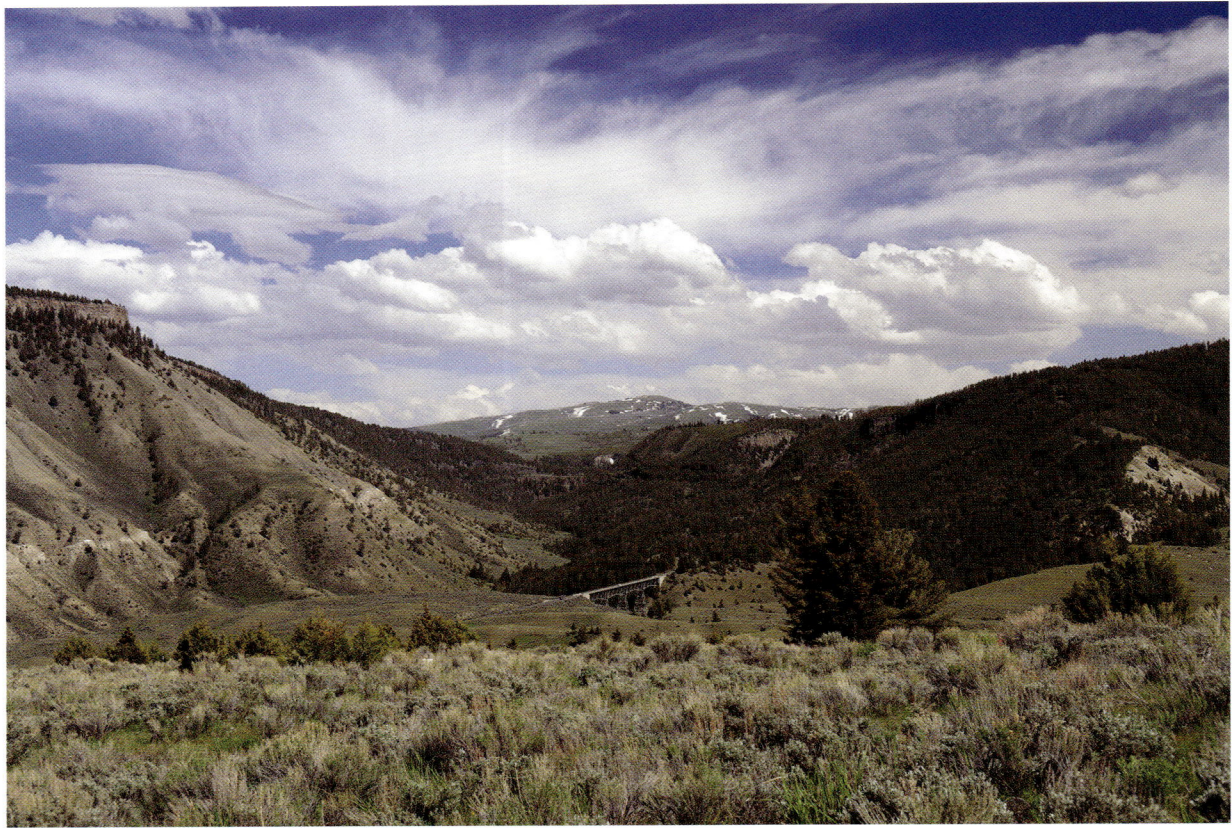

"There is a delight in the hardy life of the open. There are no words that can tell the hidden spirit of the wilderness, that can reveal its mystery, its melancholy and its charm. The nation behaves well if it treats the natural resources as assets which it must turn over to the next generation increased and not impaired in value. Conservation means development as much as it does protection."

PRESIDENT THEODORE ROOSEVELT

Gardner River Bridge

>

Mammoth Hot Springs

MAMMOTH HOT SPRINGS

"Or, as in the case of the Mammoth Hot Springs, at the north end of the park, where the building waters issue from the side of a steep hill, the deposits form a succession of higher and broader terraces of white travertine tinged with purple,... draped in front with clustering stalactites, each terrace having a pool of indescribably beautiful water upon it in a basin with a raised rim that glistens with confervæ,—the whole, when viewed at a distance of a mile or two, looking like a broad, massive cascade pouring over shelving rocks in snowy purpled foam."

JOHN MUIR
"The Yellowstone National Park," *The Atlantic Monthly,* April 1898

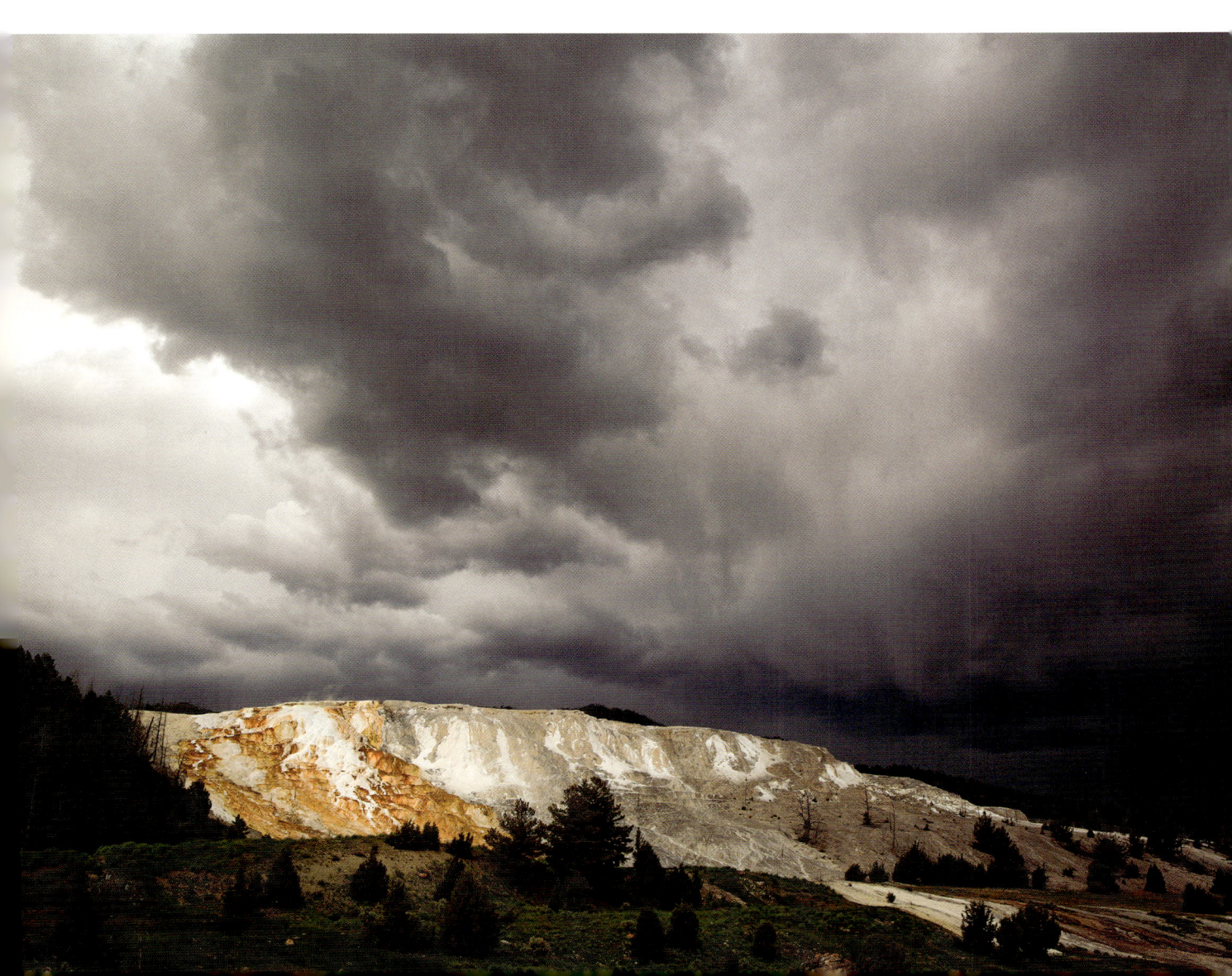

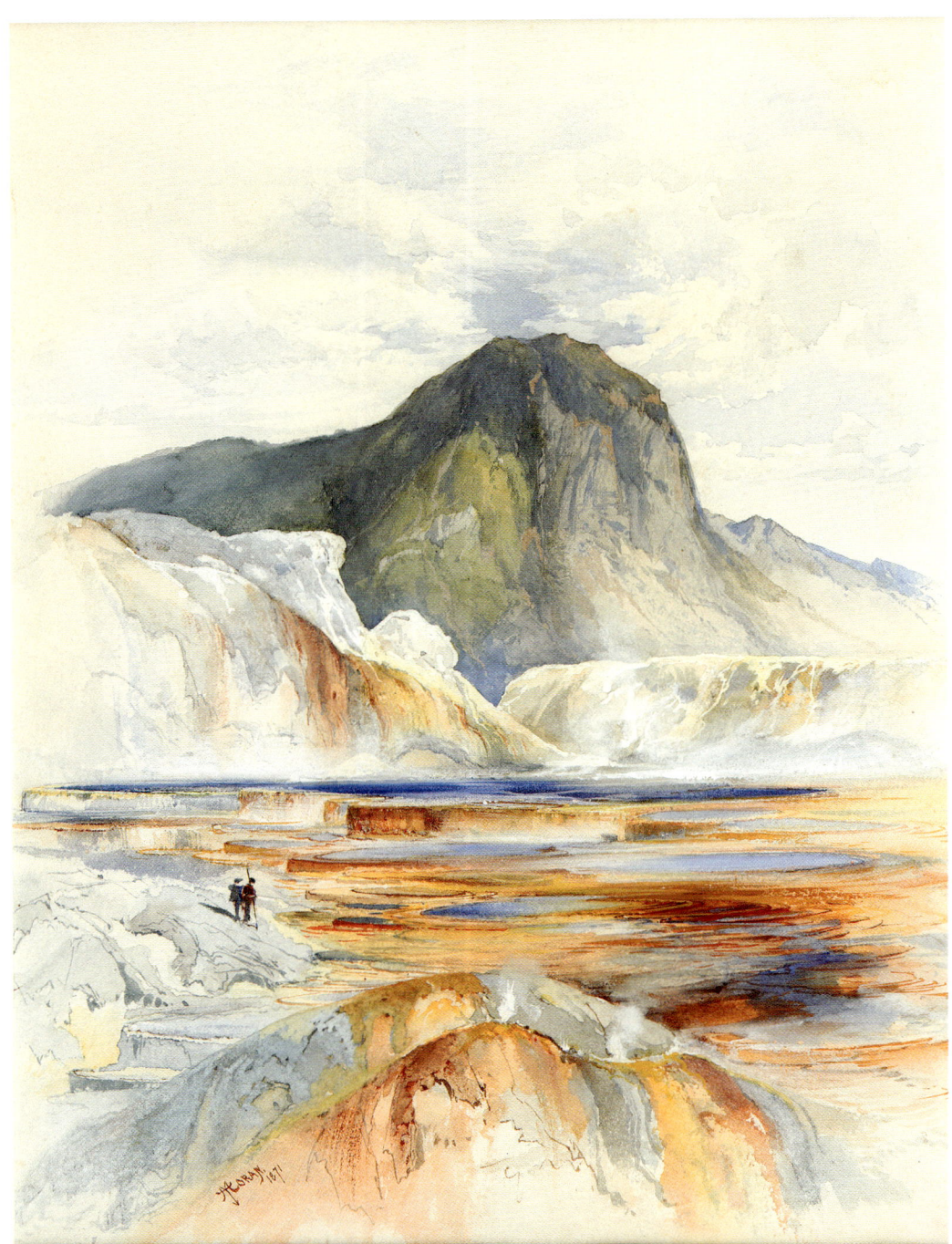

Upper Pools at the Hot Springs of
Gardiner's River, Yellowstone Valley
Thomas Moran, 1871
Gilcrease Museum, Tulsa, OK
0226.1367

>

Main Terrace

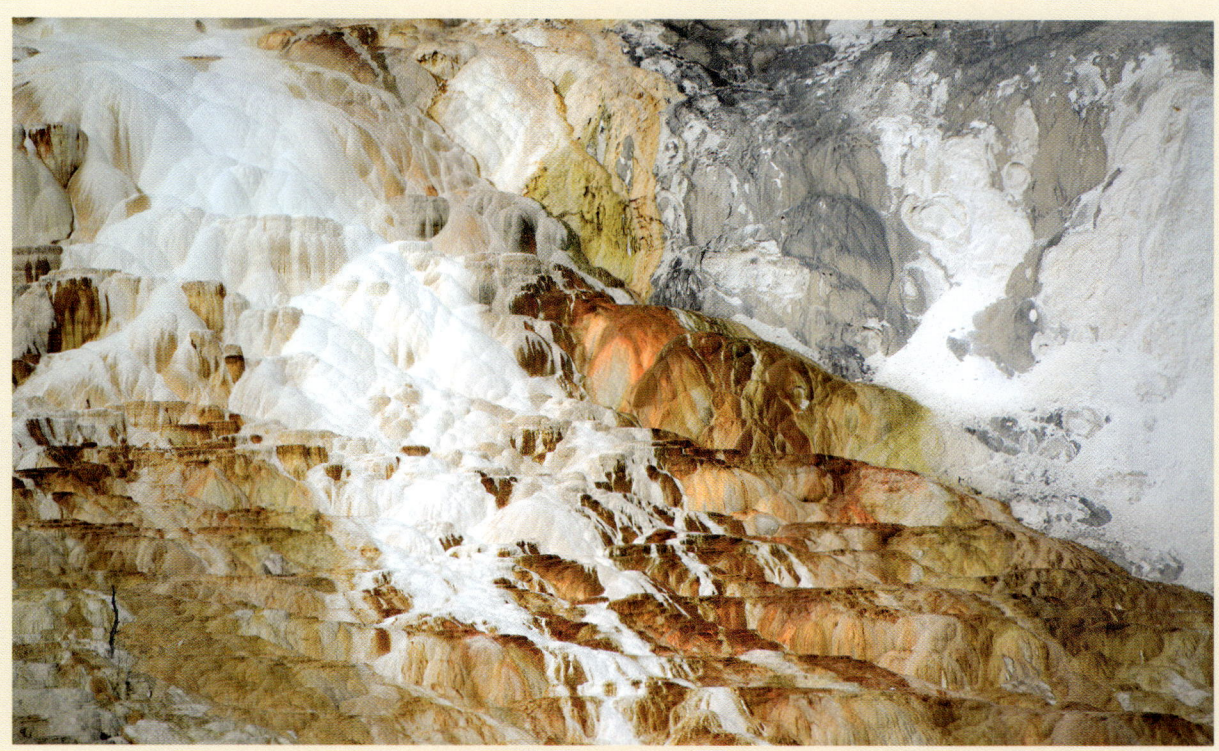

"Standing on some one of the snowy knobs that arise near the little chalky gorge called Antony's Gate, and looking down on these crystal-clear pools the eye and the senses are charmed by the soft beauty, the varied outlines, and the exquisite blending of color which they present. I had seen some of Moran's paintings of these hot pools and always had a suspicion that he had gone just a little wild in his appetite for color effect. Now that I have seen the springs I know that he stopped short of the reality."

"THE YELLOWSTONE PARK:
WONDERS OF THE MAMMOTH HOT SPRINGS BASIN"
The New York Times, July 22, 1883

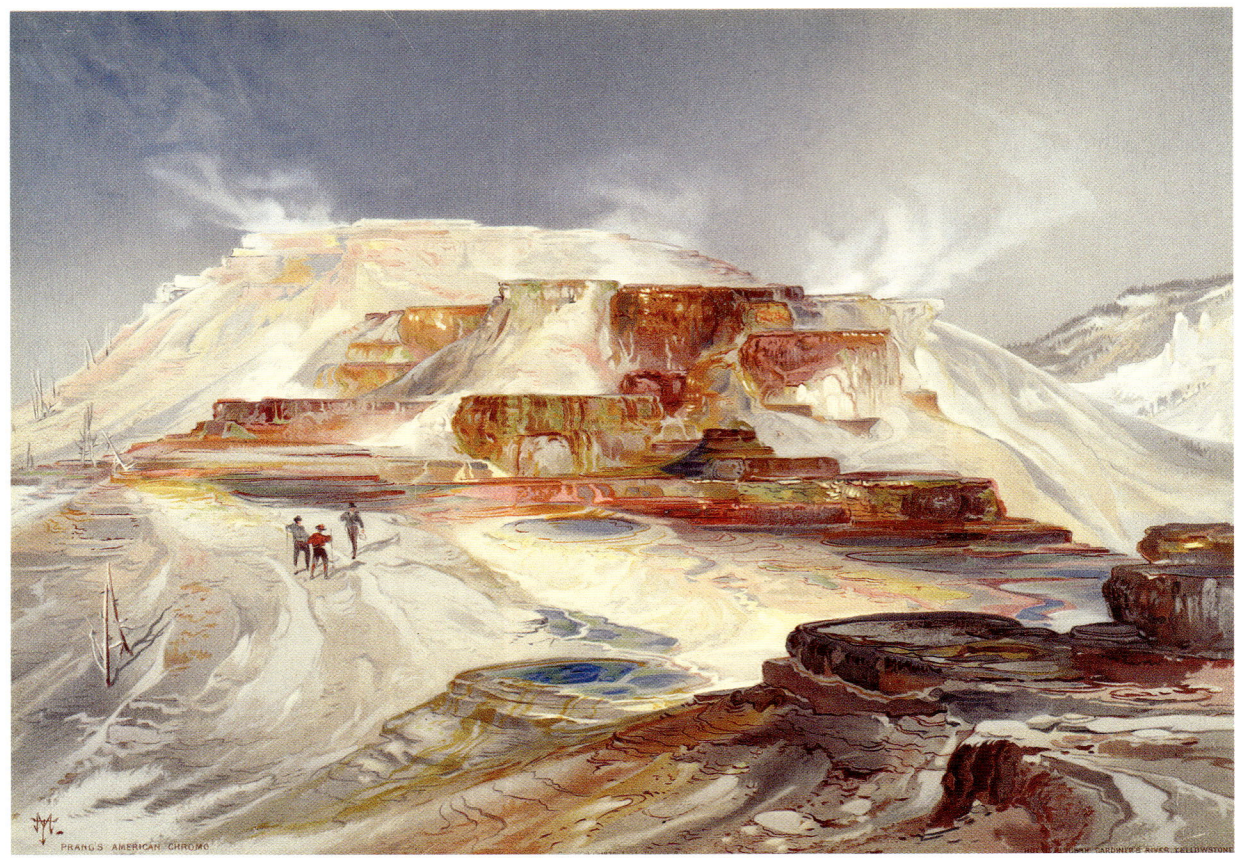

Hot Springs of Gardiner's River, Yellowstone
Thomas Moran, 1875
Gilcrease Museum, Tulsa, OK
2426.47.1

>

Canary Spring

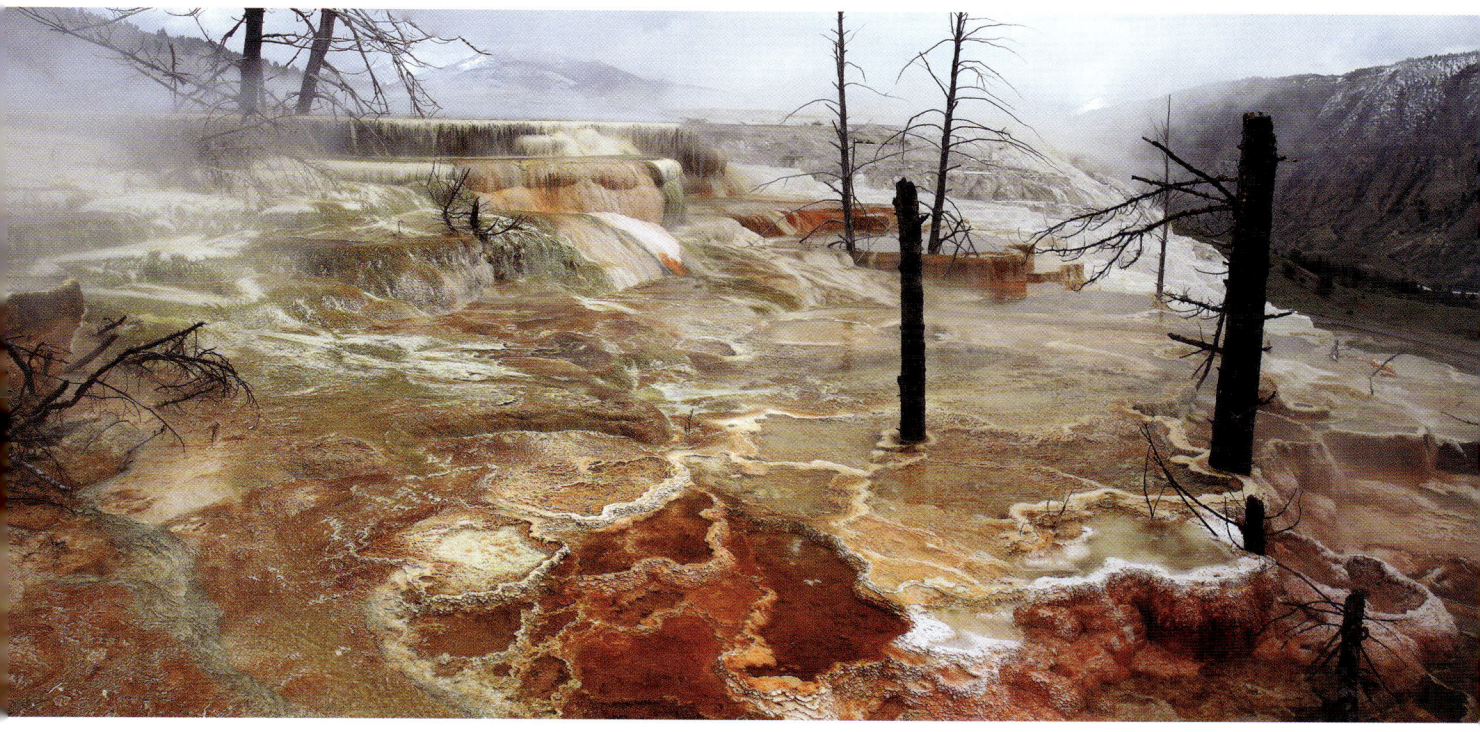

Mammoth Hot Springs is "a huge frozen waterfall, a petrified but larger Niagara, except that instead of being in a single sheet, it is broken into a series of cascades, white as snow in some places, dingy in others, here a reddish yellow, like iron-rust, and there with broad stripes of soft shrimp pink and terra cotta. . . .

"As you start to climb up the face of the terrace you experience a succession of surprises. The summit of each little cascade is found to be a beautiful pool, with scalloped edges, indented and fretted like the most beautiful coral. The steaming water in these is as clear as the air and covers the most exquisite formation, beside which, delicate lace seems coarse and tawdry. The colors are simply indescribable. The most delicate pinks and blues, vivid reds and emerald greens rapidly succeed each other. . . ."

GEORGE WOOD WINGATE
Through the Yellowstone Park on Horseback, 1886

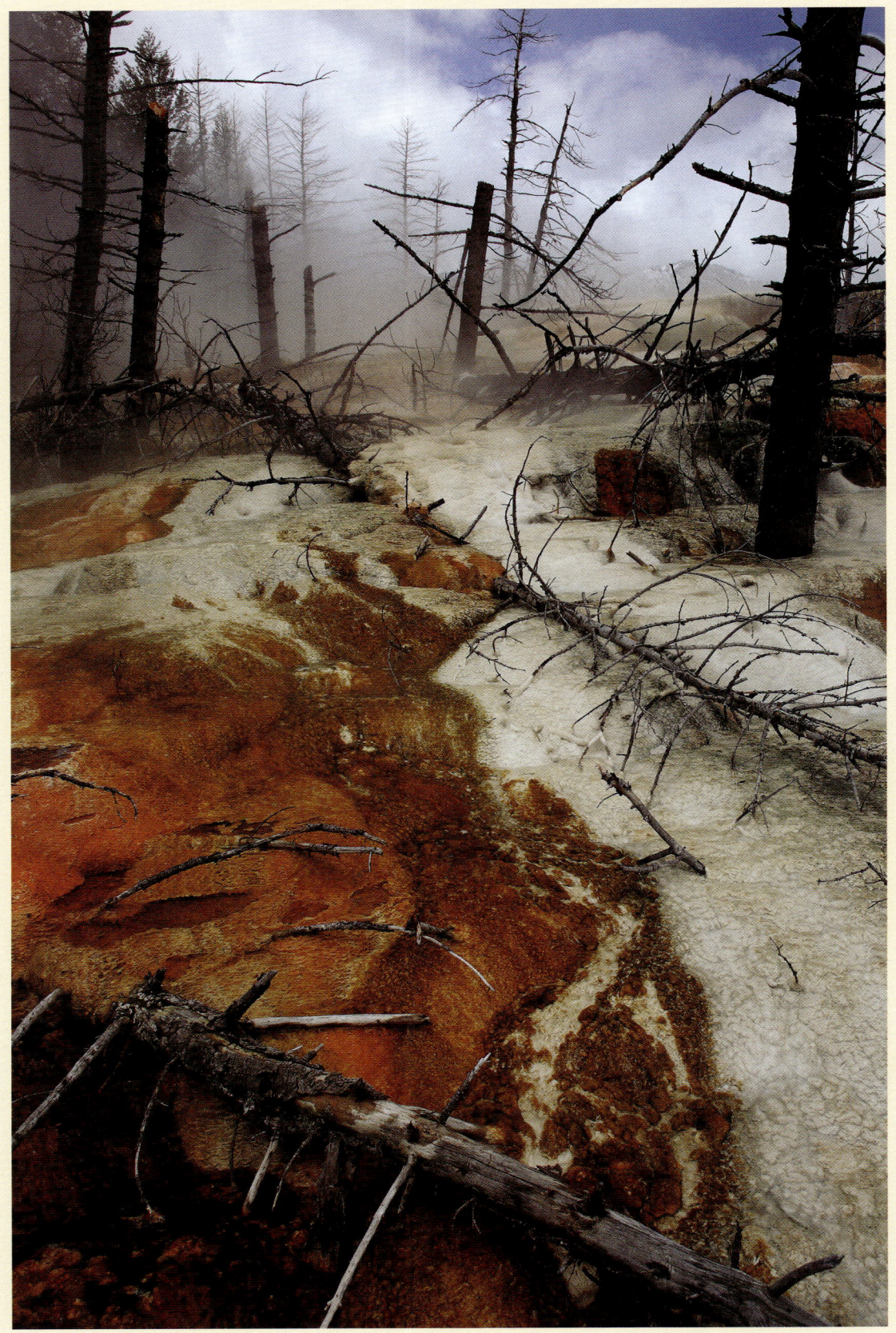

<
Canary Spring

Devil's Thumb

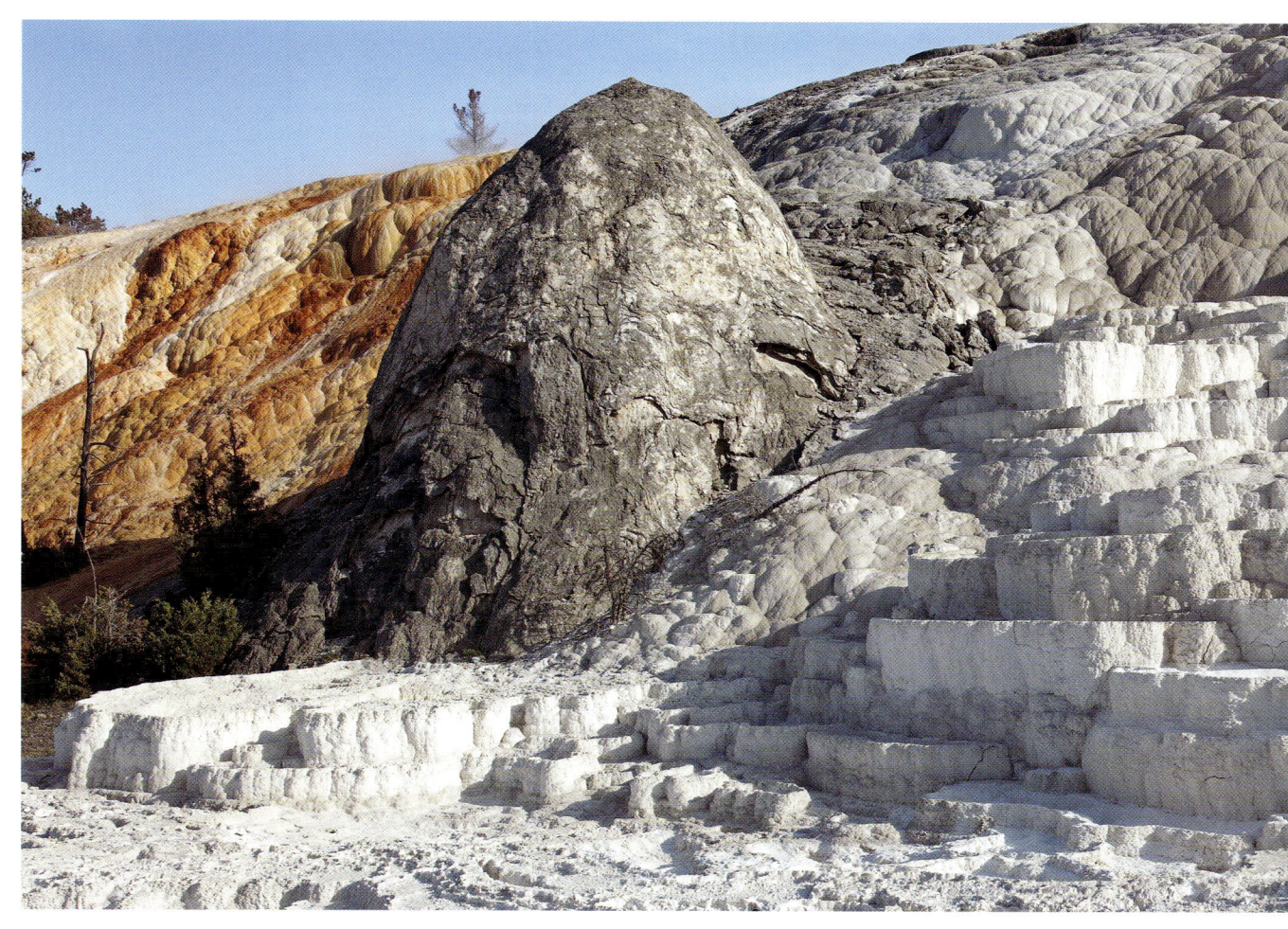

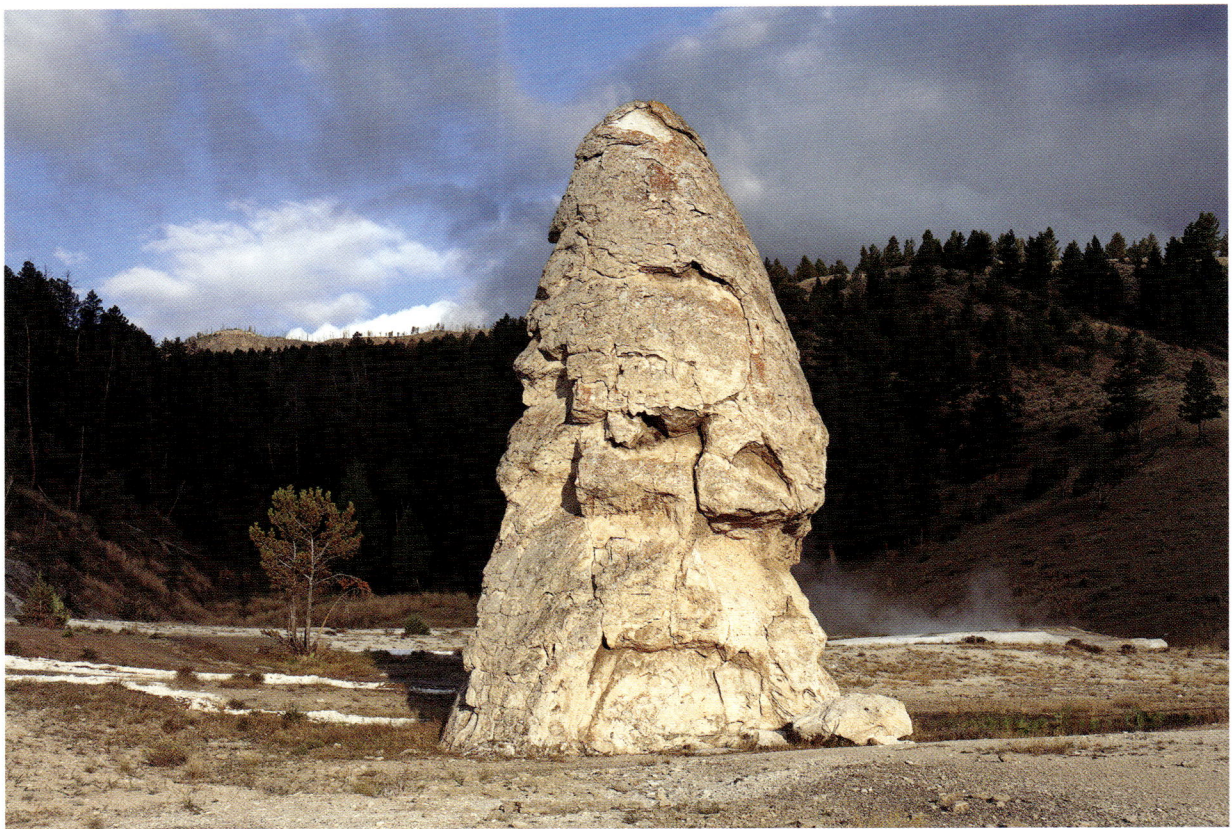

Liberty Cap

>
The Hot Springs of Gardiner's River
Extinct Geyser Crater
Thomas Moran, 1872
Gilcrease Museum, Tulsa, OK
0226.1360

Liberty Cap "looks like a silent sentinel guarding the gate of Wonderland; or like an ancient witness who could, if it would, reveal the sealed secrets of the past. It has more faces than Janus and more eyes than the fabled Argus."

G.L. HENDERSON, PARK INTERPRETER, 1888

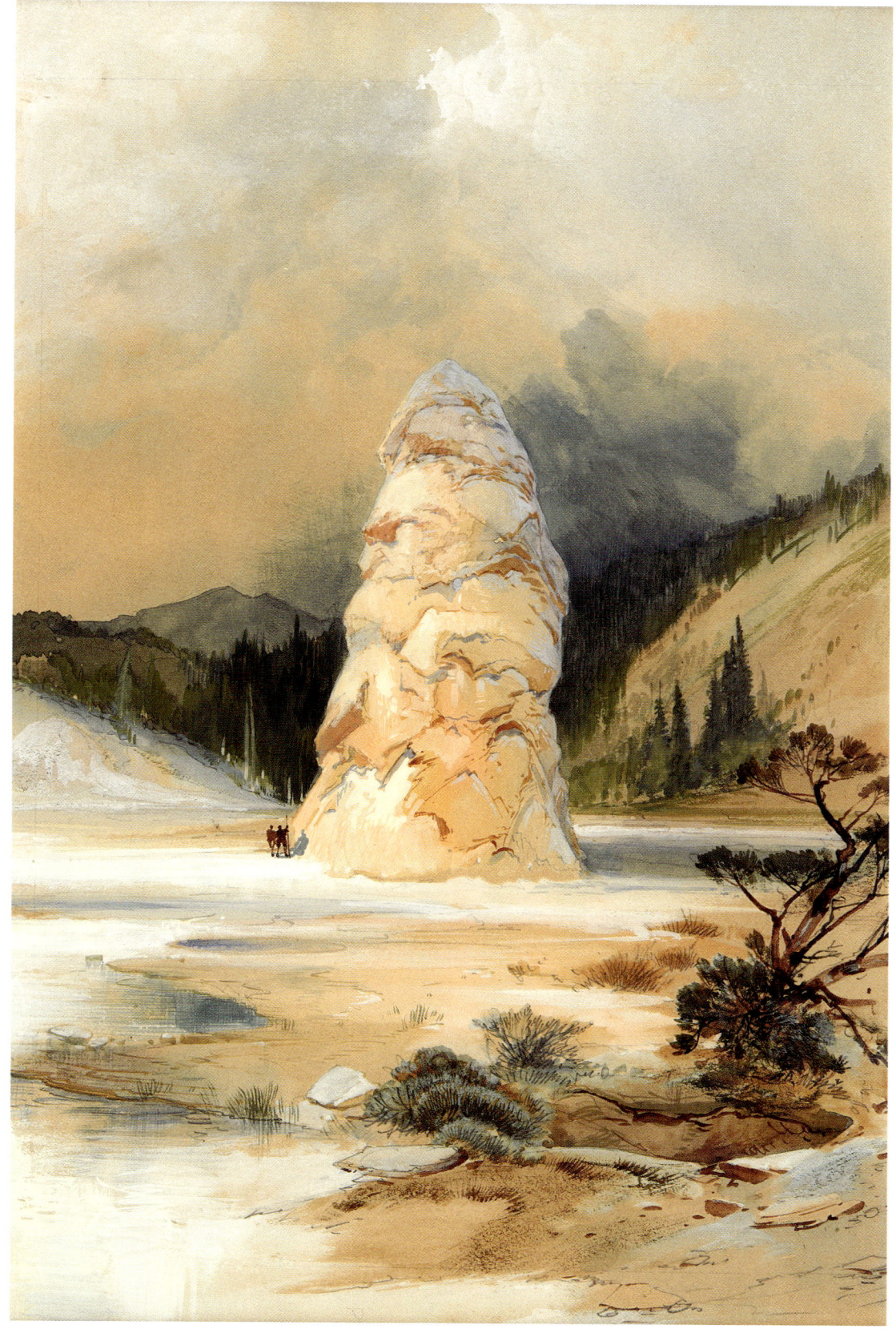

MINERVA TERRACE

"We were totally unprepared to find [Mammoth Hot Springs] so beautiful and extensive. Before us lay a high white hill, composed of calcareous sediment deposited from numerous hot springs. The whole mass looked like some grand cascade that had been suddenly arrested in its descent, and frozen."

ALBERT CHARLES PEALE, GEOLOGIST WITH THE F.V. HAYDEN SURVEY, 1872

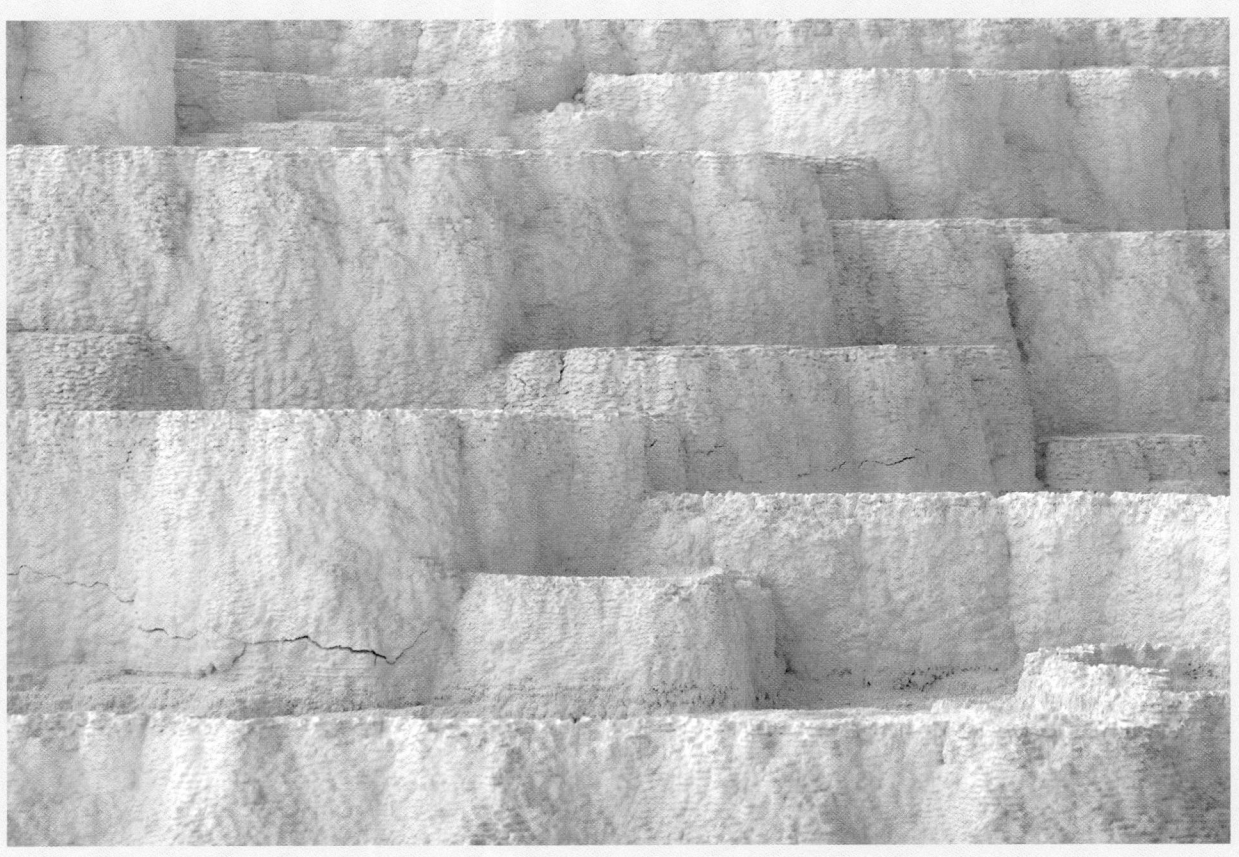

<

Minerva Terrace

Palette Spring

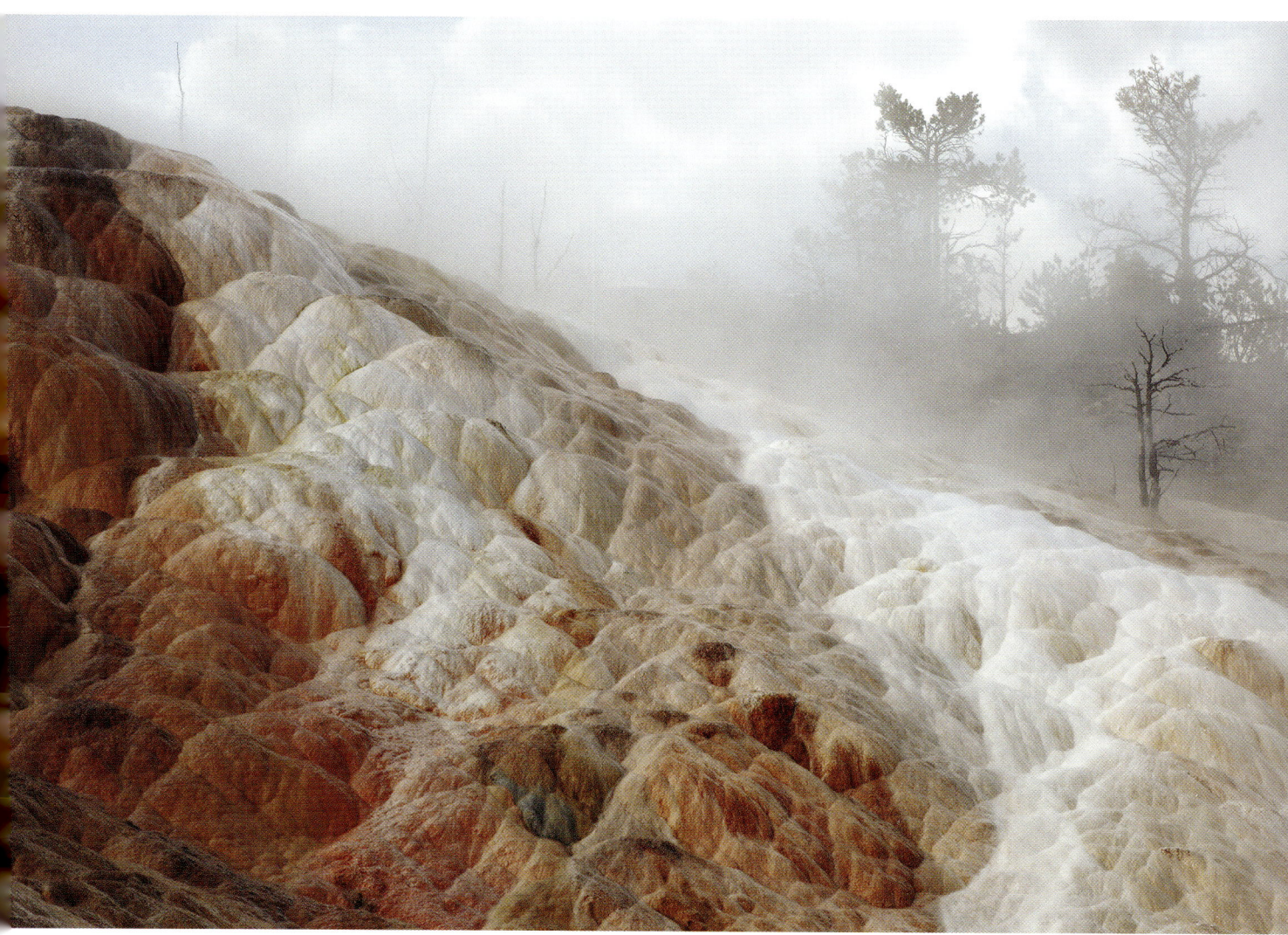

"The whole snowy mass that had looked so cold and silent under the pale moon the night before, was now glowing, gleaming, pulsating with life under the morning sun. For perhaps a hundred acres the whole surface was studded with brilliant pools, set like jewels, clear as diamonds, lovelier in color than opals, in rims of fretted frost, delicate as lace and firm as marble. Over these coralline edges trickles softly the gentle overflow of the lovely lakes—falling tremulously and without a sound over the fluted, reed-like columns of the terraces below, only to leave them harder than they were before. . . .

"Even the exquisite coloring of the water, a lovely robin's-egg blue, and the almost gorgeous coloring of the terraces where part of the deposit had formed in columns or streaks of the richest orange and red, or of the daintiest pink or creamy-yellow, failed to detract from the general effect of acres upon acres of snow and ice."

ALICE WELLINGTON ROLLINS
The Three Tetons, 1887

>
The Hot Springs of Gardiner's River "Diana's Baths"
Thomas Moran, 1872
Gilcrease Museum, Tulsa, OK
0226.1454

Palette Spring

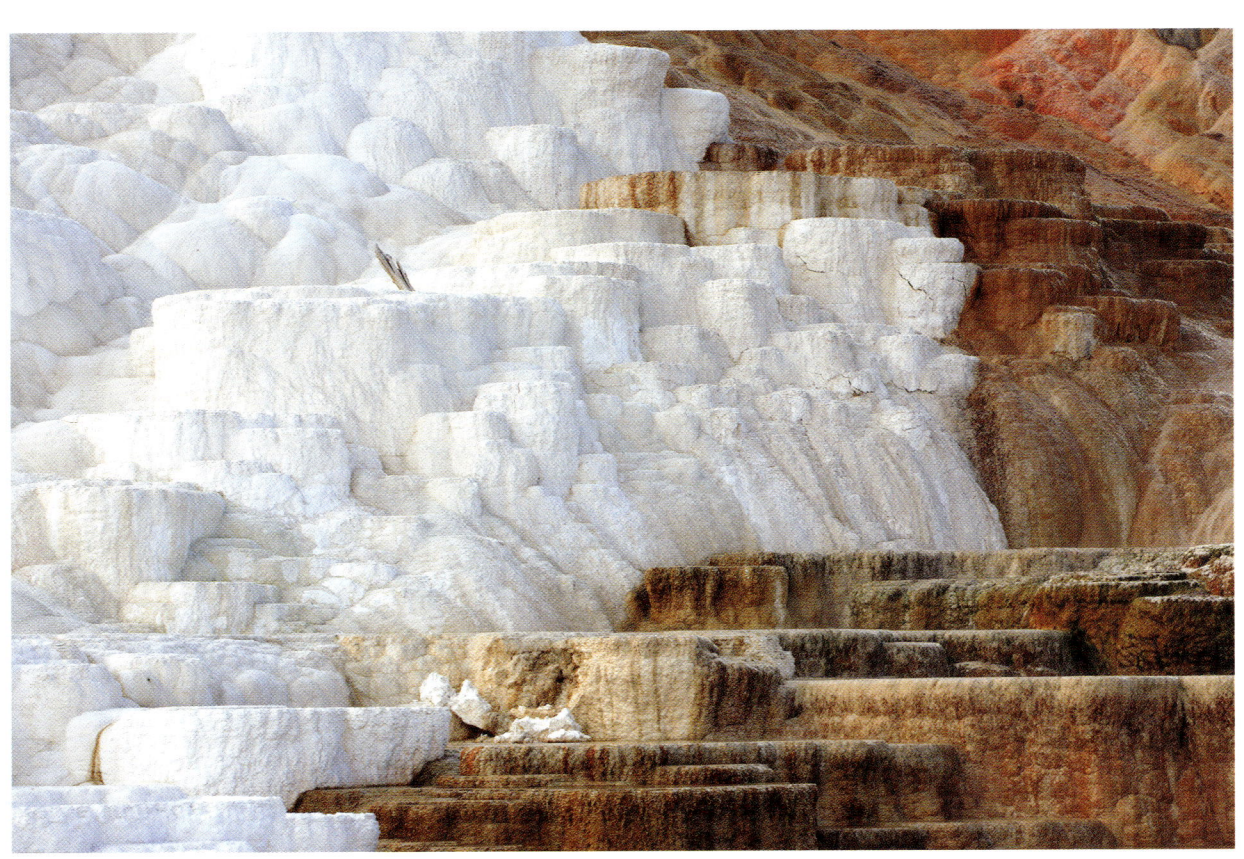

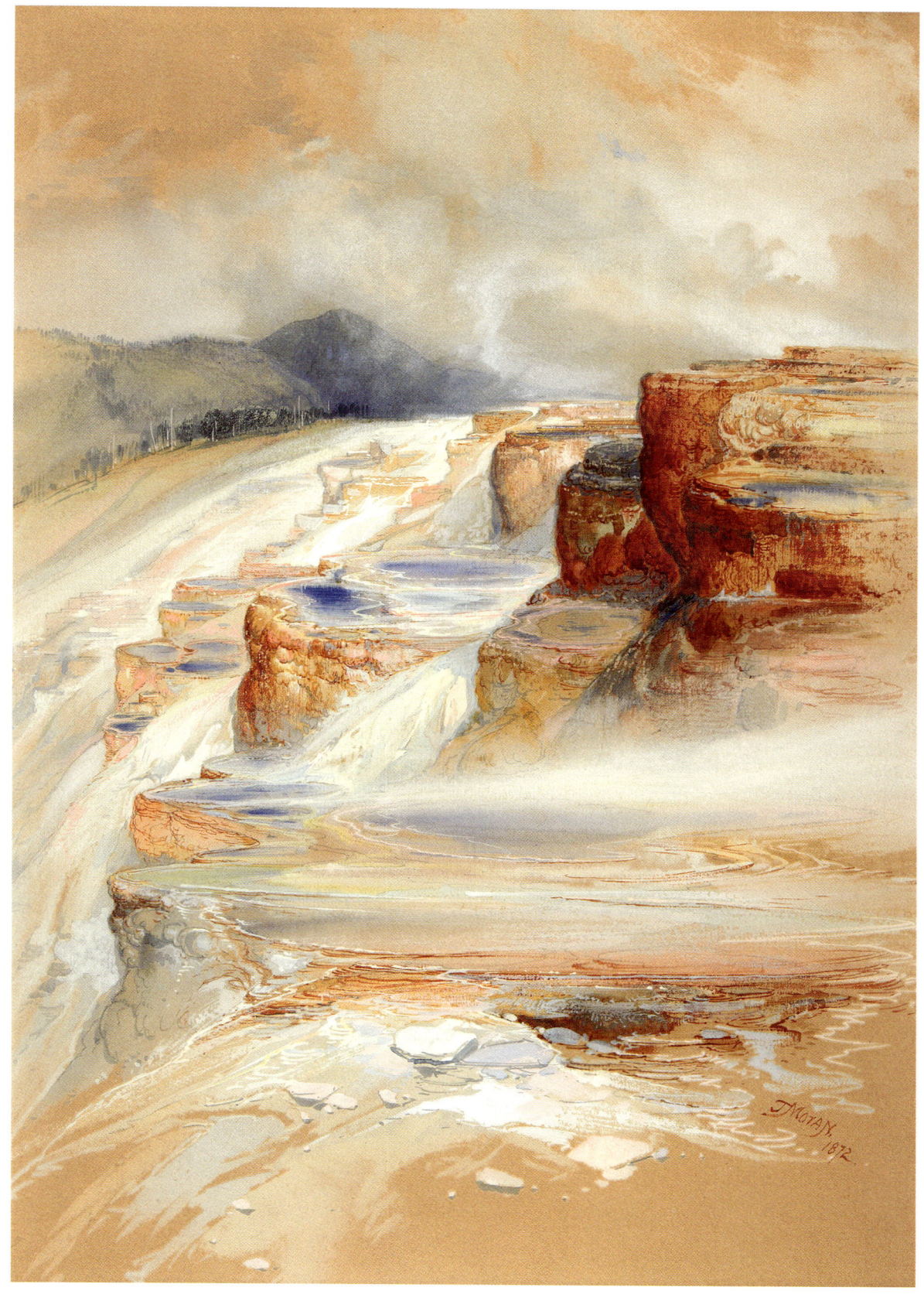

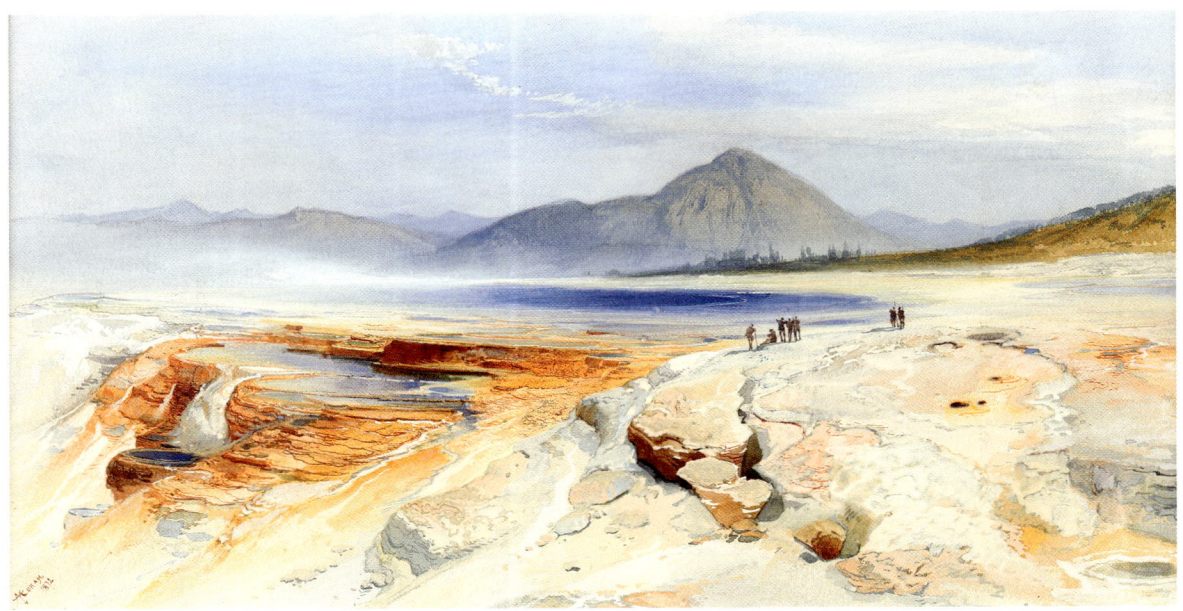

The Main Springs at Gardiner's River,
Yellowstone Valley
Thomas Moran, 1872
Gilcrease Museum, Tulsa, OK
0226.1361

Upper Terrace and Electric Peak
(10,969 ft) in the Gallatin Range

Mammoth from Upper Terrace

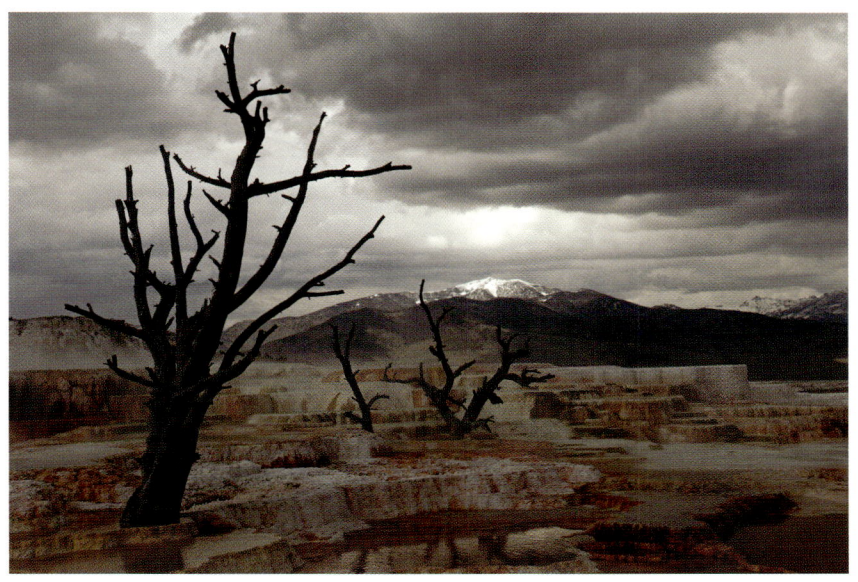

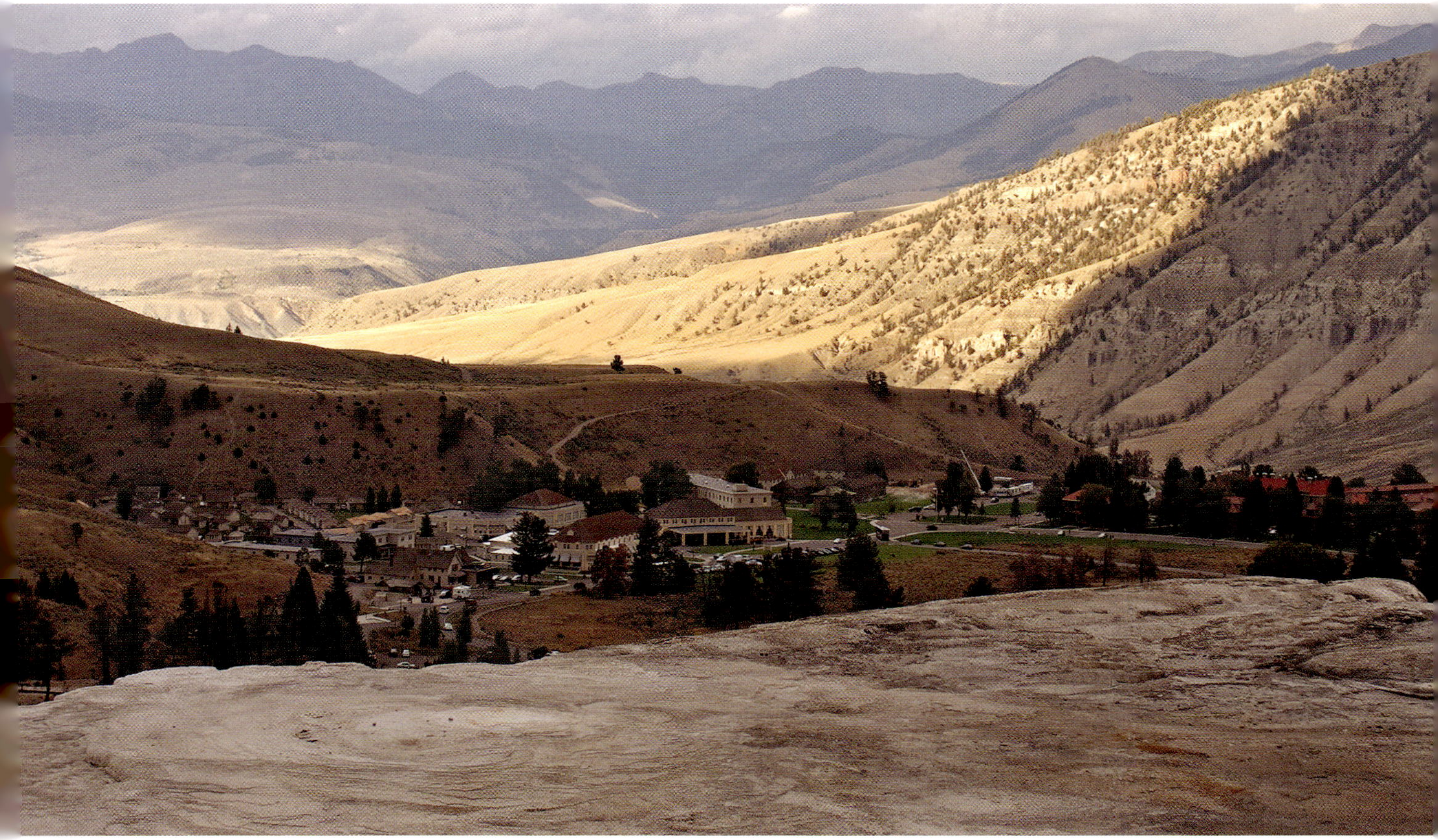

Orange Spring Mound on
Upper Terrace Drive

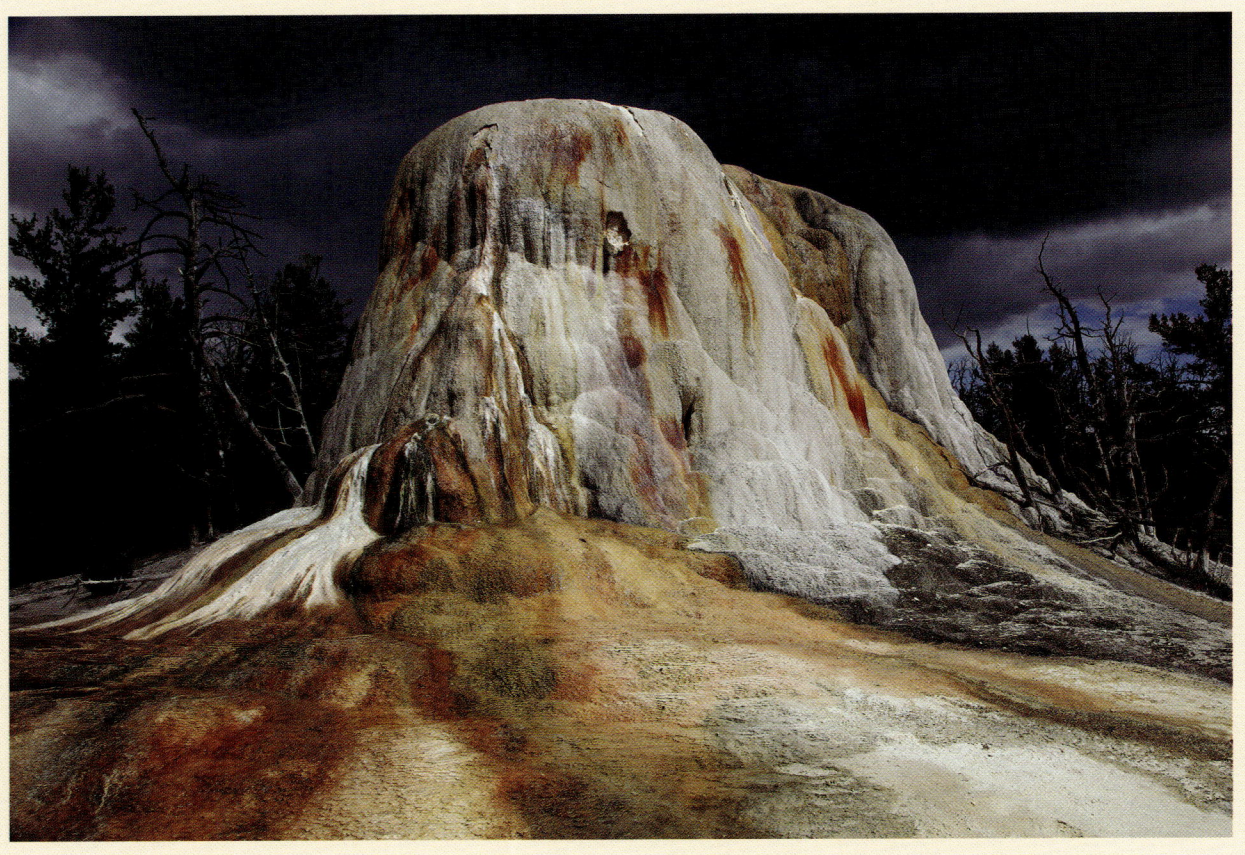

ROOSEVELT ARCH

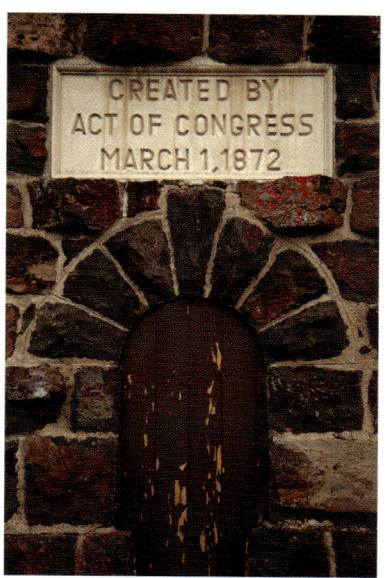

"It is a pleasure now to say a few words to you at the laying of the corner stone of the beautiful arch which is to mark the entrance to this park. Yellowstone Park is something absolutely unique in the world so far as I know. Nowhere else in any civilized country is there to be found such a tract of veritable wonderland made accessible to all visitors. : . . This Park was created, and is now administered for the benefit and enjoyment of the people . . . and with the sense on the part of every visitor that it is in part his property; that it is the property of Uncle Sam and therefore of all of us. The only way that the people as a whole can secure to themselves and their children the enjoyment in perpetuity of what the Yellowstone Park has to give, is by assuming the ownership in the name of the nation and jealously safeguarding and preserving the scenery, the forests, and the wild creatures. . . . The geysers, the extraordinary hot springs, the lakes, the mountains, the canyon and cataracts unite to make this region something not paralleled elsewhere on the globe. It must be kept for the benefit and enjoyment of all of us."

PRESIDENT THEODORE ROOSEVELT, April 24, 1903

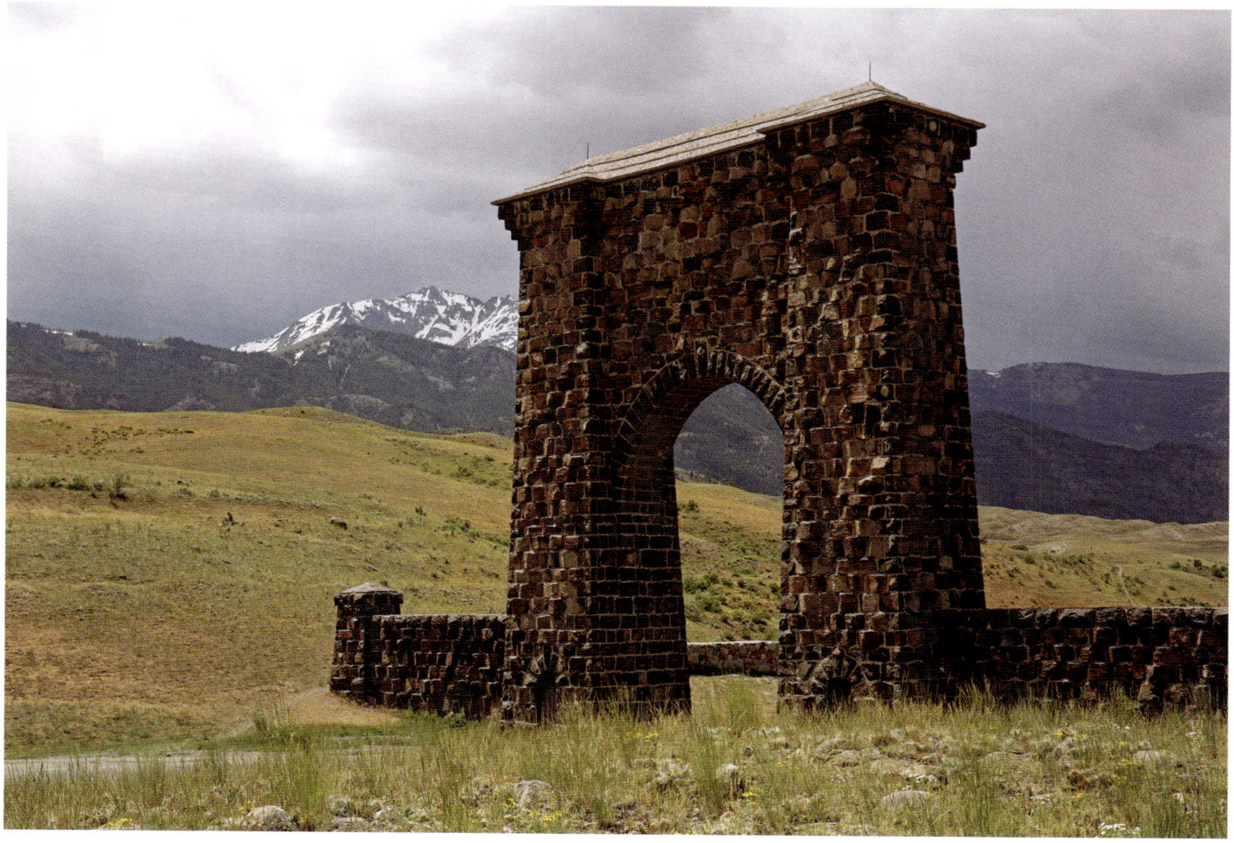

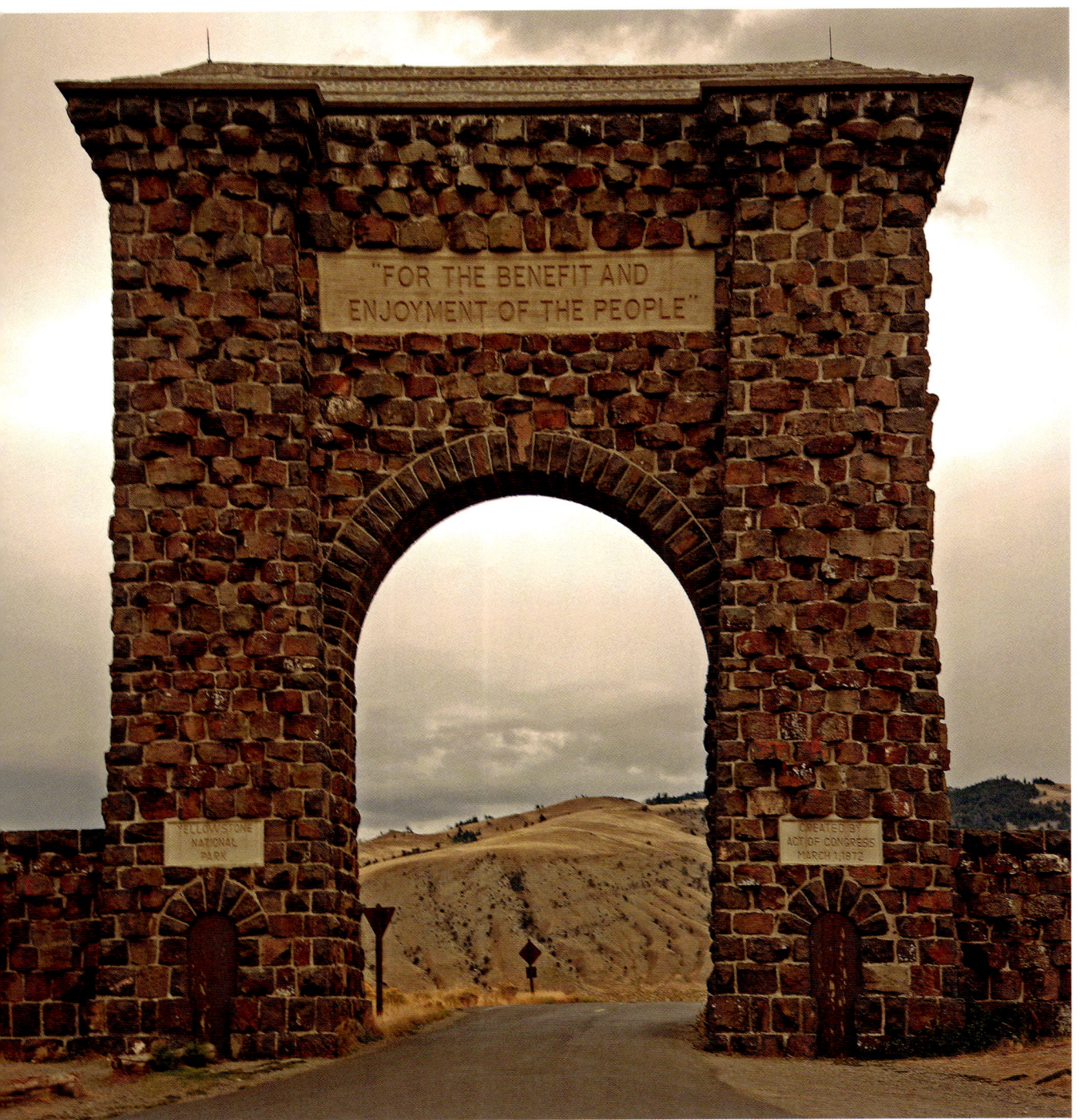

"FOR THE BENEFIT AND ENJOYMENT OF THE PEOPLE"

YELLOWSTONE NATIONAL PARK

CREATED BY ACT OF CONGRESS MARCH 1, 1872

Roosevelt Arch

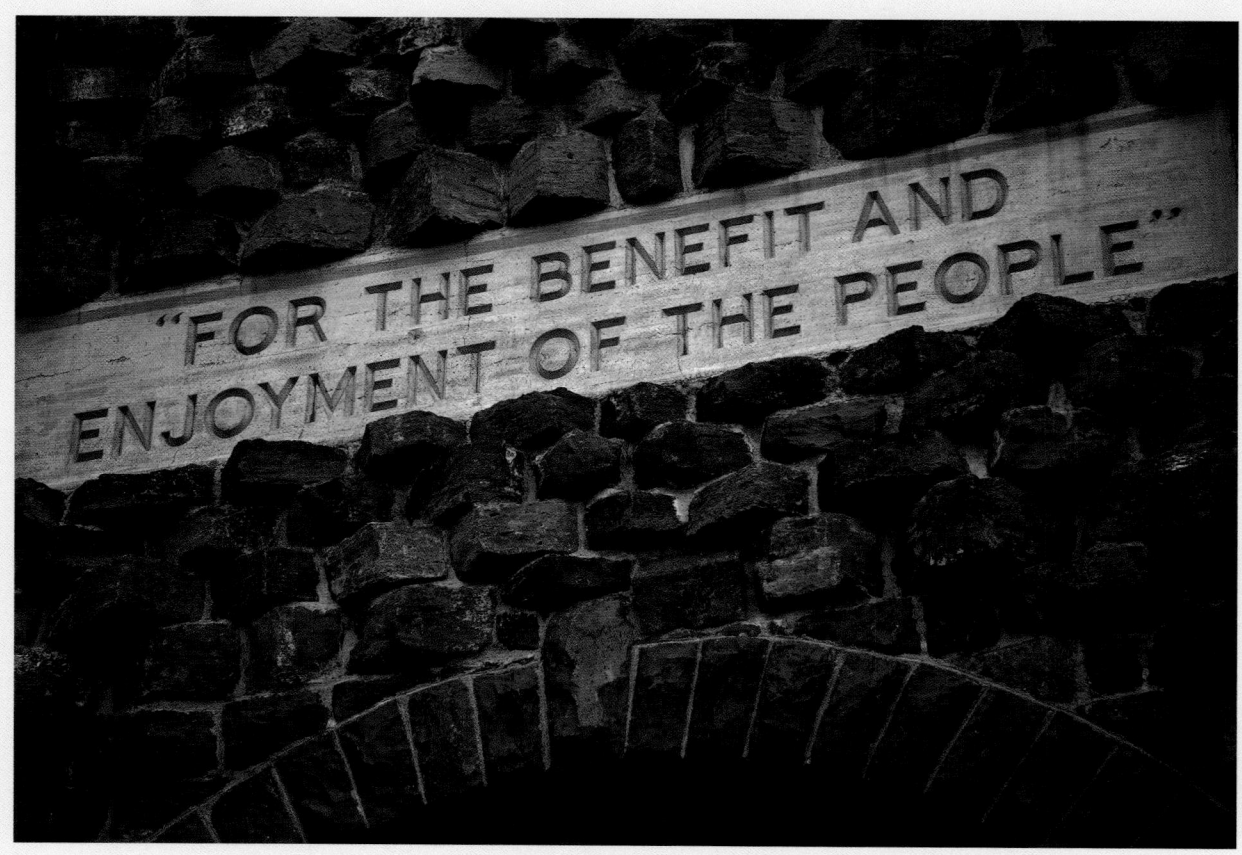

SWAN LAKE FLAT AND
ELECTRIC PEAK (10,969')

"We reached the summit of the peak about four o'clock. There was a storm cloud all about us. [Henry] Gannett was a little ahead and we saw him hurrying back to us with his hair standing on end. As he neared us we could hear a crackling noise as though there were a lot of frictional electrical machines all about him. We soon began to feel it ourselves. Gannet said [that when] he got to the summit the electricity was so strong that he was obliged to put down the gradienter and hurry down. [A.E.] Brown tried to go up and get it but got a shock on the top of his head and came back in a hurry also. We then descended about one hundred feet, having the noise all about us as though there were a lot of electrical machines about us."

ALBERT CHARLES PEALE, GEOLOGIST WITH THE F.V. HAYDEN SURVEY, 1872

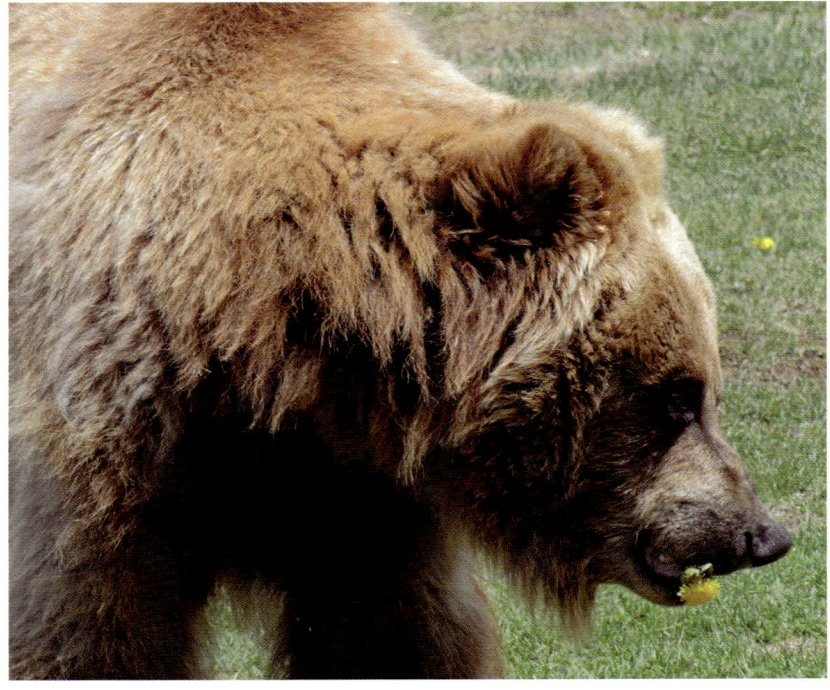

Grizzly bear

>

Swan Lake Flat and Electric Peak

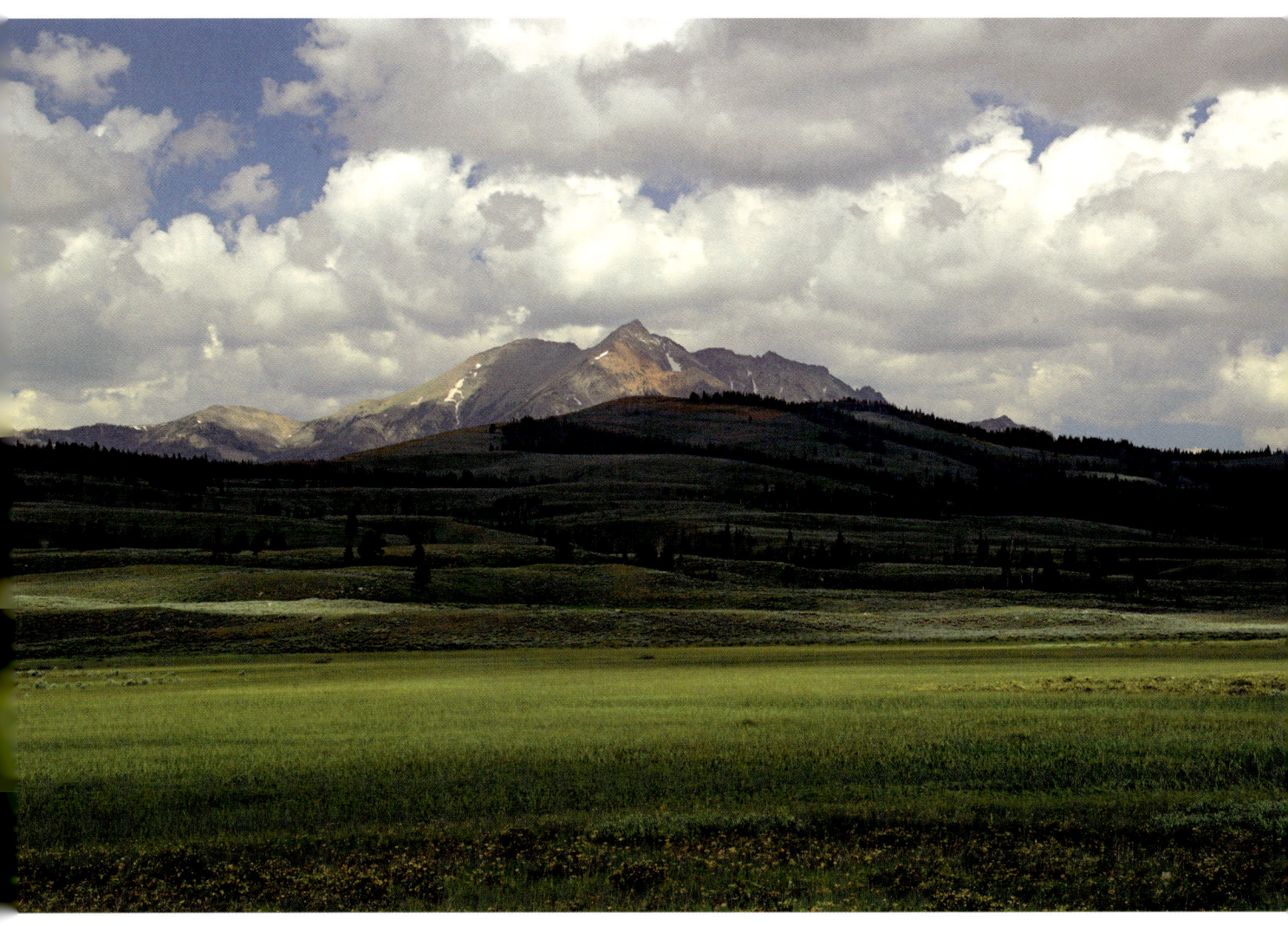

UNDINE FALLS

Undine Falls

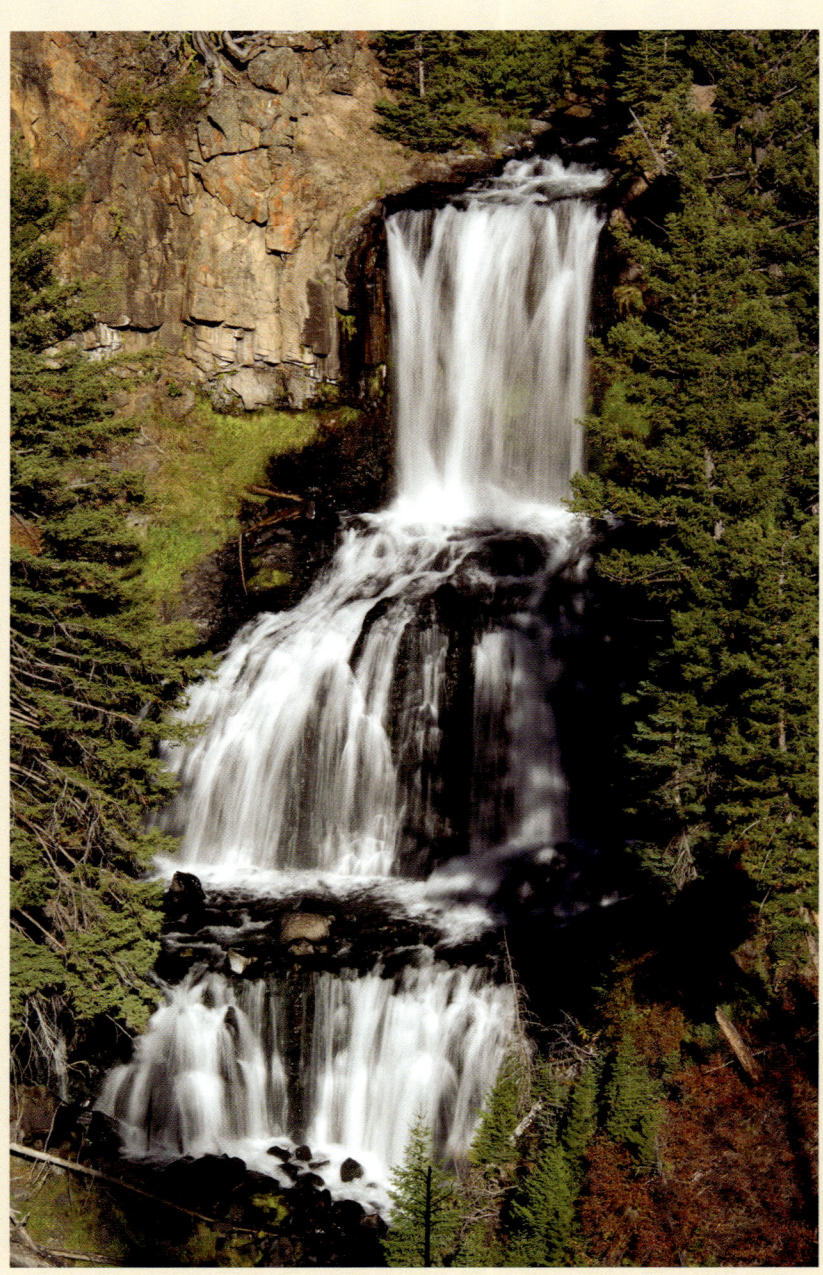

Bald eagle

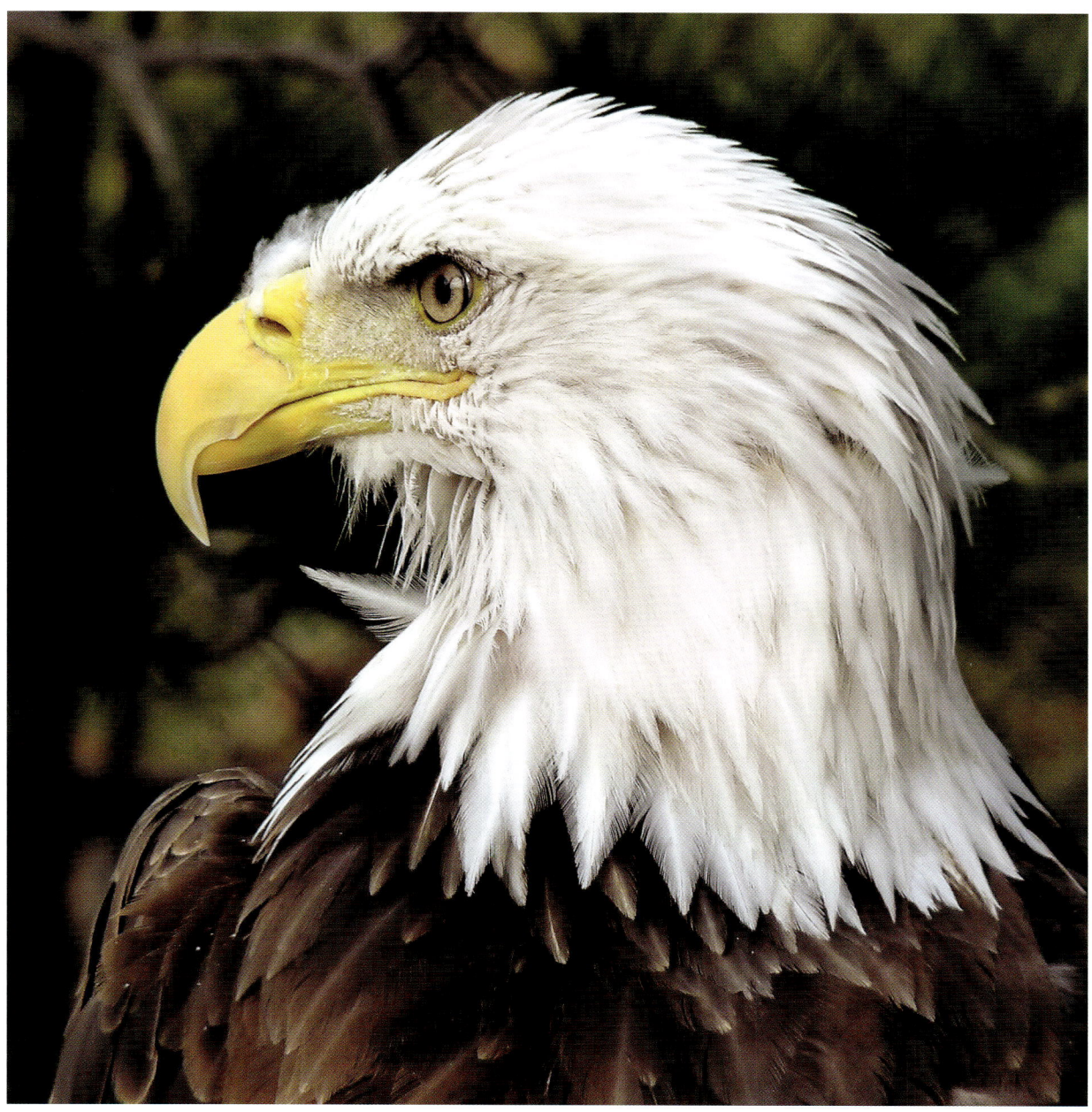

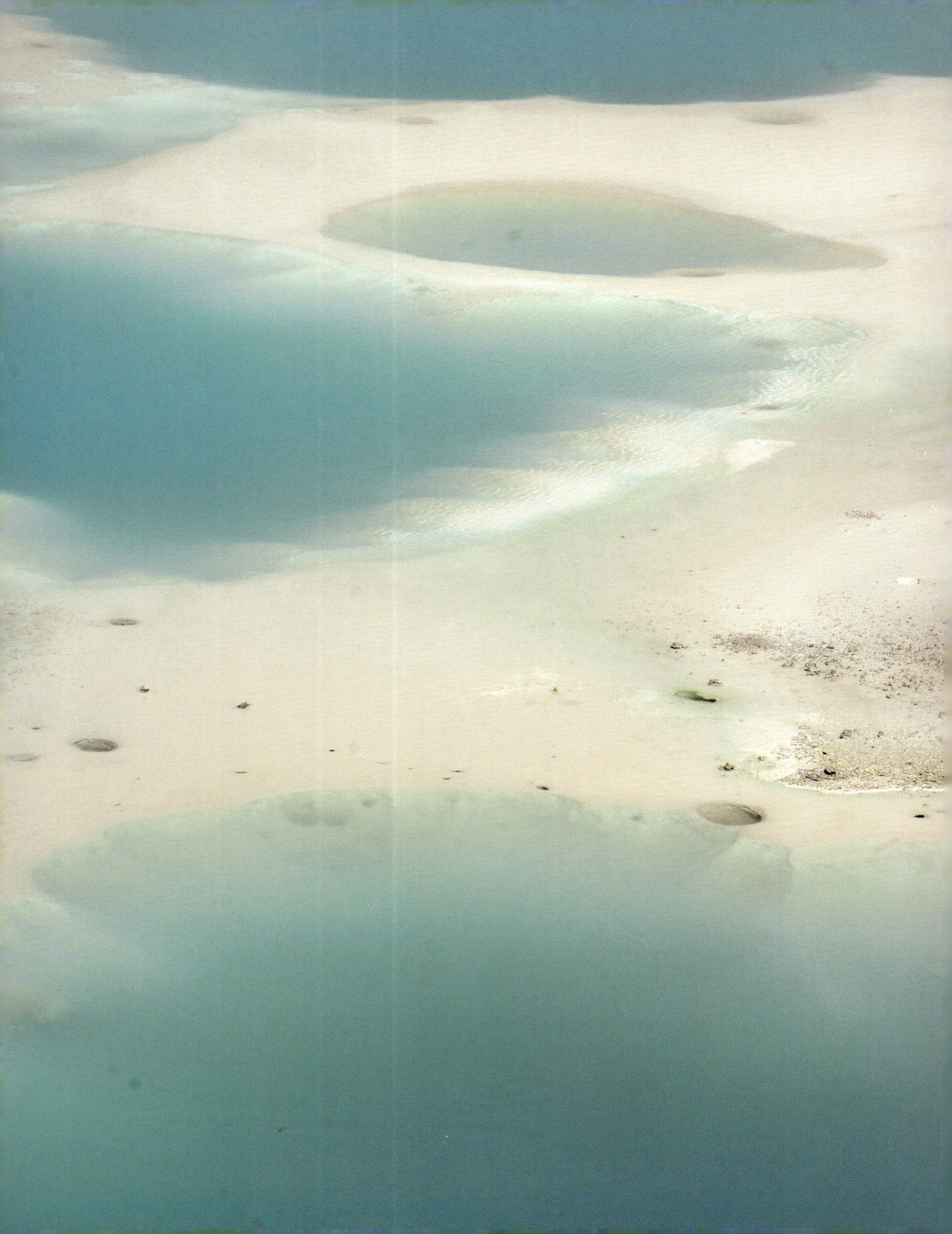

NORRIS AREA

GIBBON RIVER

NORRIS GEYSER BASIN
> PORCELAIN BASIN

Colloidal Pool

GIBBON RIVER

Gibbon River at Norris Canyon Road

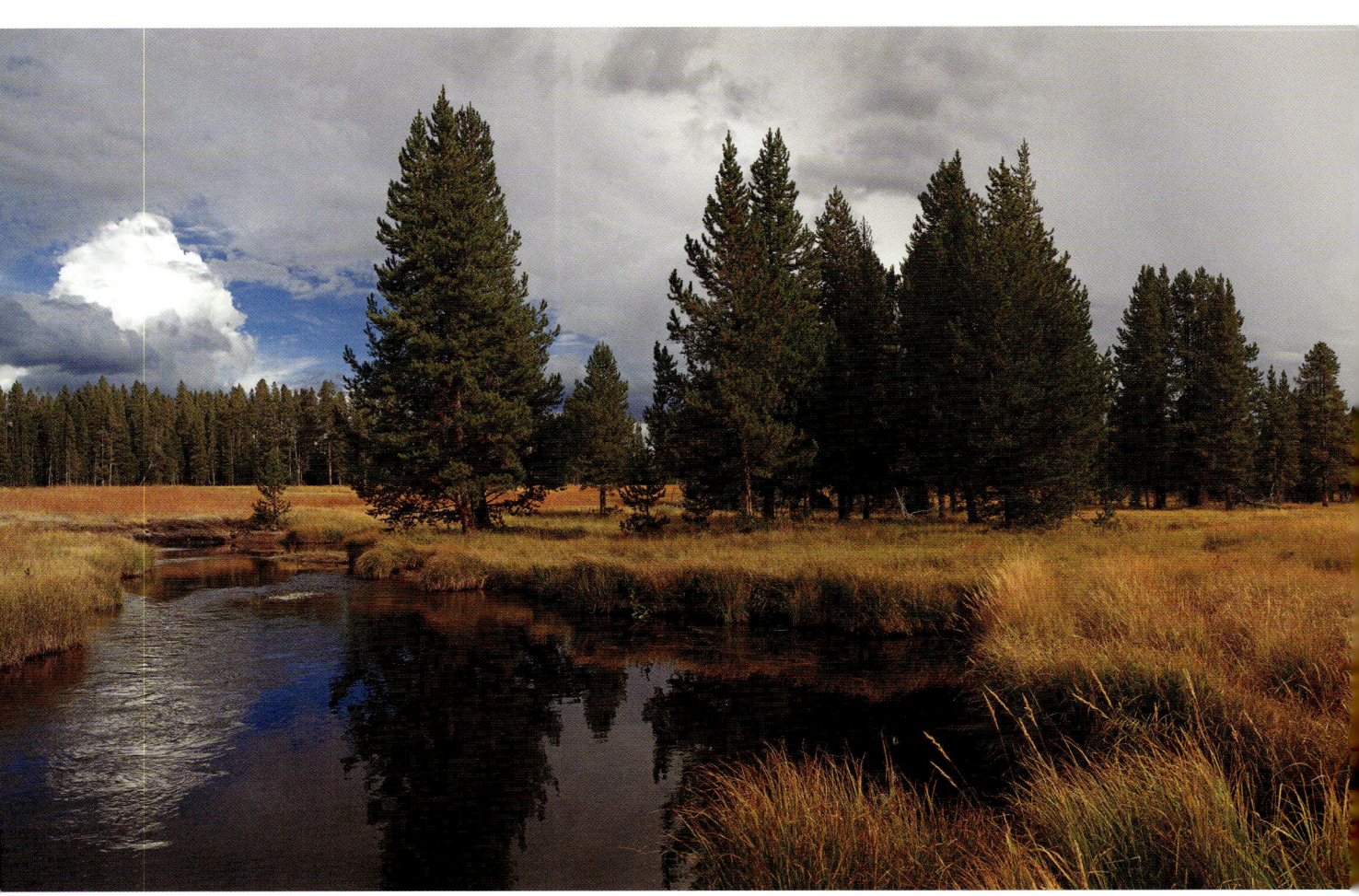

Along the Gibbon River

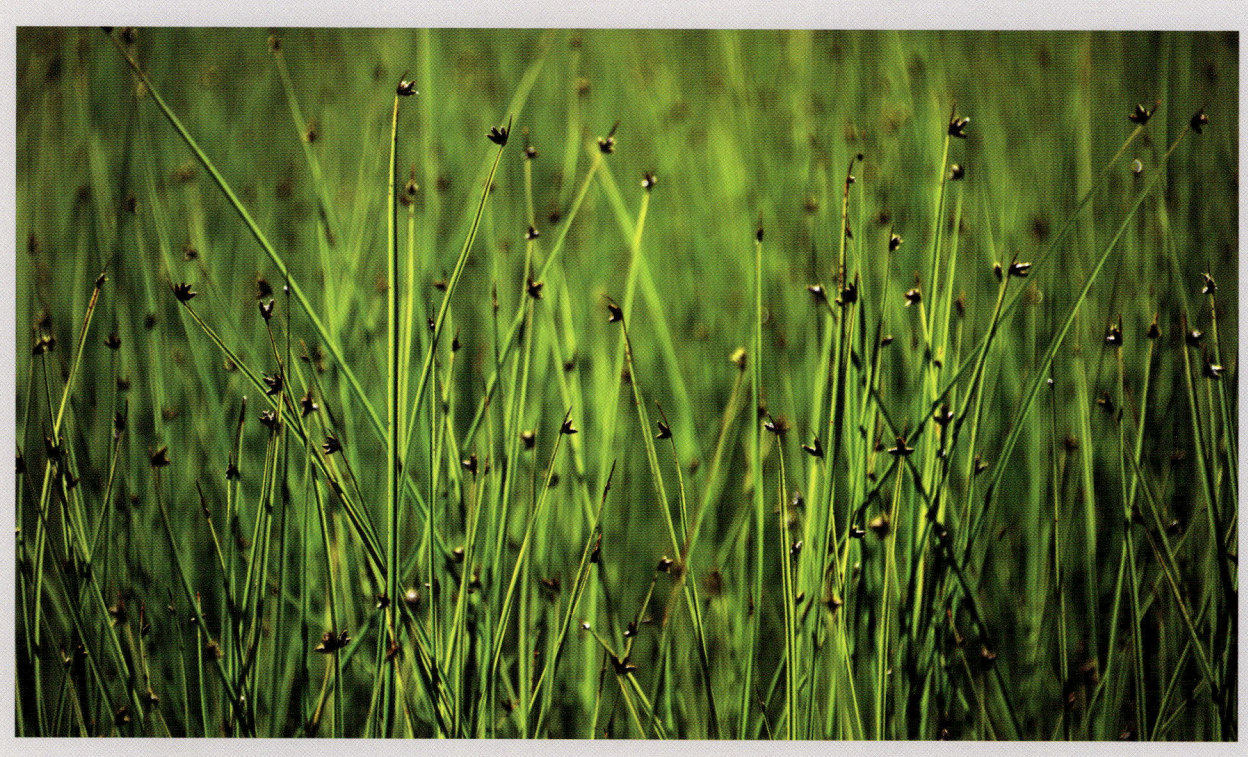

NORRIS GEYSER BASIN

Norris Geyser Basin is "a barren tract, and resembles an immense area recently swept by a terrific fire. From many places jets of steam are constantly rising."

EDWARD S. PARKINSON
Wonderland; or, Twelve weeks in and out of the United States, 1894

Norris Geyser Basin is "a valley some half a mile long and a quarter wide, white and utterly barren.... As you descend from the road into this valley, you meet on the side-hill what seems to be the gateway of the infernal regions. On the left hand is a crater or opening in the rock about the size of a large barrel, and black as ink, from which a volume of steam escapes with a roar like a dozen North River steamboats letting off steam at once, fairly shaking the solid rock around it, and giving the idea that if anything should occur to choke up this vent, the whole surrounding rock would be blown into the air....

"A short distance to the right was a mud pot, some twenty feet in diameter, filled with mud of a pale drab, which was boiling so furiously that its surface was constantly springing up in jets and spray two or three feet high, flickering and twisting like the tongues of flame from a bonfire. The sight was appalling. It seemed as if innumerable demons were struggling beneath it to escape. Certainly nothing I ever saw impressed my imagination so strongly."

GEORGE WOOD WINGATE
Through the Yellowstone Park on Horseback, 1886

"These valleys at the heads of the great rivers may be regarded as laboratories and kitchens, in which, amid a thousand retorts and pots, we may see Nature at work as chemist or cook, cunningly compounding an infinite variety of mineral messes; cooking whole mountains; boiling and steaming flinty rocks to smooth paste and mush,—yellow, brown, red, pink, lavender, gray, and creamy white,—making the most beautiful mud in the world; and distilling the most ethereal essences. Many of these pots and caldrons have been boiling thousands of years. Pots of sulphurous mush, stringy and lumpy, and pots of broth as black as ink, are tossed and stirred with constant care, and thin transparent essences, too pure and fine to be called water, are kept simmering gently in beautiful sinter cups and bowls that grow ever more beautiful the longer they are used. In some of the spring basins, the waters, though still warm, are perfectly calm, and shine blandly in a sod of overleaning grass and flowers, as if they were thoroughly cooked at last, and set aside to settle and cool. Others are wildly boiling over as if running to waste, thousands of tons of the precious liquids being thrown into the air to fall in scalding floods on the clean coral floor of the establishment, keeping onlookers at a distance. Instead of holding limpid pale green or azure water, other pots and craters are filled with scalding mud, which is tossed up from three or four feet to thirty feet, in sticky, rank-smelling masses, with gasping, belching, thudding sounds, plastering the branches of neighboring trees; every flask, retort, hot spring, and geyser has something special in it, no two being the same in temperature, color, or composition.

"In these natural laboratories one needs stout faith to feel at ease. The ground sounds hollow underfoot, and the awful subterranean thunder shakes one's mind as the ground is shaken, especially at night in the pale moonlight, or when the sky is overcast with storm clouds. In the solemn gloom, the geysers, dimly visible, look like monstrous dancing ghosts, and their wild songs and the earthquake thunder replying to the storms overhead seem doubly terrible, as if divine government were at an end. But the trembling hills keep their places. The sky clears, the rosy dawn is reassuring, and up comes the sun like a god, pouring his faithful beams across the mountains and forest, lighting each peak and tree and ghastly geyser alike, and shining into the eyes of the reeking springs, clothing them with rainbow light, and dissolving the seeming chaos of darkness into varied forms of harmony."

JOHN MUIR
"The Yellowstone National Park," *The Atlantic Monthly,* April 1898

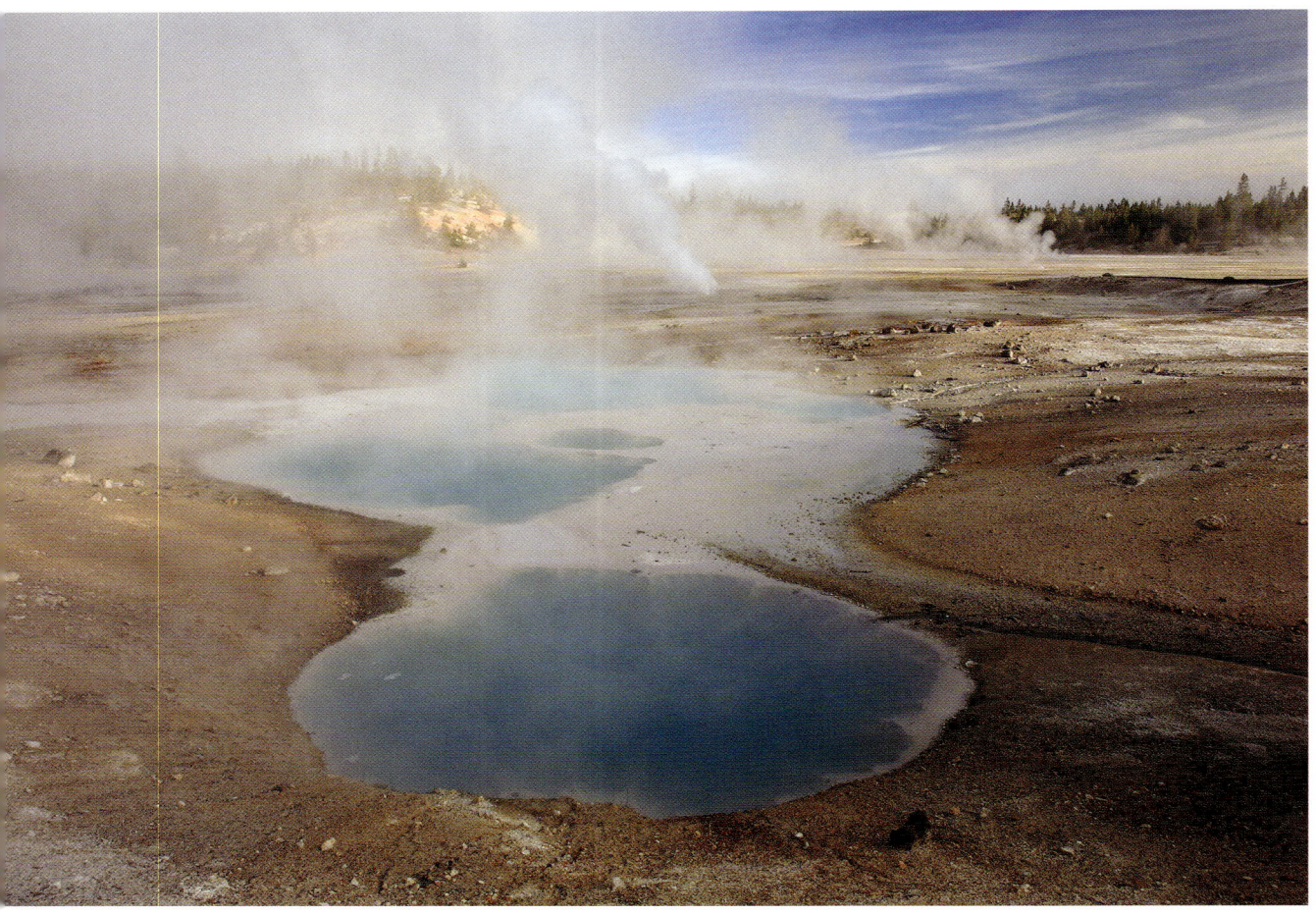

Colloidal Pool

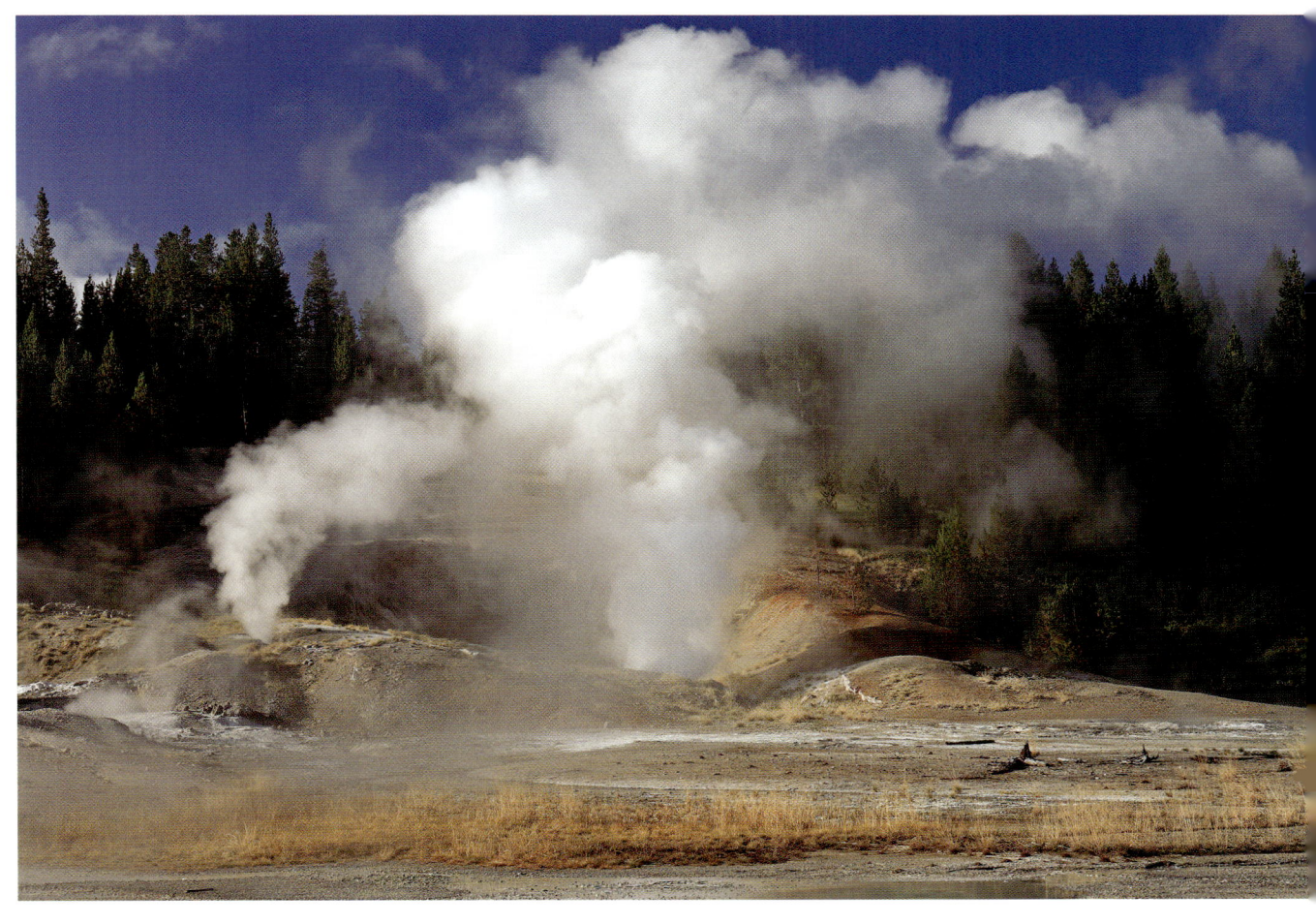

Black Growler

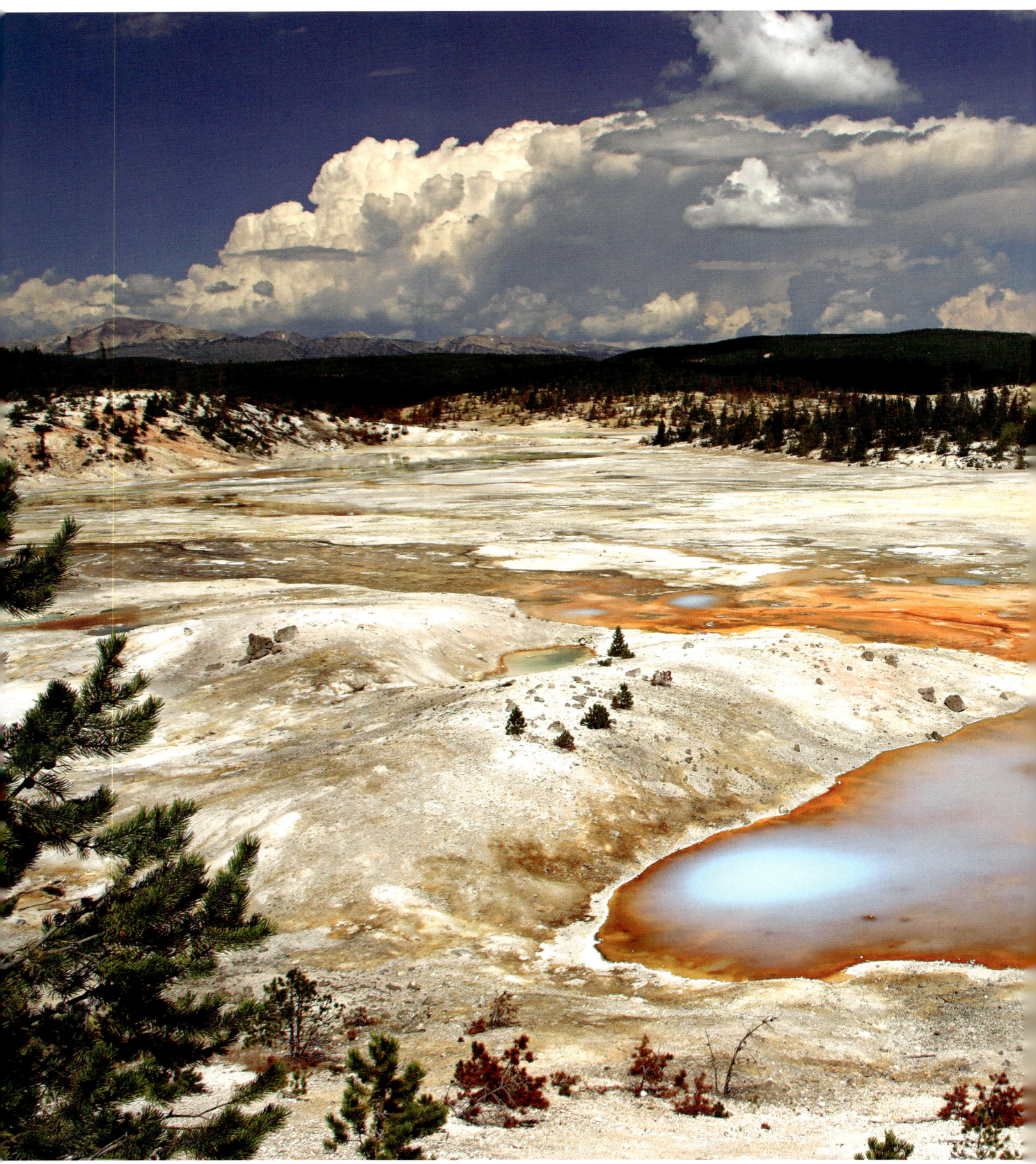

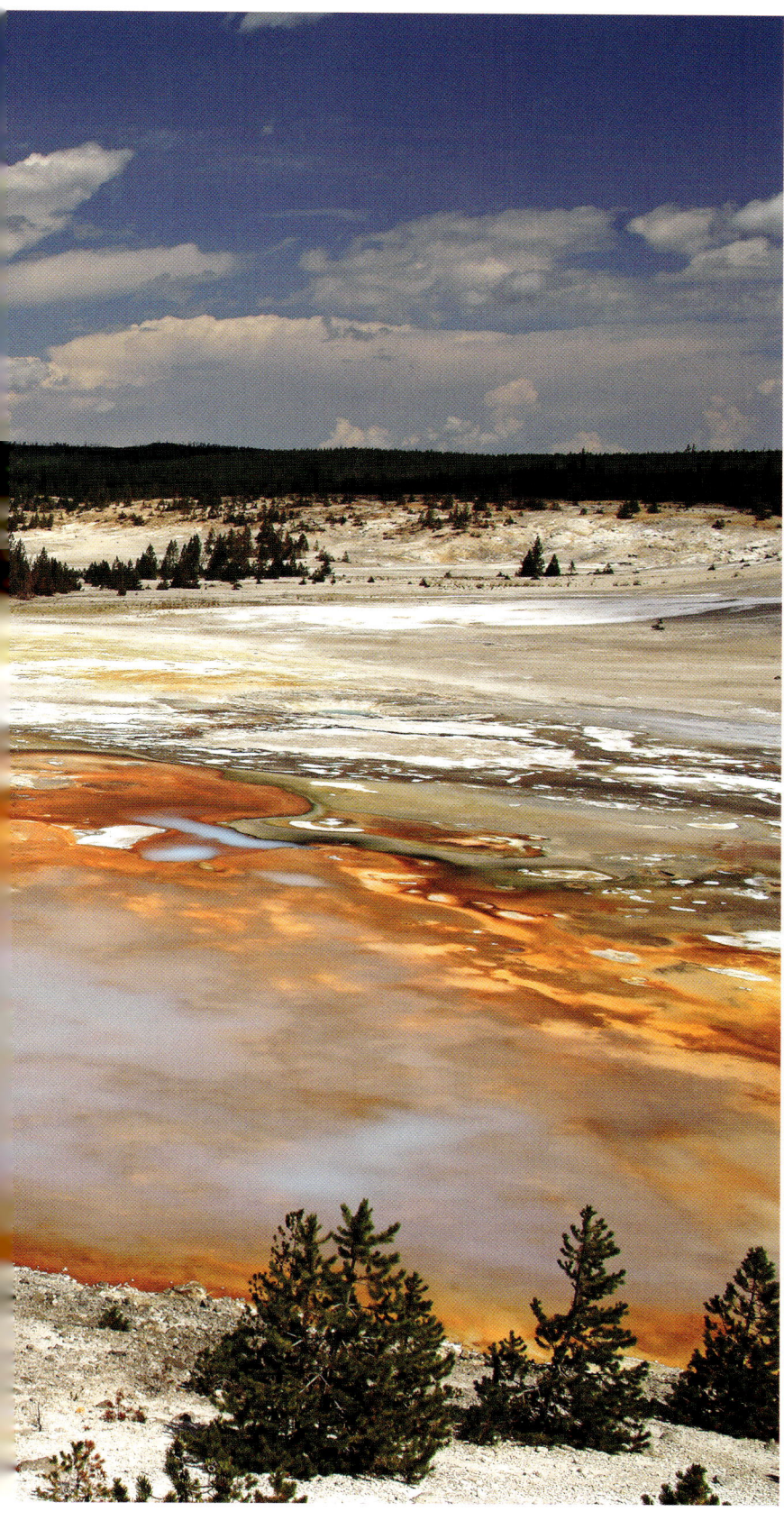

Porcelain Basin

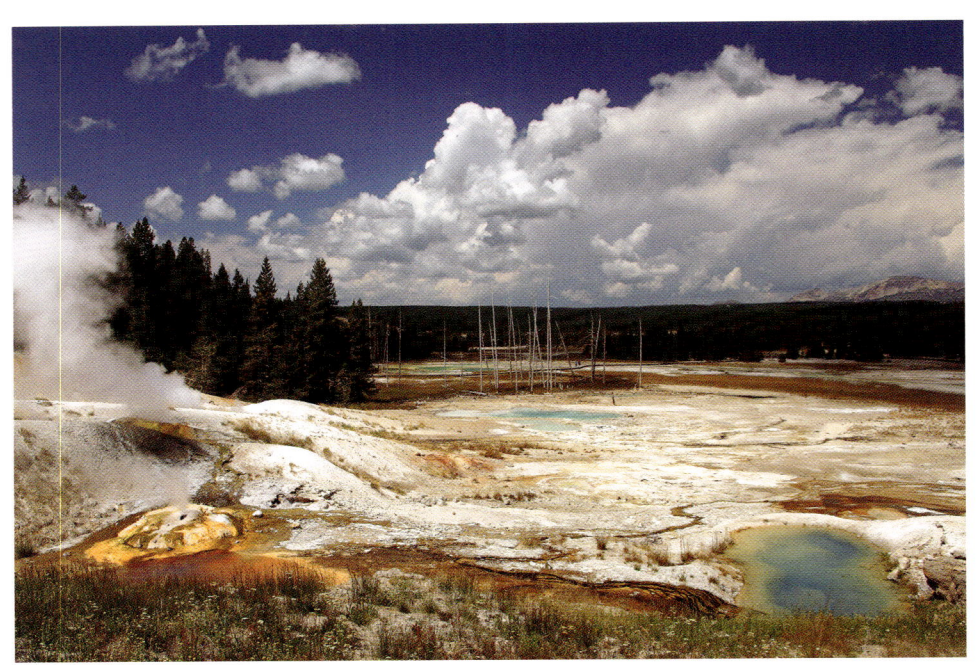

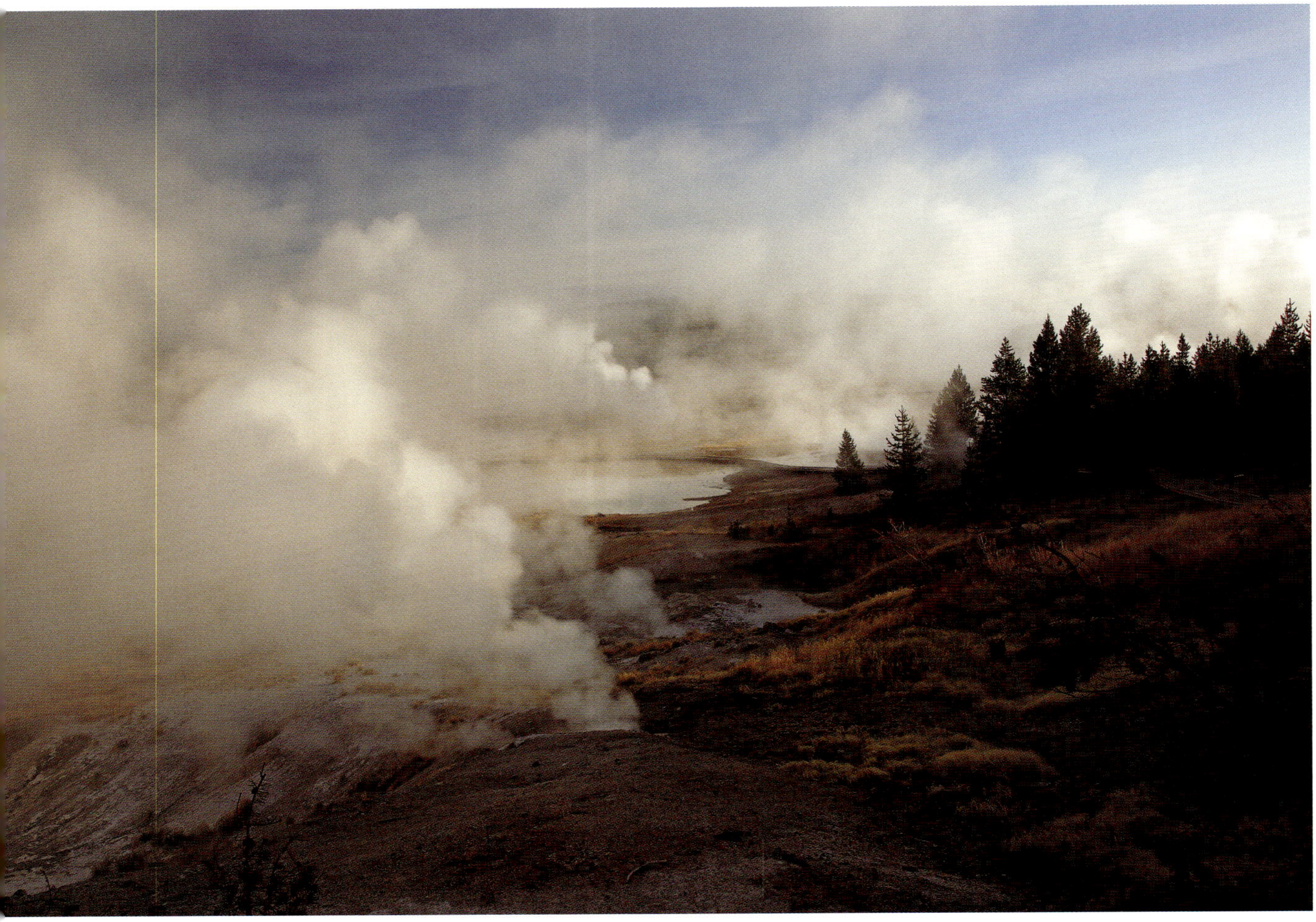

Porcelain Basin steam vents

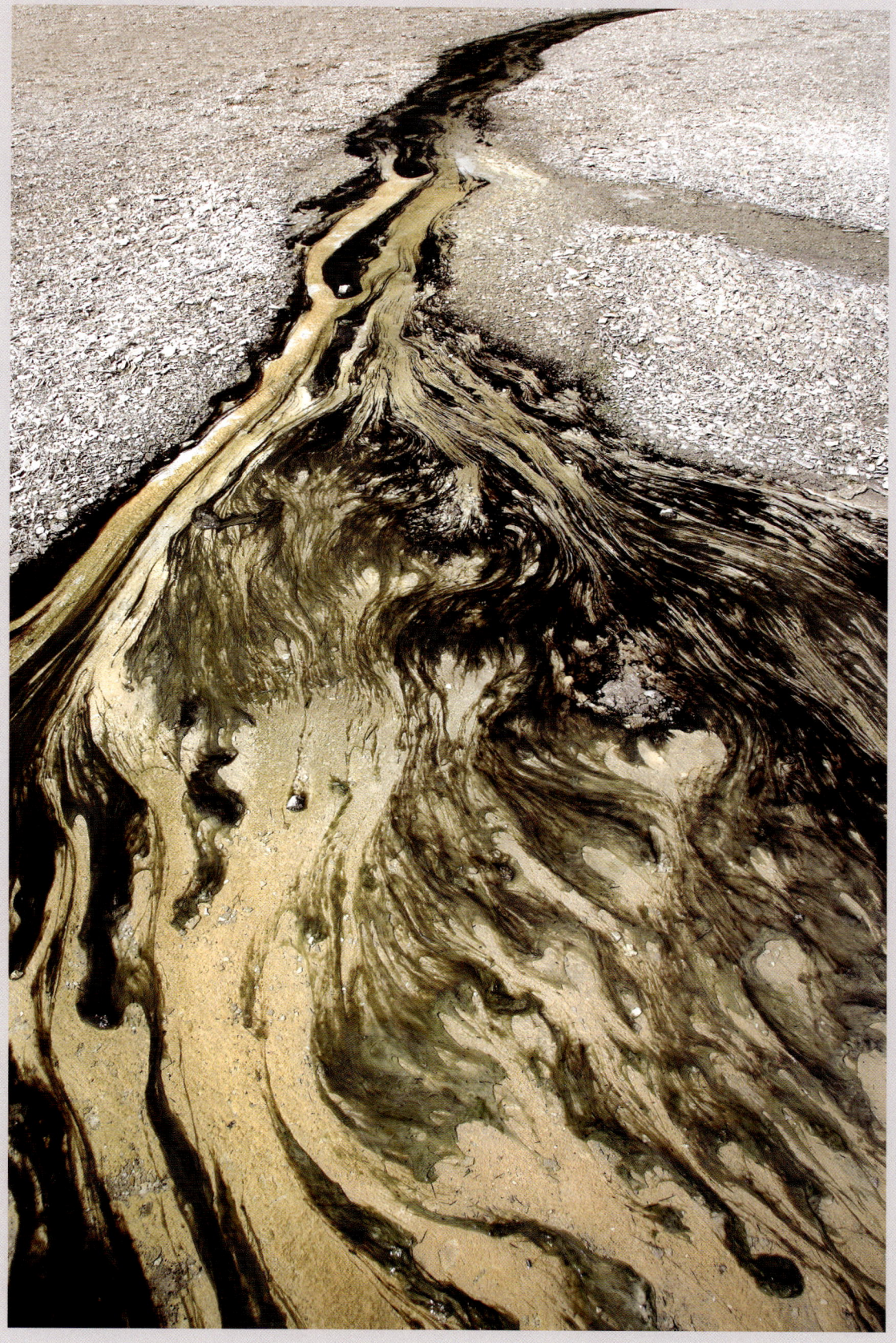

OLD FAITHFUL AREA

BISCUIT BASIN
> SAPPHIRE POOL

BLACK SAND BASIN
> CLIFF GEYSER
> EMERALD POOL
> IRON SPRING CREEK
> OPALESCENT POOL
> RAINBOW POOL
> SUNSET LAKE

LOWER GEYSER BASIN
> FIREHOLE LAKE DRIVE
> FIREHOLE RIVER
> FOUNTAIN FLAT
> FOUNTAIN PAINT POT AREA
> NEZ PERCE CREEK

MIDWAY GEYSER BASIN
> EXCELSIOR GEYSER CRATER
> FIREHOLE RIVER
> GRAND PRISMATIC SPRING
> TURQUOISE POOL
> WHISKEY FLATS

UPPER GEYSER BASIN
> ANEMONE GEYSER
> BEEHIVE GEYSER
> CASTLE GEYSER
> CHROMATIC AND BEAUTY POOLS
> CRESTED POOL
> GIANT GEYSER
> GRAND GEYSER
> GROTTO GEYSER
> LION GEYSER AND HEART SPRING
> MORNING GLORY POOL
> OLD FAITHFUL
> OLD FAITHFUL INN
> RIVERSIDE GEYSER
> SAWMILL GEYSER
> SPASMODIC GEYSER

Old Faithful

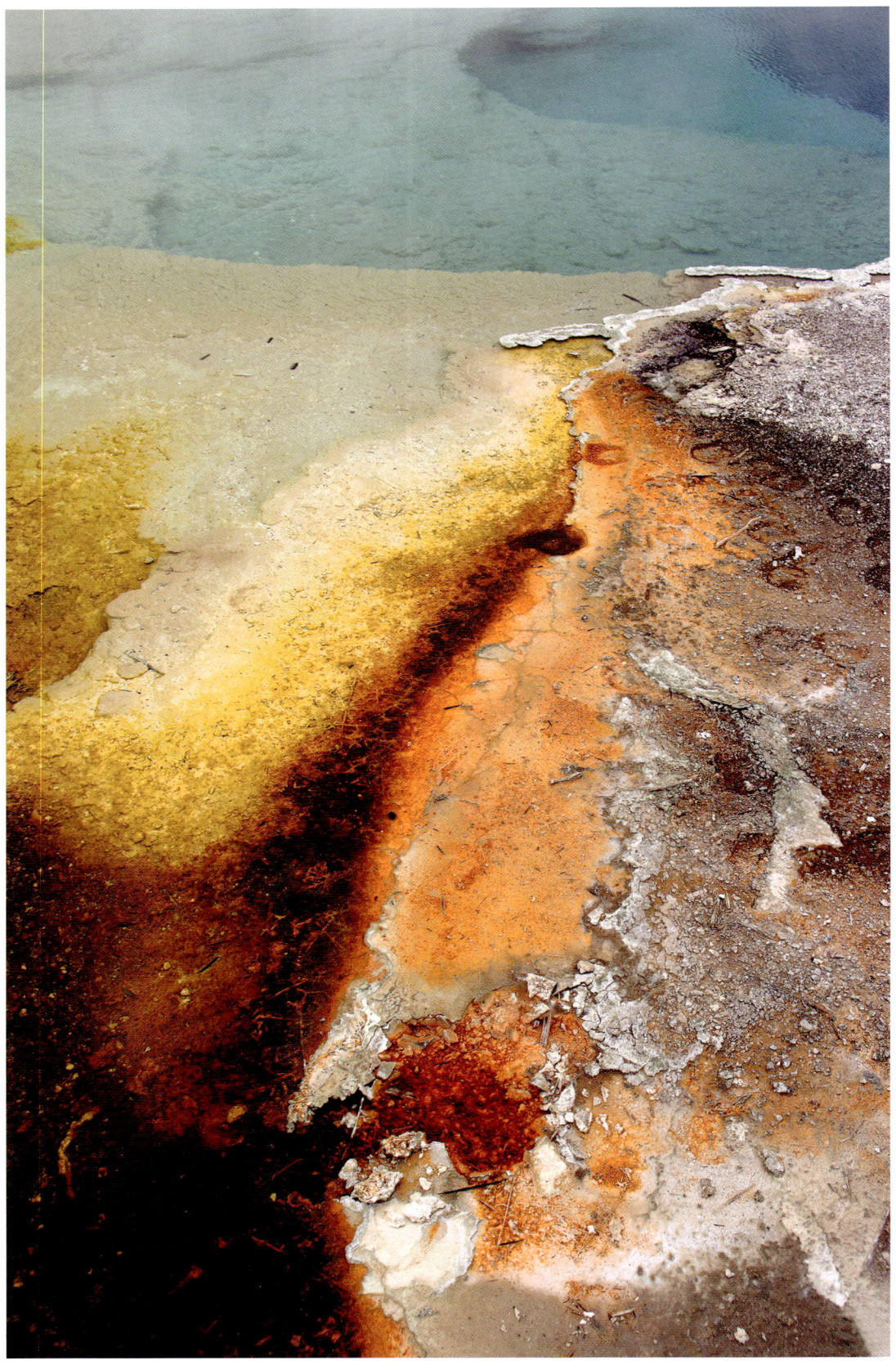

BISCUIT BASIN

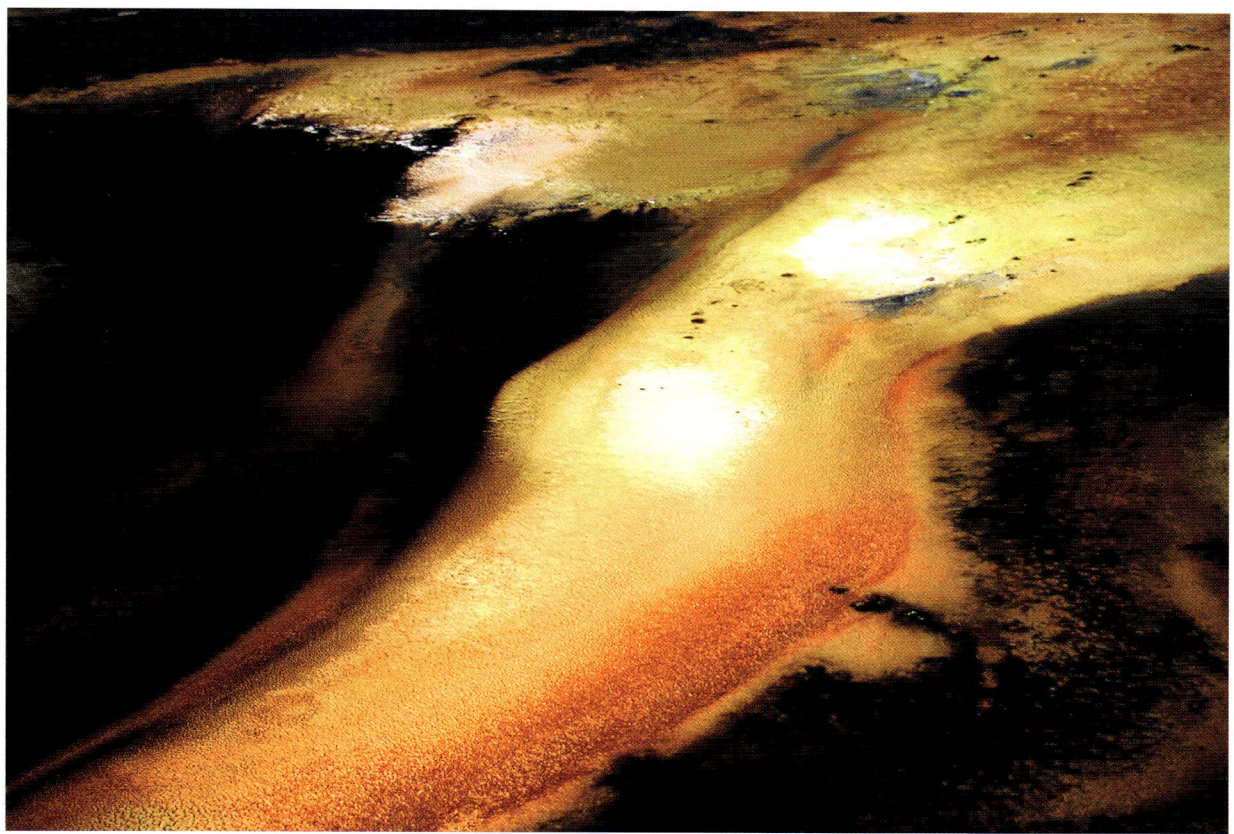

"The variously tinted sinter and travertine formations, outspread like pavements over large areas of the geyser valleys, lining the spring basins and throats of the craters, and forming beautiful coral-like rims and curbs about them, always excite admiring attention; so also does the play of the waters from which they are deposited. The various minerals in them are rich in fine colors, and these are greatly heightened by a smooth, silky growth of brilliantly colored confervæ, which lines many of the pools and channels and terraces. No bed of flower-bloom is more exquisite than these myriads of minute plants, visible only in mass, growing in the hot waters."

JOHN MUIR
"The Yellowstone National Park," *The Atlantic Monthly,* April 1898

Biscuit Basin

‹

Sapphire Pool

"The water in some of the springs presents to the eye the colors of all the precious gems known to commerce. In one spring the hue is like that of an emerald, in another like that of the turquoise, another has the ultra-marine hue of the sapphire, another has the color of the topaz; and the suggestion has been made that the names of these jewels may very properly be given to many of these springs."

NATHANIEL PITT LANGFORD
The Discovery of Yellowstone Park: Journal of the Washburn Expedition to the Yellowstone and Firehole Rivers in the Year 1870, 1905

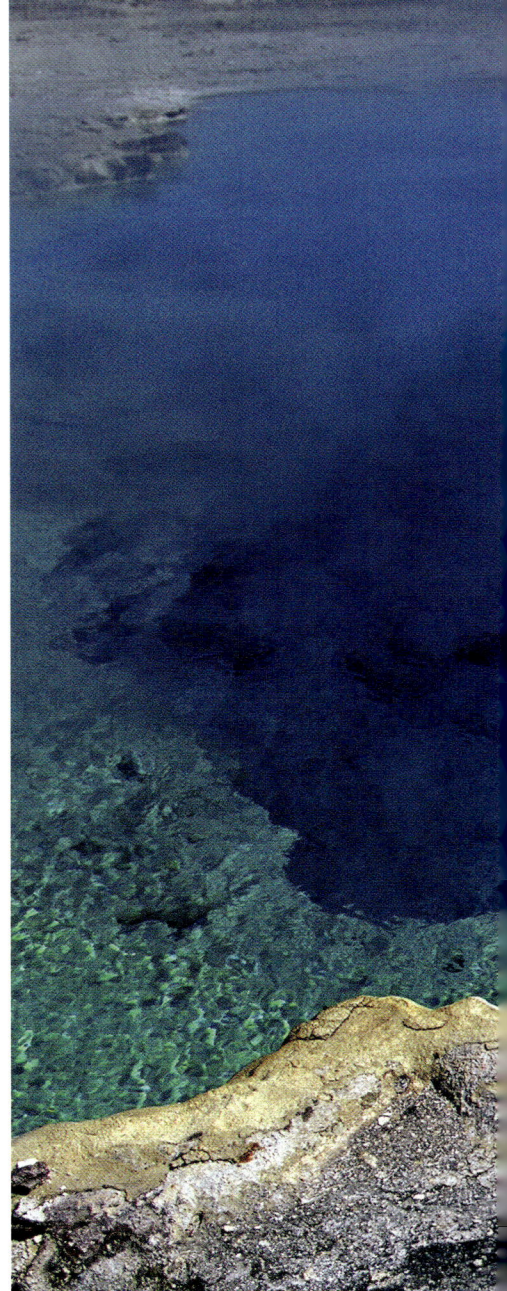

Sapphire Pool

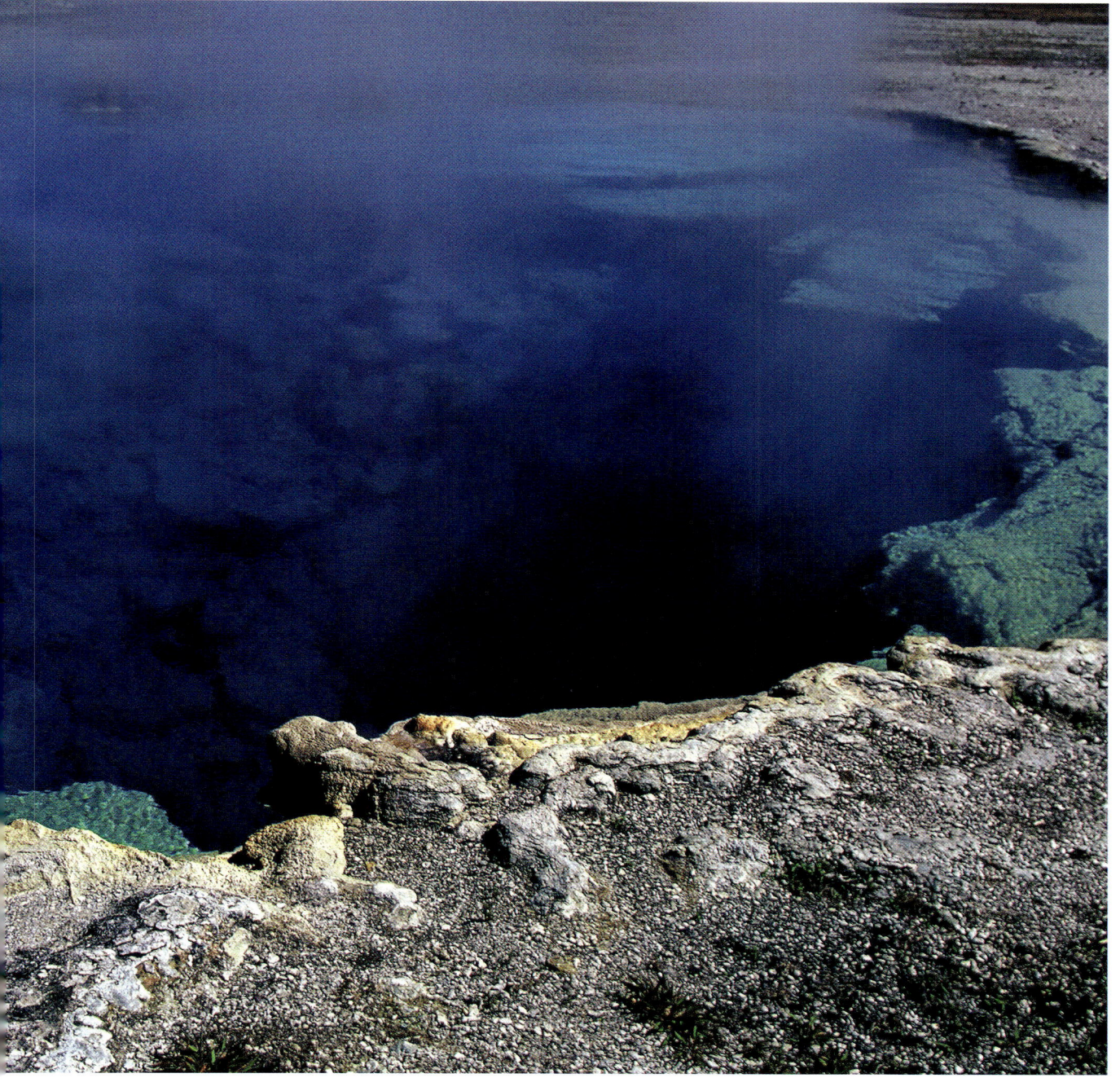

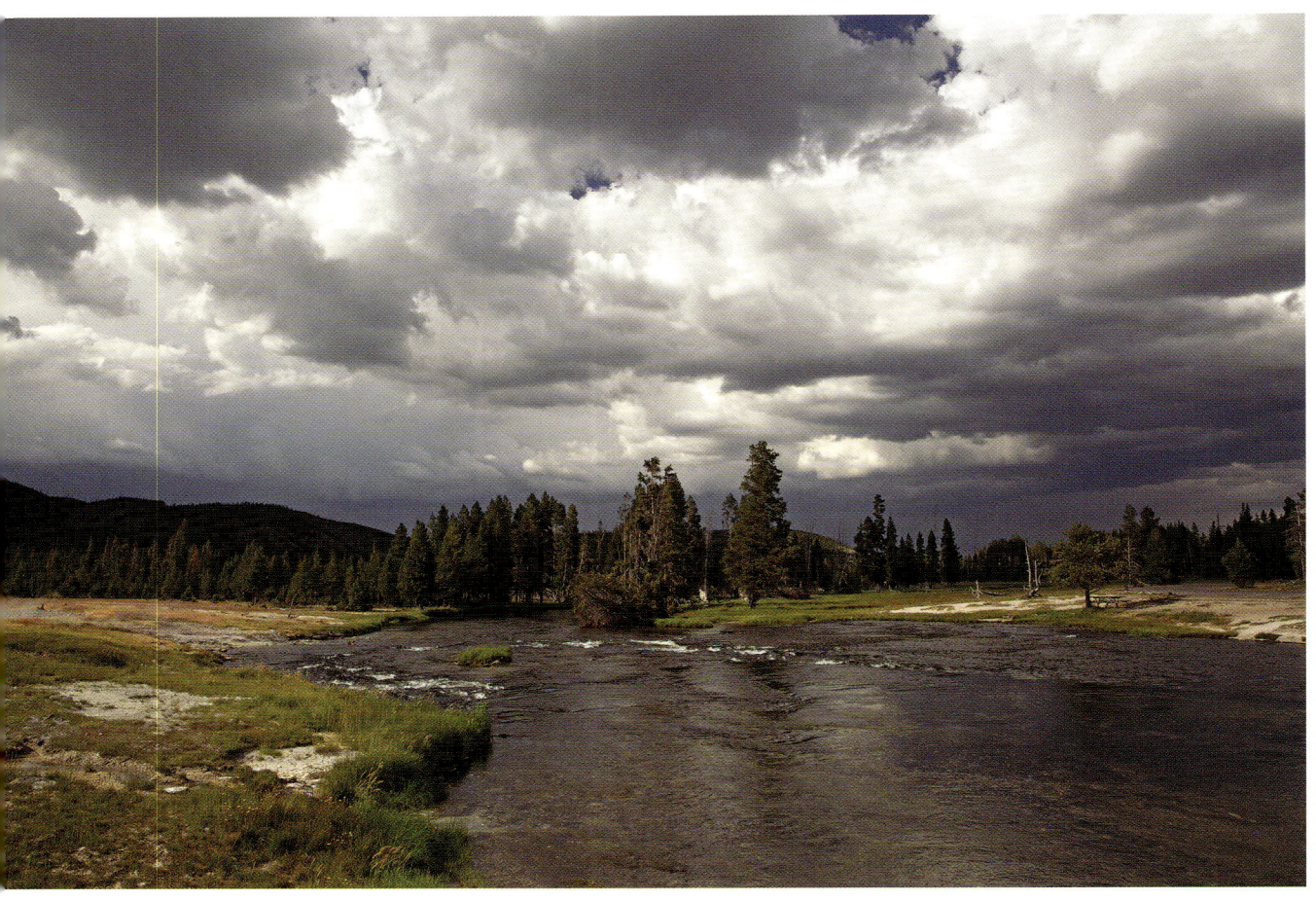

Firehole River in Biscuit Basin

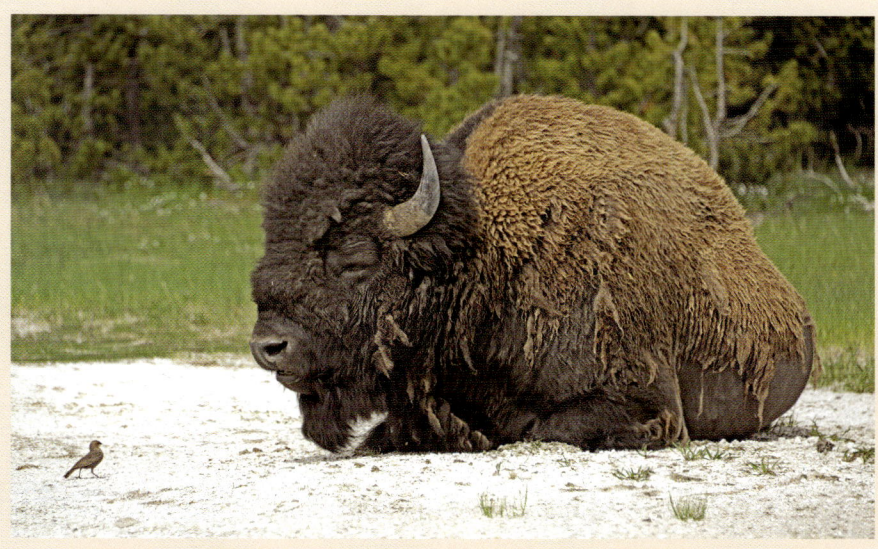

Bison and cowbird

Bison

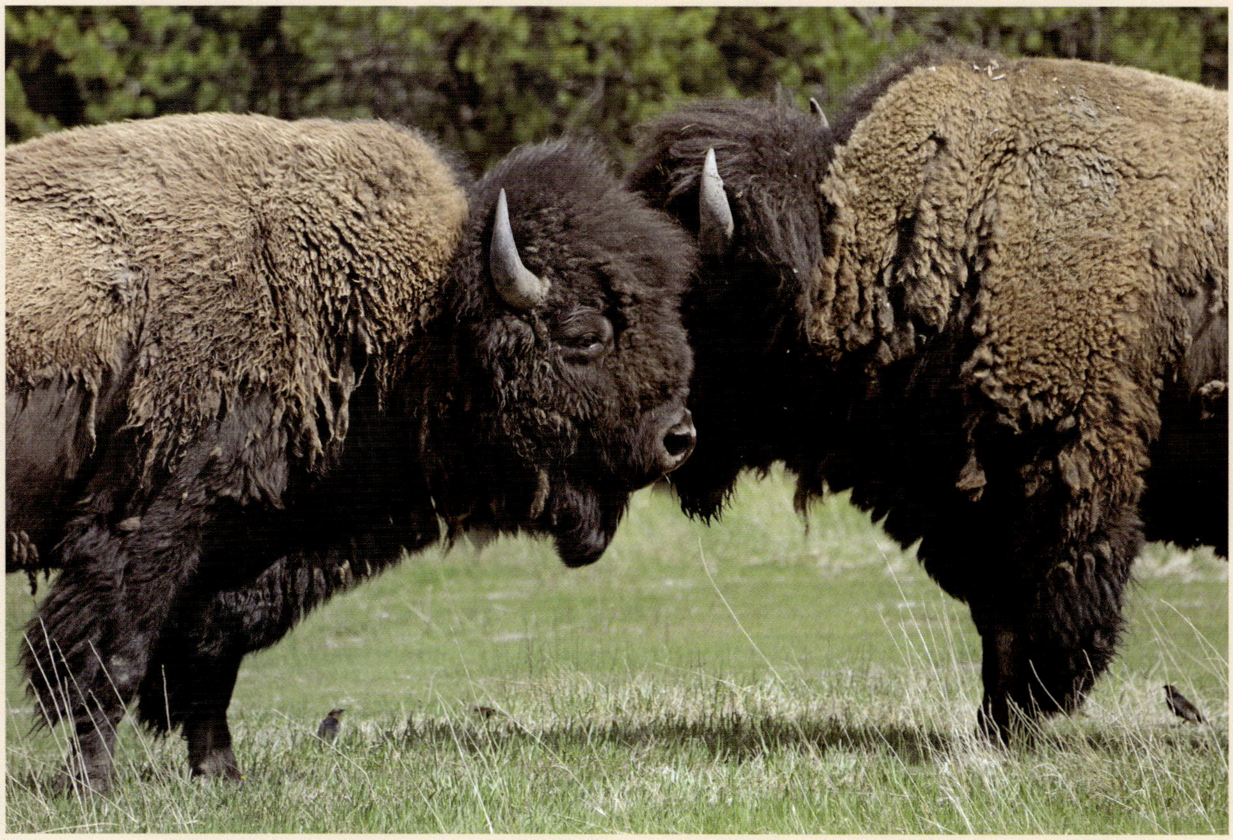

BLACK SAND BASIN

Black Sand Basin is "a deep spring of beautiful blue, surrounded on three sides by banks of black sand ten feet high; the water trickles out at the fourth side and through a channel full of variegated yellows and browns, the contrast between the blue water and black sand being very striking."

GEORGE WOOD WINGATE
Through the Yellowstone Park on Horseback, 1886

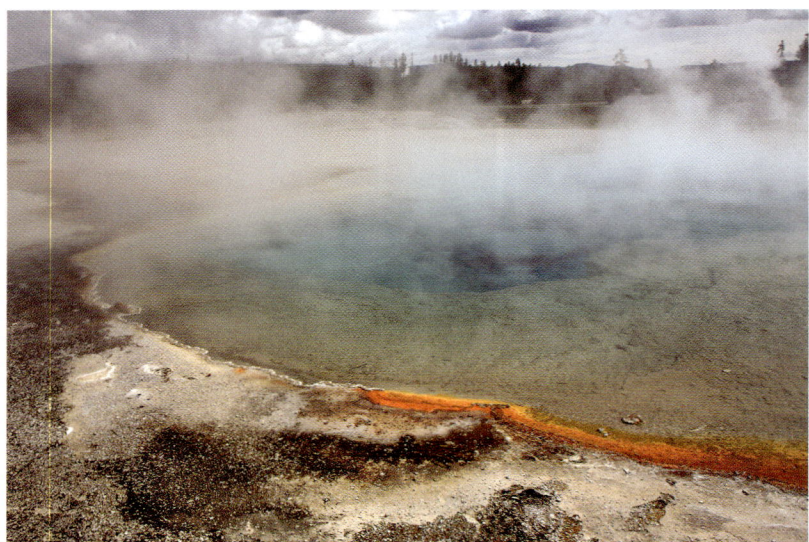

Black Sand Basin

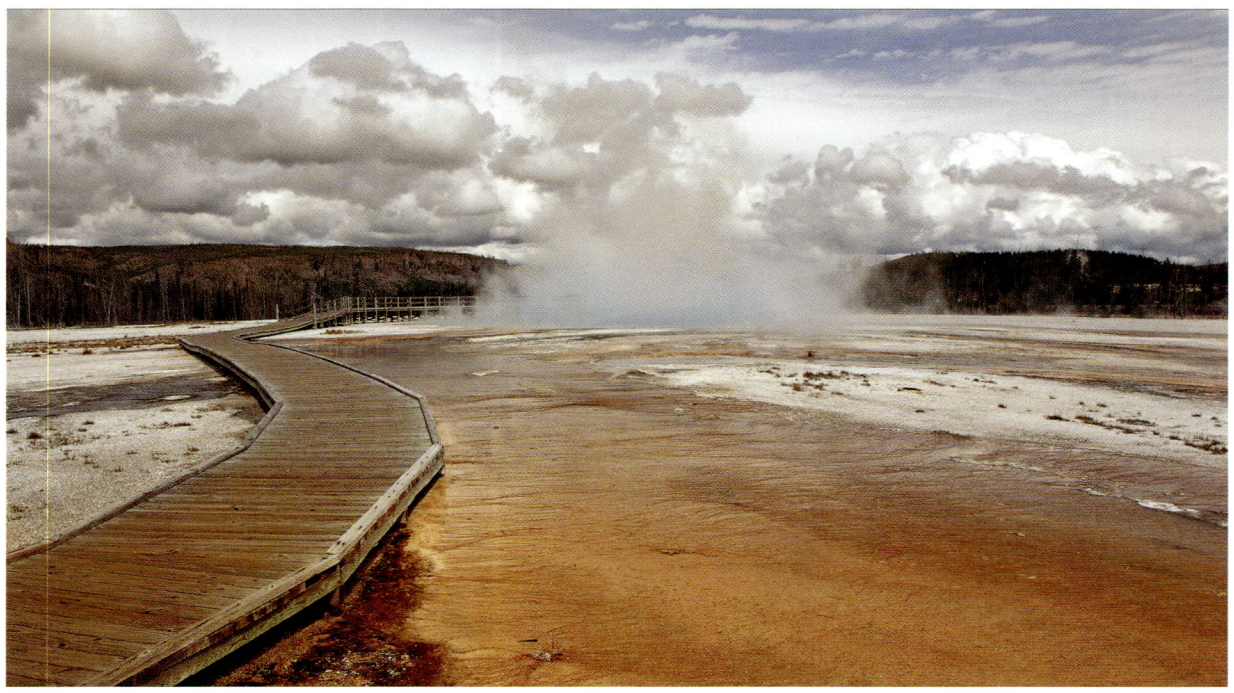

CLIFF GEYSER

"On the bank of Iron [Spring] Creek and near a sharp point in the stream not far from the Emerald, is situated Cliff Geyser, a singularly picturesque basin. It has built up from the stream a semicircular wall several feet above high-water level, the corrugated outer rim being produced during the building up of the sinter by an incessant downflow of water. According to Mr. Weed, 'the two vents of Cliff Geyser seem built up along the same fissure, though their activity is slightly different. The west vent bubbles quietly and the basin about it is lined with light gold algae. The main vent is undoubtedly a fissure one to three feet wide and five feet long, the hole being five feet below the surface of the pool.'"

ARNOLD HAGUE, GEOLOGIST AND ASSISTANT TO WALTER WEED, 1911

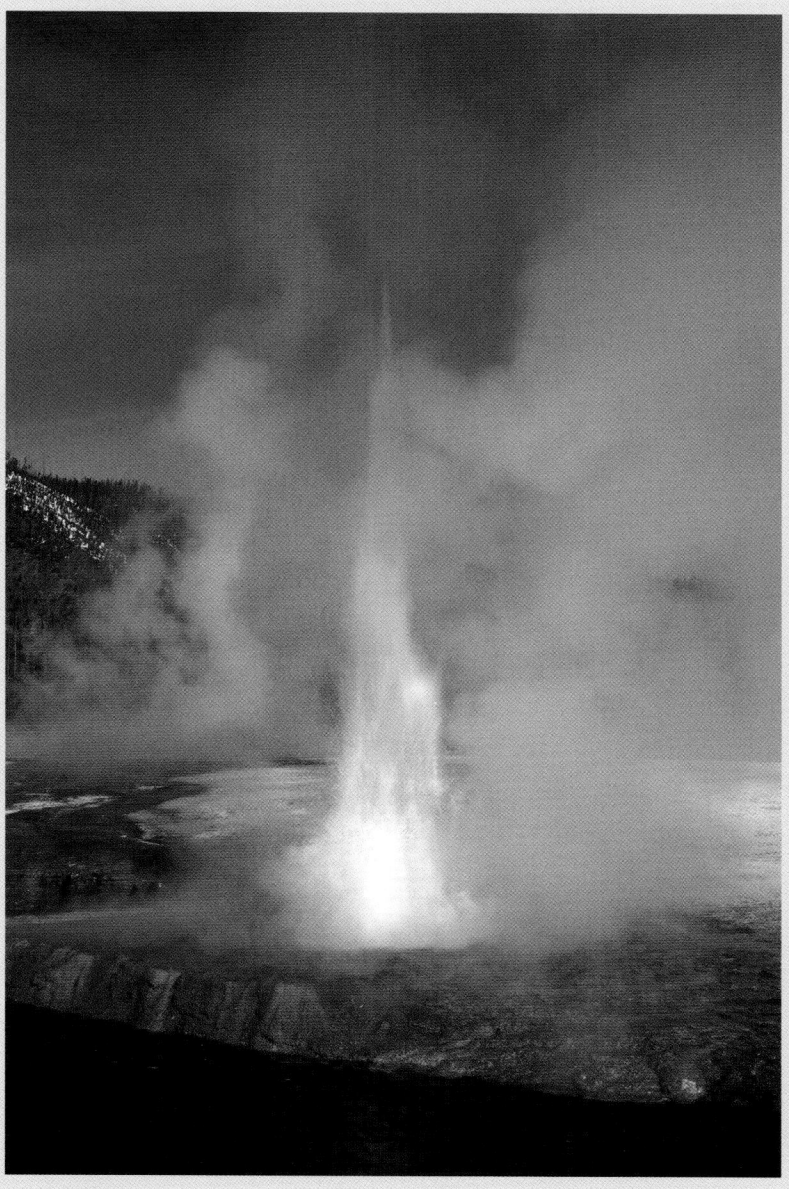

Cliff Geyser

"Fill a thin goblet with Crème de Menthe, on the top drop a few 'beads' of absinthe, and you will have a faint, only a faint idea of the glistening green glory of Emerald Pool, which can be compared to nothing unless one can imagine liquefied Chinese fire or the unknown, unnamable tones seen under the influence of an anesthetic or during delirium. Round the edges is a rim of sediment, exactly the color and apparent texture of rough-grained gold. Truly this is a jewel—an emerald set in gold! Were there nothing else to be seem in the Park, Emerald Pool would be worth the journey."

J. SANFORD SALTUS
A Week in the Yellowstone, 1895

Emerald Pool

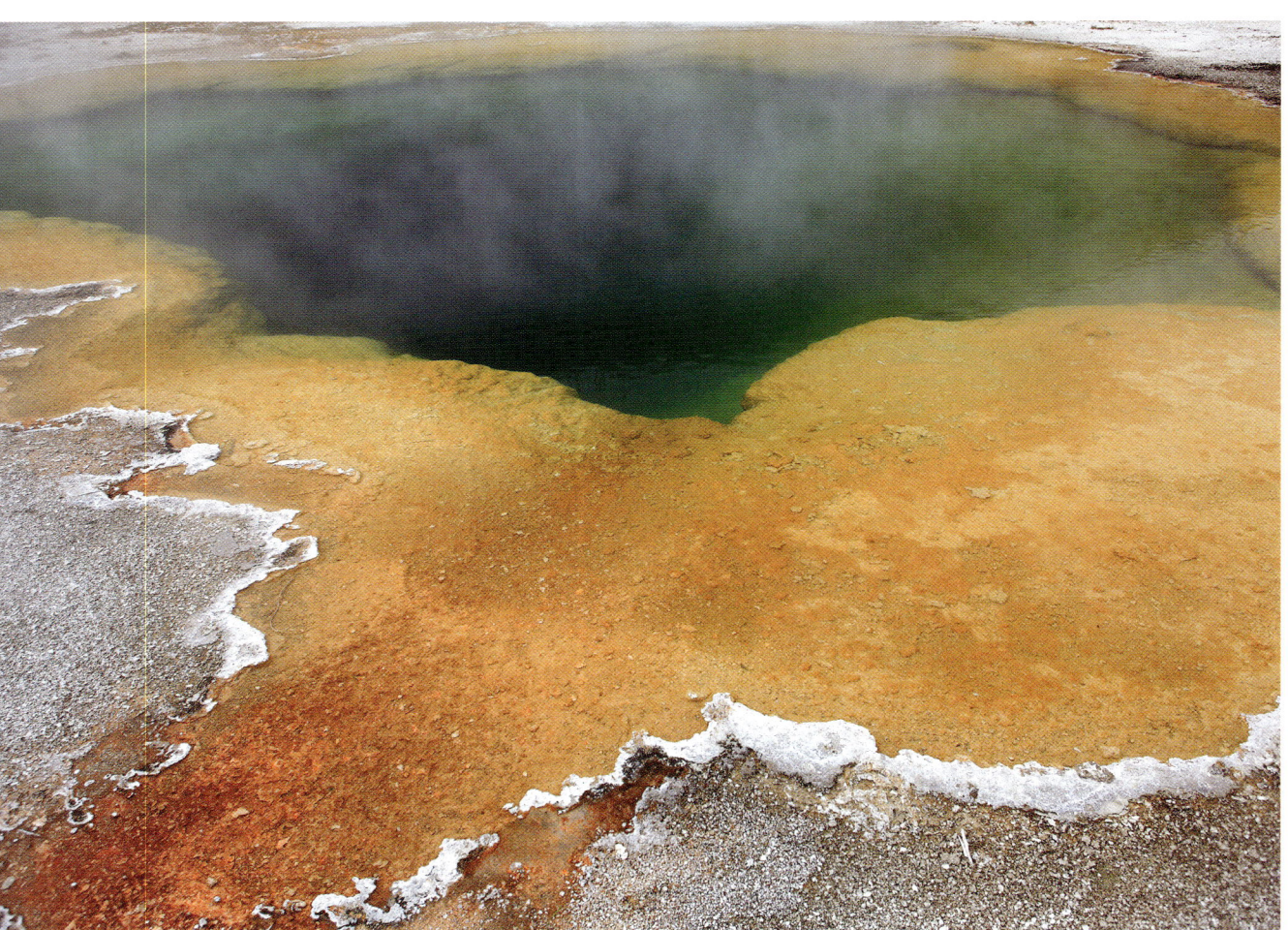

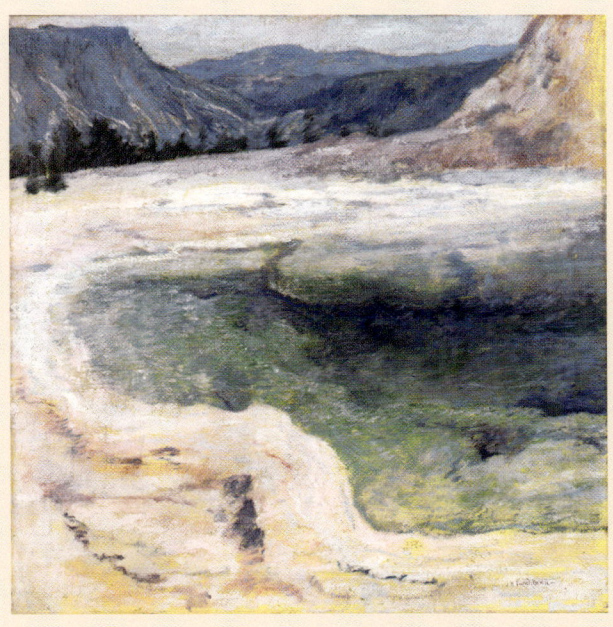

The Emerald Pool
John Henry Twachtman, 1895
The Phillips Collection, Washington, DC

Edge of the Emerald Pool, Yellowstone
John Henry Twachtman, 1895
private collection

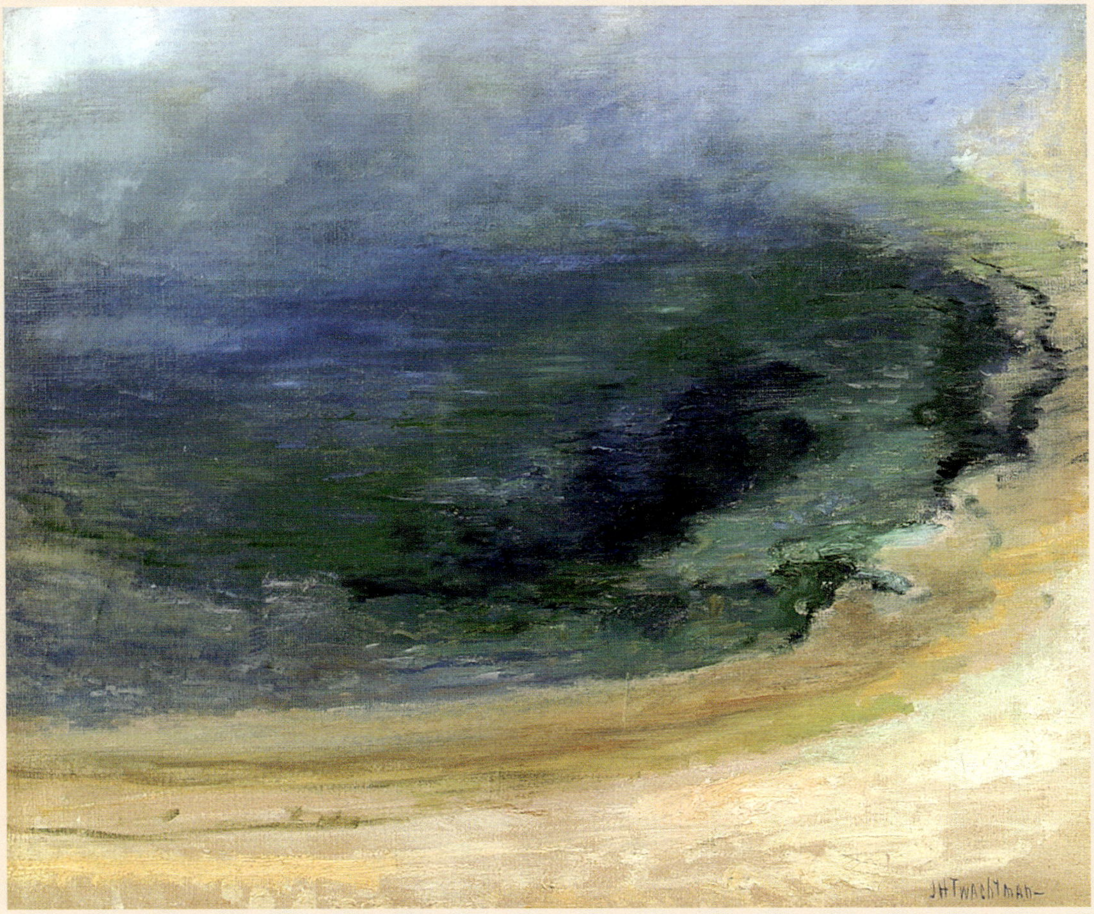

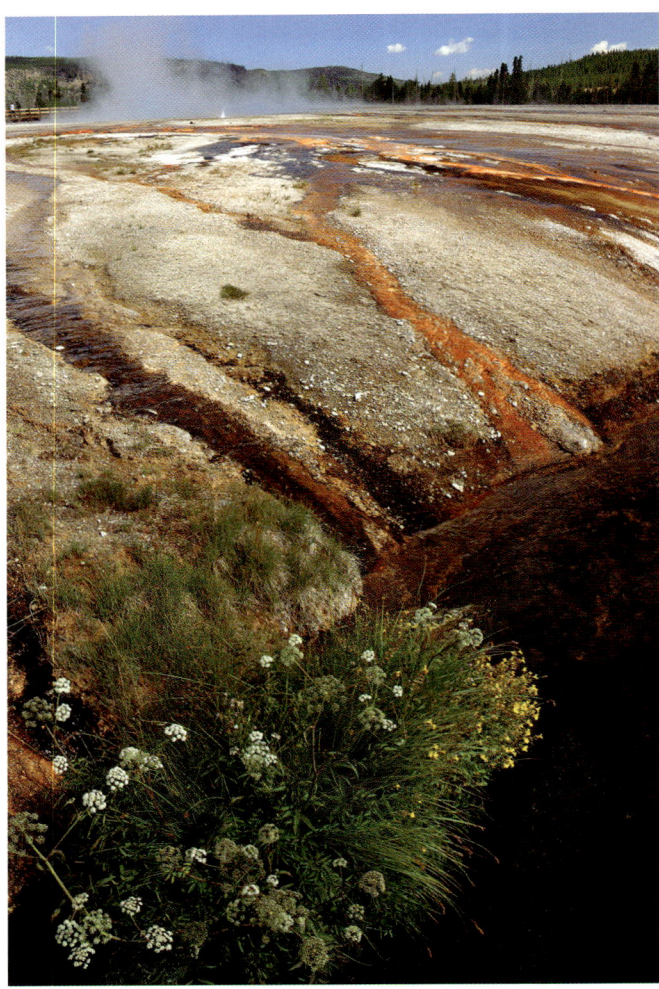

"Imagine mighty green fields splattered with lime-beds, all the flowers of the summer growing up to the very edge of the lime. That was our first glimpse of the geyser basins."

RUDYARD KIPLING
American Notes, 1891

"Neither the water nor its banks [are] in any manner more characterized by iron than other tributaries of the Firehole. Its name is . . . owing to the exceptionally large amount of reddish-brown algae accompanying its thermal waters."

ARNOLD HAGUE, GEOLOGIST AND ASSISTANT TO WALTER WEED, 1911

OPALESCENT POOL

Opalescent Pool "revealed an opalescent azure as lovely as the sky above."

<

Iron Spring Creek

Opalescent Pool

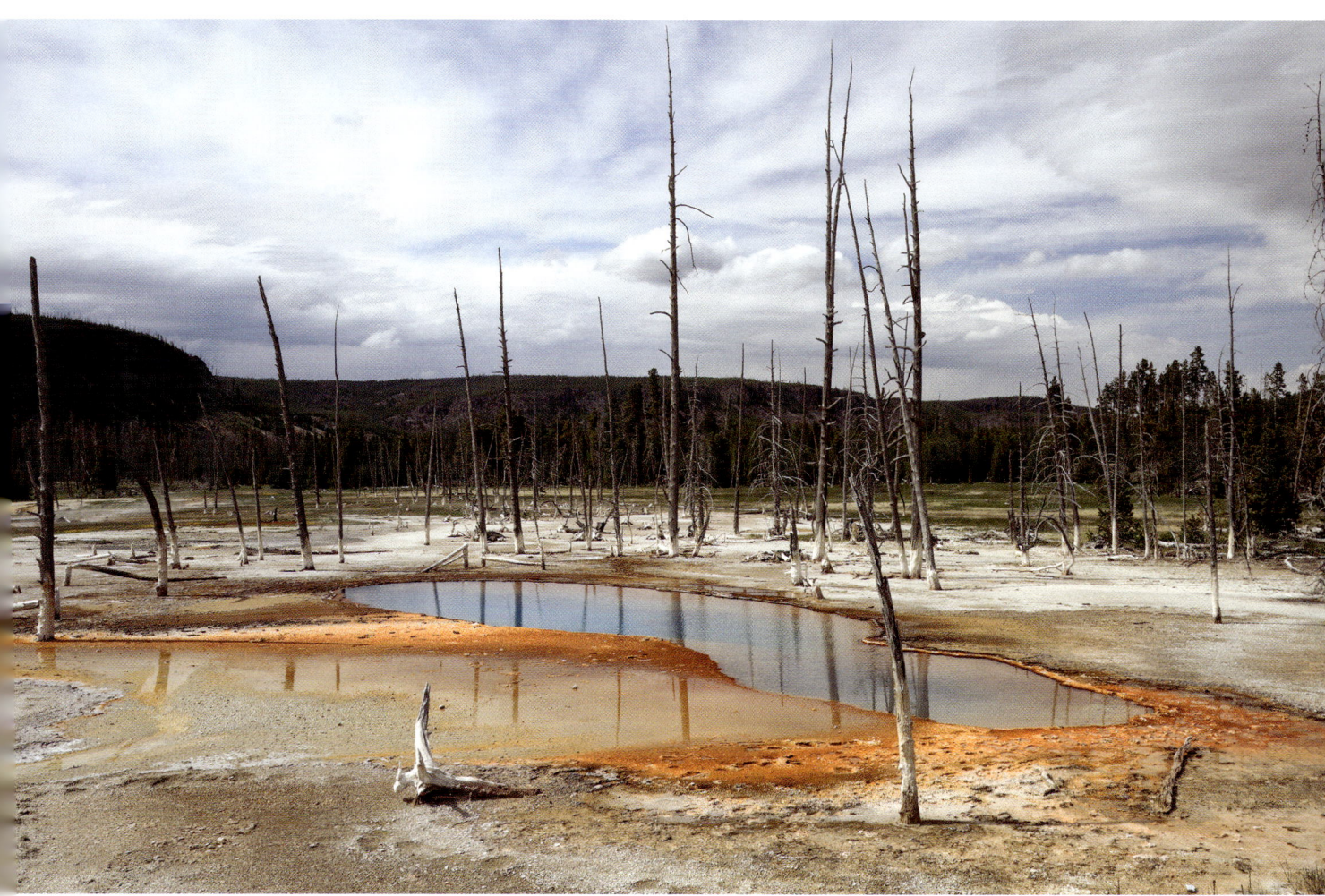

RAINBOW POOL

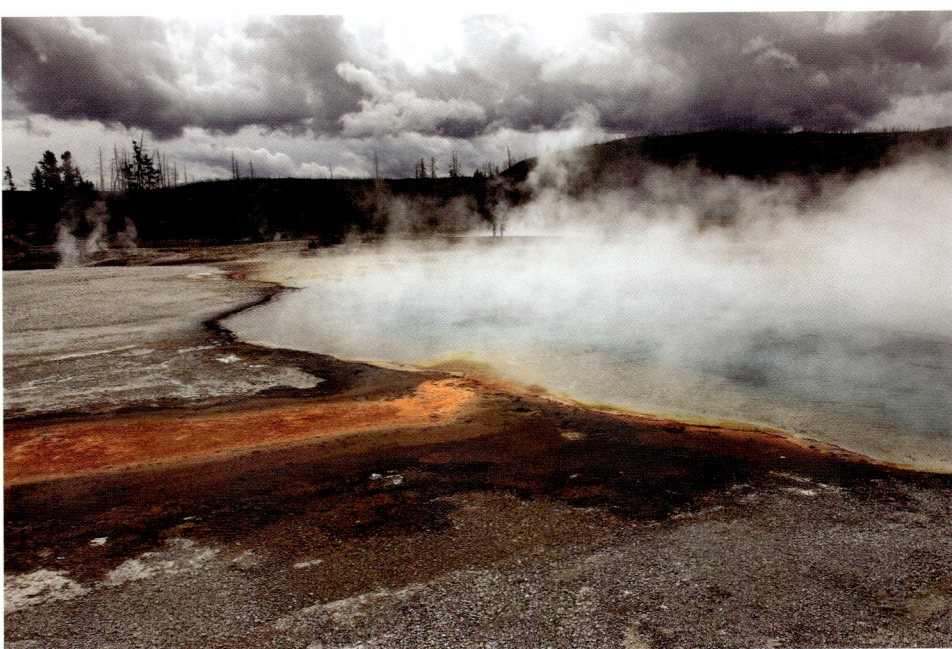

Rainbow Pool

Sunset Lake

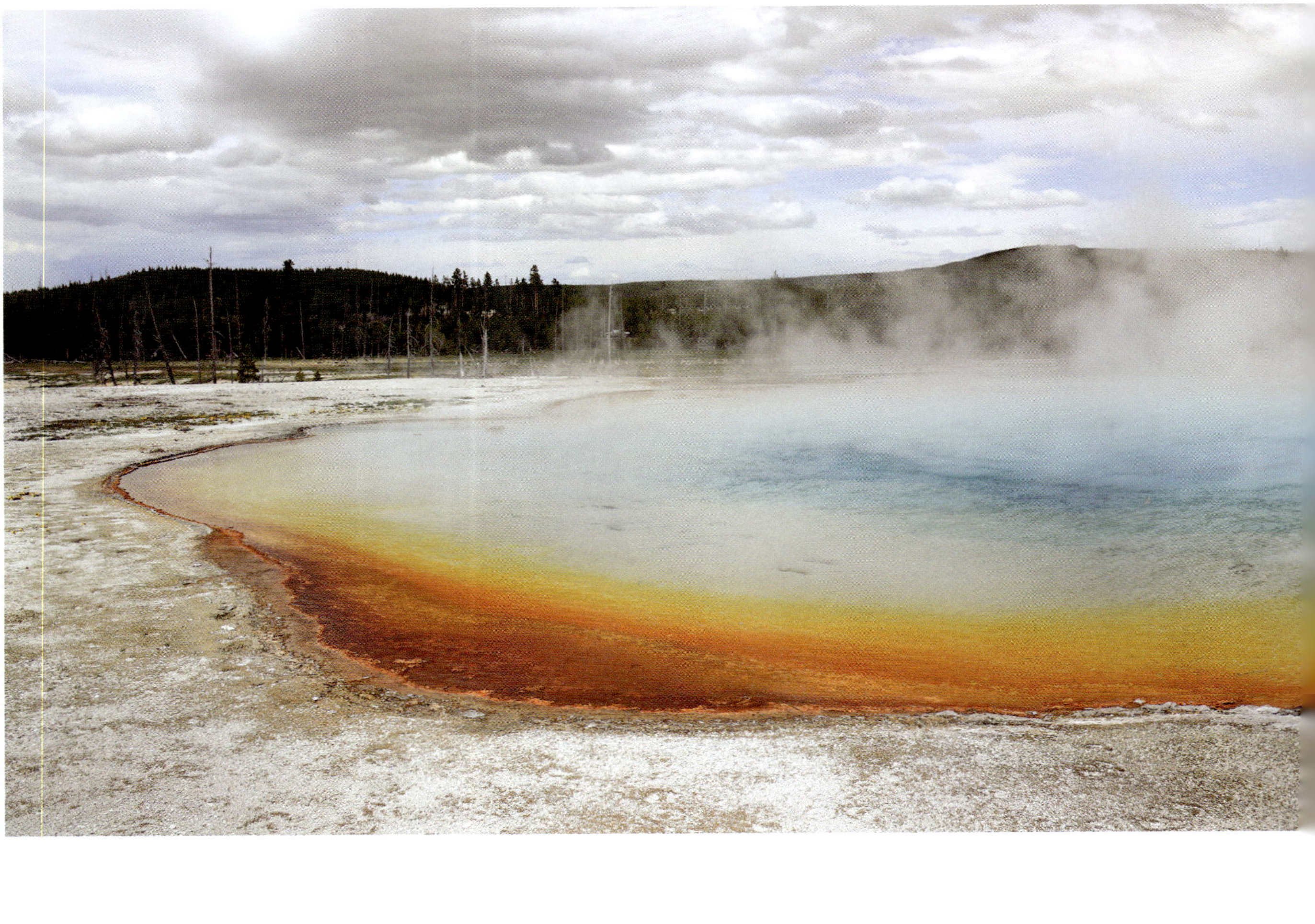

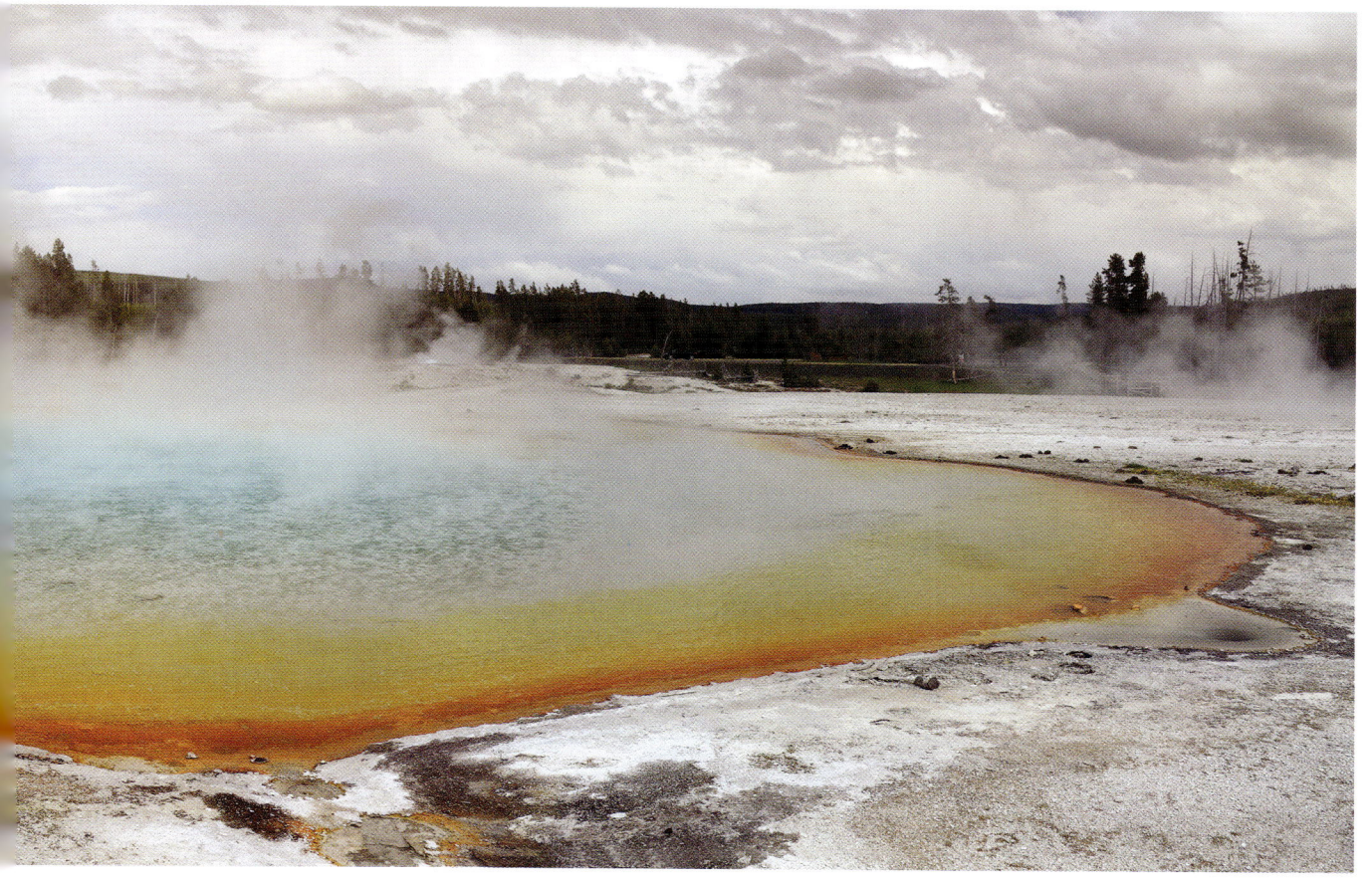

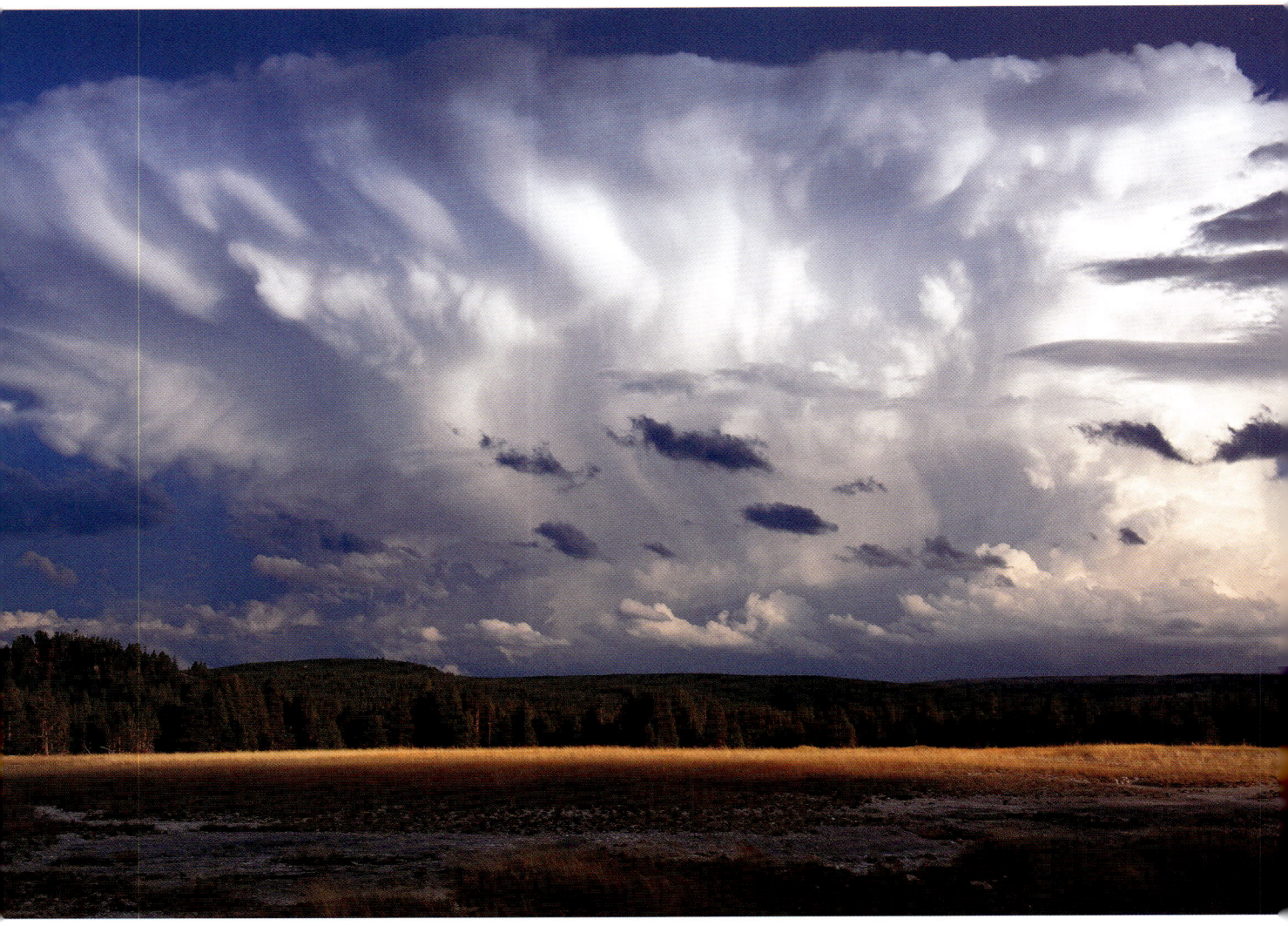

FIREHOLE LAKE DRIVE

Firehole Spring is "one of the most beautiful of the gas-aqueous variety [of springs]. Its action is incessant but variable. Every few seconds there arise great globes that seem to revolve like chariot wheels as they rise toward the surface. Then they come faster and faster until they seem to glide into each other and rise into one magnificent dome of liquid splendor, upon which the sunlight is reflected with a glory of coloring that equals the rainbow's prismatic hues."

G.L. HENDERSON, PARK INTERPRETER, 1888

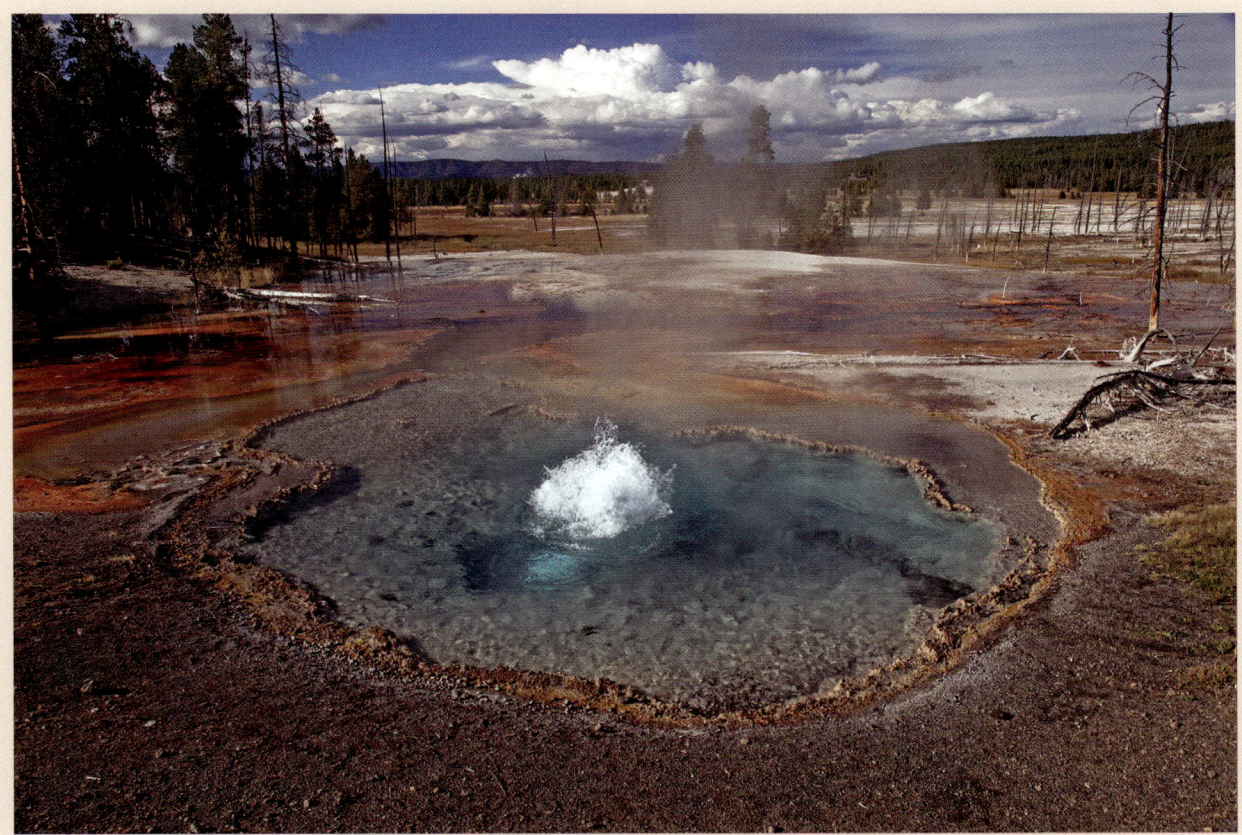

Firehole Spring

<
Lower Geyser Basin

GREAT FOUNTAIN GEYSER

Great Fountain Geyser erupts with "exquisite jets and columns of water, enormous in quantity sent upward. Jets from the central part of the basin reached the height of one hundred forty or one hundred fifty feet, the cluster of jets breaking from the main columns in dartlike points and trembling into the surrounding pools in showers of crystal drops."

WILLIAM HENRY HOLMES, GEOLOGIST WITH THE F.V. HAYDEN SURVEY, 1872

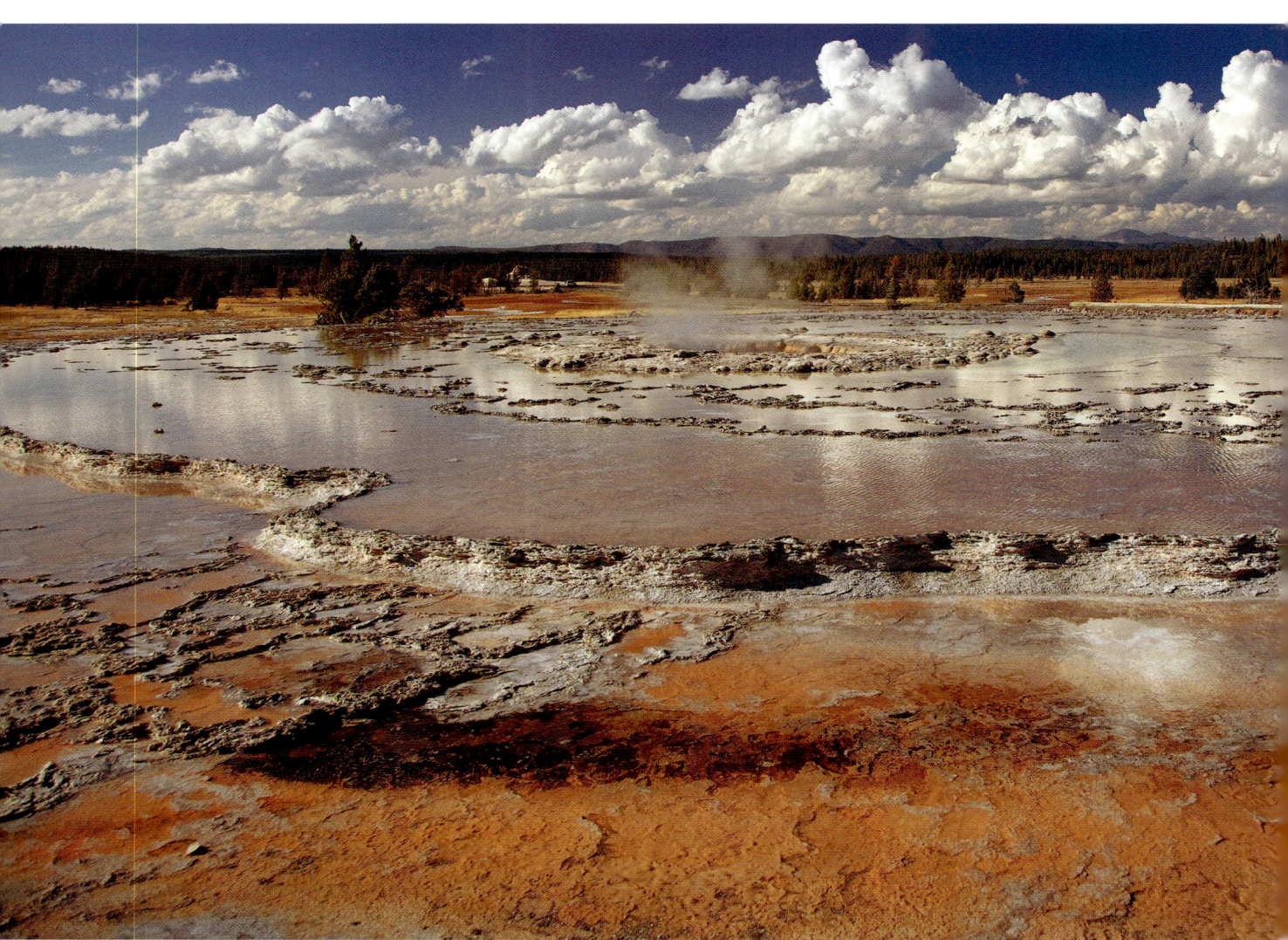

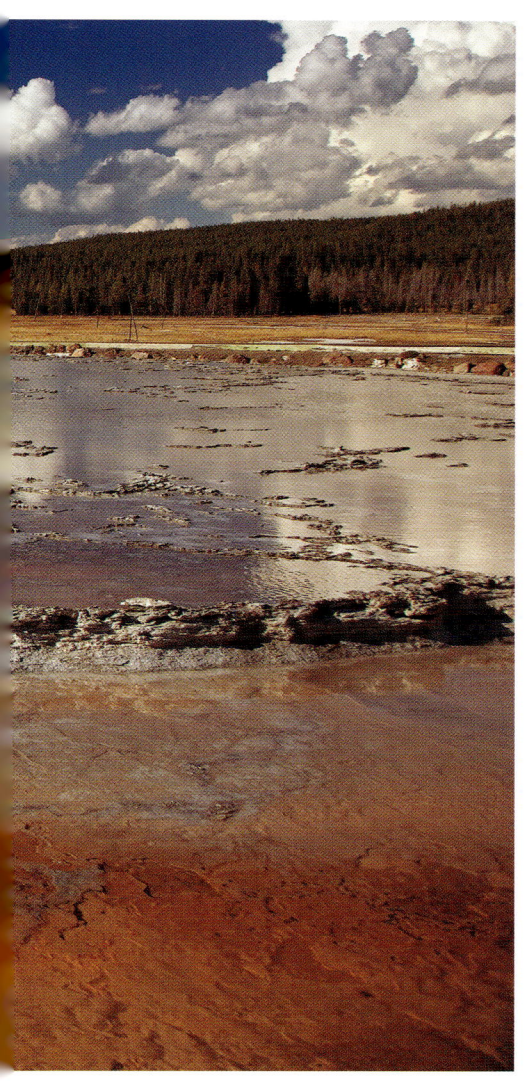

<

Great Fountain Geyser terrace

Great Fountain Geyser

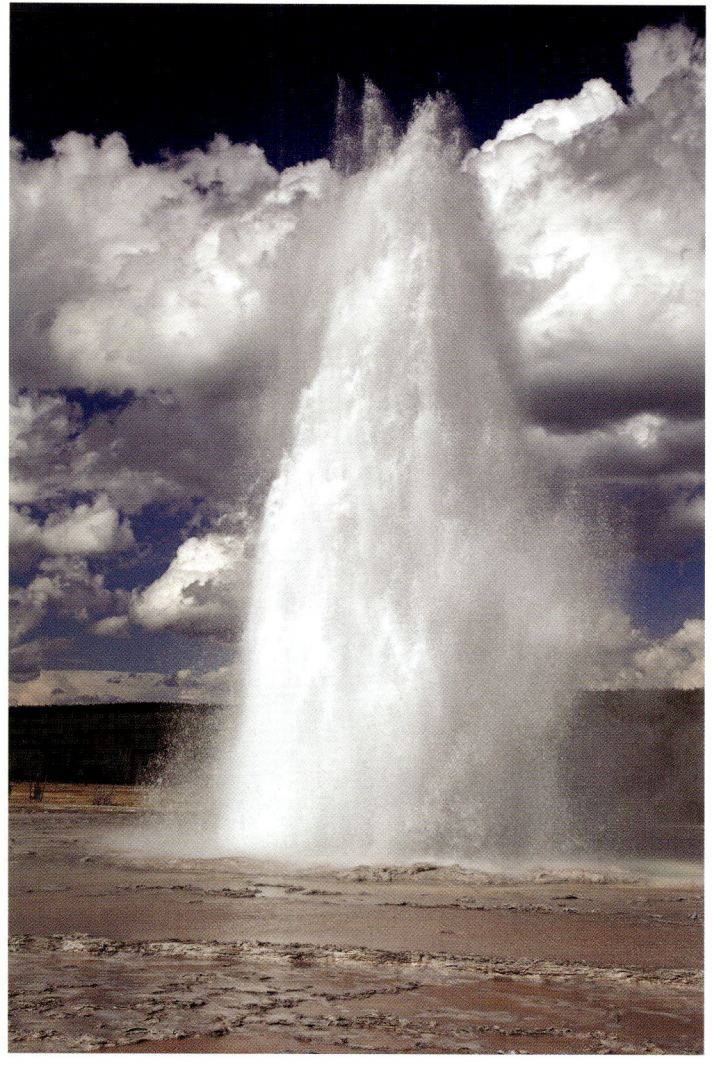

"Our attention was at once attracted by water and steam escaping, or being thrown up from an opening. . . . Soon this geyser was in full play. The setting sun shining into the spray and steam drifting toward the mountains, gave it the appearance of burnished gold, a wonderful sight. We could not contain our enthusiasm: with one accord we all took off our hats and yelled with all our might."

FOLSOM-COOK-PETERSON EXPEDITION, 1869

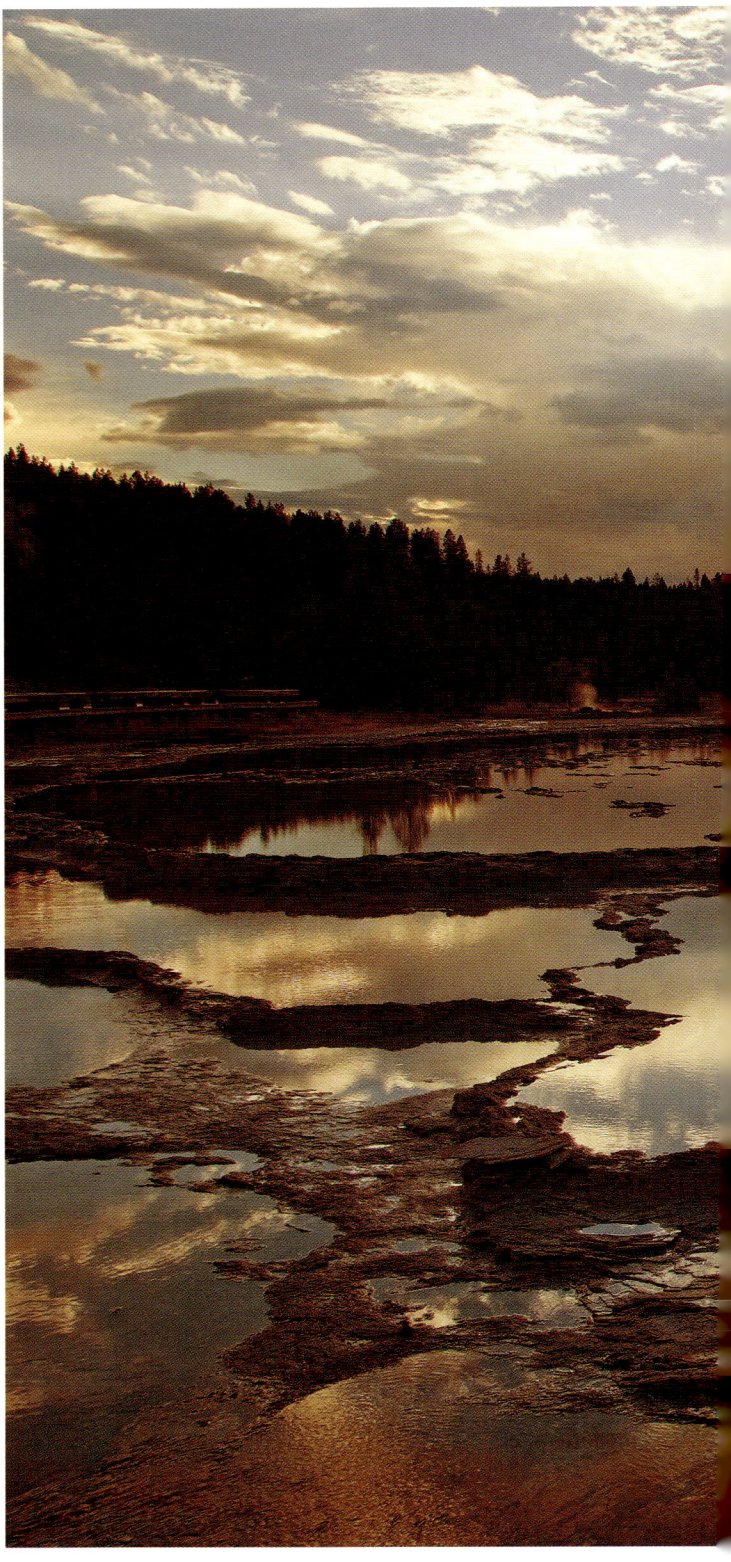

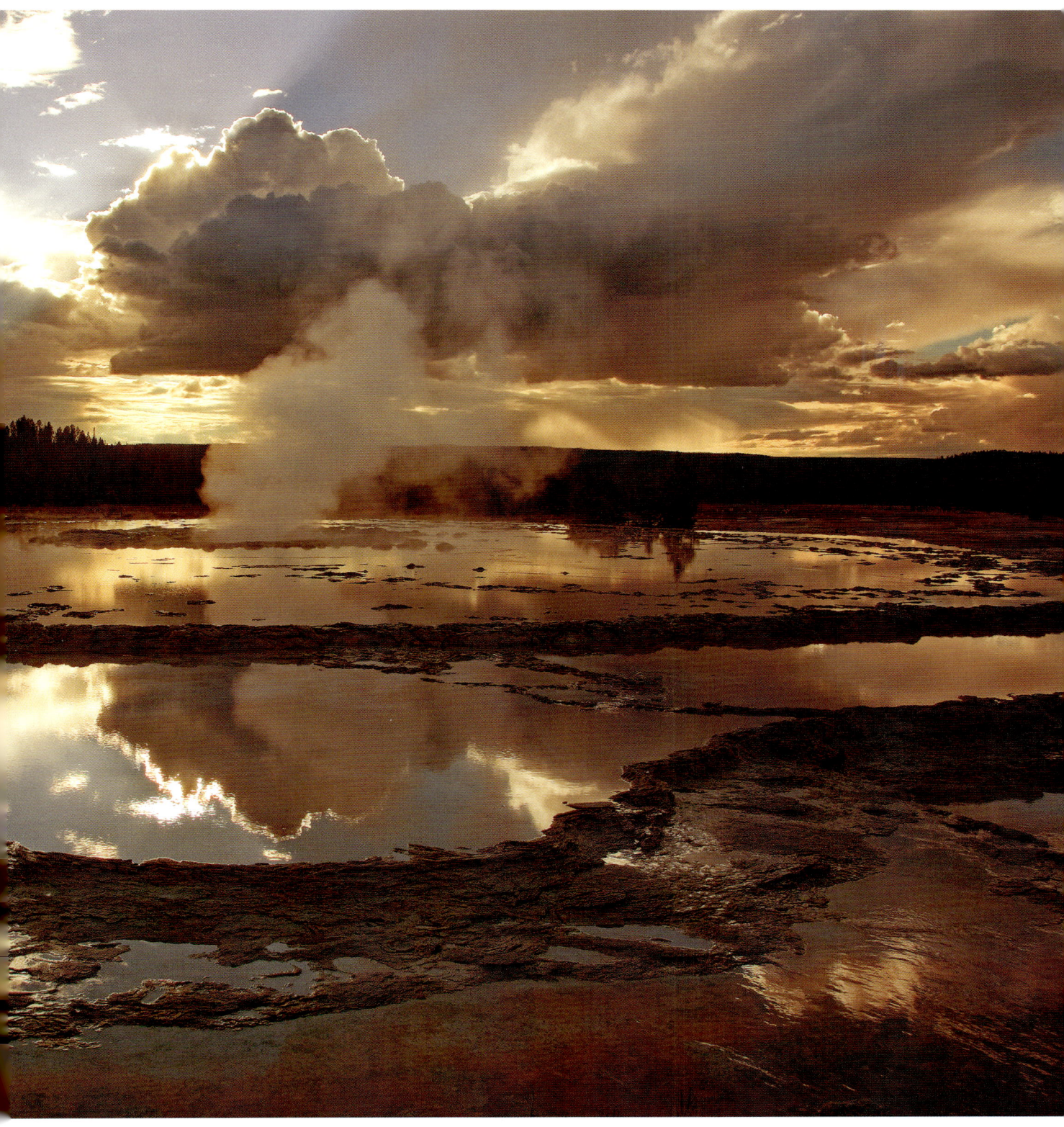

HOT LAKE

WHITE DOME GEYSER

"We could not help feeling that we were lifted between heaven and hell, for while the seething, sulphurous lakes were on each side and far beneath us, the placid sky hung in grandest beauty above us."

CALVIN CLAWSON, JOURNALIST, 1871

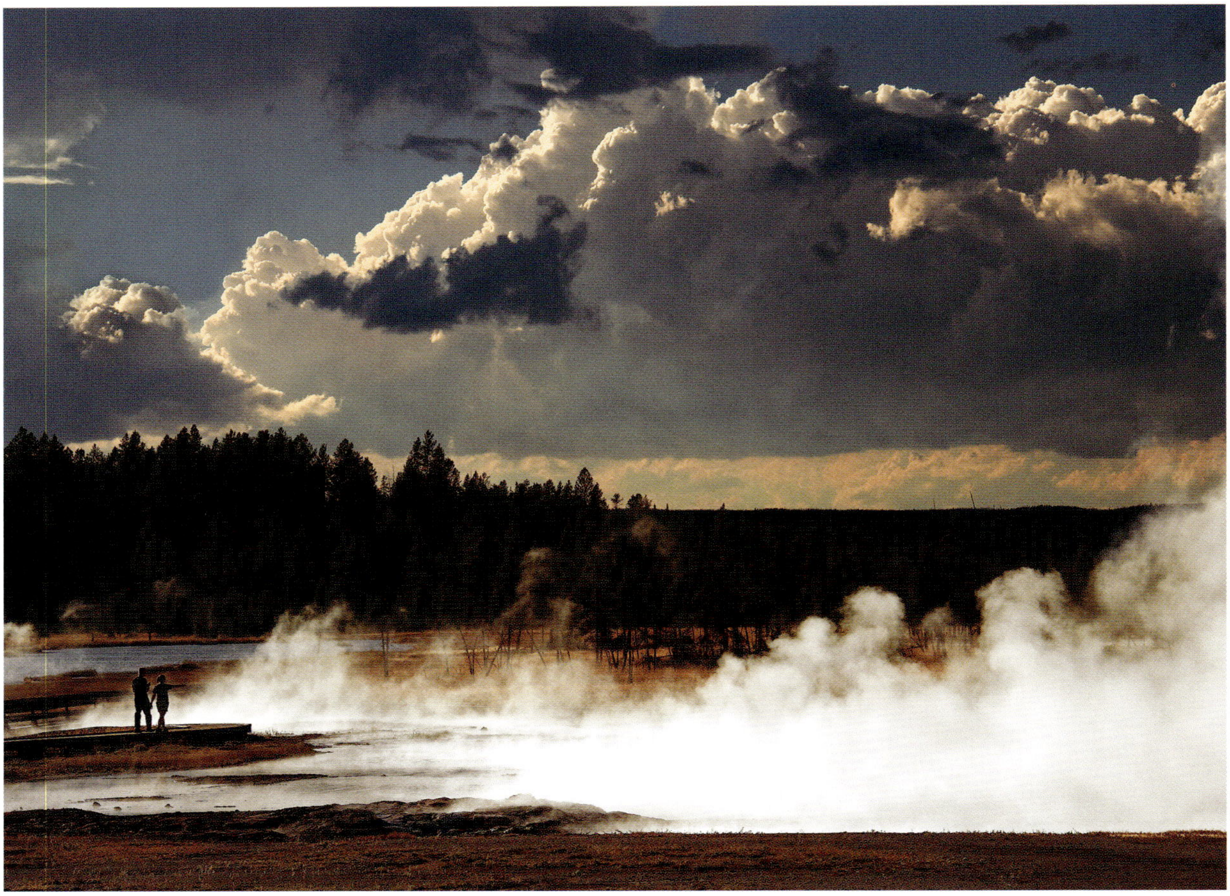

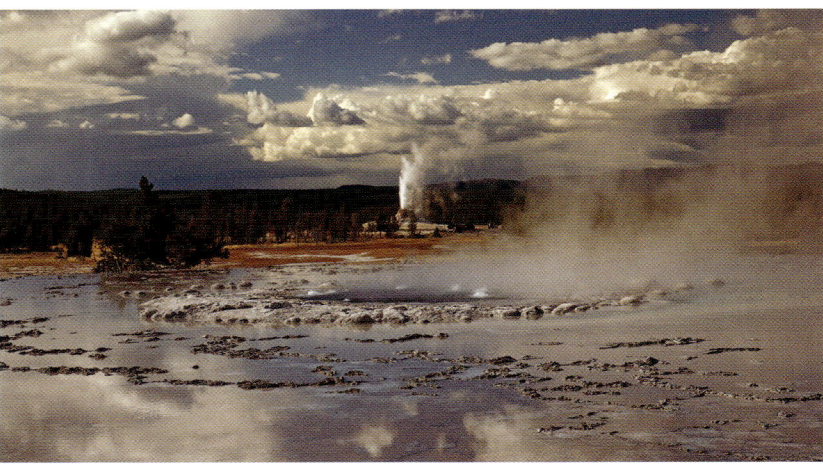

Hot Lake

White Dome Geyser and Great Fountain Geyser terrace

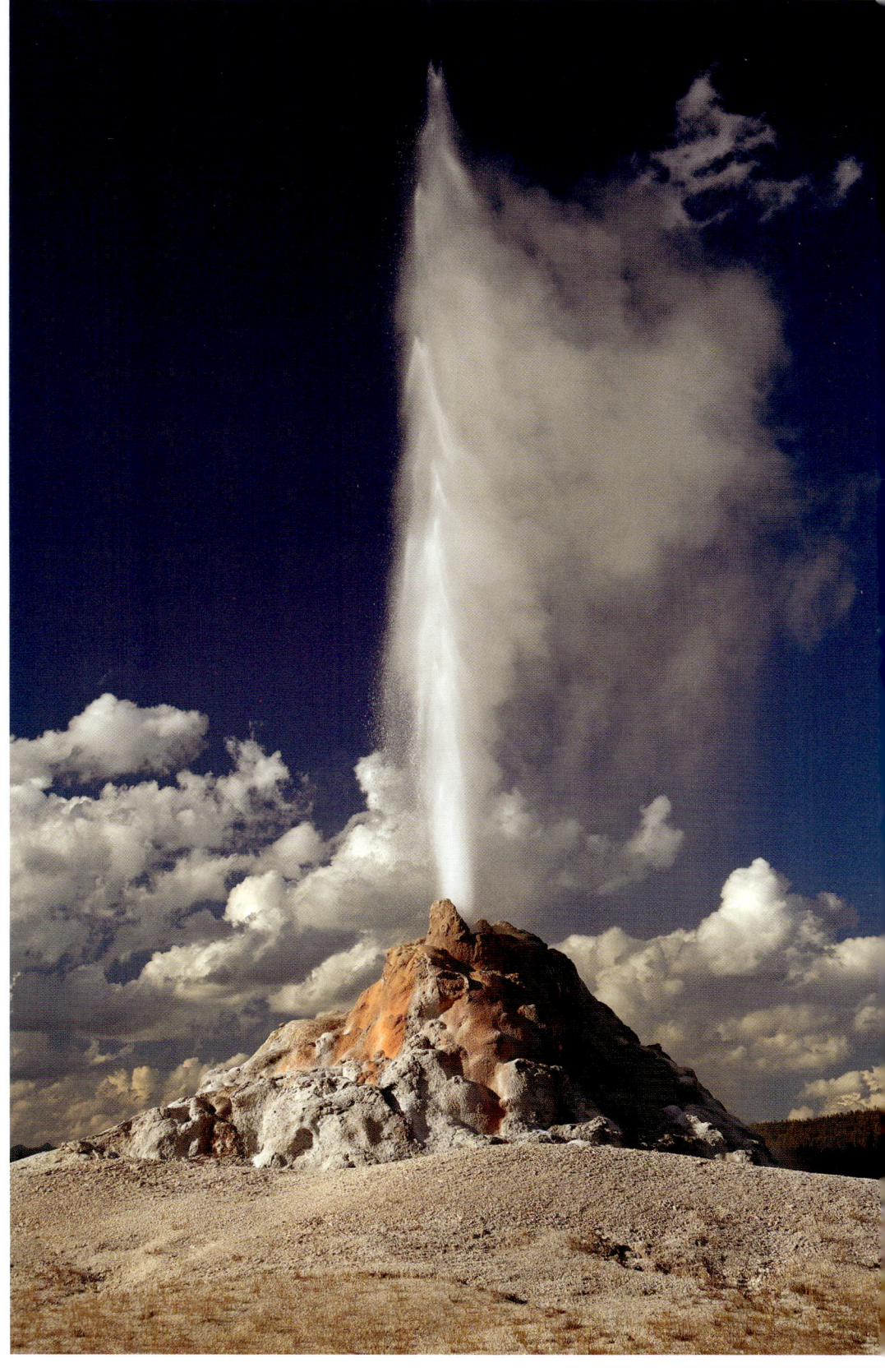

White Dome Geyser

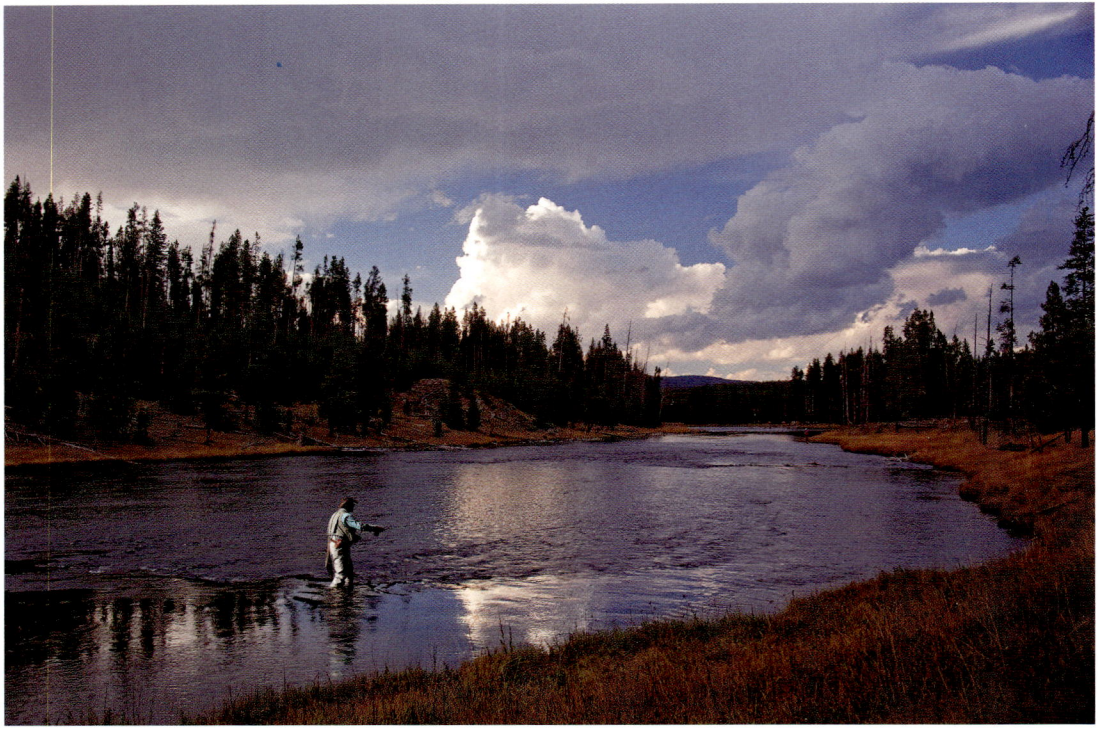

Firehole River

"Early in the afternoon we crossed the mountain and our eyes for the first time beheld 'Wonderland.' Vast columns of steam were ascending from the many geysers and boiling springs which abound in the valley."

EDWARD S. PARKINSON
Wonderland; or, Twelve weeks in and out of the United States, 1894

"Throughout the area of the valley, a space of nearly four miles square, and as far as the eye could reach in the dim light, there was hardly a space from which a misty column, white and spectral, was not slowly rising and mounting until it seemed to meet the skies. These white and mysterious columns with their steady, upward movement appeared in the gray light of early dawn like an army of spirits assembling; and gave one a most vivid idea of the Judgment Day, 'when the trumpet shall sound and the dead shall be raised.'"

GEORGE WOOD WINGATE
Through the Yellowstone Park on Horseback, 1886

FOUNTAIN FLAT

"The so-called geyser basins . . . are mostly open valleys on the central plateau that were eroded by glaciers after the greater volcanic fires had ceased to burn. Looking down over the forests as you approach them from the surrounding heights, you see a multitude of white columns, broad, reeking masses, and irregular jets and puffs of misty vapor ascending from the bottom of the valley, or entangled like smoke among the neighboring trees, suggesting the factories of some busy town or the campfires of an army. These mark the position of each mush pot, paint pot, hot spring, and geyser, or gusher, as the Icelandic word means. And when you saunter into the midst of them over the bright sinter pavements, and see how pure and white and pearly gray they are in the shade of the mountains, and how radiant in the sunshine, you are fairly enchanted. So numerous they are and varied, Nature seems to have gathered them from all the world as specimens of her rarest fountains, to show in one place what she can do."

JOHN MUIR
"The Yellowstone National Park," *The Atlantic Monthly,* April 1898

Fountain Flat

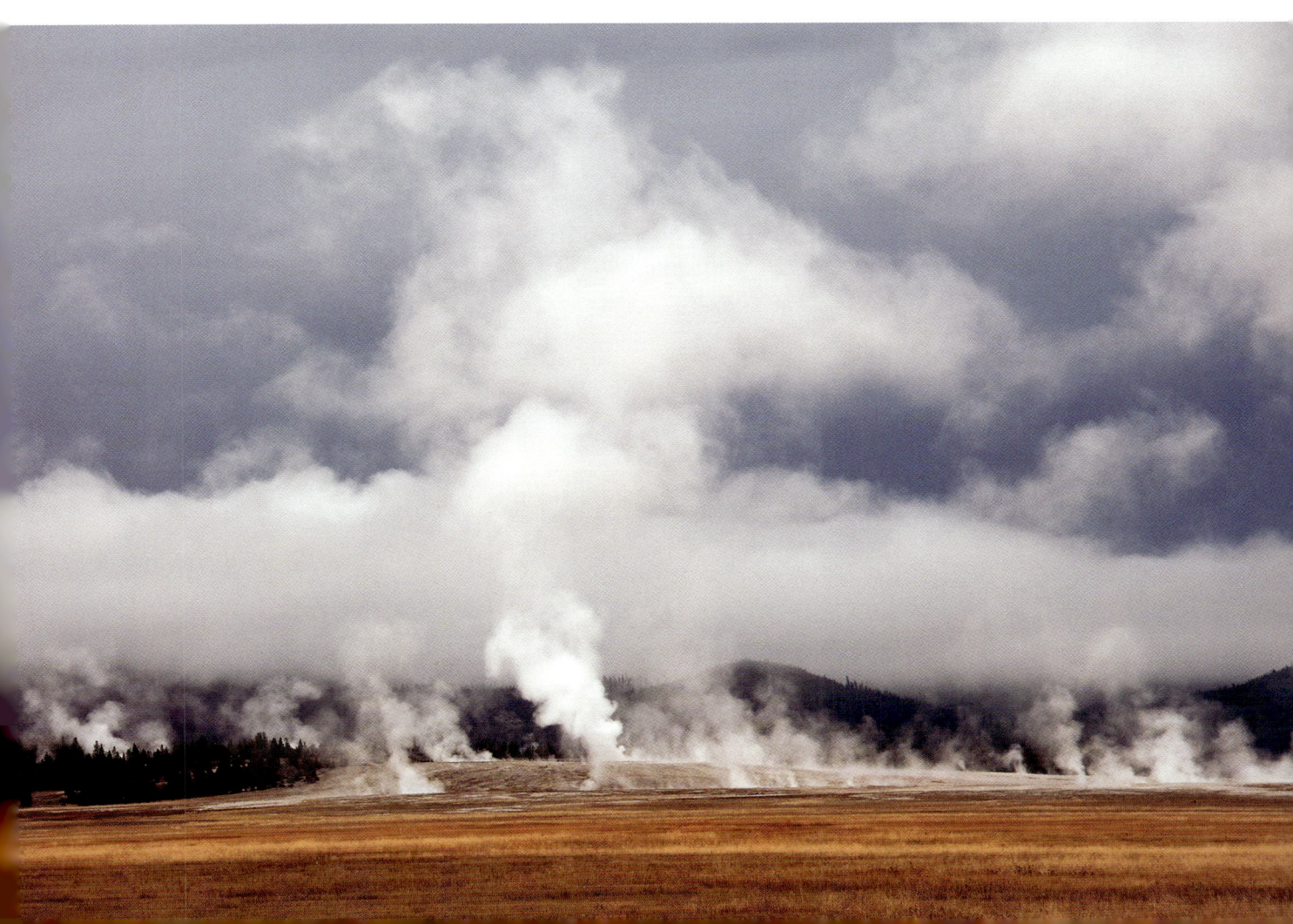

Nez Perce Creek

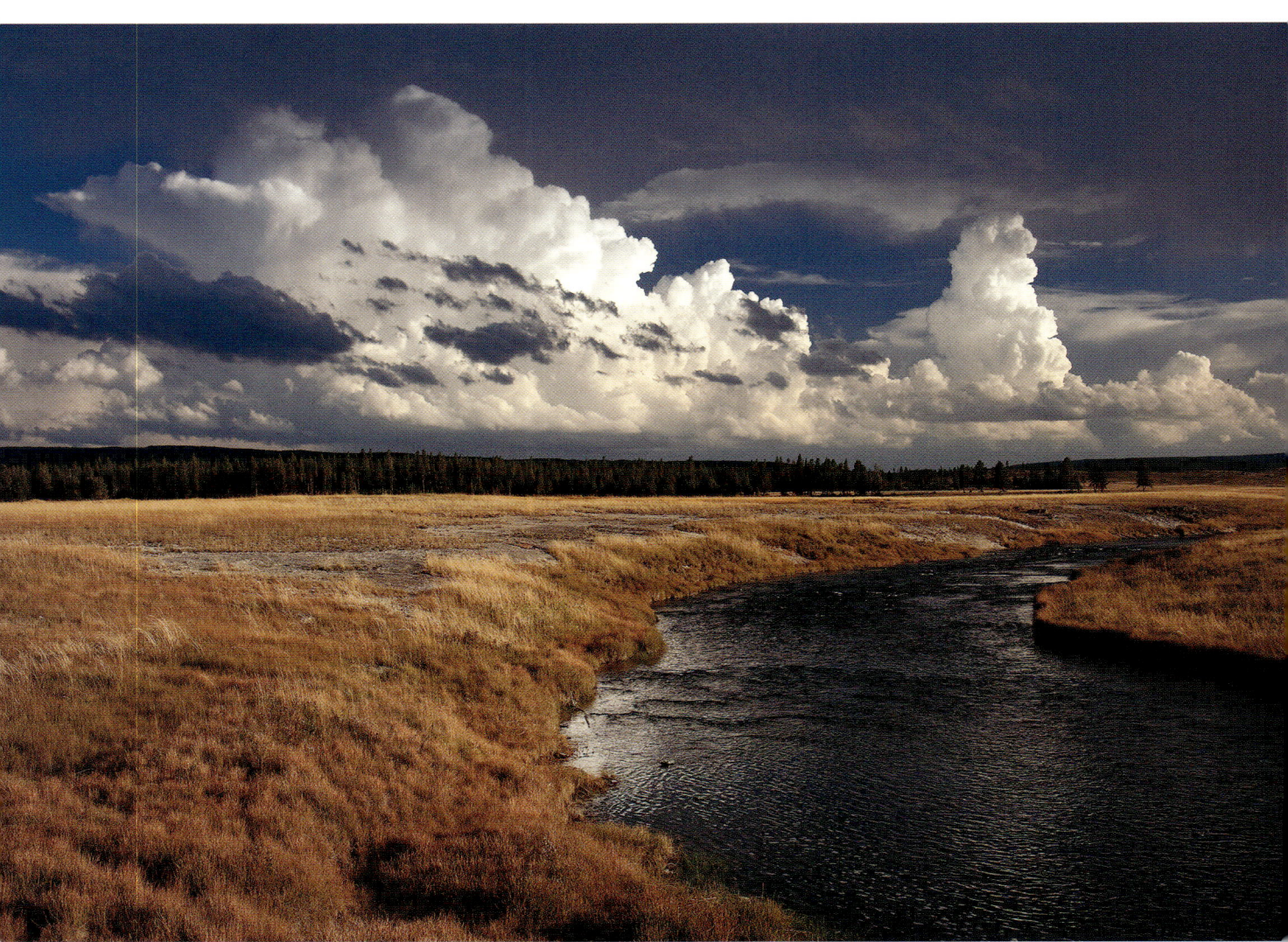

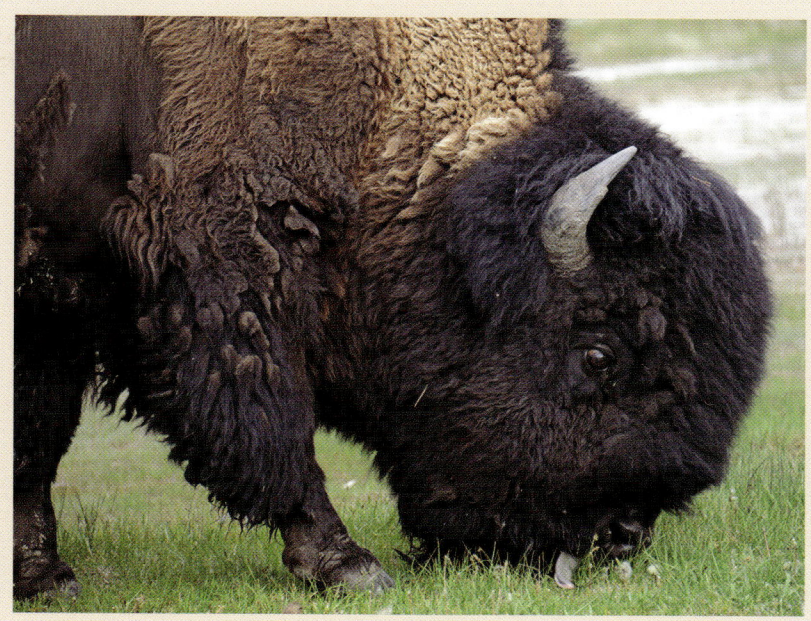

Bison

Fountain Paint Pot Area

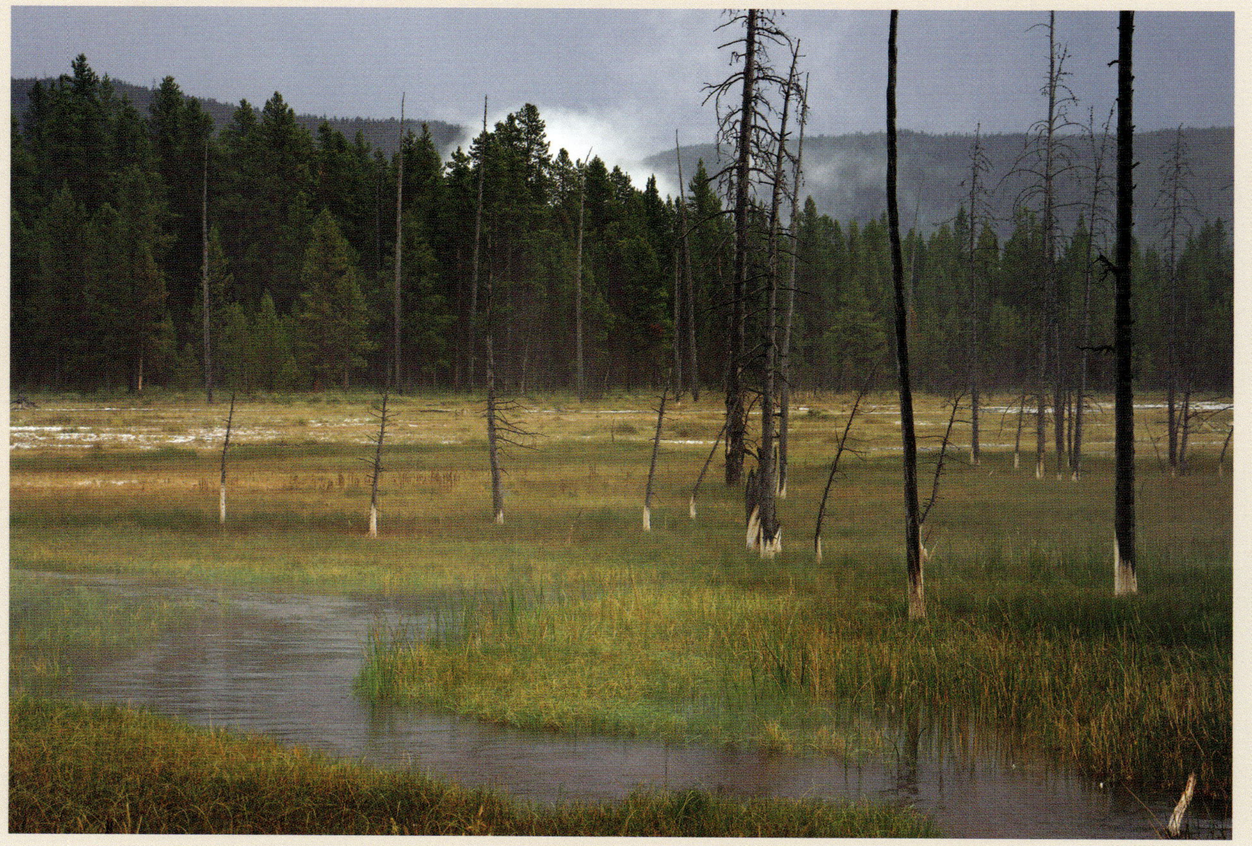

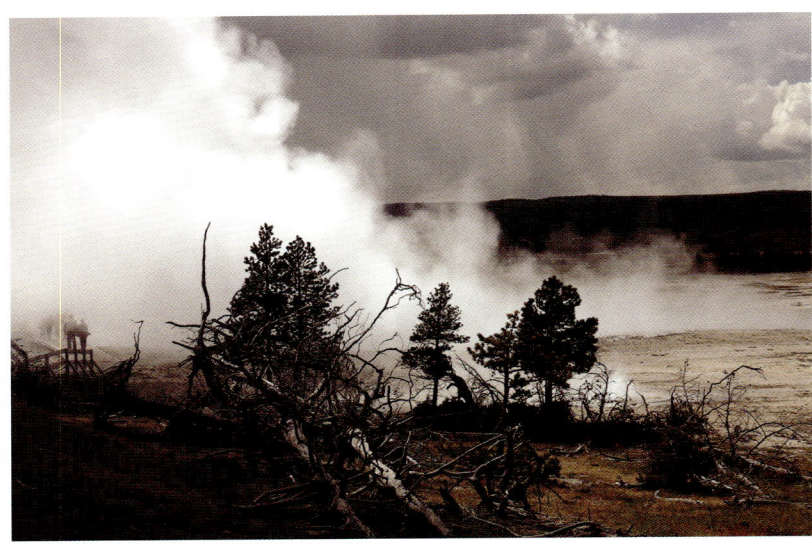

Fountain Paint Pot Area

Silex Spring

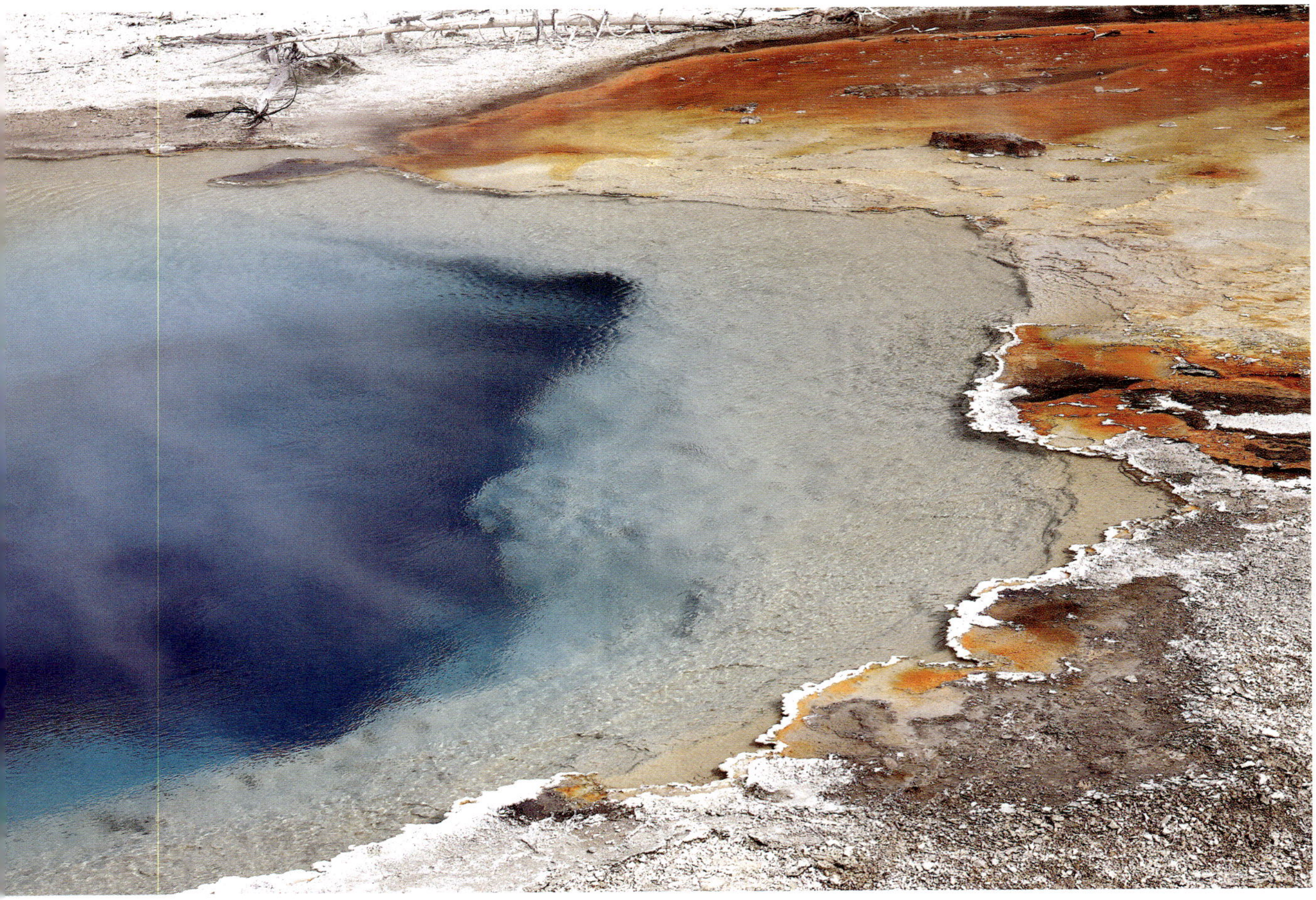

"We passed hot streams boiling in the forest; saw whiffs of steam beyond these, and yet other whiffs breaking through the misty green hills in the far distance."

RUDYARD KIPLING
American Notes, 1891

Lower Geyser Basin near Whiskey Flats

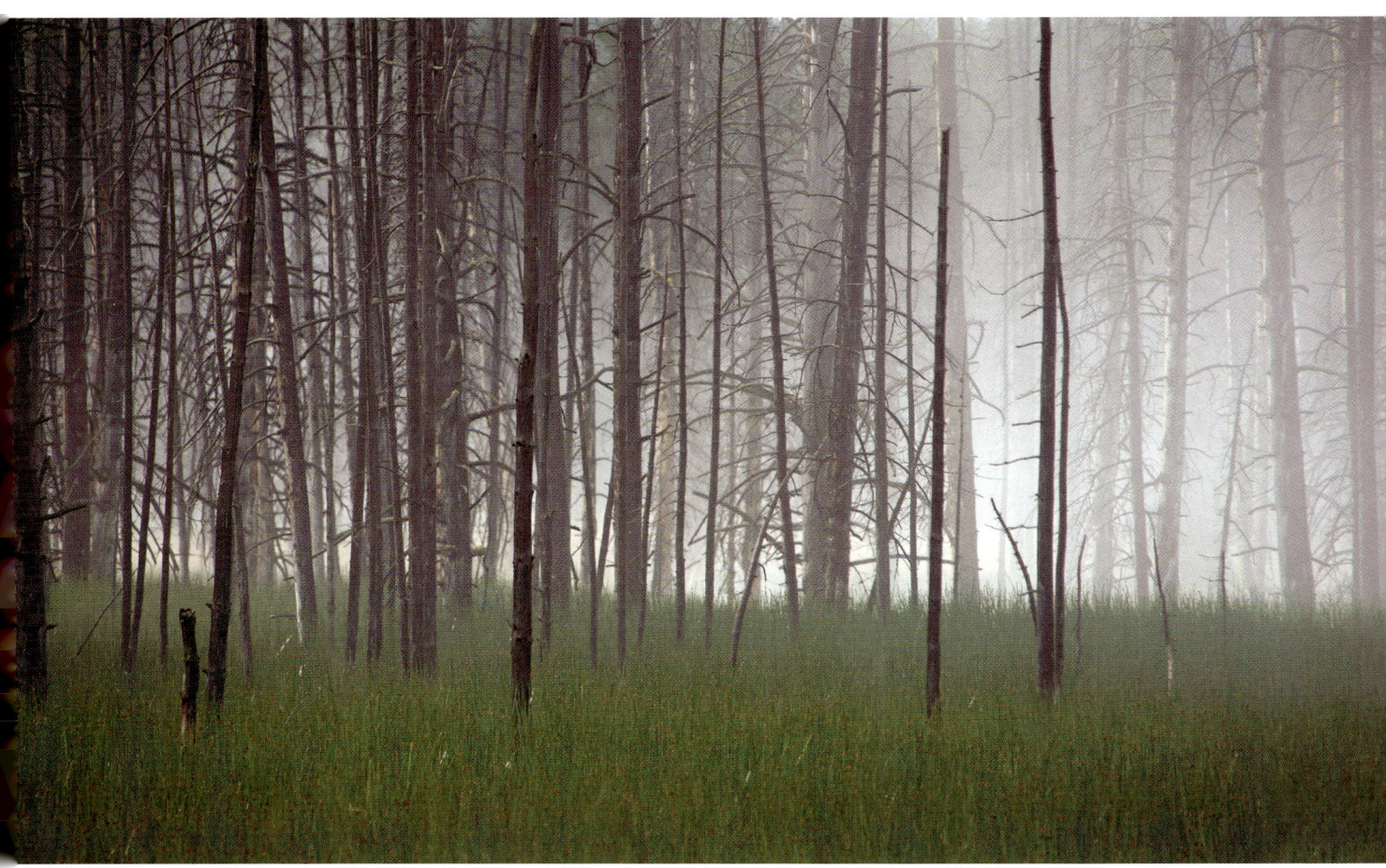

MIDWAY GEYSER BASIN

"A cloud of steam on the opposite side of the river announced our arrival at what . . . is popularly known as Hell's Half Acre. Fording the rapid and stony Firehole, our ponies clambered up the rocky bank on the other side, and after tying them to some trees, a few steps brought us to the edge of the Excelsior, the largest geyser in the world. This is emphatically 'a terror,' if the expression may be permitted.

"Imagine a pit like a huge cellar, two hundred and fifty feet in diameter, sunk fifteen to twenty feet deep in the solid rock and full of water, boiling and seething like the most gigantic caldron conceivable, while from the whole surface a column of steam is constantly ascending high in air and almost concealing the water below.

"On the river side, half the rocky bank has been swept away by some terrific eruption, and through the gap thus formed a stream of boiling water the size of a brook rushes into the river. The other banks overhang the basin and seem tottering to their fall. As one of the men remarked, 'It looks as if the whole business might go up at any minute, and if it does so when we are here, it will be a case of "Good-bye, John."'

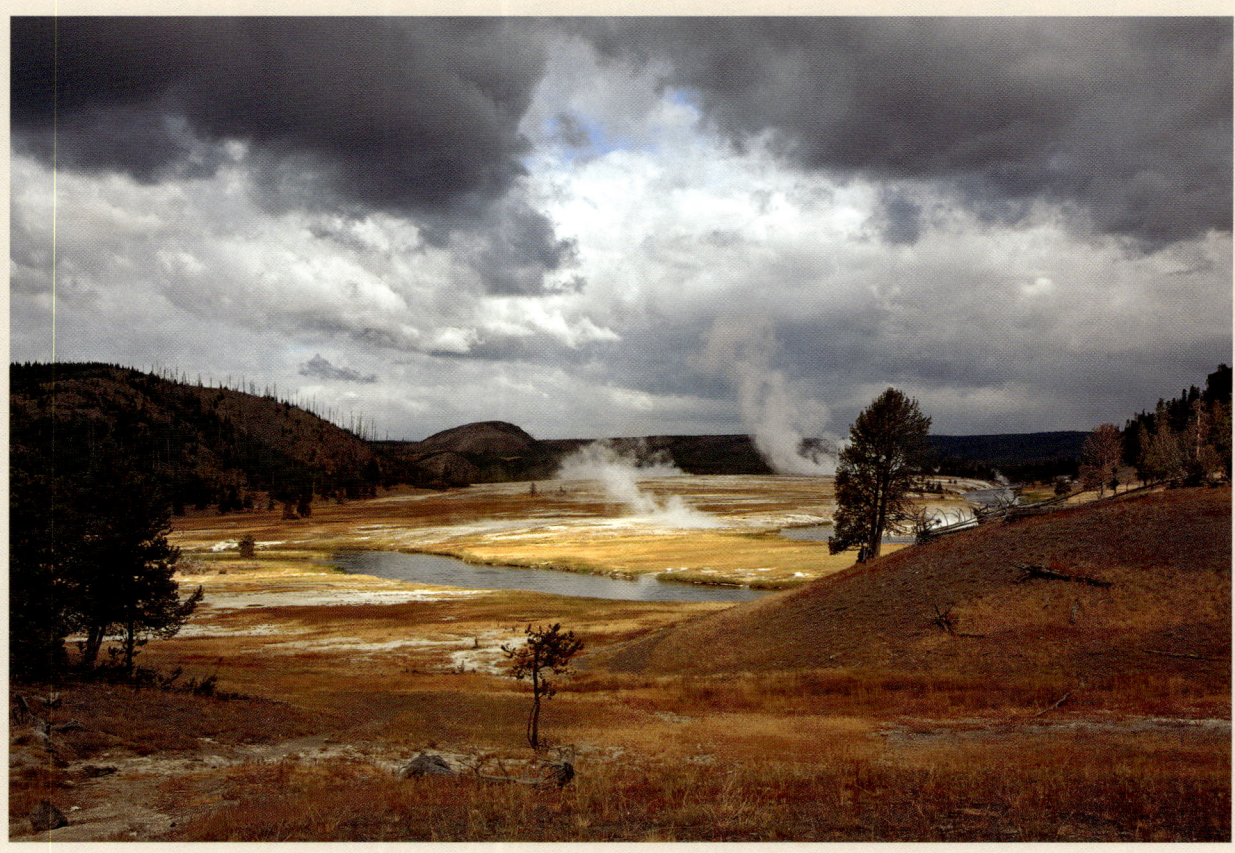

"The eruptions of the Excelsior are rare. I could learn of but two men who had actually seen one. These reported that the column was sixty feet in diameter and ascended three hundred feet; the volume of water was so great as to sweep away all the bridges over the Firehole River; the roar sounded like an earthquake, and huge stones were scattered all over the neighborhood. On the other hand, a good deal of incredulity was expressed on the subject by men who ought to know the truth. The remark of one of this class, a stage driver, sums up their version.

"'I have heard,' said he, 'lots of stories about the Excelsior, a guisen, from men who have heard somebody else tell about it. But I a'int seen no one who has seen it with his own eyes, and I don't expect to. In my opinion, it never did guise and it a'int never agoin' to.'

"This was the first time I ever heard the verb 'to guise,' but it struck me as quite appropriate.

"Language fails me to fitly describe the beauty of the Grand Prismatic Spring, which adjoins this geyser. General Terry expressed to me the opinion that this was the most beautiful thing in the Park. Its dimensions are immense (two hundred and fifty by three hundred feet). Although hot, its surface is placid. The colors are indescribable. In the center it is of the deepest, darkest blue, which softly shades off near the edges into a beautiful green. Closer to the shore the tints change into yellow, then to orange, then to dark red, brown, and yellow on a white ground. These colors are formed apparently by the different deposits under the water, and all are strikingly vivid and distinct.

"As the steam which rises slowly from it is blown here and there by the wind, the surface is exposed first in one place and then in another, and the eye falls in succession upon color after color, so strangely contrasted, so vivid and yet so beautiful, as they glisten in the bright sunshine, that it seems more like magic than anything which really exists in nature.

"To the north is another spring called the Turquoise, which is a hundred feet square, and a perfect turquoise blue. This would be beautiful elsewhere, but fades into insignificance when compared with the glories of its prismatic neighbor.

"The outlets from these springs are almost as beautiful as the springs themselves. As the Prismatic softly pulsates, it sends a gentle flow of water over its beautifully scalloped edges, which gathers into pools of softly variegated colors, while the Turquoise emits a small meandering stream through various channels of white, salmon color, and yellow."

Firehole River above Midway Geyser Basin

GEORGE WOOD WINGATE
Through the Yellowstone Park on Horseback, 1886

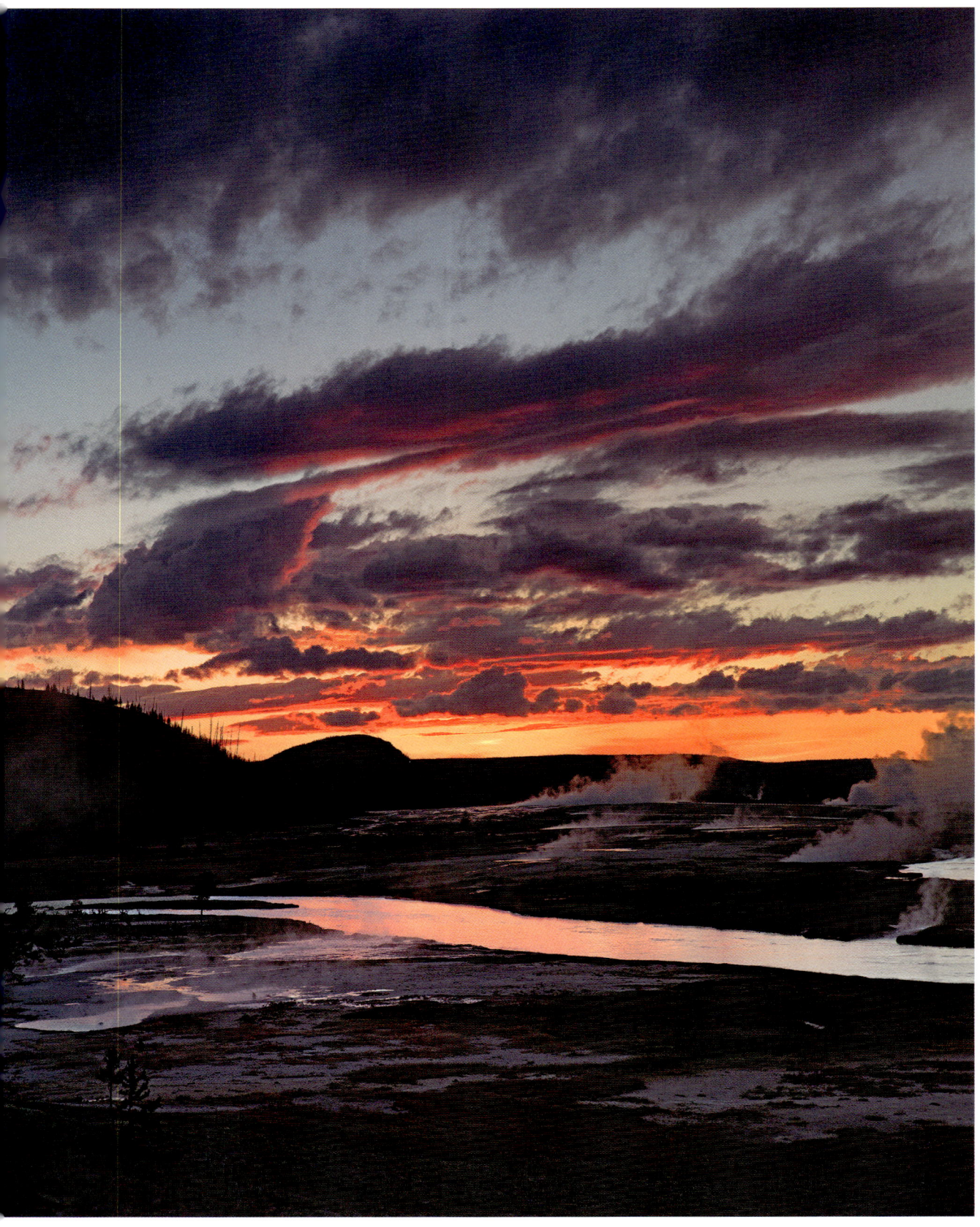

"Once upon a time there was a carter who brought his team and a friend into the Yellowstone Park without due thought. Presently they came upon a few of the natural beauties of the place, and that carter turned his team into his friend's team, howling, 'Get out o' this, Jim. All hell's alight under our noses!'

"And they called the place Hell's Half-Acre to this day to witness if the carter lied.

"We, too, the old lady from Chicago, her husband, Tom, and the good little mares, came to Hell's Half-Acre, which is about sixty acres in extent, and when Tom said, 'Would you like to drive over it?'

"We said, 'Certainly not, and if you do we shall report you to the park authorities.'

"There was a plain, blistered, peeled, and abominable, and it was given over to the sportings and spoutings of devils who threw mud, and steam, and dirt at each other with whoops, and halloos, and bellowing curses.

"The places smelled of the refuse of the pit, and that odor mixed with the clean, wholesome aroma of the pines in our nostrils throughout the day."

RUDYARD KIPLING
American Notes, 1891

"Instead of tiny pools, there is here a great lake with its basin rimmed with so many and such rich colors, and its water of such deep and heavenly tints, that the very vapor from it is tinged by reflection with hues of pale blue or delicate pink. From this lake runs a phenomenal little brook. The water in the lake is of limpid turquoise blue; for a few yards the water of the brook is thick and white like cream; for a few more yards it runs over a bed distinctly and brightly crimson; then for a few yards more its course is marked by a perfectly defined band of brilliant yellow. There is a definite break in each color; they do not run into each other. The same water drops in its course entirely different deposits.

"Here, too, is the horrible crater of the greatest geyser in the world, the Excelsior, whose eruptions are fortunately few, when it sends three hundred feet into the air water enough to wash away bridges over small streams below, rumbling with a roar to be heard for miles, and scattering over acres rocks of a hundred pounds in weight. The crater is dreadful enough when not in action; but into this seething, burning, frightful abyss of boiling horror, a little rill of clear, perfectly cold water, fed from the snowy uplands in the distance, drops gently, unceasingly, unafraid."

ALICE WELLINGTON ROLLINS
The Three Tetons, 1887

Midway Geyser Basin

EXCELSIOR GEYSER CRATER

"Near the Prismatic Spring is the great Excelsior Geyser, which is said to throw a column of boiling water sixty to seventy feet in diameter to a height of from fifty to three hundred feet, at irregular periods. This is the greatest of all the geysers yet discovered anywhere. The Firehole River, which sweeps past [Excelsior Geyser], is, at ordinary stages, a stream about one hundred yards wide and three feet deep; but when the geyser is in eruption, so great is the quantity of water discharged that the volume of the river is doubled, and it is rendered too hot and rapid to be forded."

JOHN MUIR
"The Yellowstone National Park," *The Atlantic Monthly,* April 1898

"The earth quaked and rumbled under our feet with such violence as to almost, throw us down. Then up went Old Excelsior! You should have witnessed that display. It was grand, magnificent! The water was thrown up at a height of over four hundred feet and with such an awful shower of rocks that we all fled for our lives. Some of the rocks thrown up must have weighed three hundred pounds. The edge of the crater, around its entire circumference was torn up to a depth of twelve feet. The volume of water projected was simply enormous. It raised the Firehole River fully six inches."

LOUIS RICHARD HUNTER, PARK VISITOR, 1888

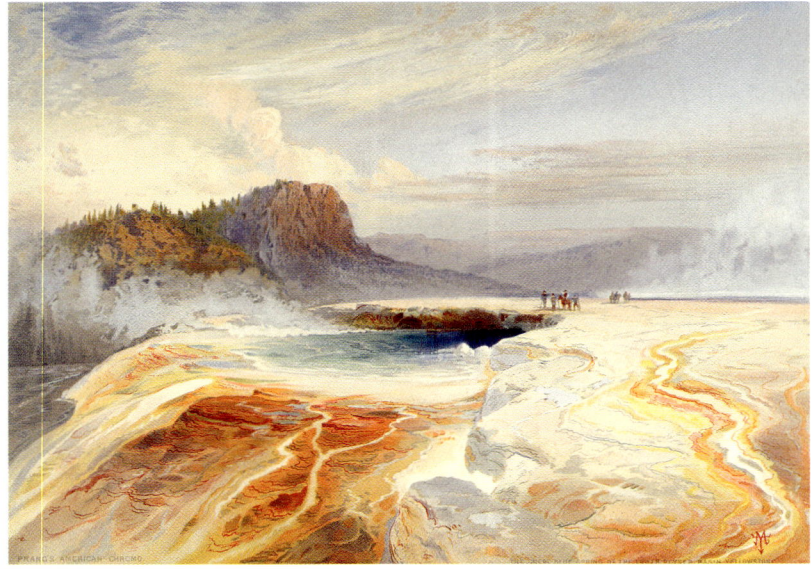

The Great Blue Spring of the Lower Geyser Basin, Yellowstone
Thomas Moran, 1875
Gilcrease Museum, Tulsa, OK
2426.47.2

>
Excelsior Geyser Crater

"The close of each eruption was accompanied by violent earthquake shocks that tore down the geyserite walls and added much both to the danger and sublimity of the spectacle. These masses of broken wall were at each eruption hurled into the air several hundred feet above the topmost waves, clashing together in their descent . . . with a deafening noise that was most terrific. . . . As the waters rose into a vast dome the hissing noise increased until the rocks broke through, and then all was clatter and confusion for a few seconds, and while the water sank back with a gurgling noise, from three to seven shocks were so strong as to render it necessary for lookers-on to support each other to avoid falling."

G.L. HENDERSON, PARK INTERPRETER, 1888

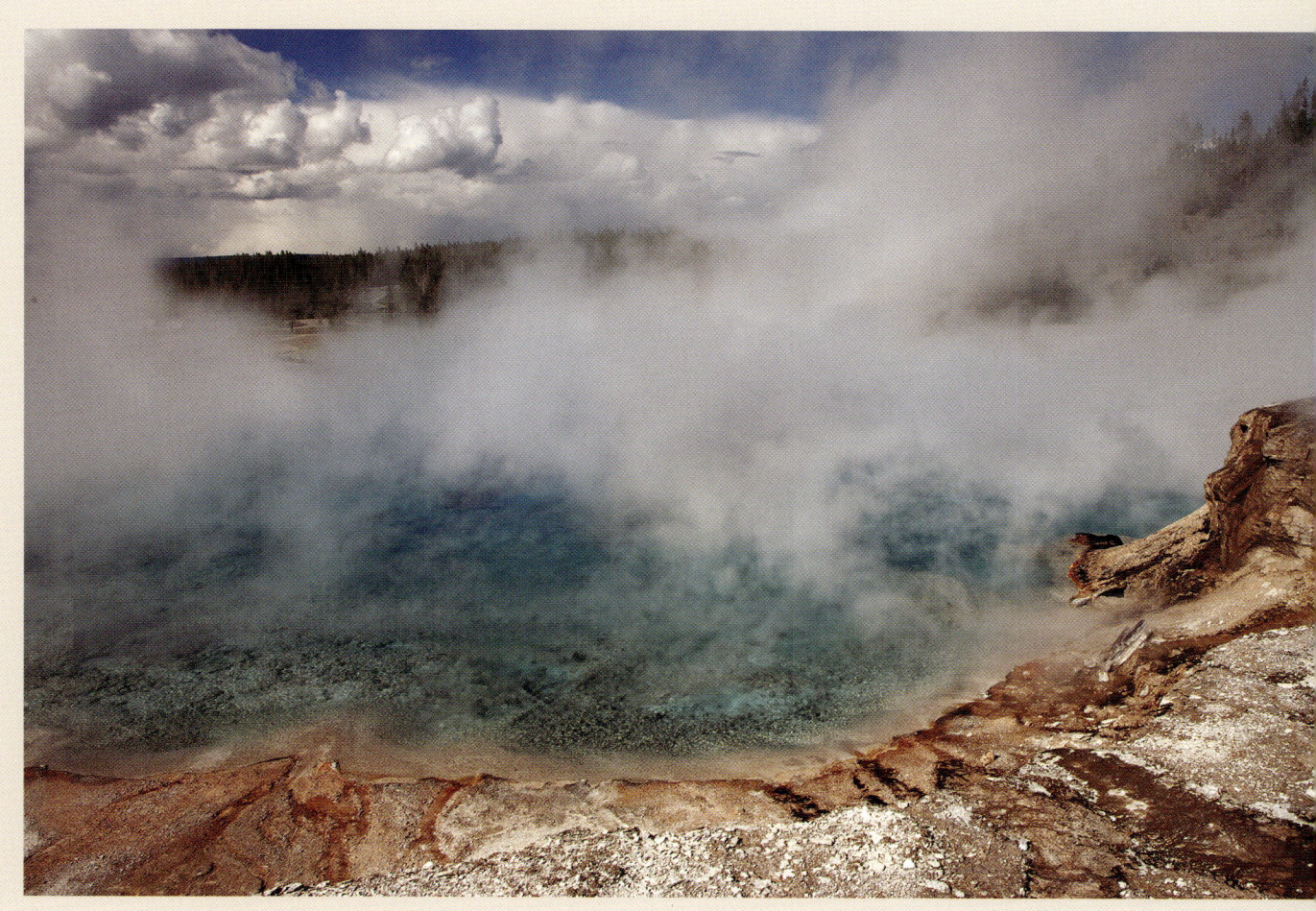

FIREHOLE RIVER

"The overflow from [Grand Prismatic Spring] pours over the slope in small channels, or spreads over broad surfaces, where the evaporation of the water has deposited a crust of a marvelous combination of tints. The coloring is very vivid, and of many shades, from bright scarlet to delicate rose, mingled with bright and creamy yellows, and vivid green from the minute vegetation."

FERDINAND VANDEVEER HAYDEN,
The Yellowstone National Park, and the Mountain Regions of Portions of Idaho, Nevada, Colorado, and Utah, 1876

Firehole River at Midway Geyser Basin

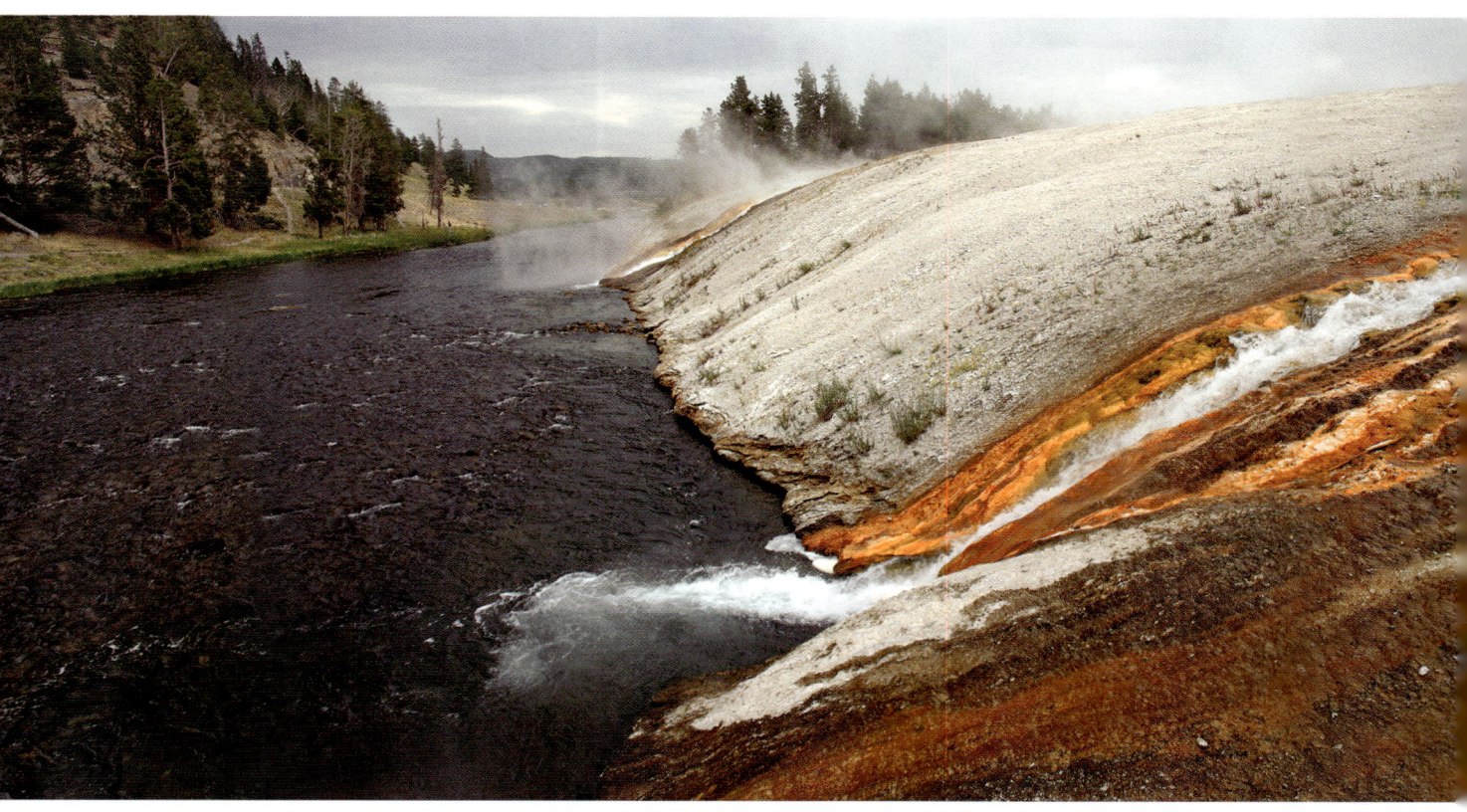

"Mr. [Cornelius] Hedges and I forded the Firehole River a short distance below our camp. The current, as it dashed over the boulders, was swift, and, taking off our boots and stockings, we selected for our place of crossing what seemed to be a smooth rock surface in the bottom of the stream, extending from shore to shore. When I reached the middle of the stream I paused a moment and turned around to speak to Mr. Hedges, who was about entering the stream, when I discovered from the sensation of warmth under my feet that I was standing upon an incrustation formed over a hot spring that had its vent in the bed of the stream. I exclaimed to Hedges: 'Here is the river which [Jim] Bridger said was *hot at the bottom.*'"

NATHANIEL PITT LANGFORD
The Discovery of Yellowstone Park: Journal of the Washburn Expedition to the Yellowstone and Firehole Rivers in the Year 1870, 1905

Midway Geyser Basin and the Firehole River

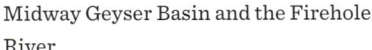

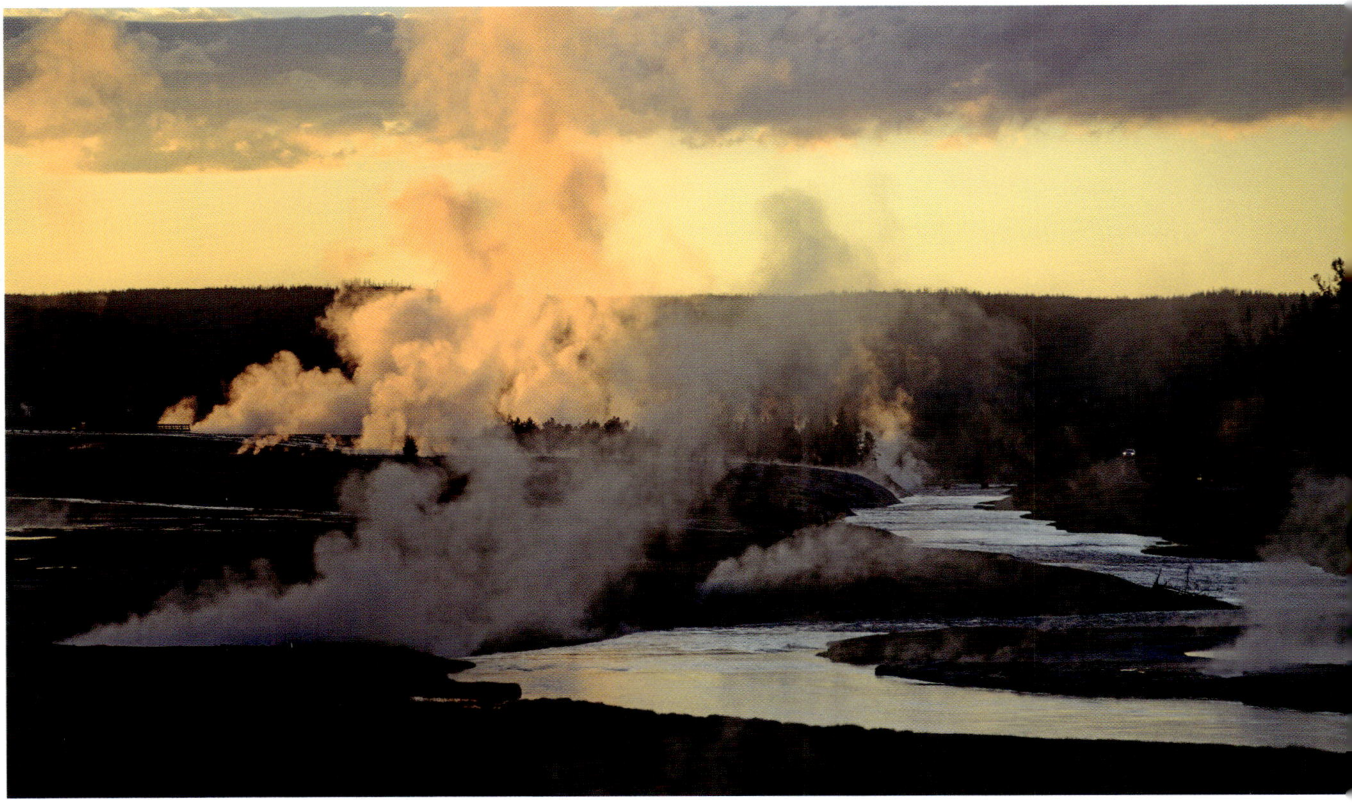

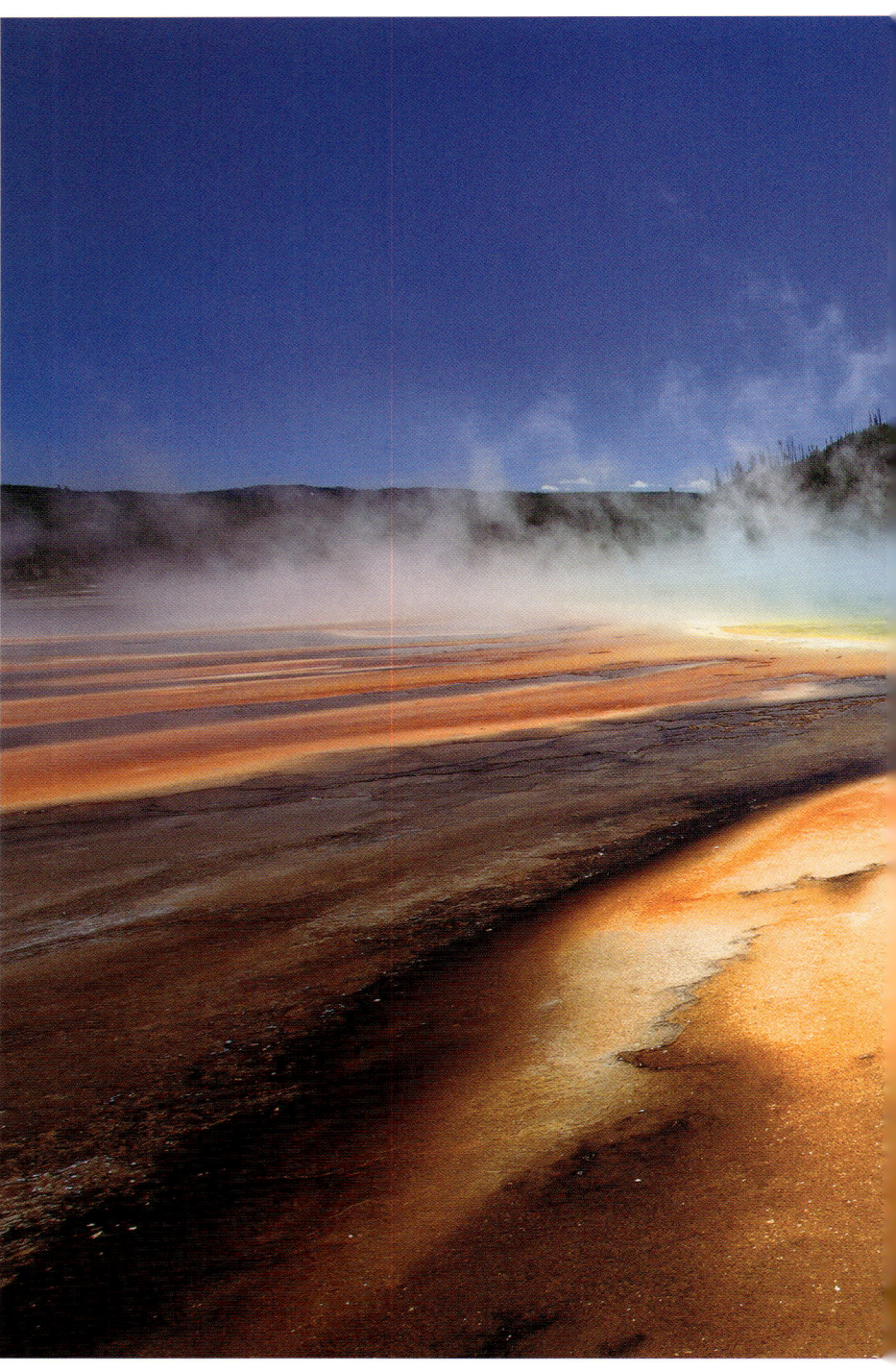

Grand Prismatic Spring

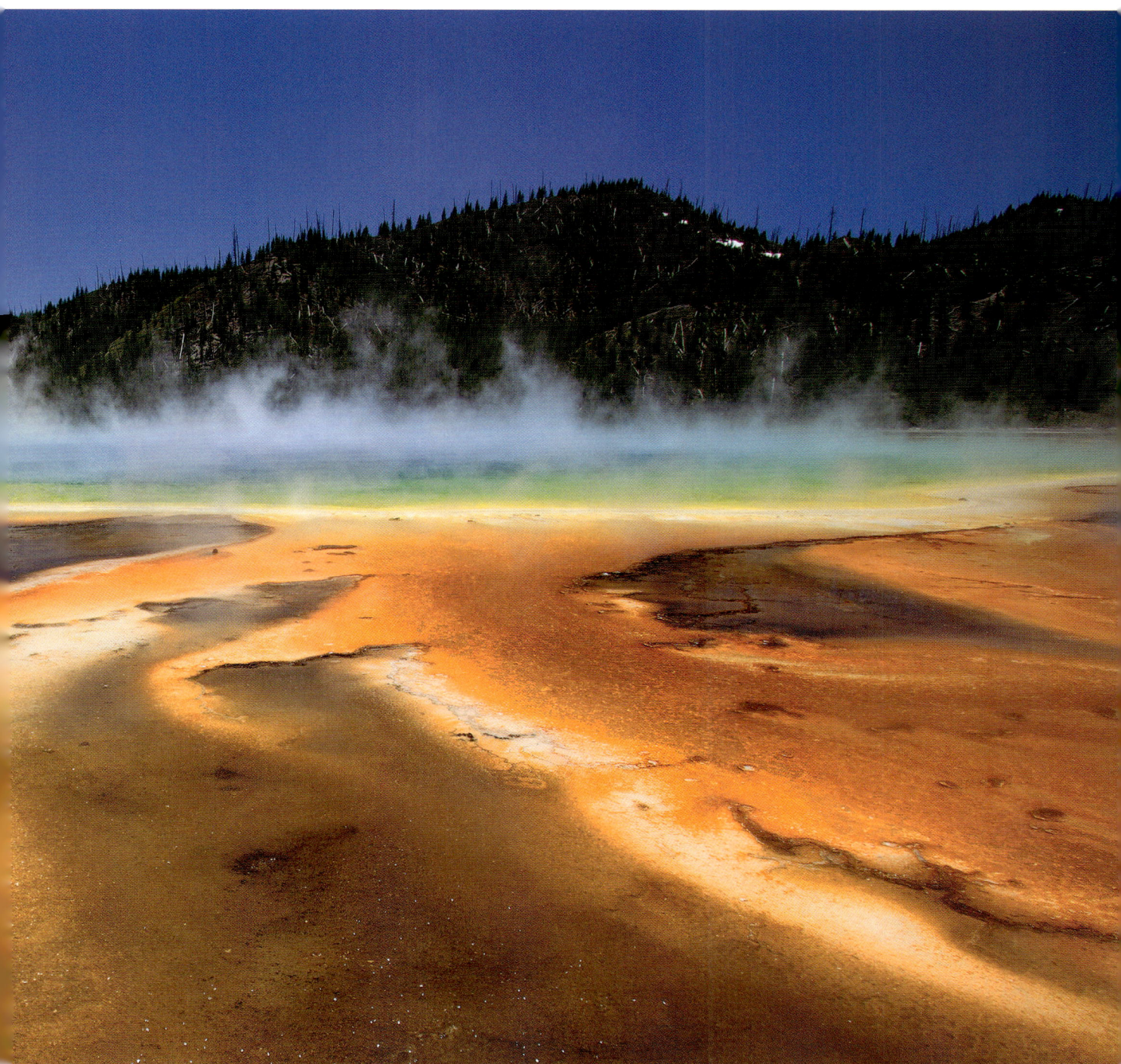

"This section is known as Hell's Half Acre, from the great number of boiling springs in the vicinity. Prismatic lake [Grand Prismatic Spring] is perhaps a couple of hundred yards west from the Excelsior, and receives its name from the many colors visible on its surface. The water in the centre of the lake is deep blue, gradually shading off to green. When the shallower portion of the lake is reached it assumes a yellow color, which deepens to a distinct orange. The formation around the rim of the basin is a brilliant red. The constantly rising volumes of steam are tinged with the colors that are so prominent in the pool, and form one of the most pleasing effects of the Park."

EDWARD S. PARKINSON
Wonderland; or, Twelve weeks in and out of the United States, 1894

"The largest and one of the most wonderfully beautiful of the springs is the Prismatic. . . . With a circumference of three hundred yards, it is more like a lake than a spring. The water is pure deep blue in the centre, fading to green on the edges, and its basin and the slightly terraced pavement about it are astonishingly bright and varied in color. This one of the multitude of Yellowstone fountains is of itself object enough for a trip across the continent. No wonder that so many fine myths have originated in springs; that so many fountains were held sacred in the youth of the world, and had miraculous virtues ascribed to them. Even in these cold, doubting, questioning, scientific times many of the Yellowstone fountains seem able to work miracles."

JOHN MUIR
"The Yellowstone National Park," *The Atlantic Monthly,* April 1898

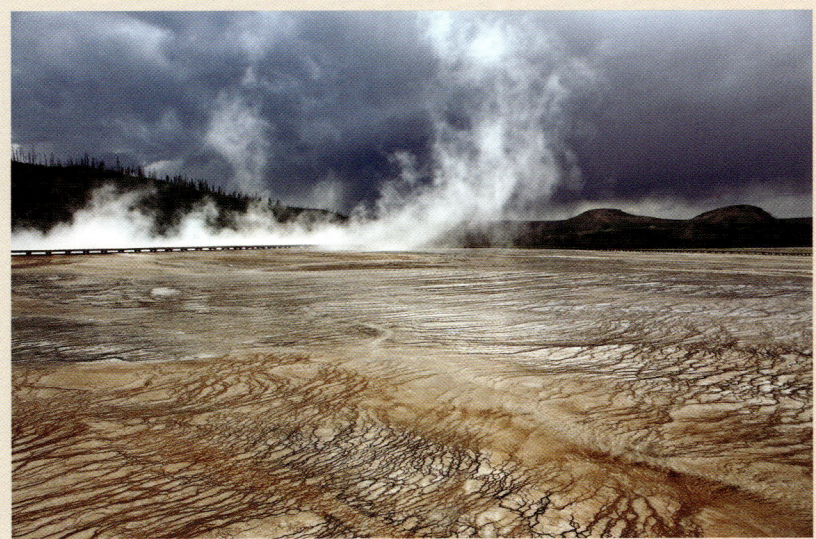

Grand Prismatic Spring boardwalk

>
Grand Prismatic Spring runoff

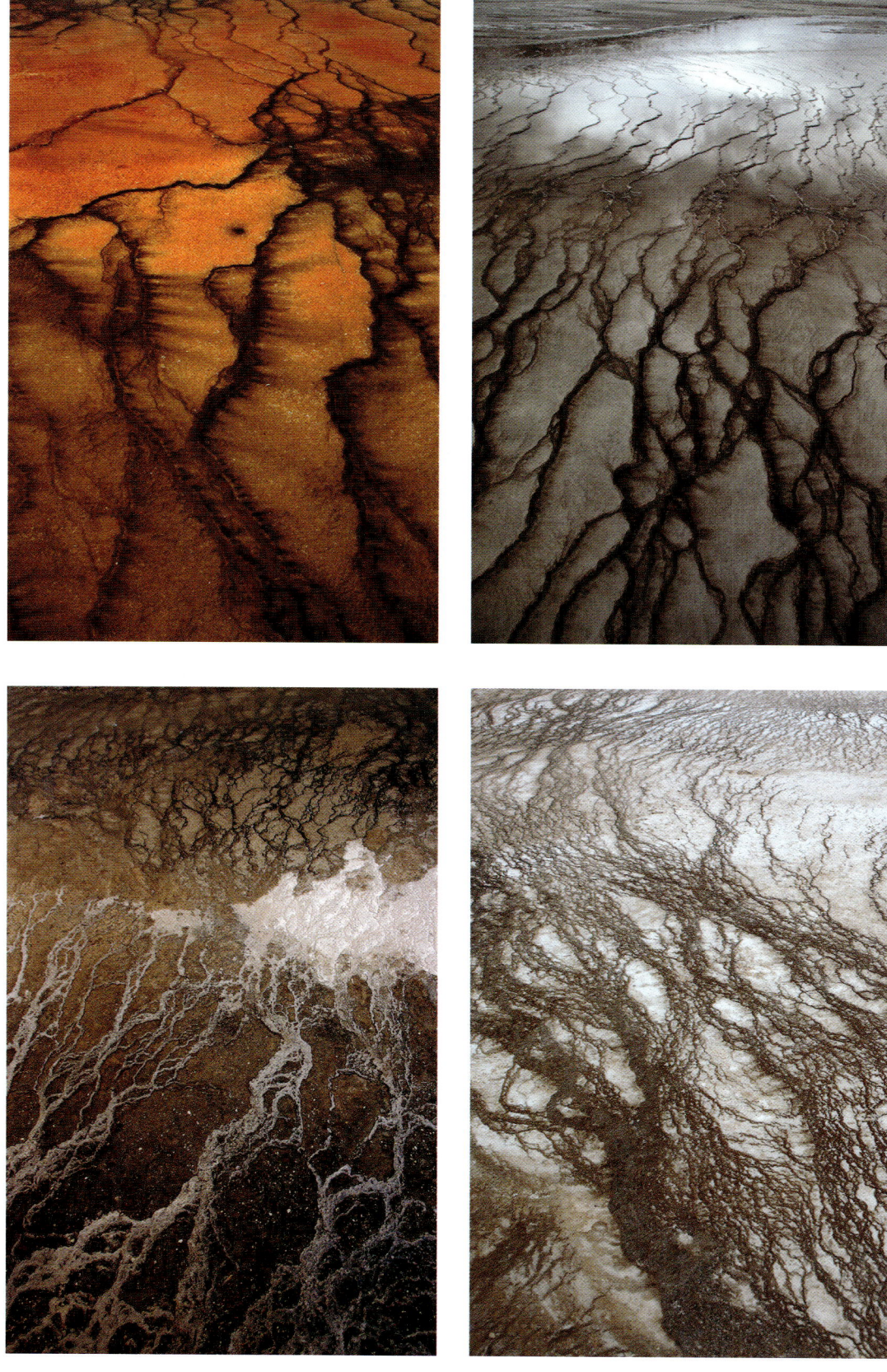

"a magnificent forest of pines and firs all growing straight as a ship's mast, and growing but a few feet apart"

THOMAS MORAN, PAINTER, 1871

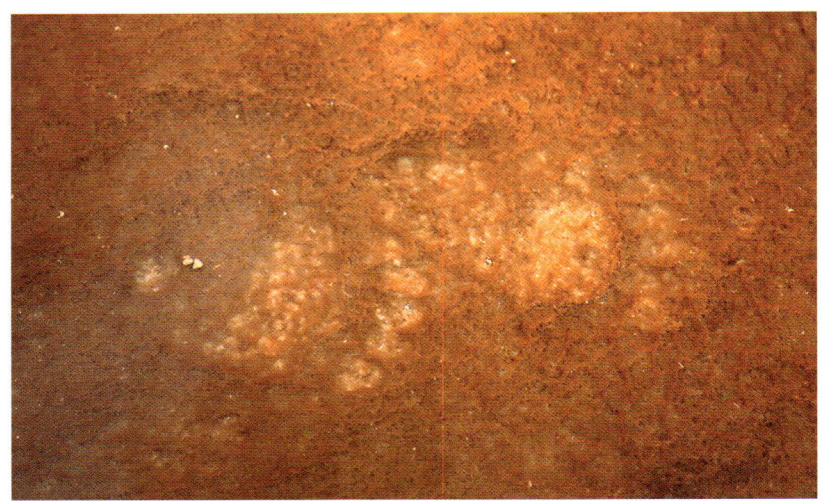

Bear tracks in Grand Prismatic Spring

Lodgepole pines

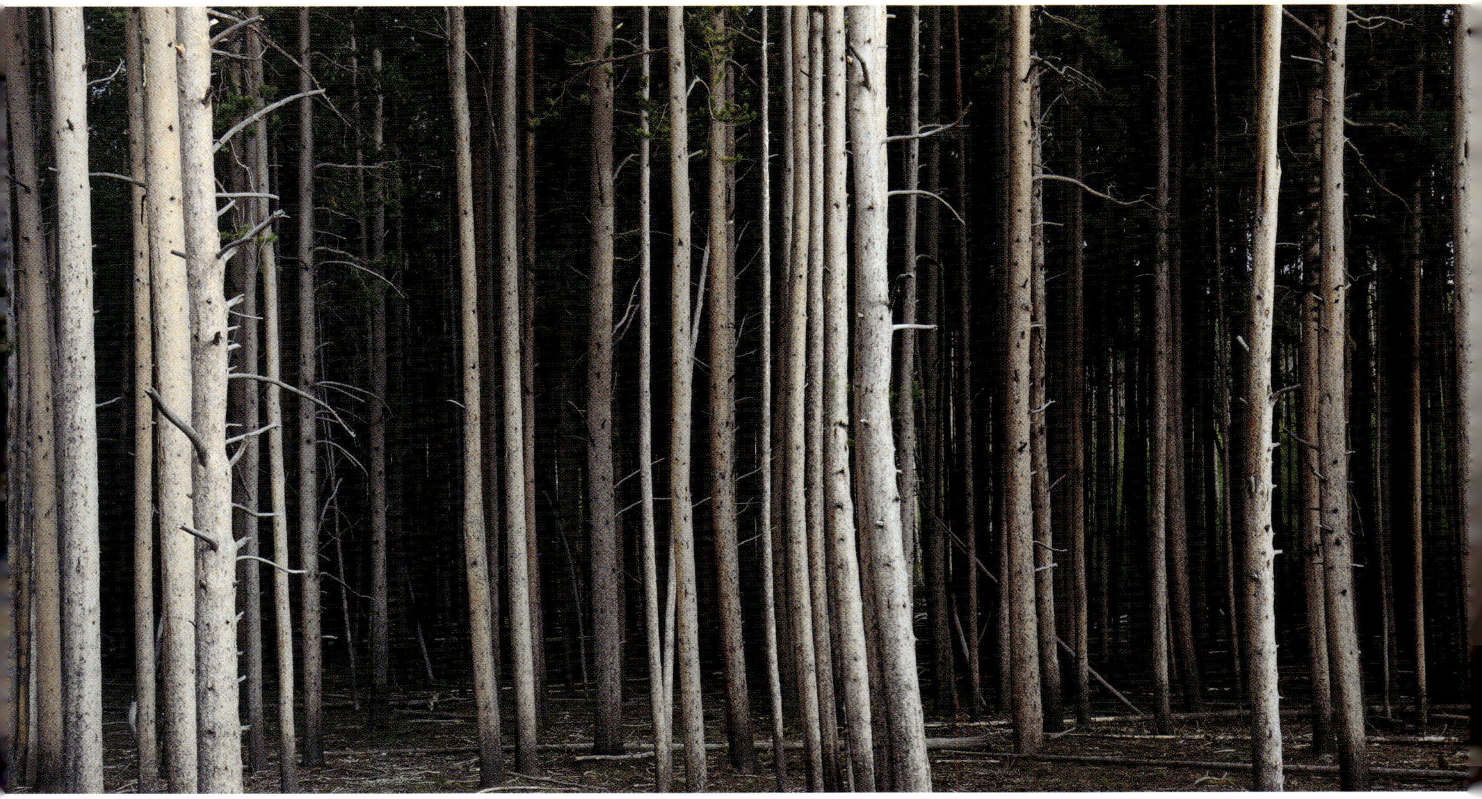

Turquoise Pool

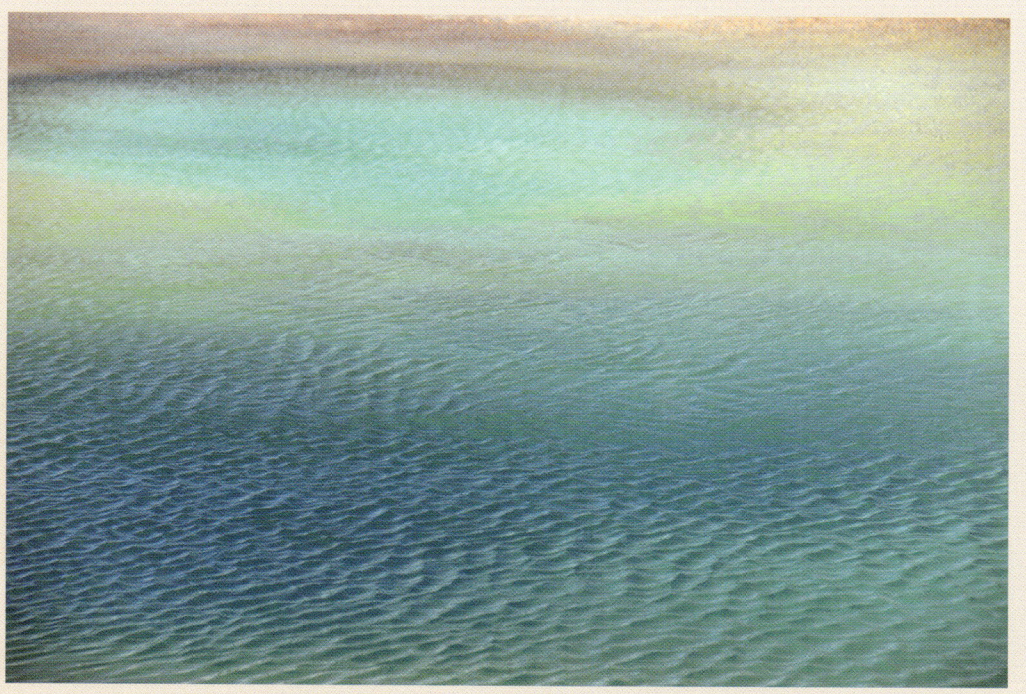

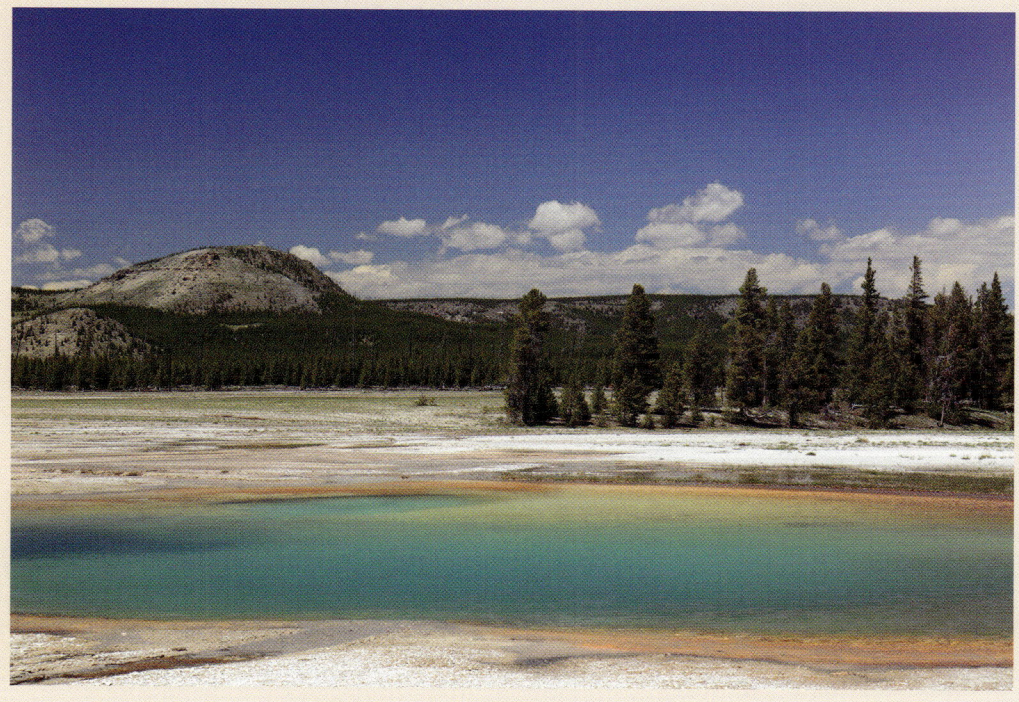

"It is a perfect gem. If by some means it could be solidified it would rival in beauty the most precious of stones. At a distance it looks like a block of sapphire."

"Boiling," *The Brooklyn Daily Eagle,* August 15, 1883

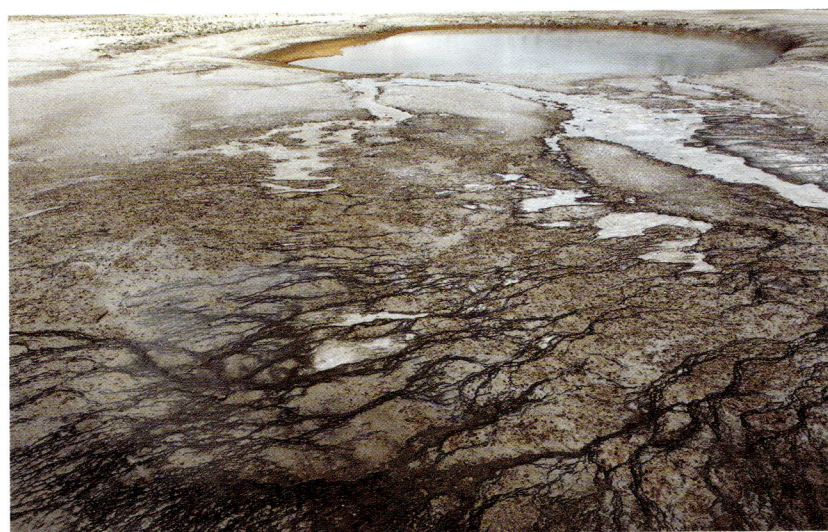

Turquoise Pool

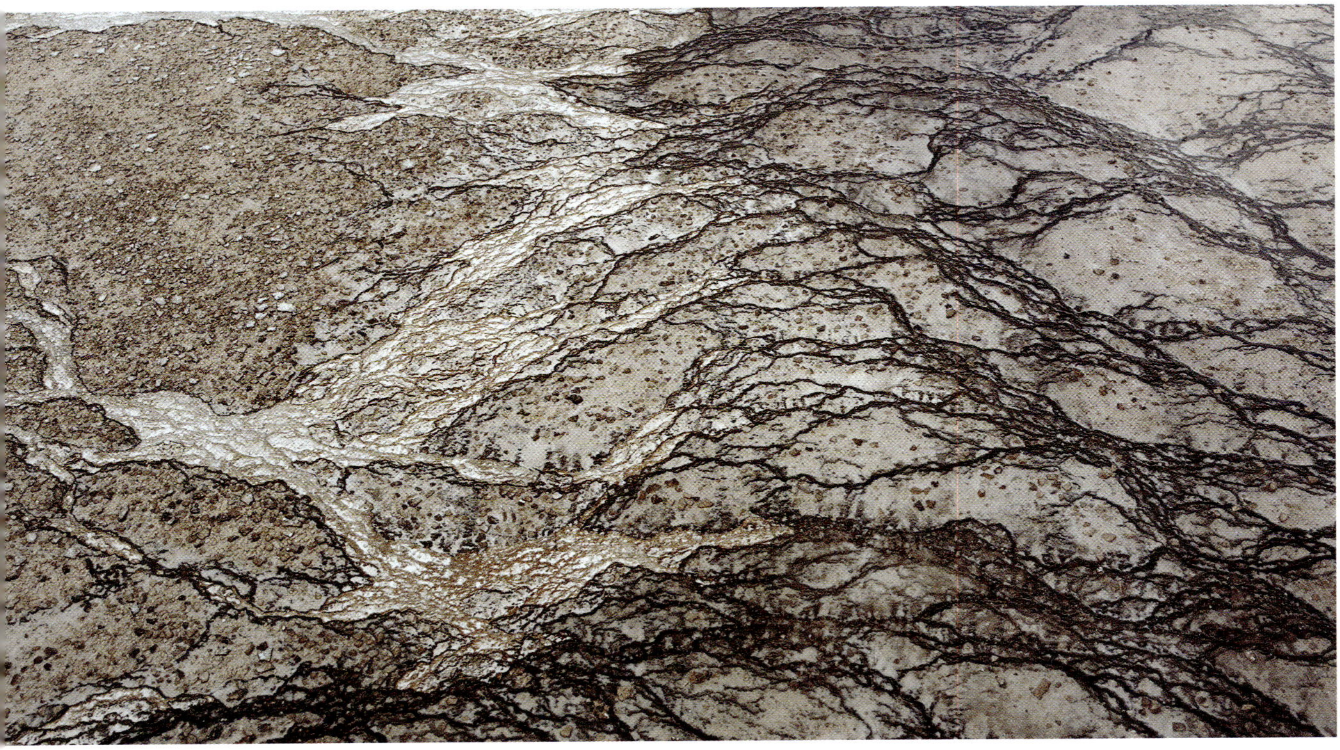

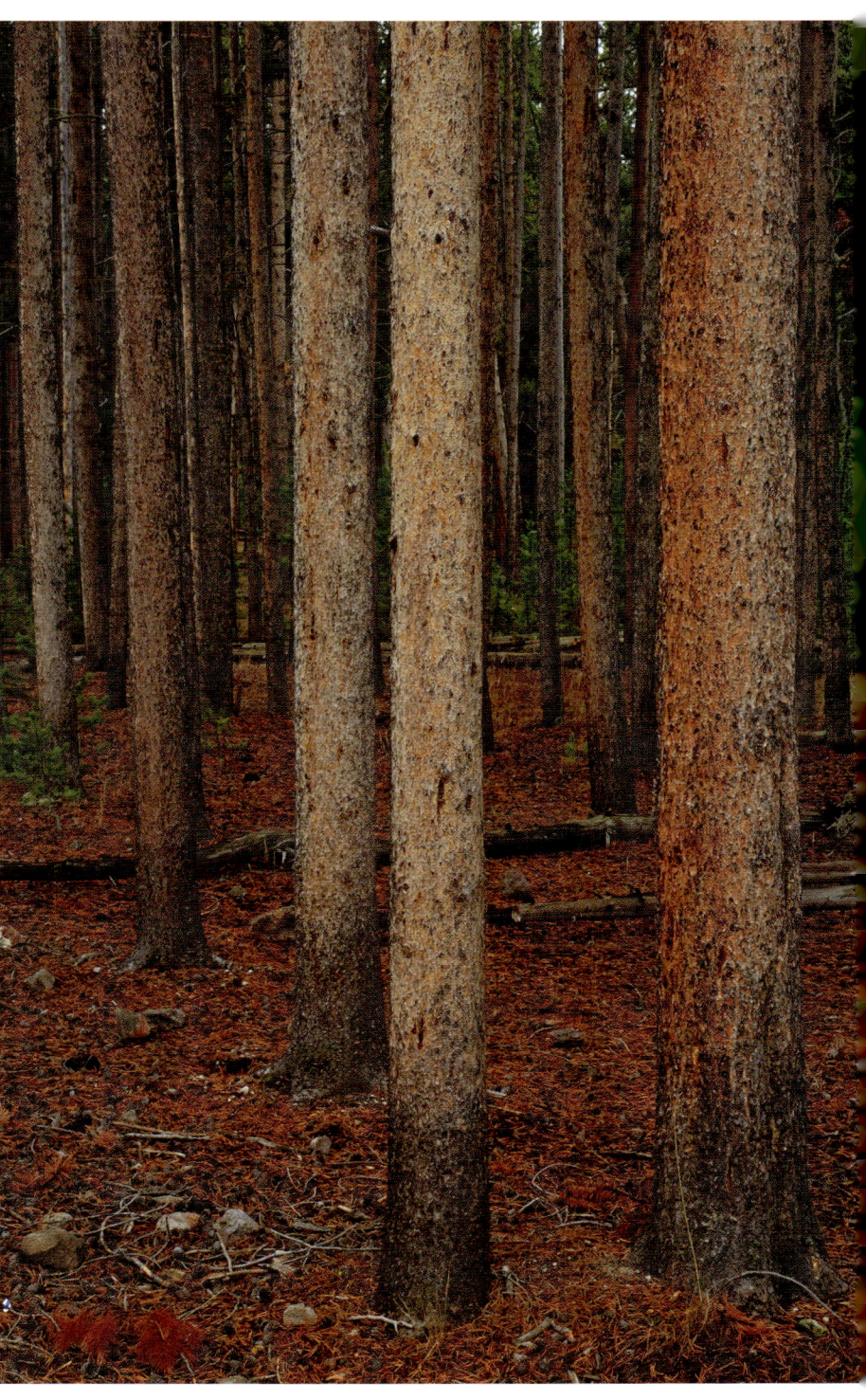

Whiskey Flats picnic area

UPPER GEYSER BASIN

Upper Geyser Basin "is a cleared space of three or four miles, in which there are said to be nearly five hundred springs and geysers, twenty-six of them being unequalled on the surface of the globe for size, splendor, and the tremendous flood of water they send forth."

ALICE WELLINGTON ROLLINS
The Three Tetons, 1887

"We had within a distance of fifty miles seen what we believed to be the greatest wonders on the continent. We were convinced that there was not on the globe another region where within the same limits Nature had crowded so much of grandeur and majesty with so much of novelty and wonder. Judge, then, of our astonishment on entering this basin, to see at no great distance before us an immense body of sparkling water, projected suddenly and with terrific force into the air to the height of over one hundred feet. We had found a real geyser. In the valley before us were a thousand hot springs of various sizes and character, and five hundred craters jetting forth vapor. In one place the eye followed through crevices in the crust a stream of hot water of considerable size, running at nearly right angles with the river, and in a direction, not towards, but away from the stream. We traced the course of this stream by the crevices in the surface for twenty or thirty yards. It is probable that it eventually flows into the Firehole, but there is nothing on the surface to indicate to the beholder the course of its underground passage to the river.

"On the summit of a cone twenty-five feet high was a boiling spring seven feet in diameter, surrounded with beautiful incrustations, on the slope of which we gathered twigs encased in a crust a quarter of an inch in thickness. On an incrusted hill opposite our camp are four craters from three to five feet in diameter, sending forth steam jets and water to the height of four or five feet. But the marvelous features of this wonderful basin are its spouting geysers, of which during our brief stay of twenty-two hours we have seen twelve in action. Six of these threw water to the height of from fifteen to twenty feet, but in the presence of others of immense dimensions they soon ceased to attract attention.

"Of the latter six, the one we saw in action on entering the basin ejected from a crevice of irregular form, and about four feet long by three wide, a column of water of corresponding magnitude to the height of one hundred feet. Around this crevice or mouth the sediment is piled in many capricious shapes, chiefly indented globules from six inches to two feet in diameter. Little hollows in the crust filled with water contained small white spheres of tufa, of the size of a nutmeg, formed as it seemed to me around some nuclei.

"We gave such names to those of the geysers which we saw in action as we think will best illustrate their peculiarities. The one I have just described General Washburn has named Old Faithful, because of the regularity of its eruptions, the intervals between which being from sixty to sixty-five minutes, the column of water being thrown at each eruption to the height of from eighty to one hundred feet.

"The Grotto, so named from the singularly winding apertures penetrating the sinter surrounding it, was at rest when we first discovered it. Externally it presented few indications of its character as a geyser. Private Williamson, one of our escorts, crawled through an aperture and looked into the discharging orifice. When afterwards, he saw it belching forth a column of boiling water two feet in diameter to the height of sixty feet, and a scalding stream of two hundred square inches flowing from the cavern he had entered a short time before, he said that he felt like one who had narrowly escaped being summarily cooked.

"The Castle is on the summit of an incrusted elevation. This name was given because of its resemblance to the ruins of some old tower with its broken down turrets. The silicious sinter composing the formation surrounding it takes the form of small globules, resembling a ripe cauliflower, and the massive nodules indicate that at some former period the flow of water must have been much larger than at present. The jet is sixty feet high by four feet in diameter, and the vent near it, which is in angry ebullition during the eruption, constantly flows with boiling water.

"One of the most wonderful of the springs in this basin is that of ultra-marine hue directly in front of the Castle Geyser. [Crested Pool] It is nearly round, having diameters of about twenty and twenty-five feet, the sides being corrugated and funnel-shaped, and at the depth of thirty feet opening out into a cavern of unfathomable depth, the rim of the spring having beautifully escalloped edges. It does not boil over, but a very small stream of water flows from it, and it is not affected in its appearance by the spouting of the geyser in its immediate proximity. There is evidently no connection between this spring and the geyser.

"The Giant is a rugged deposit presenting in form a miniature model of the Colosseum. It has an opening three feet in diameter. A remarkable characteristic of this geyser is the duration of its discharges, which yesterday afternoon continued for more than an hour in a steady stream about three feet in diameter and one hundred and forty feet high.

"Opposite our camp, on the east side of the Firehole River, is a symmetrical cone resembling an old-fashioned straw beehive with the top cut off. It is about five feet in diameter at its base, with an irregular oval-shaped orifice having escalloped edges, and of twenty-four by thirty-six inches interior diameter. No one supposed that it was a geyser, and until this morning, among so many wonders, it had escaped a second notice. Suddenly, while we were at breakfast this morning, a column of water shot from it, which by quite accurate triangular measurement proved to be two hundred and nineteen feet in height. Our method of triangulation was as follows: A point on the surface of the ground was marked, which was in a direct line with a branch of a tree near by, and of the top of the column of water when at its greatest height. Having obtained the perpendicular height of the branch of the tree from the ground, and the distance from this perpendicular to the point of observation and to the geyser cone, we were enabled to make a very accurate calculation of the height of the column of water. We named this geyser the 'Bee Hive.'"

NATHANIEL PITT LANGFORD
The Discovery of Yellowstone Park: Journal of the Washburn Expedition to the Yellowstone and Firehole Rivers in the Year 1870, 1905

ANEMONE GEYSER

"Most of the spring borders are low and daintily scalloped, crenelated, and beaded with sinter pearls . . .."

JOHN MUIR
"The Yellowstone National Park," *The Atlantic Monthly,* April 1898

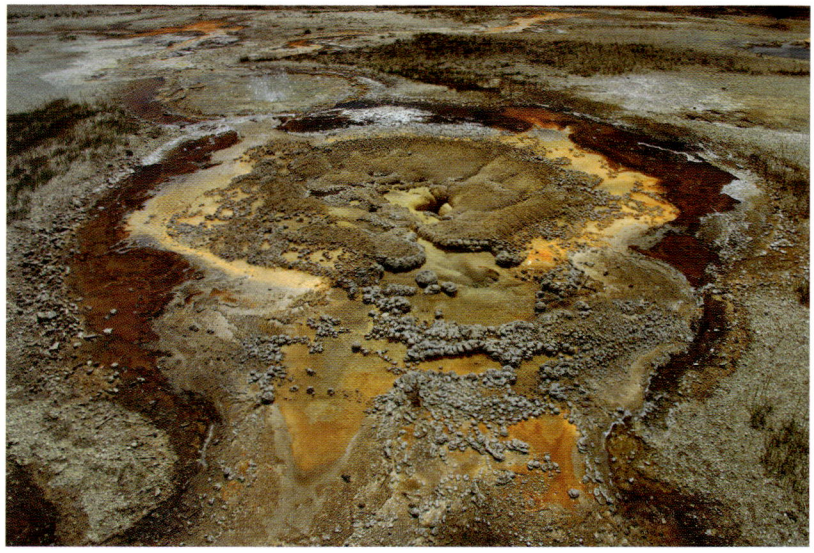

Anemone Geyser

BEEHIVE GEYSER

"The Beehive—named for the shape of its mound—was quite small, but threw its water higher than any other geyser we saw. The stream was less than two feet in diameter, and ascended two hundred and twenty feet, from accurate measurement by triangulation. It remained in action only a few moments."

WALTER TRUMBALL
Overland Monthly, June 1871

"In full action, the Beehive has no superior for beauty of its jet and sharpness of outline."

ARNOLD HAGUE, GEOLOGIST AND ASSISTANT TO WALTER WEED, 1911

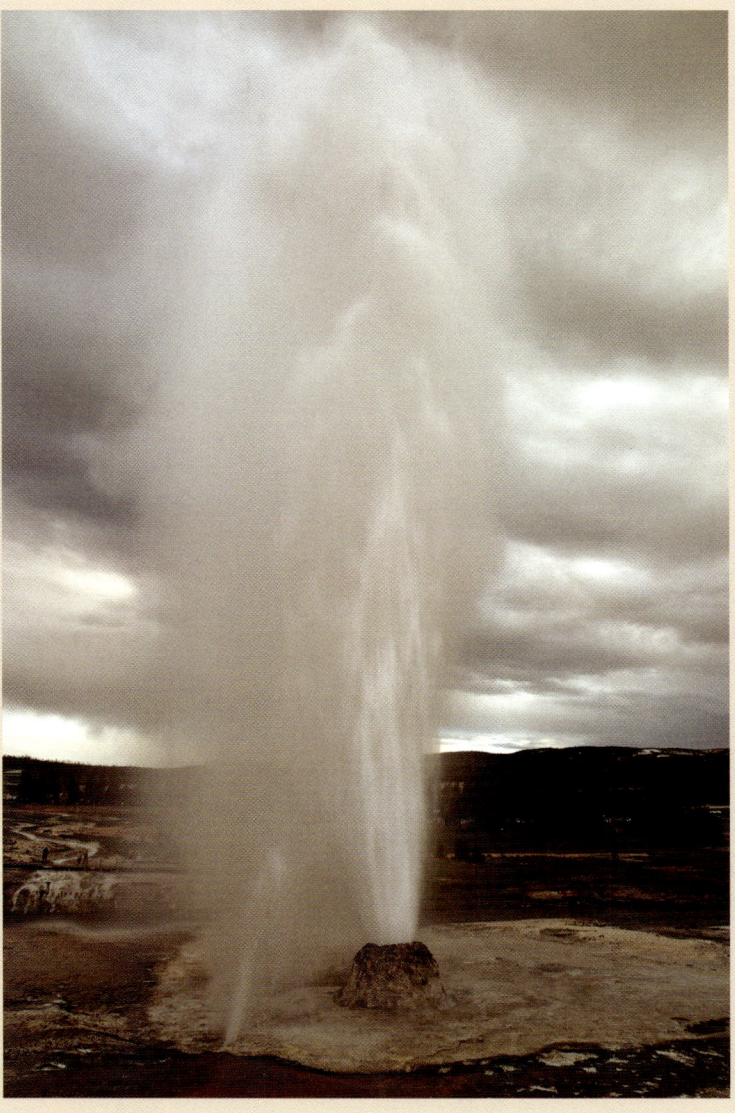

Beehive Geyser

CASTLE GEYSER

"Near the bank of the river, and a half a mile below camp, rose on the farther margin of a marshy lake the Castle Crater, the largest formation in the valley. The calcareous knoll on which it stands is forty feet in height, and covers several acres. The crater is built up from its center, with irregular walls of spherical nodules, in forms of wondrous beauty, to a castellated turret, forty feet in height and two hundred feet in circumference at the base. The outer rim, at its summit, is formed in embrasures between large nodules of rock, of the tint of ashes of roses, and in the center is a crater three feet in diameter, bordered and lined with a frostwork of saffron. From a distance it strongly resembles an old feudal tower partially in ruins. This great crater is continually pouring forth steam, the condensation of which keeps the outside walls constantly wet and dripping. The deposit is silver-gray in color, and the structure is wonderful in its massiveness, completion, and exquisite tracery of outline."

LIEUTENANT GUSTAVUS C. DOANE
Yellowstone Expedition of 1870

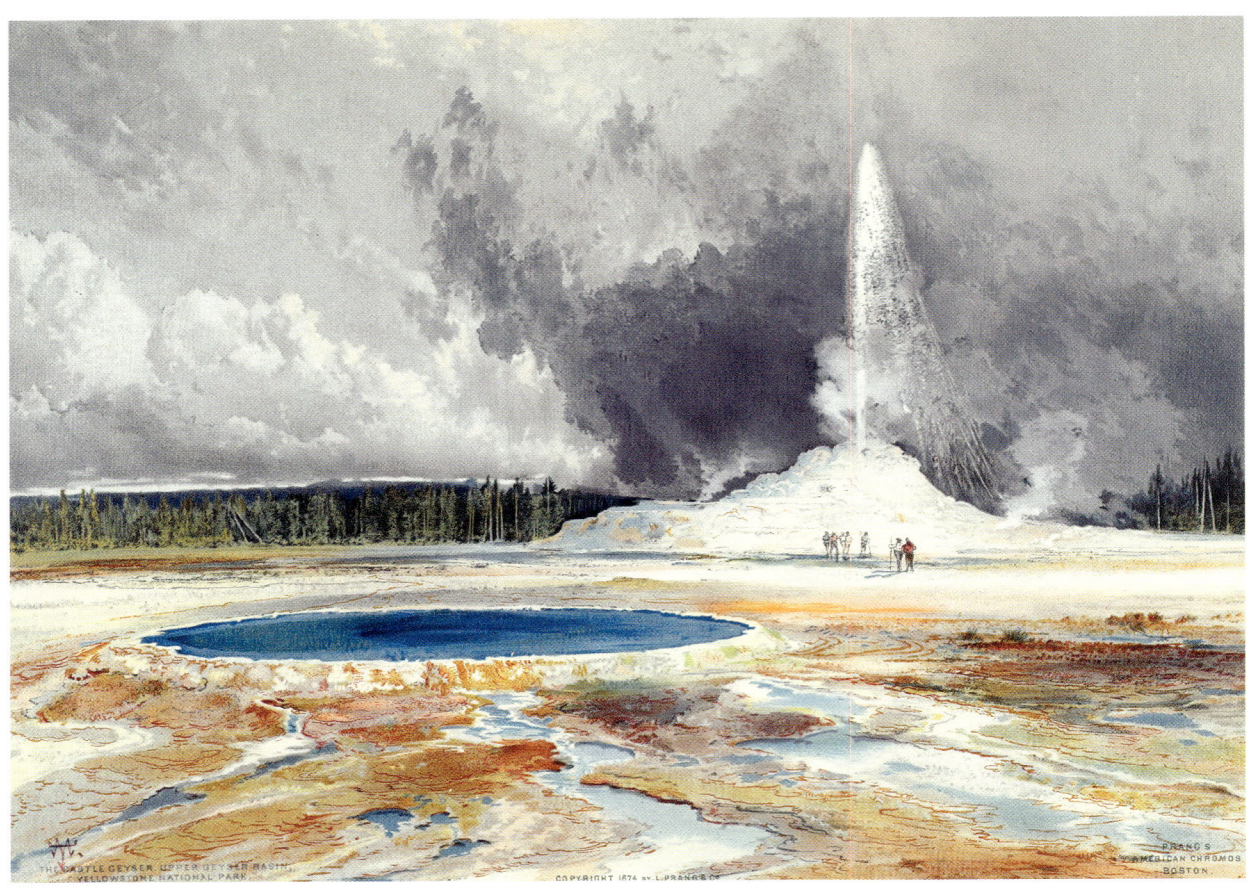

"About the crater of The Castle was the largest cone, or mass of incrustations, in the basin. For a hundred yards around, the ground, flooded with subsilica, of glittering whiteness, sloped gradually up to the cone, which itself rose thirty feet, nearly perpendicular. It was quite rugged and efflorescent, and on its outer sides had a number of benches. . . . We called it The Castle, on account of its size and commanding appearance. It was in action a short time on the morning after our arrival, but only threw water about thirty feet high. The water did not retain the shape of a column, like that thrown out by Old Faithful, but rather splashed up and slopped over. This geyser did not appear to be doing its best, but only spouted a little in a patronizing way, thinking to surprise us novices sufficiently without any undue exertion on its part."

WALTER TRUMBALL
Overland Monthly, June 1871

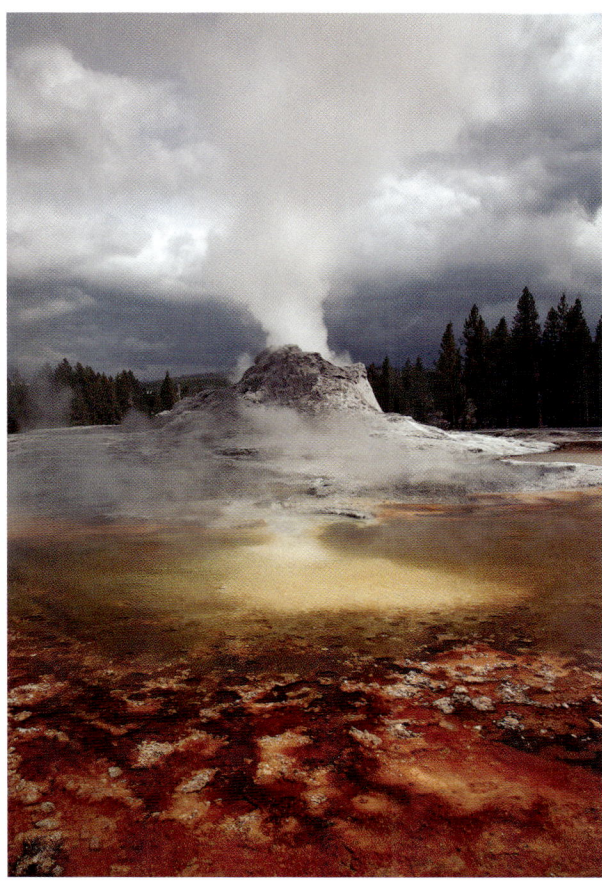

<
The Castle Geyser, Upper Geyser
Basin, Yellowstone National Park
Thomas Moran, 1874
Gilcrease Museum, Tulsa, OK
2426.47.3

Castle Geyser

CHROMATIC AND BEAUTY POOLS

Chromatic Pool and neighboring Beauty Pool share a heating system. Their colors change as water temperature varies, shifting from blue, green, yellow, and orange with hotter water to dark rusty red and brown when the water temperature falls.

1. Blue and clear waters are extremely hot and at times may exceed the boiling point (199 degrees F [93 degrees C] at this elevation.) Archaea

2. 163 degrees F (73 degrees C) or lower Cyanobacteria

3. 144 degrees F (62 degrees C) or lower Fungi

4. 140 degrees F (60 degrees C) or lower Algae

5. 133 degrees F (56 degrees C) or lower Protozoa

6. 122 degrees F (50 degrees C) or lower Mosses, crustaceans, and insects

7. 80 degrees F (27 degrees C) or lower Trout

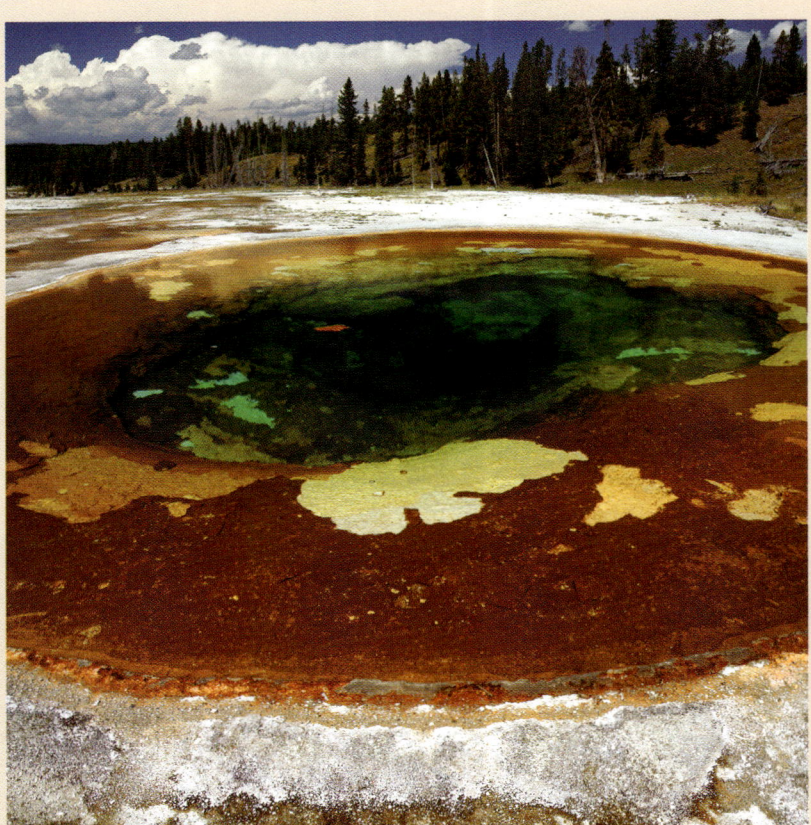

Beauty Pool

>

Chromatic Pool

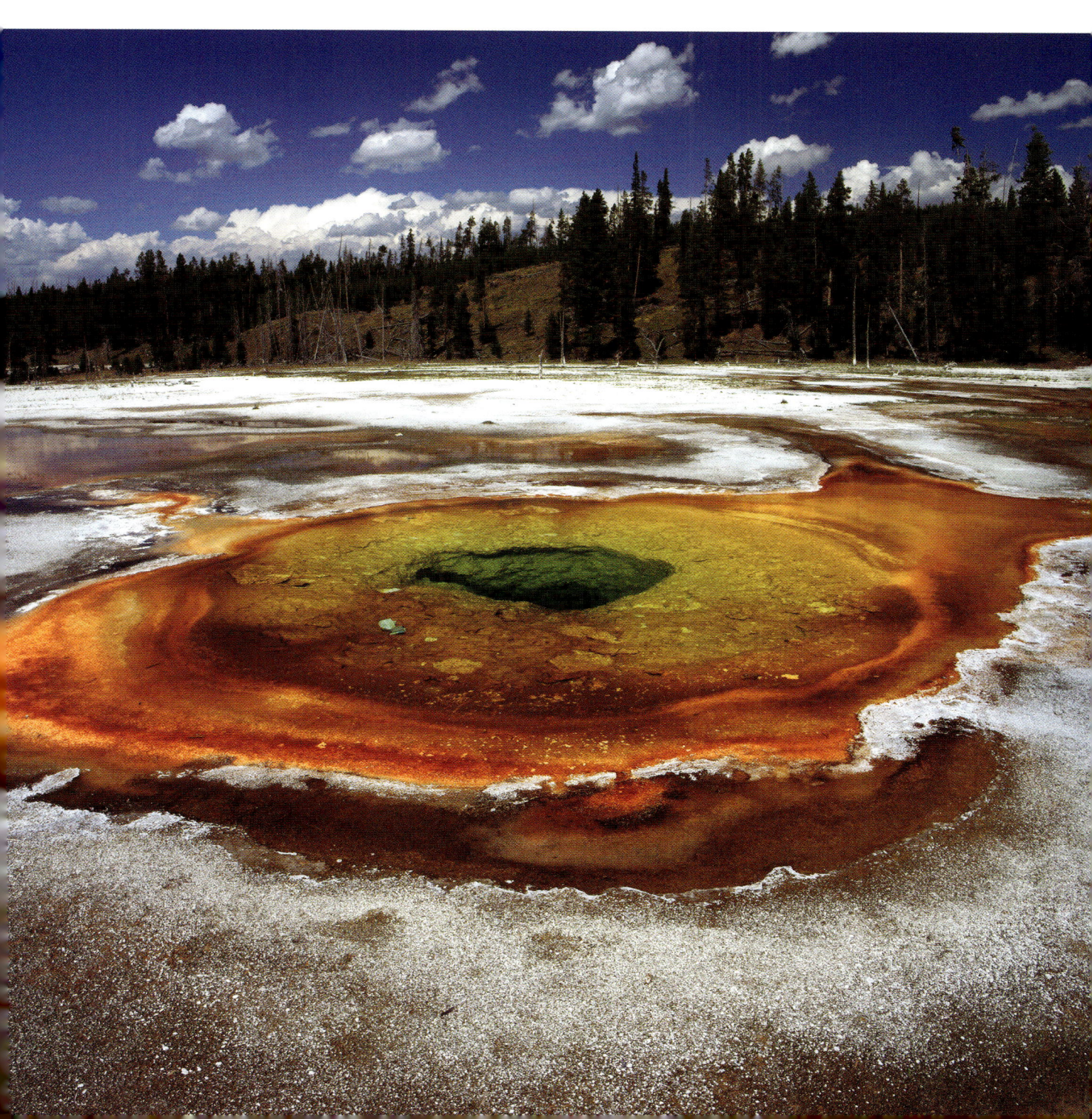

CRESTED POOL

Crested Pool is "a beautiful spring, transparent and of a lovely blue, its walls lined with dazzling white."

GEORGE WOOD WINGATE
Through the Yellowstone Park on Horseback, 1886

"Upon the same mound, a few steps from the Castle, is one of those calm, lovely prismatic springs, the most beautiful in the whole geyser region. For delicacy of coloring and beauty of ornamentation it surpasses any we visited. It is more quiet than others, yet its surface is gently rippled by constant vibrations. The handsomely-scalloped rim rises seven or eight inches above the water, describes a complete circle of about sixty feet, and inside is festooned and embroidered in many a fantastic design. The water is unnaturally transparent, and one can look an unknown depth into its fairy regions, discovering caves, bowers, castles, and grottoes, painted in every color of brightest rainbow, and magically carved. . . . It seems as if our eyes would never cease feasting upon its unearthly beauty; there was an intense longing to know what mysterious treasures lie hidden deep down in its tranquil bosom; and as we regretfully, unsatisfiedly retired to rest, we wondered who would care if we explored its deepest recesses—to return to earth never again."

HARRY J. NORTON
Wonderland Illustrated, 1873

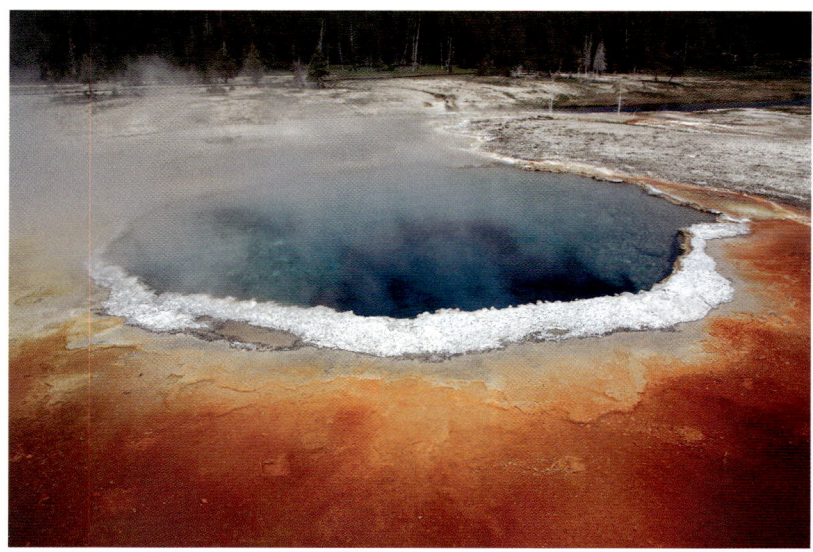

Crested Pool

"A few hundred yards farther down the stream is a crater of flinty rock, in shape resembling a huge shattered horn, broken off half way from its base. It is twelve feet in height, with a solid base; its sides have a curvilinear slope, tagged edges, and its cavity or nozzle is seven feet in diameter. During its quiescent state the boiling water can be seen in its chambers at a depth of forty feet, the action of the steam and water together producing a loud rumbling sound. Near and acting in concert with it are half a dozen smaller craters from two to eight feet in height constantly full of water, and boiling violently from two to six feet into the air. This great geyser played several times while we were in the valley, on one occasion throwing constantly for over three hours a stream of water seven feet in diameter from ninety to two hundred feet perpendicularly. While playing it doubled the size of the Firehole River, running at its maximum about twenty-five hundred inches of water."

LIEUTENANT GUSTAVUS C. DOANE
Yellowstone Expedition of 1870

"We rounded and limped over a low spur of hill, and came out upon a field of aching, snowy lime rolled in sheets, twisted into knots, riven with rents, and diamonds, and stars, stretching for more than half a mile in every direction.

"On this place of despair lay most of the big, bad geysers who know when there is trouble in Krakatoa, who tell the pines when there is a cyclone on the Atlantic seaboard, and who are exhibited to visitors under pretty and fanciful names.

"The first mound that I encountered belonged to a goblin who was splashing in his tub.

"I heard him kick, pull a shower-bath on his shoulders, gasp, crack his joints, and rub himself down with a towel; then he let the water out of the bath, as a thoughtful man should, and it all sunk down out of sight till another goblin arrived.

"You will understand that these foolish stories are introduced in order to cover the fact that this pen cannot describe the glories of the Upper Geyser Basin."

RUDYARD KIPLING
American Notes, 1891

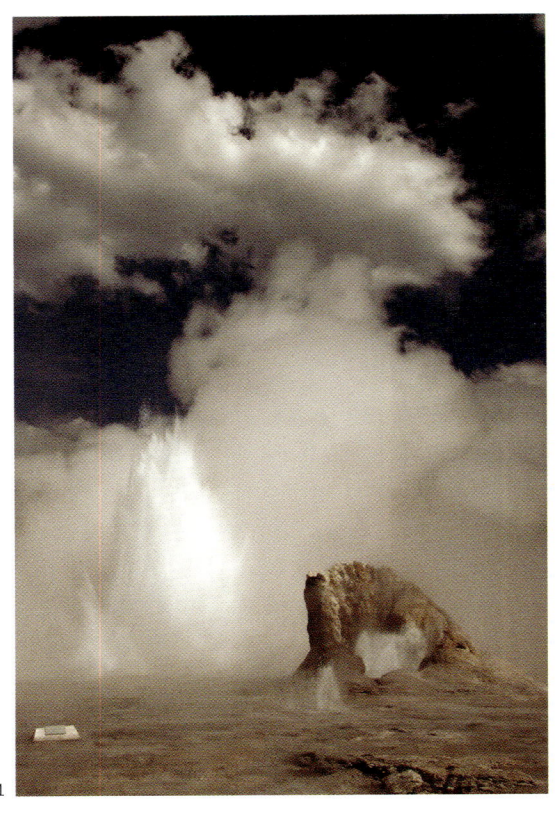

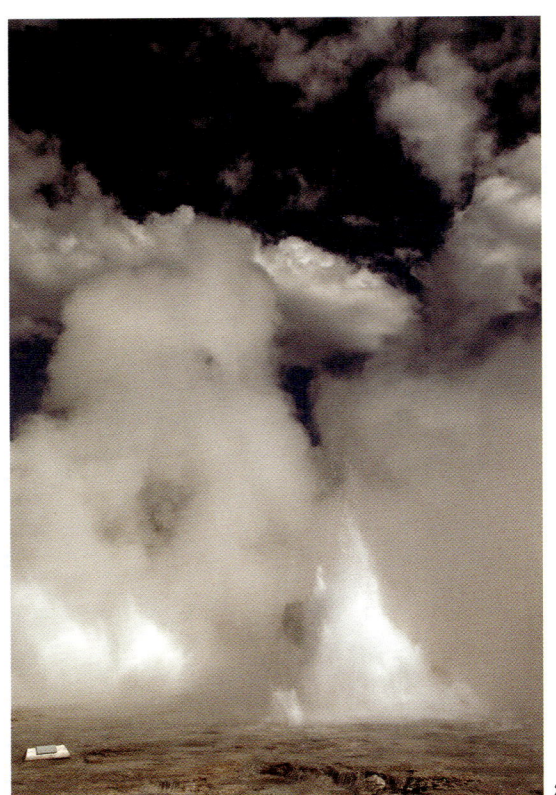

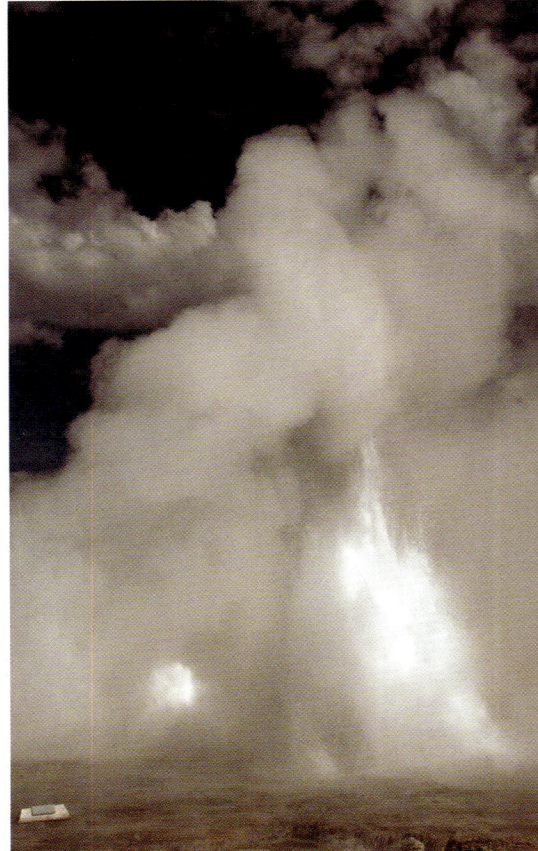

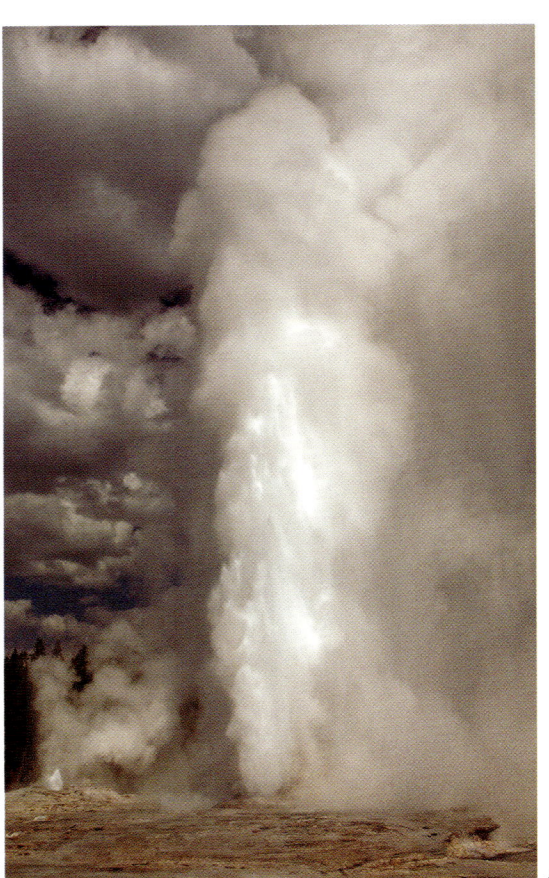

1

2

3

4

"The mound around The Giant was about twelve feet high, and had a piece knocked out of one side of [its] crater, which was shaped like a hollow cylinder, and six feet in diameter. The Giant discharged a column of water, of the same size as its crater, to a height of a hundred feet. It played as if through an immense hose. We thought it deserved to be called The Giant, as it threw out more water than any other geyser which we saw in operation."

WALTER TRUMBALL
Overland Monthly, June 1871

A rare eruption of Giant Geyser on September 8, 2007

1.
3:36:12 pm—In front of Giant's cone, Feather and Feather Satellite geysers are erupting. Their presence indicates that a Giant hot period is in progress. Behind and to the left of Giant's cone, Mastiff Geyser is in eruption, which almost always indicates that Giant will erupt also. Water is rising in Giant's cone; an eruption is imminent.

2.
3:38:01 pm—Water is surging over the top of Giant's cone and spilling out onto the platform. Giant is now erupting.

3.
3:38:04 pm—Giant is starting to build height. Though lower, Mastiff is still erupting.

4.
3:40:25 pm—Giant is on its way! Mastiff is tapering off.

5.
3:41:28—In the initial phase, an eruption can reach a height of more than 220 feet and may last as long as an hour and a half. However, Giant does not maintain its maximum height for the entire time. Mastiff is steaming; its eruption has ended.

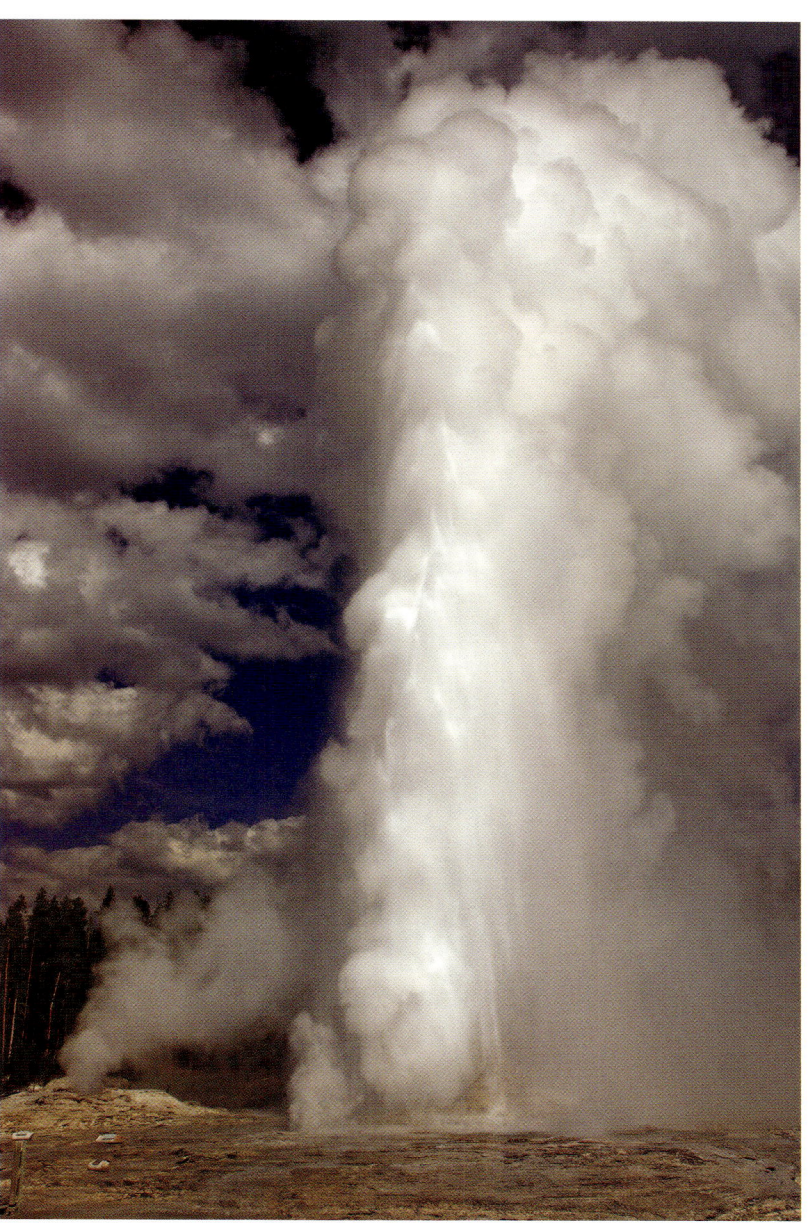

5

"We remained in camp. . .to see the eruption of as many of the great geysers as possible, particularly the Grand. This was on the side of the river opposite our camp and close to the hillside. Near it is a small geyser called the Turban. When this fills up and begins to work actively it is an indication that the Grand is getting ready for business. It was now pounding away and the Grand was overdue.

"The geysers in this basin (except the Grand) differ from the others we had seen in having regular craters, or cones, composed of rough rock, of varied shapes and rising from three to twenty feet above the ground. The Turban, however, is an exception, its crater being sunk, so that if a man stood in it, his head would be below the surface of the ground . . . .

"Night came without the expected eruption of the Grand having occurred, and as we were obliged to leave in the morning, we went to bed

Grand Geyser draws a crowd.

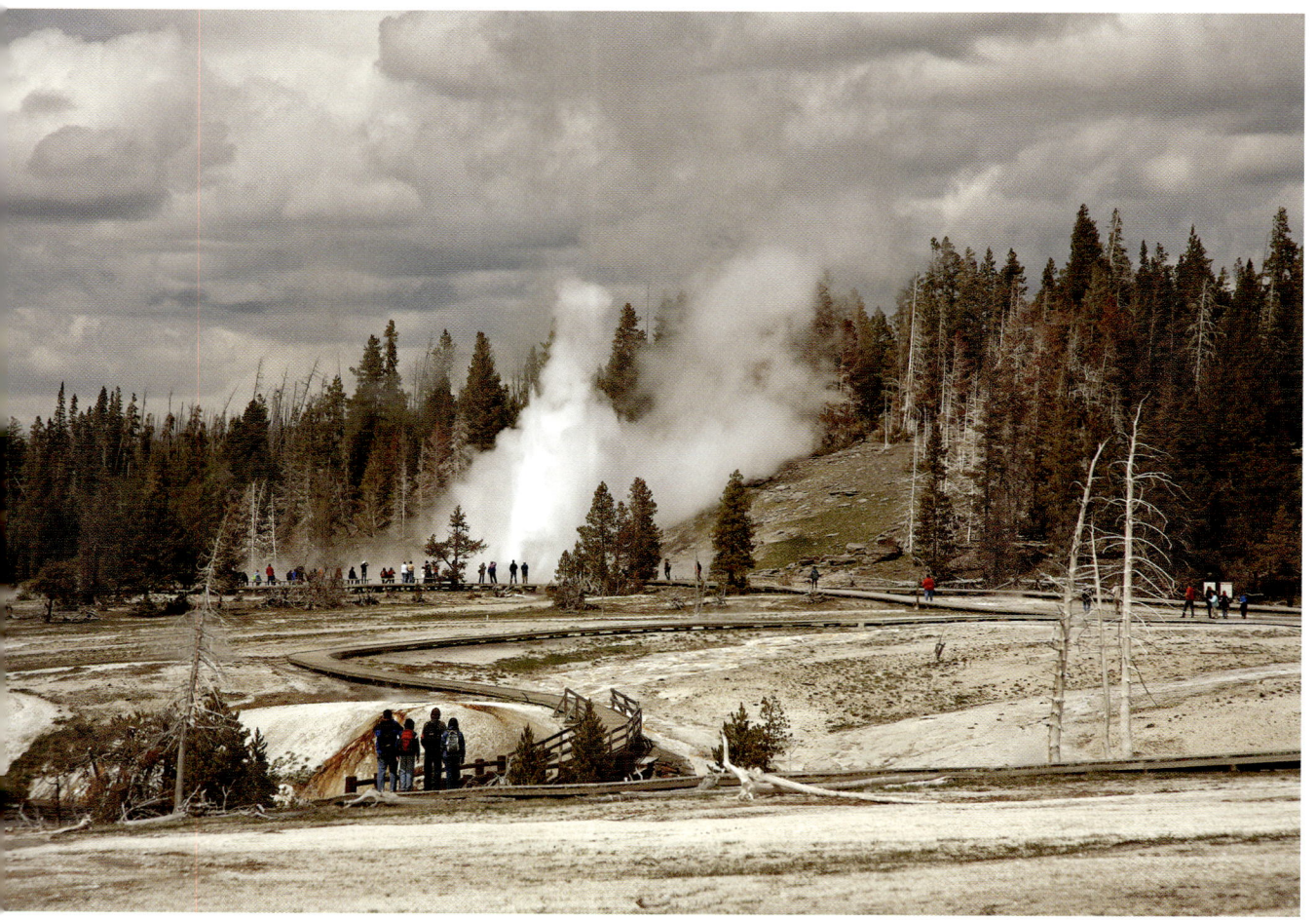

disappointed. Just at daybreak the cry went through the camp, 'Turn out, turn out, the Grand is going.' Then there was indeed a scurry from our camp and from one or two adjoining. Everybody scrambled to their feet, struggled into the first available garments and ran down the bank of the river, across the little foot-bridge and up the slope beyond at the top of their speed, buttoning as they ran and all filled with great excitement, for the Grand was at last in full operation.

"Some were wrapped in blankets, others in shawls, or overcoats, some were in their shirt-sleeves and several hatless. But everything was forgotten in the magnificent sight before us.

"Although the geyser tube of the Grand is small, not over four feet in diameter, its eruption seemed to spread so as take in the whole diameter of the pool, making a column fully fifteen feet in diameter. This enormous mass of water, far larger than we had yet seen, shot straight upward to the height of two hundred and thirty feet (or more than two-thirds the height of Trinity Church steeple) accompanied with tremendous billowy clouds of steam which mounted to double that height, and which, as they were condensed into spray fell all around in a drizzling rain. The rumbling and roaring of the escaping steam and water were terrific. The column seemed to maintain its height by a series of jets, which appeared to be constantly forced up through the central mass. After spouting with great vigor for some five or six minutes, it faltered and subsided. But the water had scarcely attained its original level when it was thrown upward to its previous height with even greater fury and volume than before. We counted seven distinct eruptions, occupying altogether over half an hour. While they were going on, the Turban was also in full operation, sometimes throwing the water it ejected into the basin of the Grand.

"Finally, the water in both geysers sank out of sight in their tubes with a loud gurgle, leaving them perfectly empty and so hot that their rocky interior dried instantly.

"While we were watching this sublime and awe-inspiring sight, and which in itself was sufficient reward for our whole journey, the wind veered several times. We lost no time in shifting our positions to conform to its direction, for the fall of the water to leeward would have swept a person away like a feather, besides scalding him to death.

"Not until the display was over, did we become for the first time aware of our motley apparel; and then all had a good laugh over each other's ludicrous appearance."

GEORGE WOOD WINGATE
Through the Yellowstone Park on Horseback, 1886

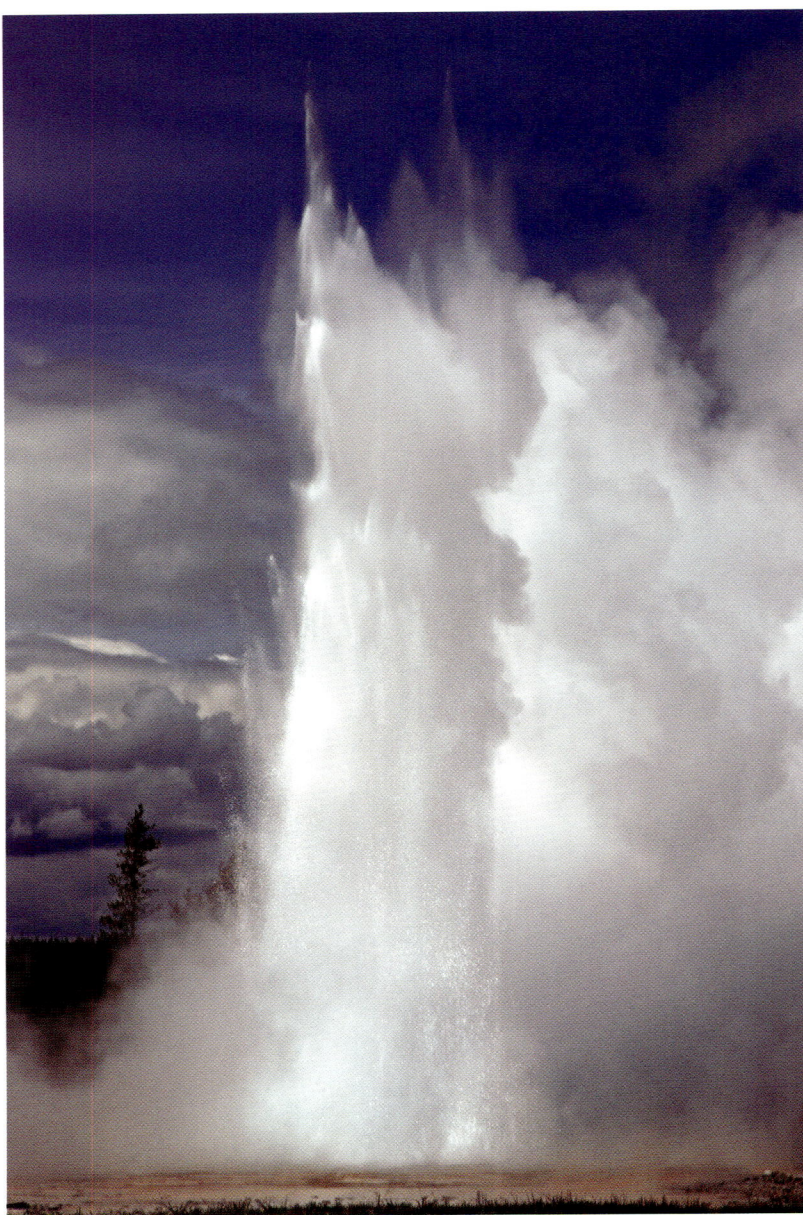

Grand Geyser

>

Grand Geyser mud

"Opposite camp, on the other side of the river, is a high ledge of stalagmite, sloping from the base of the mountain down to the river; numerous small knolls are scattered over its surface. The craters of boiling springs from fifteen to twenty-five feet in diameter; some of these throw water the height of three and four feet. In the summit of this bank of rock is the grand geyser of the world, a well in the strata twenty by twenty-five feet in diametric measurements, the perceptible elevation of the rim being but a few inches, and when quiet having a visible depth of one hundred feet. The edge of the basin is bounded by a heavy fringe of rock, and stalagmite

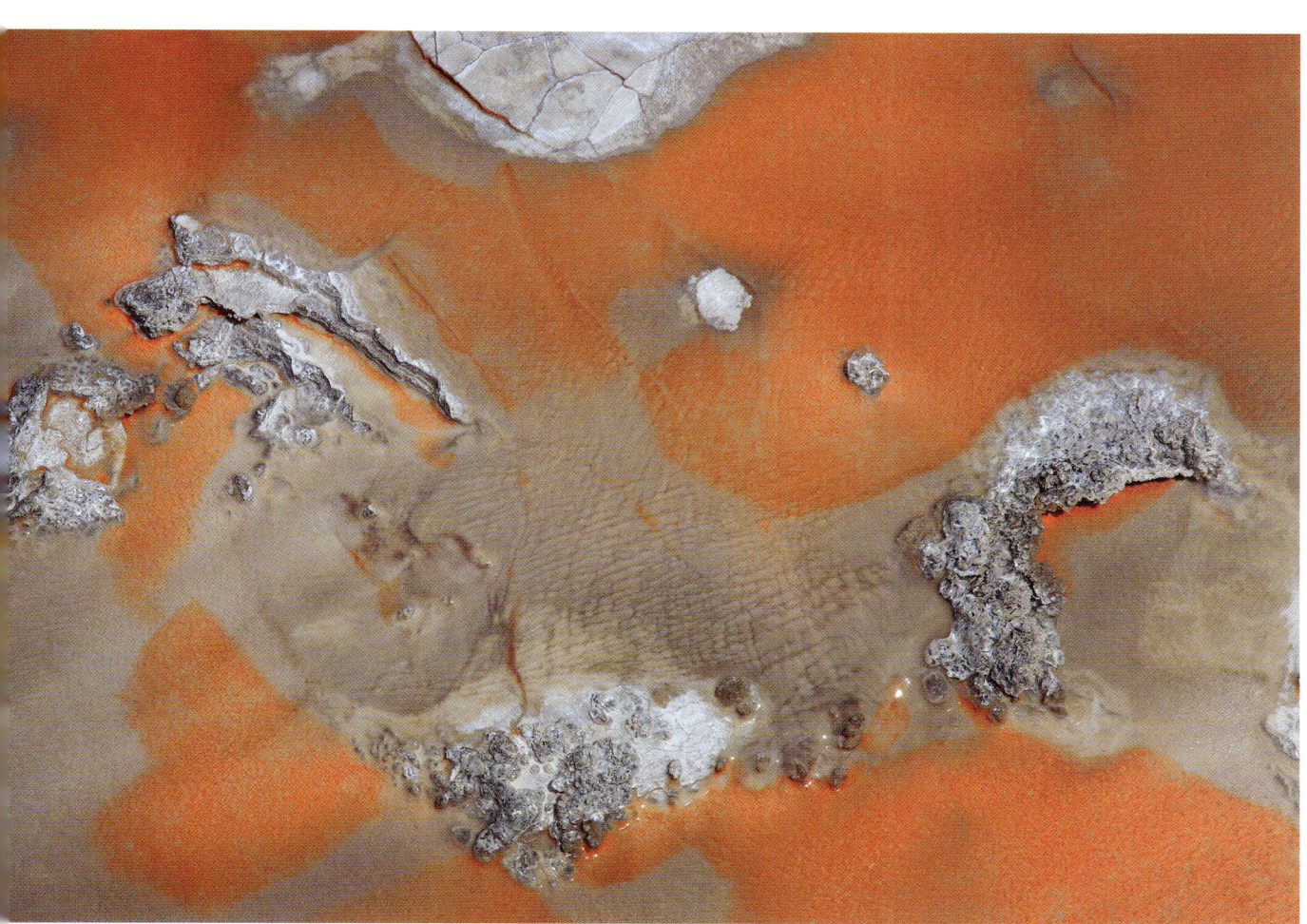

in solid layers is deposited by the overflowing waters. When an eruption is about to occur the basin suddenly fills with boiling water to within a few feet of the surface, then suddenly, with heavy concussions, immense clouds of steam rise to the height of five hundred feet. The whole great body of water, twenty by twenty-five feet, ascends in one gigantic column to the height of ninety feet, and from its apex five great jets shoot up, radiating slightly from each other, to the unparalleled altitude of two hundred fifty feet from the ground. The earth trembles under the descending deluge from this vast fountain, a thousand hissing sounds are heard in the air; rainbows encircle the summits of the jets with a halo of celestial glory. The falling water plows up and bears away the shelly strata, a seething flood pours down the slope and into the river. It is the grandest, the most majestic, and the most terrible fountain in the world."

LIEUTENANT GUSTAVUS C. DOANE
Yellowstone Expedition of 1870

>

Grotto Geyser

The Grotto Geyser; Firehole Basin
Thomas Moran, 1872
Gilcrease Museum, Tulsa, OK
0226.1359

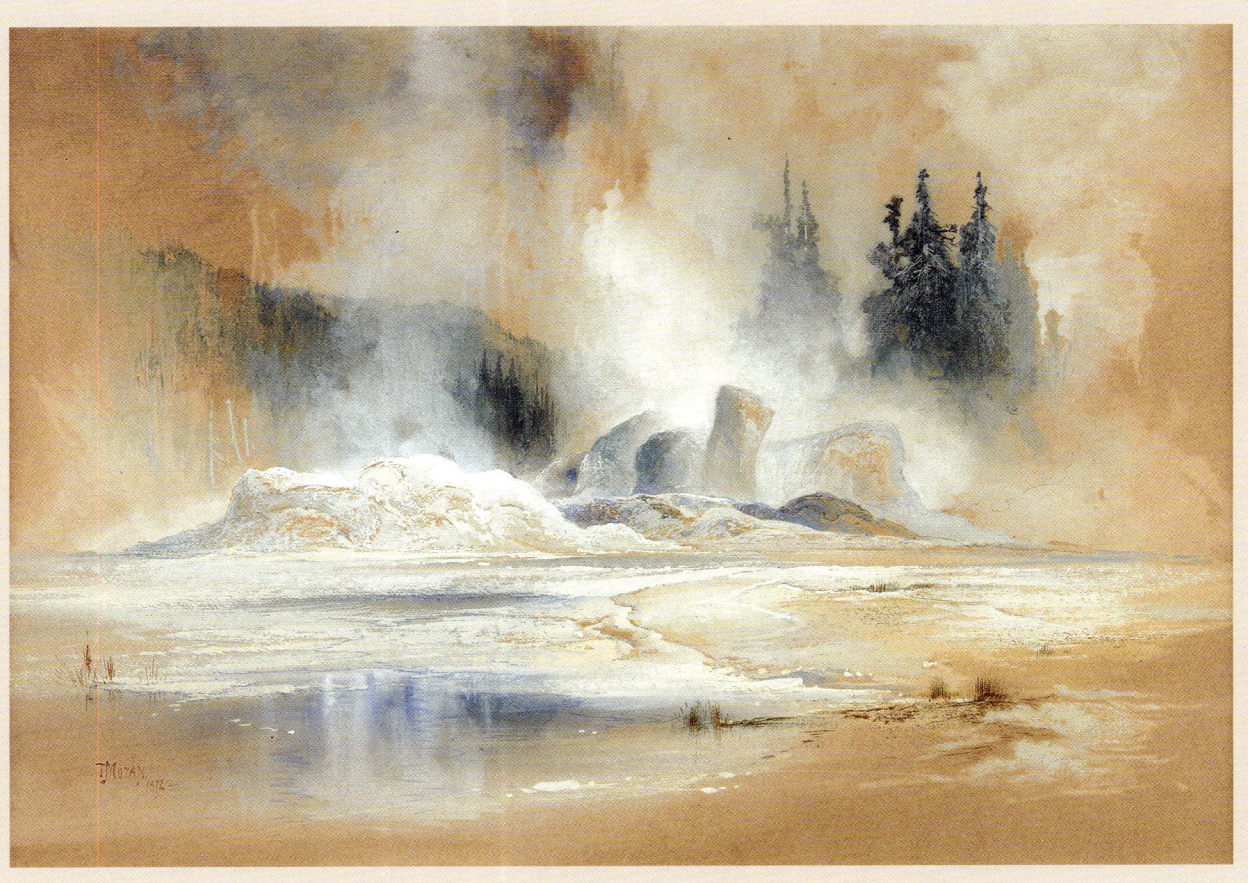

"A beautiful arched spray, called by us the Grotto, with several apertures
... each making so many vents for the water and steam."

GENERAL HENRY D. WASHBURN
Explorations in a New and Wonderful Country, 1870

"fantastic arches crusted with opals and lined with mother-of-pearl"

ALICE WELLINGTON ROLLINS
The Three Tetons, 1887

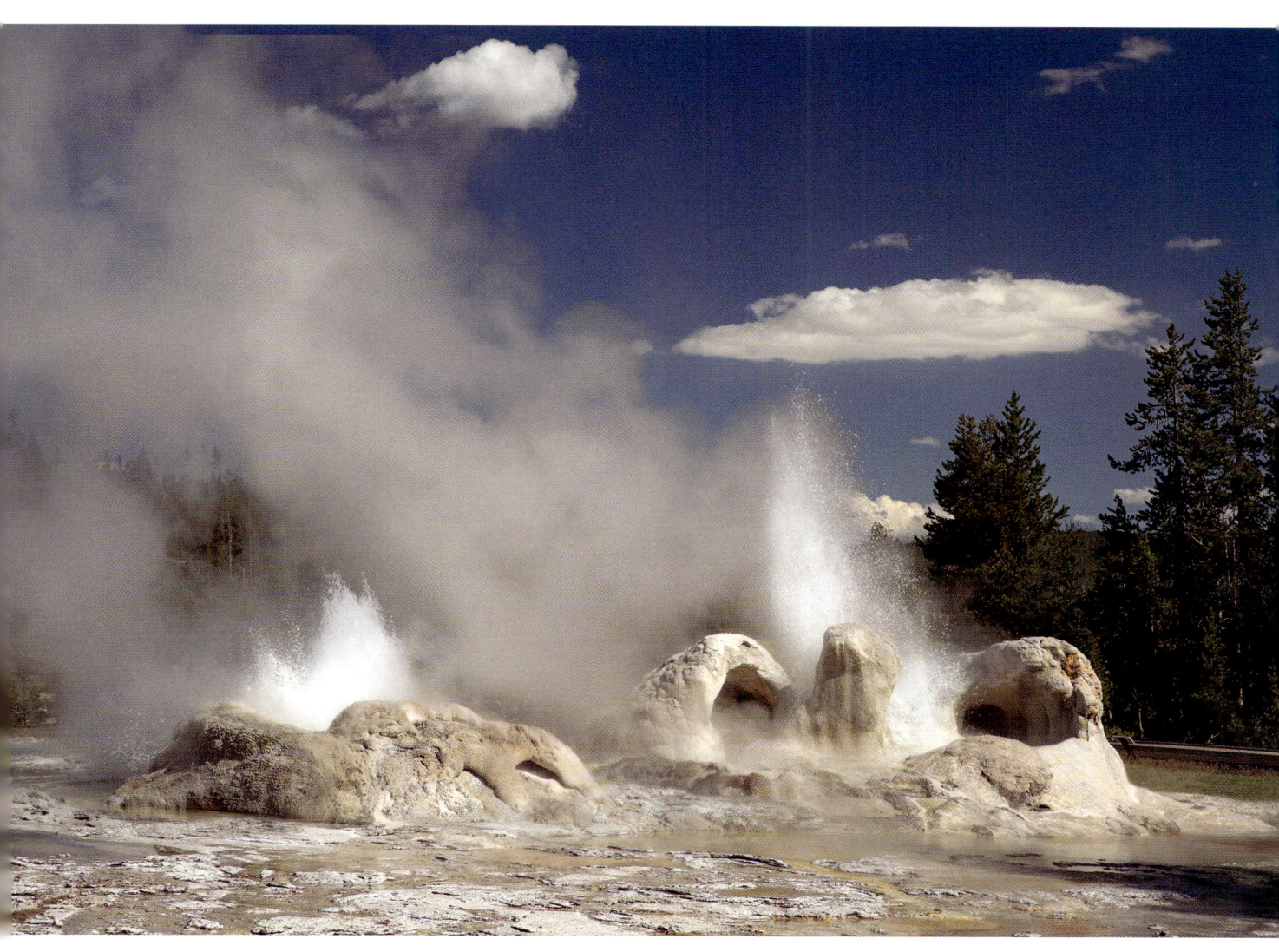

"The clump of geysers known as the Lion and Lioness and Cubs are close together and derive their name from the growling noise which they emit even when not in a state of eruption."

GEORGE WOOD WINGATE
Through the Yellowstone Park on Horseback, 1886

"We drifted on, up that miraculous valley. On either side of us were hills from a thousand or fifteen hundred feet high, wooded from crest to heel. As far as the eye could range forward were columns of steam in the air, misshapen lumps of lime, mist-like preadamite monsters, still pools of turquoise-blue, stretches of blue corn-flowers, a river that coiled on itself twenty times, pointed bowlders of strange colors, and ridges of glaring, staring white."

RUDYARD KIPLING
American Notes, 1891

Lion Geyser and Heart Spring

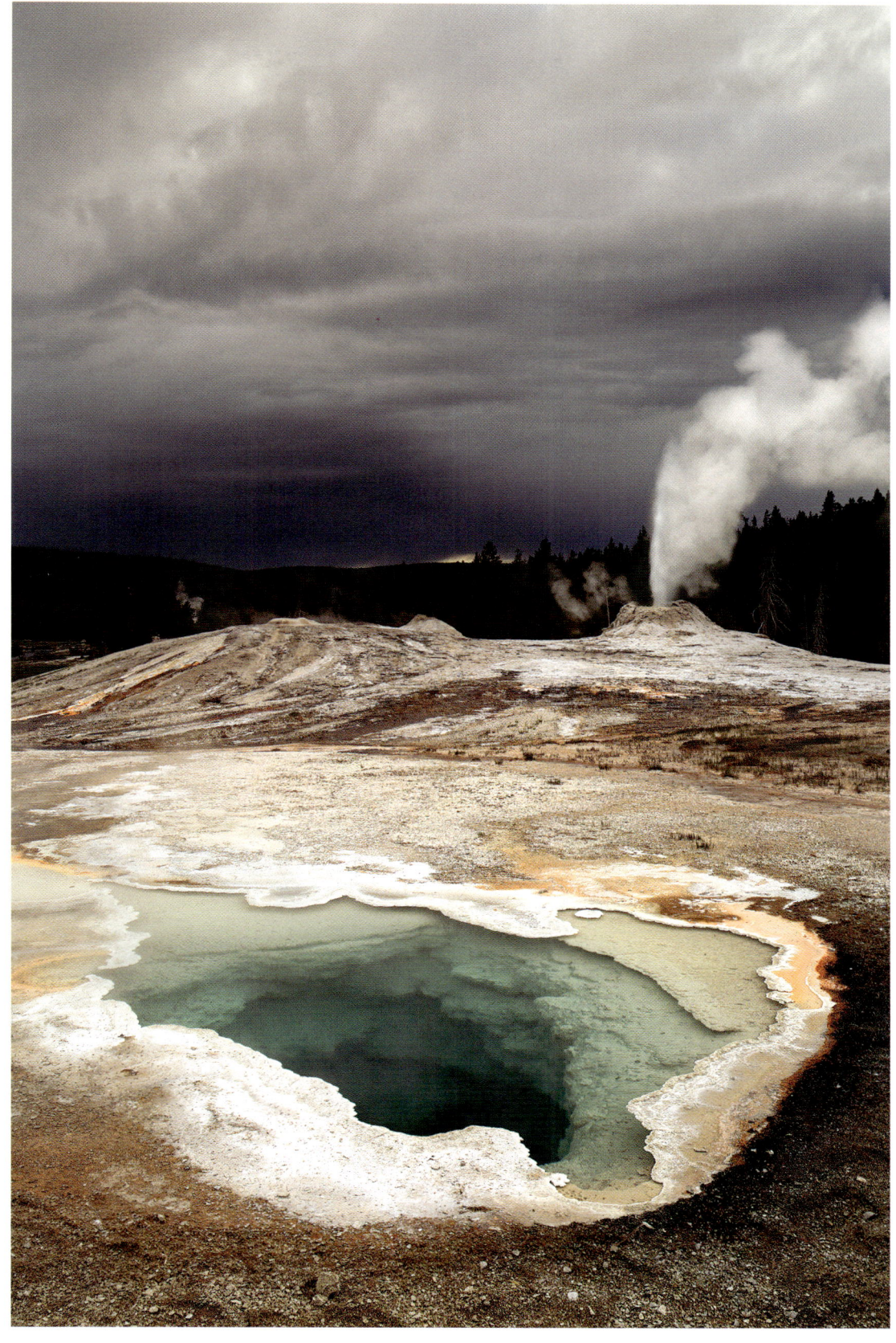

Morning Glory Pool "is exquisitely named; for it is precisely like a morning-glory flower. Its long and slender throat, like the tube of the blossom, reaching from unknown depth below, branches out in ever-widening snowy walls forming at last a perfectly symmetrical and exquisite chalice, which is filled with water of the loveliest, clearest, robin's-egg blue. The rim of the chalice is delicately and regularly scalloped, like the flower, and is edged with a tiny line of hard coral from the deposit."

ALICE WELLINGTON ROLLINS
The Three Tetons, 1887

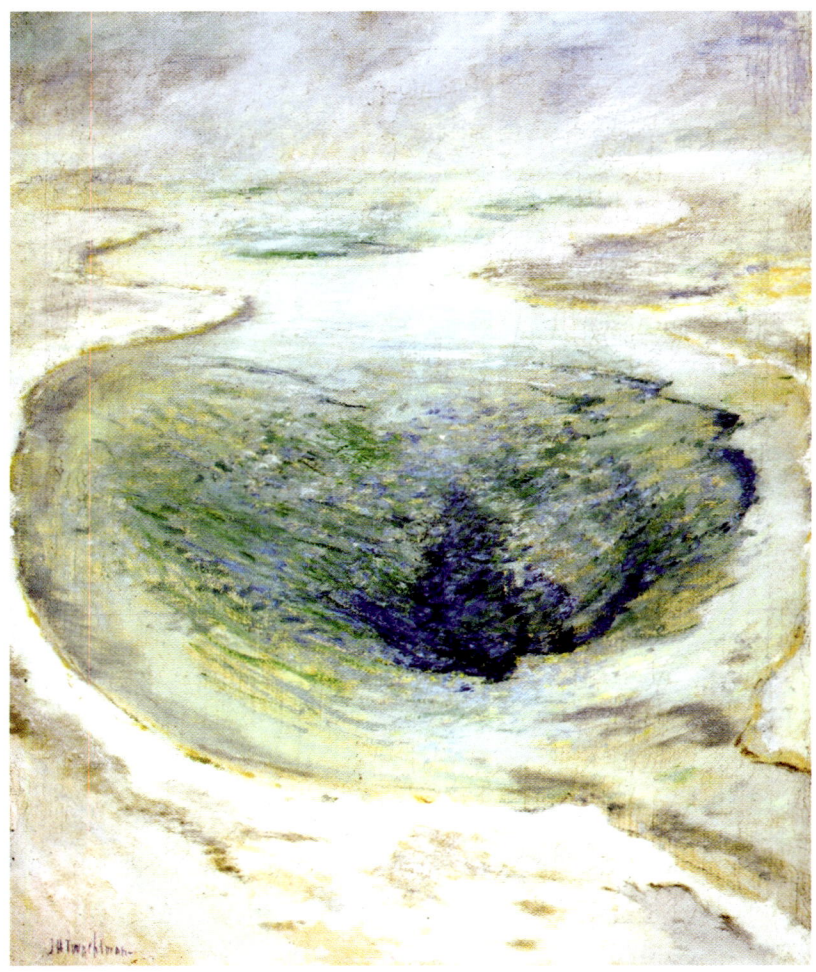

Morning Glory Pool, Yellowstone
John Henry Twachtman, 1895
private collection

>

Morning Glory Pool

"a cerulean jewel set in the earth"

MODE WINEMAN, AUTHOR

"a diaphanous cupful of limpid sky"

CHARLES WARREN STODDARD, AUTHOR

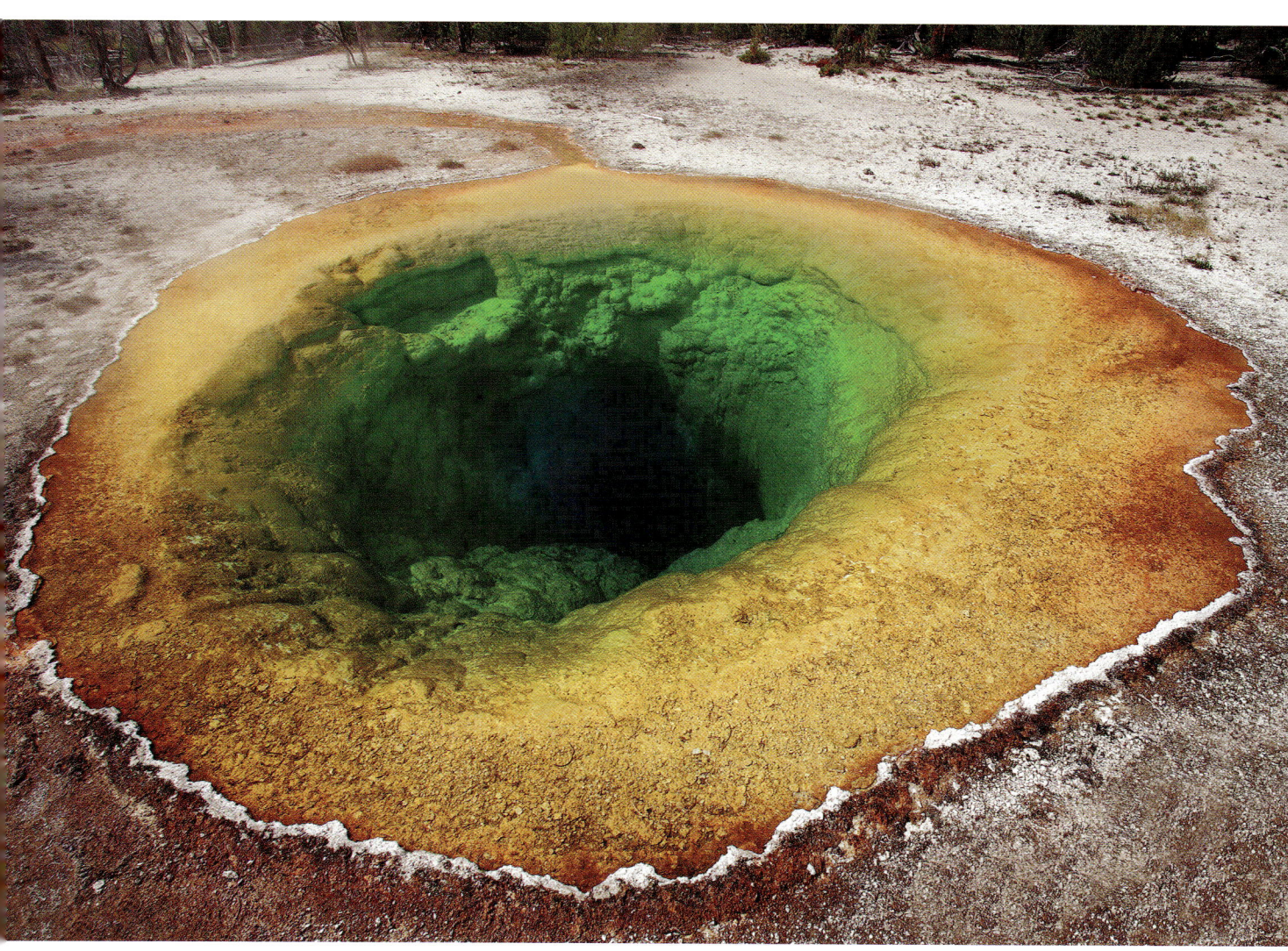

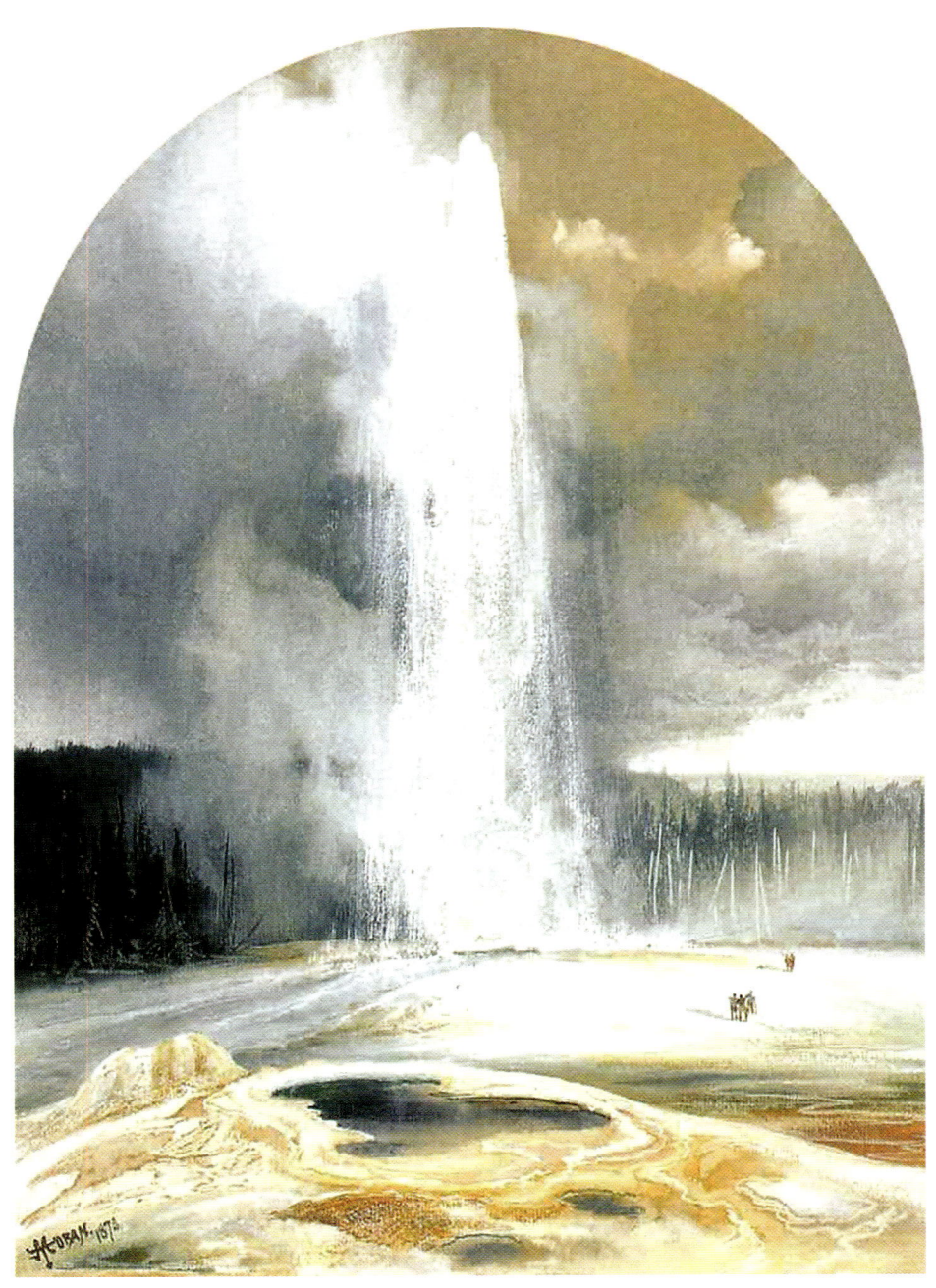

"While the tents were being pitched and the horses picketed, we walked down to Old Faithful, which was then nearly due.

"A gentle ascent, broken into low steps or terraces over which little streams of water were meandering and forming shallow pools here and there, is crowned with an irregular mass of rock some six feet high and twenty feet in diameter, in the center of which is a hole the size of a hogshead. All around is barren rock of a whitish gray and rough, like a nutmeg grater. The little pools formed in it by the geyser water are of brilliant colors and full of beautiful formations like frostwork. As a friend of mine said, 'they were like an emerald-tinted stream, flowing in a trough

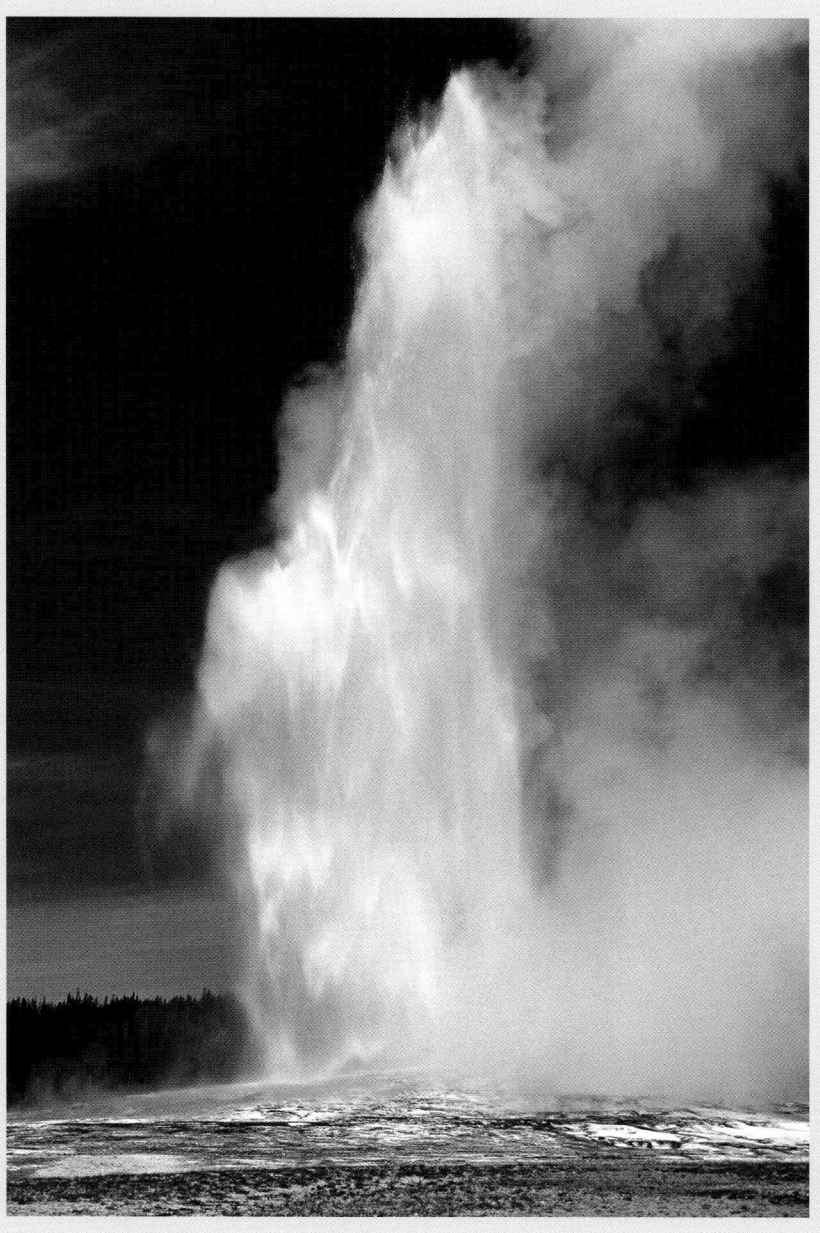

<
Old Faithful
Thomas Moran, 1873

Old Faithful

of gold.' The crater itself is composed of globular masses of a peculiar rounded appearance, like huge beaded cushions.

"While we waited (being careful to keep on the windward side) the crater filled up with hot water, which boiled and tossed and churned itself into foam and then sank away again, then with a gasp and a subdued growl the water shot up two or three feet, and fell back, but not quite so far and again tossed itself into foam. Another louder rumble, and it went up a foot higher than before and fell back again; then another still louder and the height of six feet was attained, then, just as the water was apparently subsiding, came a tremendous and appalling roar and a mass of seething, scalding water, the entire diameter of the crater, shot boldly up, and up, and up, in jet after jet until a solid column was created one hundred and thirty feet high, (which is just about the height of the Equitable Building in Broadway) and which gracefully waved in the wind and fell like a cataract opposite us, while the steam rising from it seemed to reach the very heavens.

"No language can depict the grandeur of the sight. At the first roar we all retreated precipitately to a safe distance. But seeing the regularity of the movement of the water, we gradually approached to within twenty feet. After playing about four minutes, the column wavered and gradually fell, and then with a great gurgle the water disappeared down the tube of the crater, leaving the latter perfectly empty, but so hot that all traces of water instantly disappeared. We tried to look over the edge and to peer into the depths below, but the stones were too hot to touch, and the steam, which came up from the crater could not be breathed. While the water from these geysers contain far less lime and other materials in solution than that of the Mammoth Springs, it still contains some. With one exception all the craters of the Great Geysers are situated on little knolls raised some distance above the rock surrounding them, which must have been built up by the water. Many persons write their names in the little pools, through which the water ejected from Old Faithful finds its way, but no names over two years old were legible, the others have been gradually covered by the deposit from the water. . . .

"While each geyser has its peculiarities, Old Faithful is the most interesting. Its eruptions are certain, almost to the minute; and although some others throw the water they eject to a much greater height, yet, the sight presented by its magnificent column rearing itself majestically upward and then gracefully waving in the breeze, cannot well be surpassed."

GEORGE WOOD WINGATE
Through the Yellowstone Park on Horseback, 1886

Old Faithful
Albert Bierstadt, 1881-1886

"Old Faithful stands picturesquely, setting a noble example to his followers in beauty, sublimity, and punctuality."

ALICE WELLINGTON ROLLINS
The Three Tetons, 1887

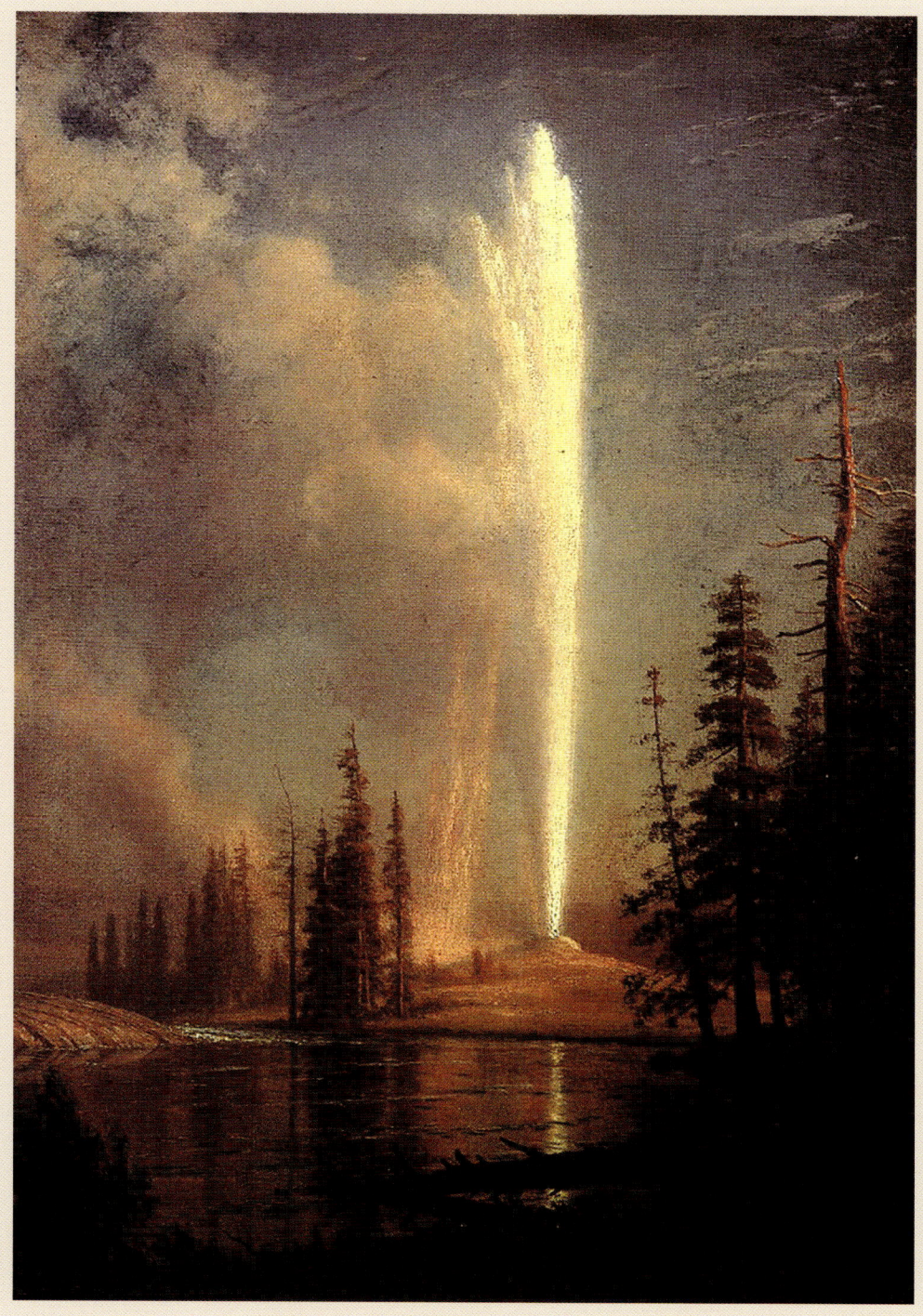

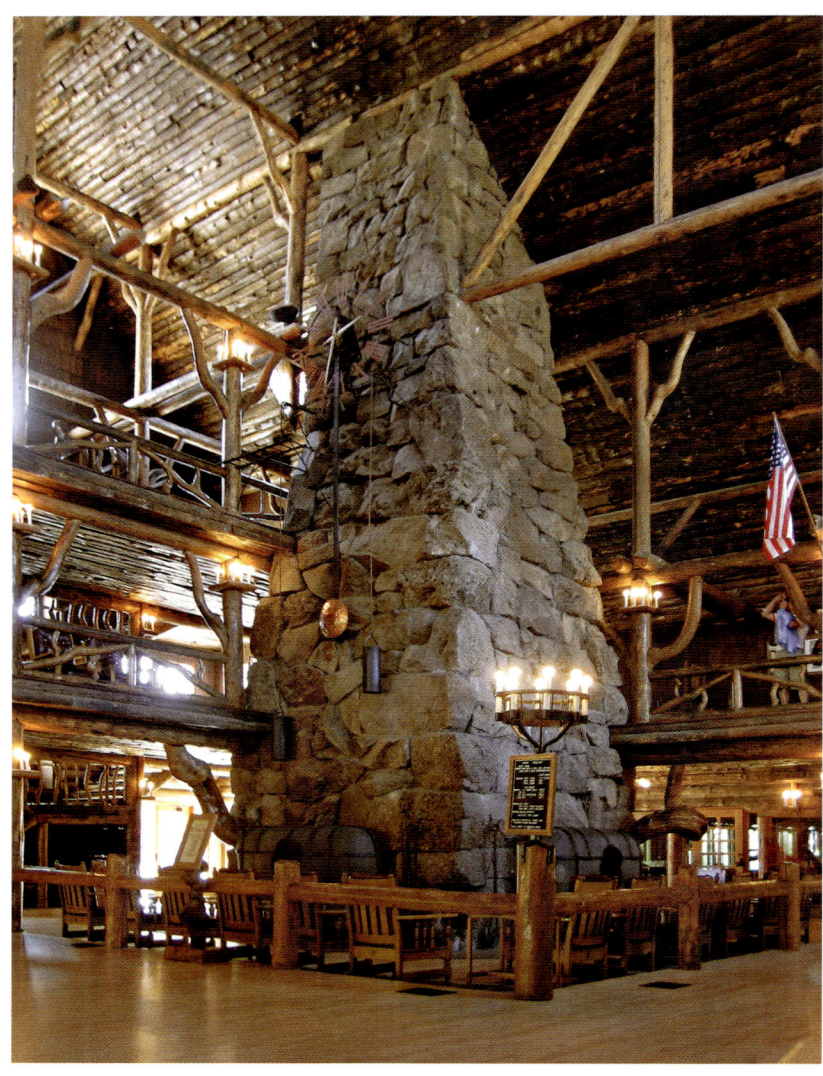

Old Faithful Inn

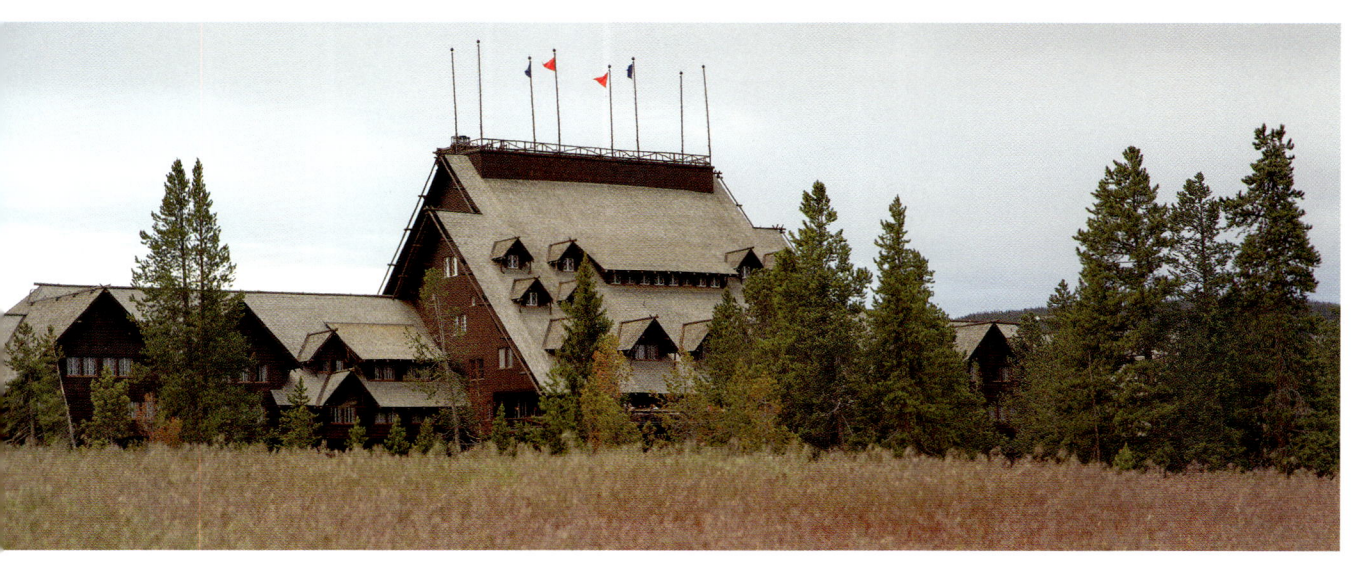

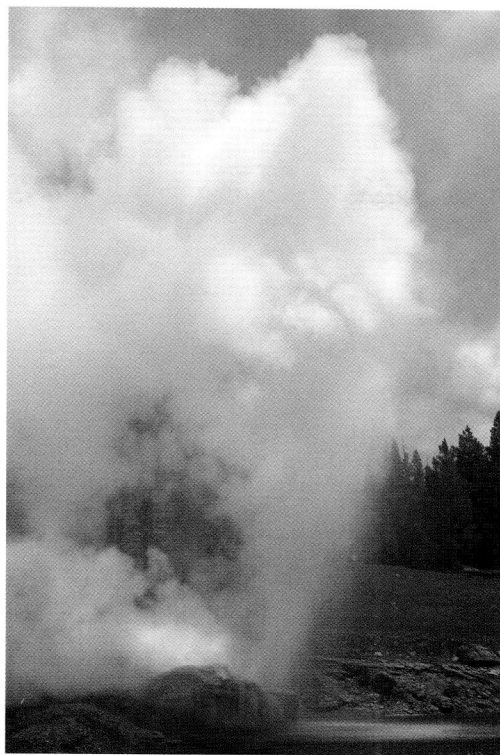

Riverside Geyser

"The buggy had pulled up close to a rough, broken, blistered cone of spelter stuff between ten and twenty feet high. There was trouble in that place—moaning, splashing, gurgling, and the clank of machinery. A spurt of boiling water jumped into the air, and a wash of water followed.

"I removed swiftly. The old lady from Chicago shrieked. 'What a wicked waste!' said her husband.

"I think they call it the Riverside Geyser. Its spout was torn and ragged like the mouth of a gun when a shell has burst there. It grumbled madly for a moment or two, and then was still. I crept over the steaming lime—it was the burning marl on which Satan lay—and looked fearfully down its mouth. You should never look a gift geyser in the mouth.

"I beheld a horrible, slippery, slimy funnel with water rising and falling ten feet at a time. Then the water rose to lip level with a rush, and an infernal bubbling troubled this Devil's Bethesda before the sullen heave of the crest of a wave lapped over the edge and made me run.

"Mark the nature of the human soul! I had begun with awe, not to say terror, for this was my first experience of such things. I stepped back from the banks of the Riverside Geyser, saying, 'Pooh! Is that all it can do?'

"Yet for aught I knew, the whole thing might have blown up at a minute's notice, she, he, or it being an arrangement of uncertain temper."

RUDYARD KIPLING
American Notes, 1891

SAWMILL GEYSER

"At times the water in the bowl takes on a characteristic rotary motion, while from the vent issues a shrill whistle suggestive of a factory or mill."

ARNOLD HAGUE, GEOLOGIST AND ASSISTANT TO WALTER WEED, 1911

"Every few minutes a little geyser . . . called the Sawmill, would apparently get itself into a frantic state of excitement, sending up a small but beautiful jet of water with a noise like a saw mill in active business."

GEORGE WOOD WINGATE
Through the Yellowstone Park on Horseback, 1886

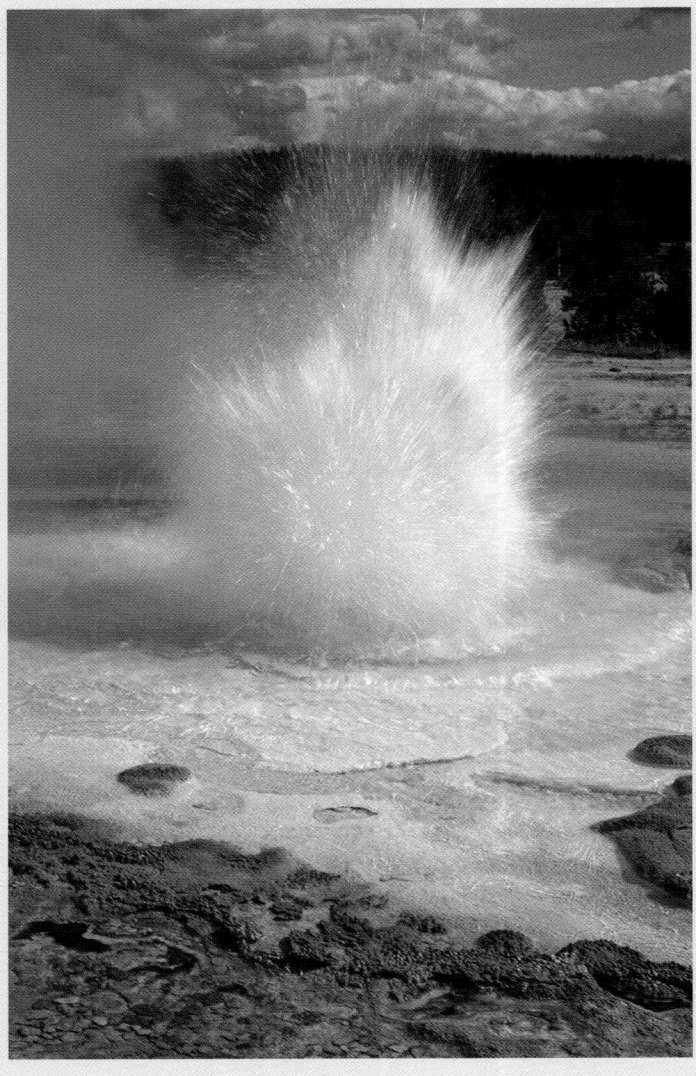

Sawmill Geyser

SPASMODIC GEYSER

"All around the geysers the ground was covered with incrustations and subsilica, and immediately about the vent of most of them the incrustations rose several feet above the surrounding level, assuming grotesque and fanciful shapes."

WALTER TRUMBALL
Overland Monthly, June 1871

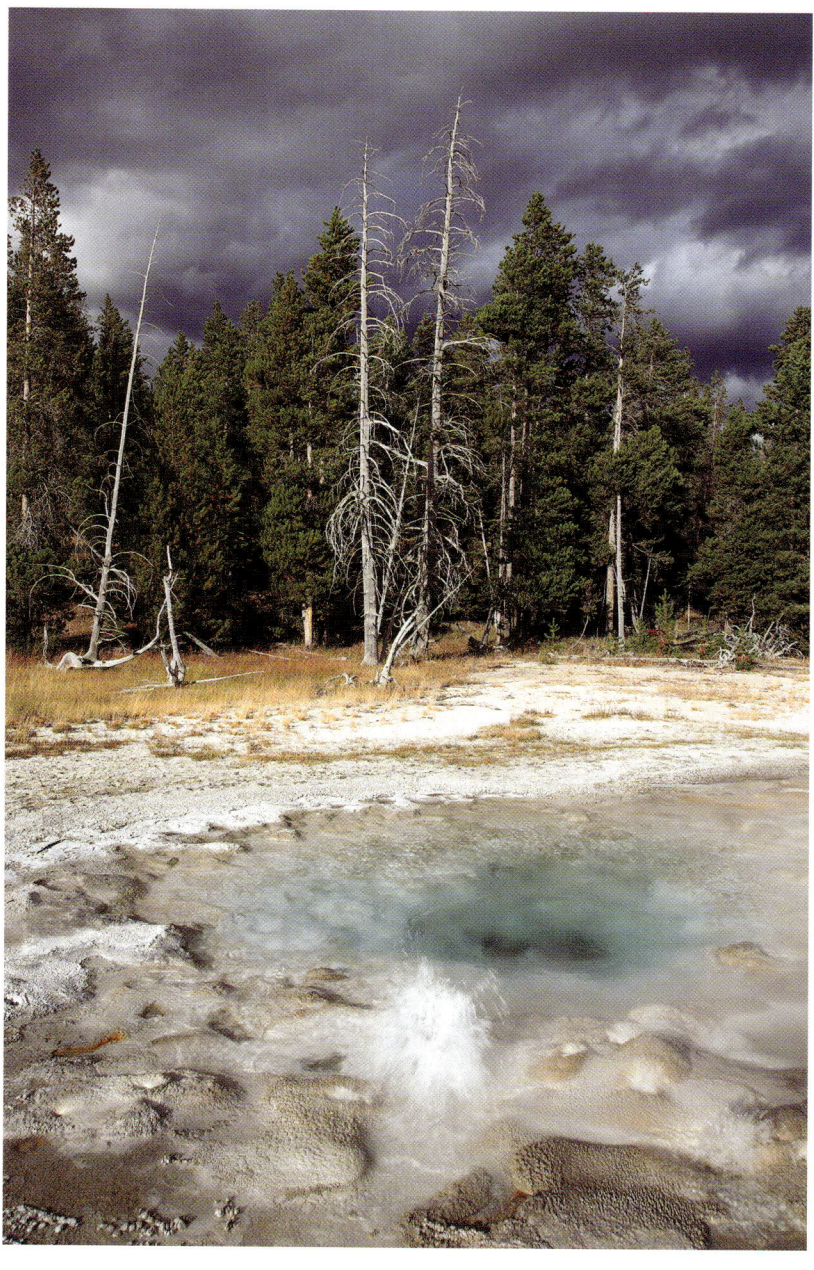

Spasmodic Geyser

"Holes and large pools (the relics of ancient and inactive geysers) are met every few feet, from which mysterious, gurgling, gasping noises are heard, and which render it necessary to take heed of one's steps."

GEORGE WOOD WINGATE
Through the Yellowstone Park on Horseback, 1886

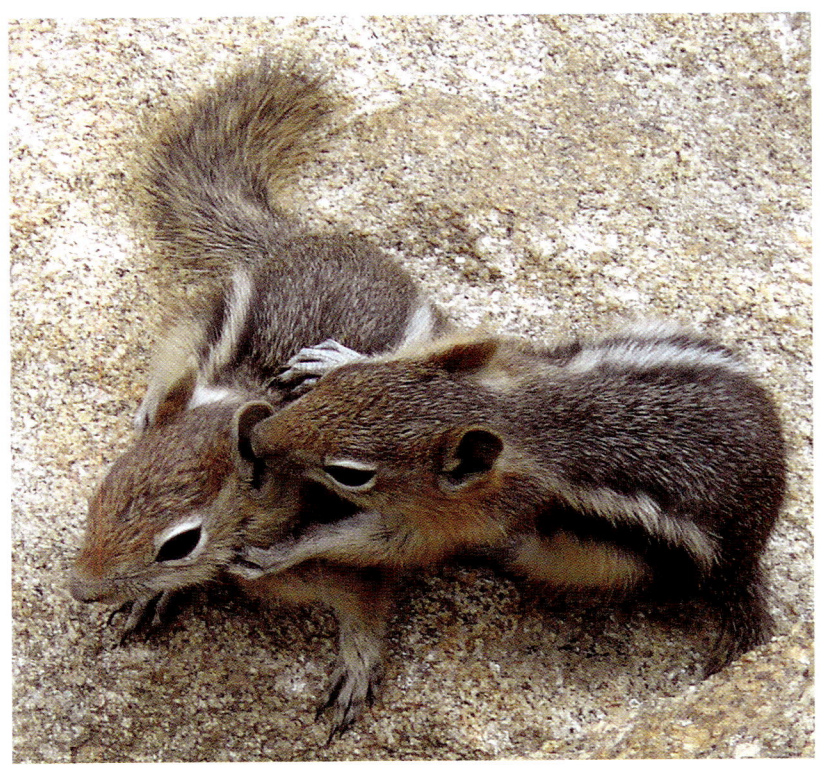

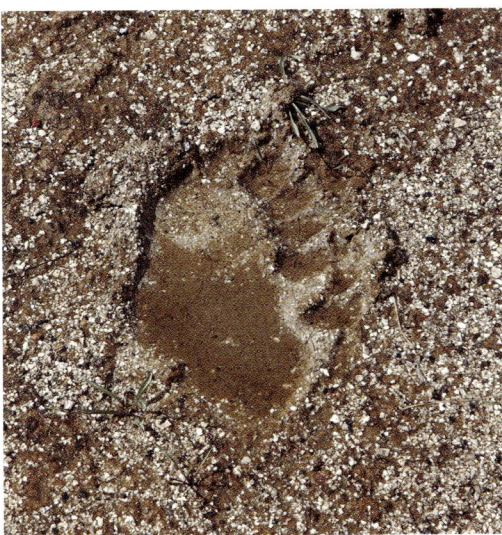

Golden-mantled ground squirrels

Bear track

"I have now described seven of the largest geysers seen in the Firehole Basin, and the description falls far short of the reality. To do justice to the subject would require a volume. The geysers of Iceland sink to insignificance beside them; they are above the reach of comparison. We could not distinguish, on every occasion, the geysers from the other hot springs, except by seeing them play, and doubtless there are many besides in the valley of great size, which we saw when quiet, and classed as boiling springs. They all vary in times, force, deposits, and colors of water. The number of springs of all kinds in the valley is not less than fifteen hundred; and, with the exception of Bluestone Springs, scarcely any two are exactly alike. Taken as an aggregate, the Firehole Basin surpasses all other great wonders of the continent. It produces an effect on the mind of the beholder utterly staggering and overpowering. During the night we were several times awakened by the rush of steam and the hissing of the waters, as the restless geysers spouted forth in the darkness. A constant rumbling, as of machinery in labor, filled the air, which was damp and warm throughout the night."

Upper Geyser Basin, Firehole River
John Henry Renshawe, 1883

LIEUTENANT GUSTAVUS C. DOANE
Yellowstone Expedition of 1870

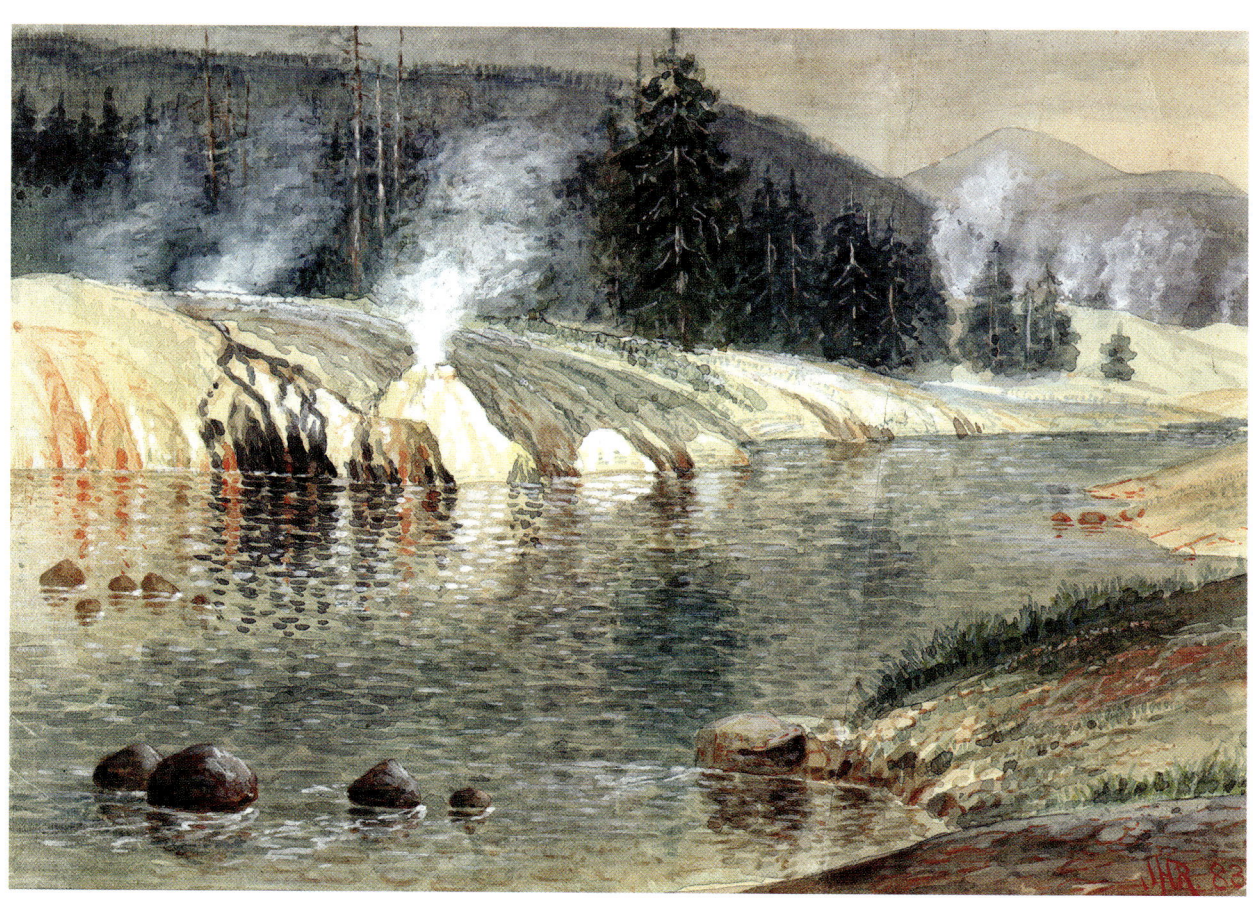

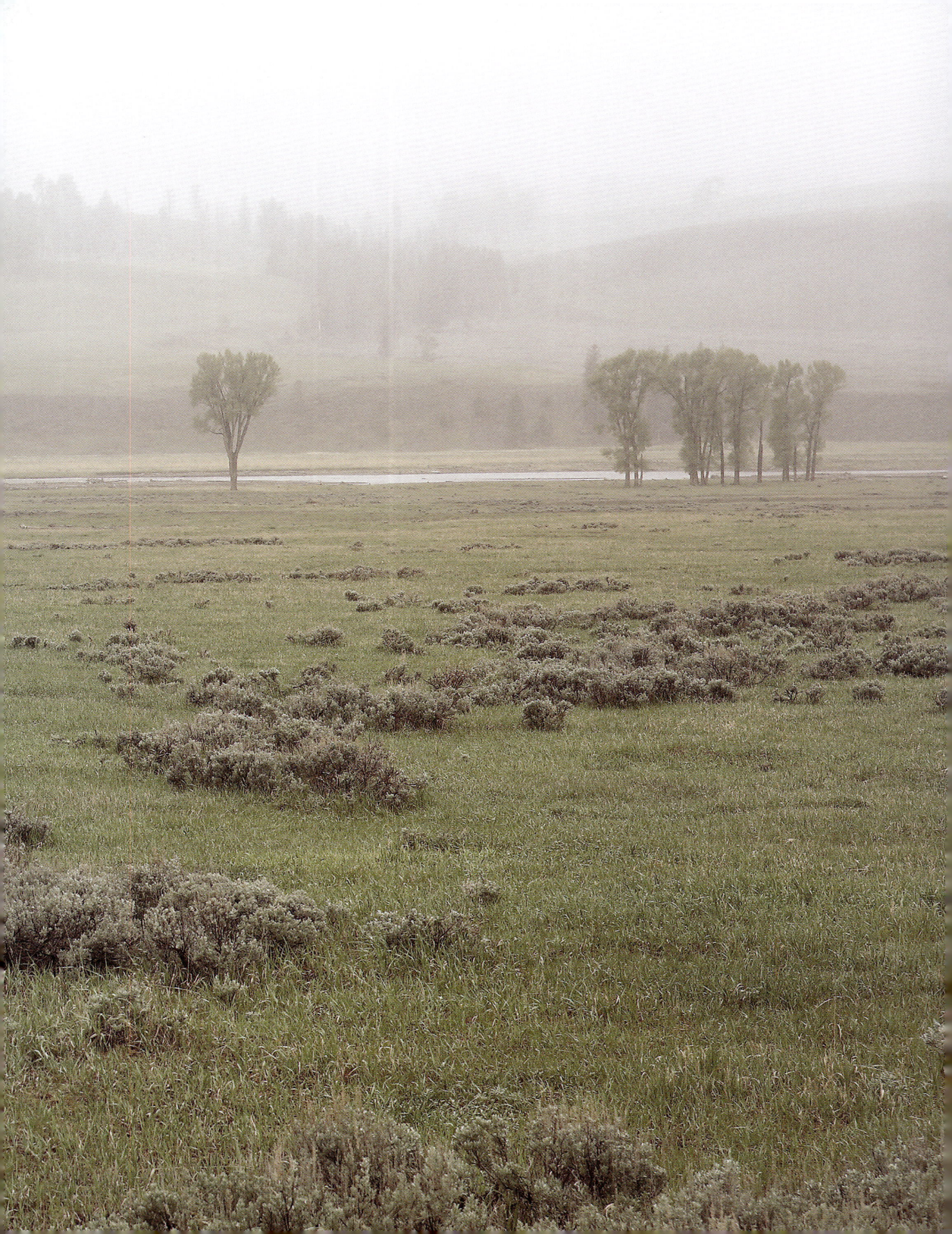

TOWER-ROOSEVELT
AREA

LAMAR RIVER

LAMAR VALLEY

TOWER FALL

Lamar Valley

LAMAR RIVER

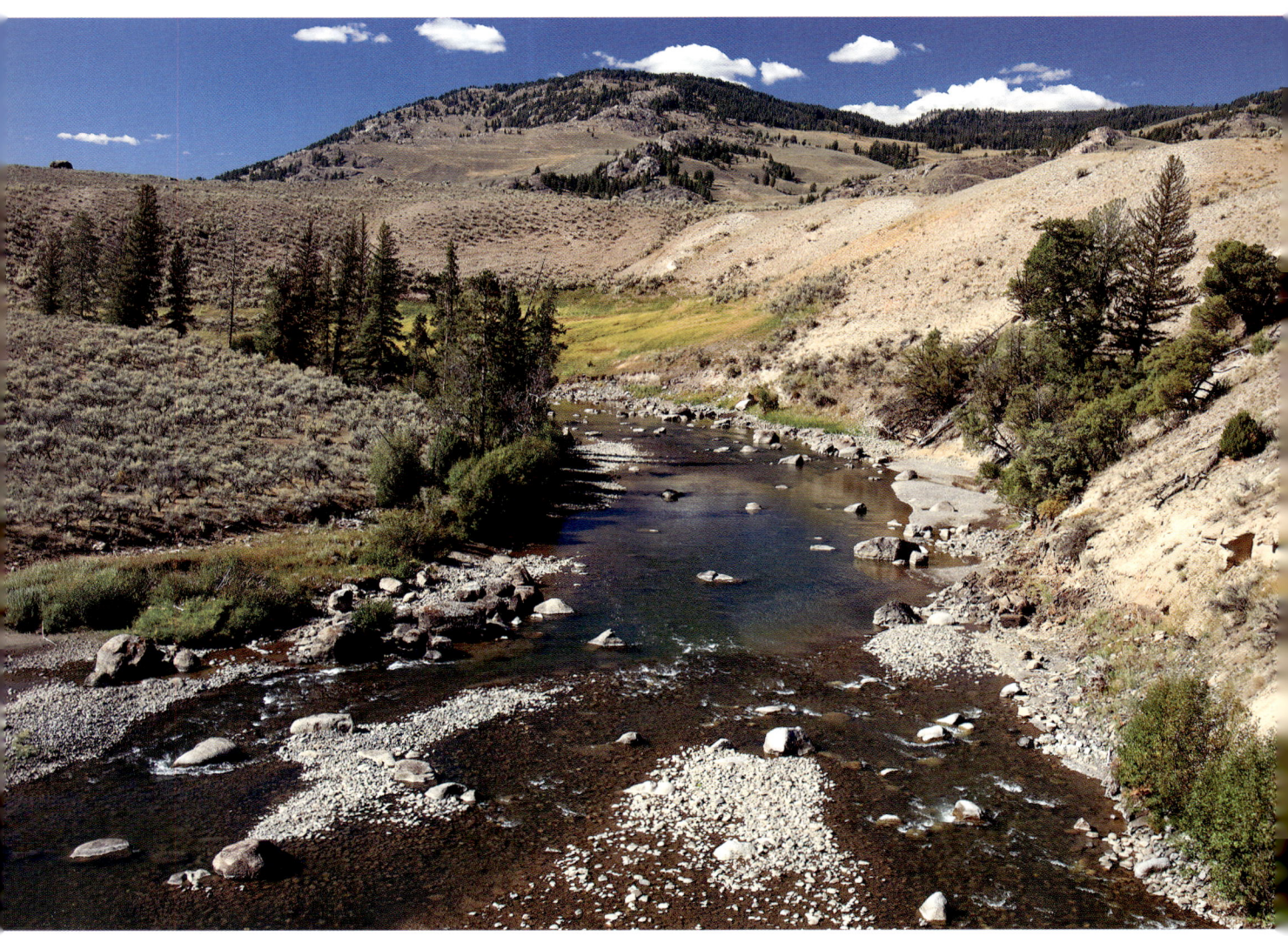

LAMAR VALLEY

"The mountains . . . are rugged, grand, picturesque and immense by turns, and colored by nature with a thousand gorgeous hues."

NATHANIEL PITT LANGFORD
The Discovery of Yellowstone Park: Journal of the Washburn Expedition to the Yellowstone and Firehole Rivers in the Year 1870, 1905

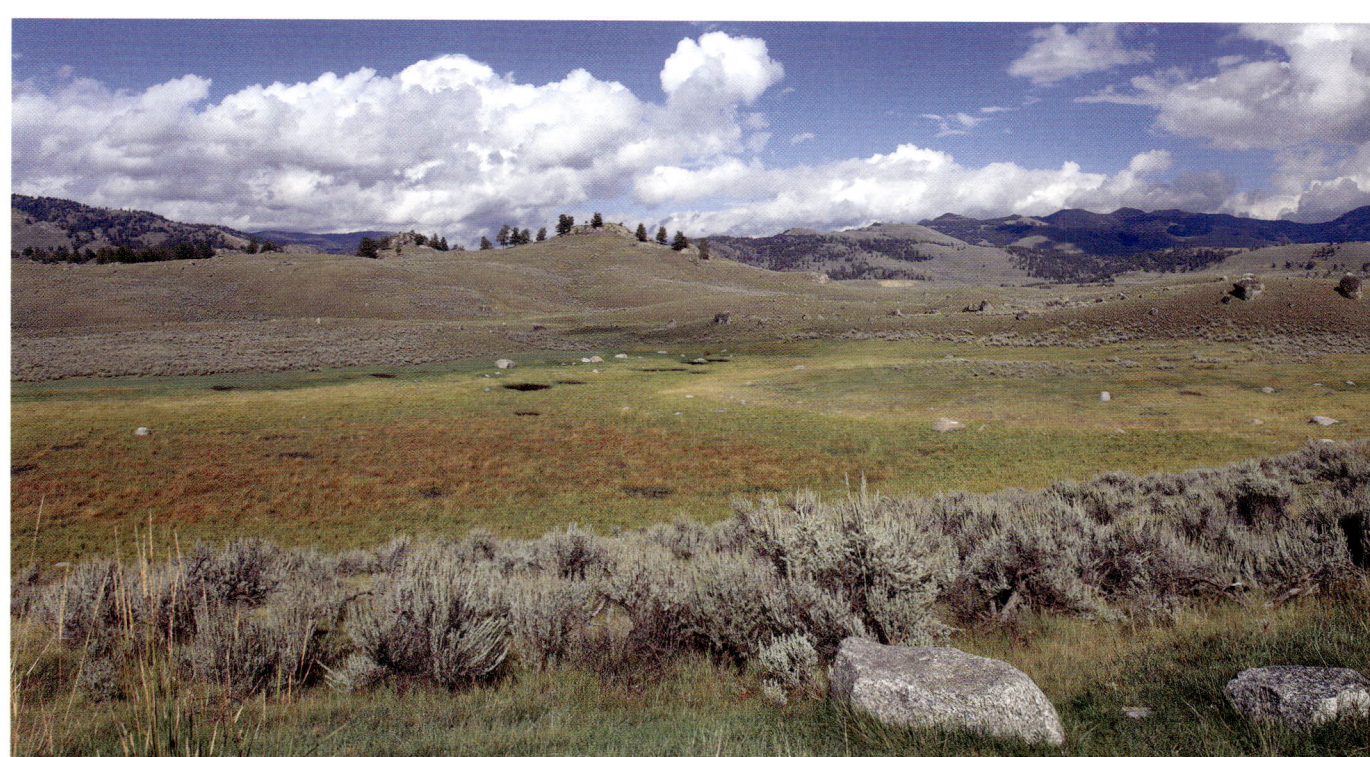

Lamar Valley in spring

‹

Lamar River

"There is something in the wild romantic scenery of this valley which I cannot nor will I attempt to describe, but the impressions made upon my mind while gazing from a high eminence on the surrounding landscape one evening as the sun was gently gliding behind the western mountain and casting its gigantic shadows across the vale were such as time can never efface from my memory."

OSBORNE RUSSELL
Journal of a Trapper-Nine Years in the Rocky Mountains (1834-1843), 1921

Overlook near Chittendon Road

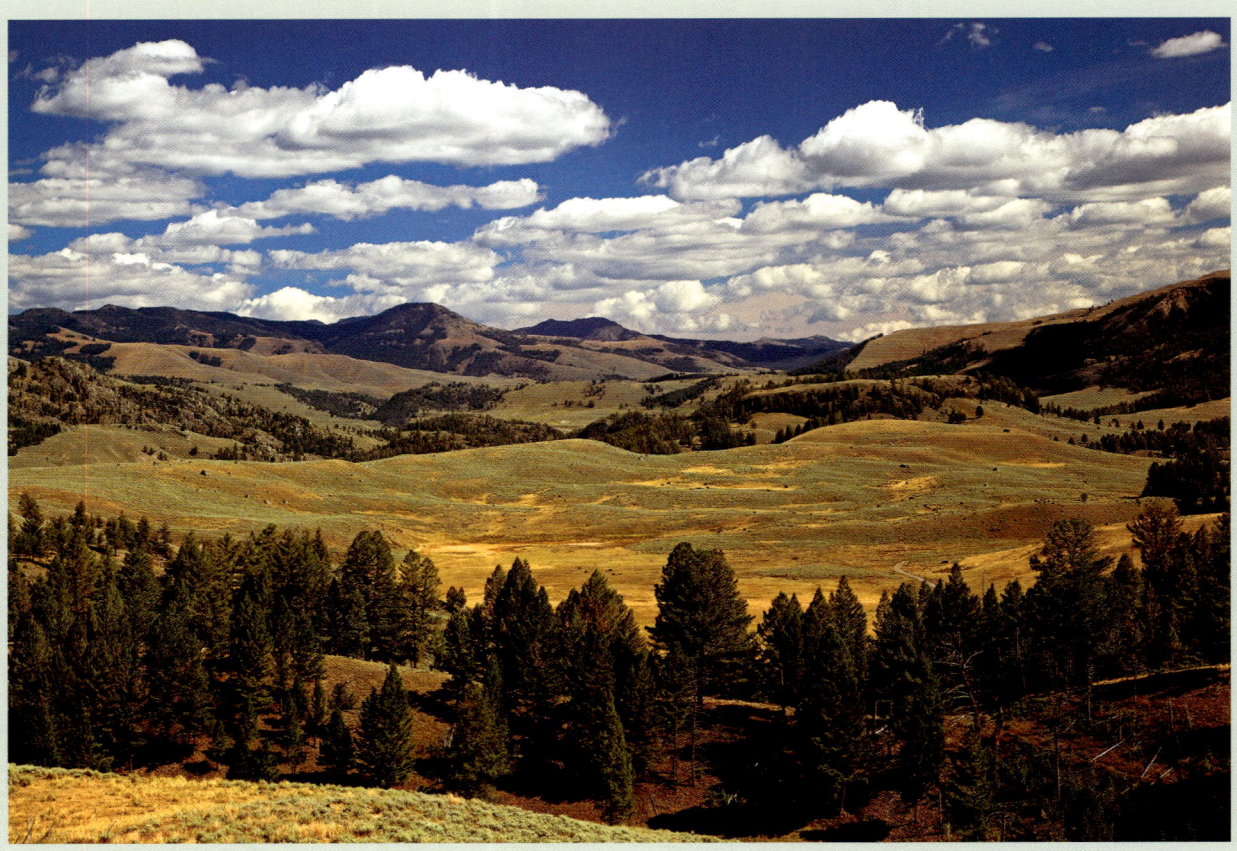

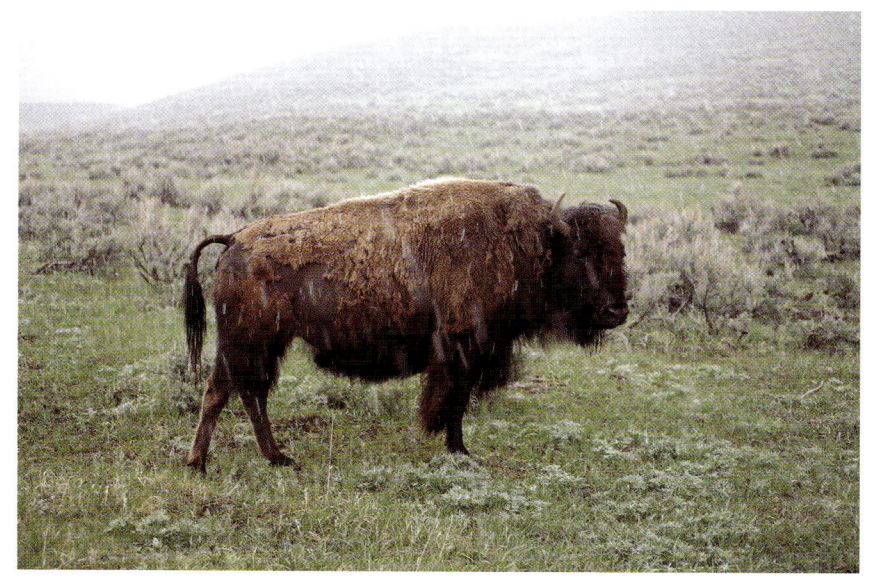

Bison

Lamar Valley in autumn

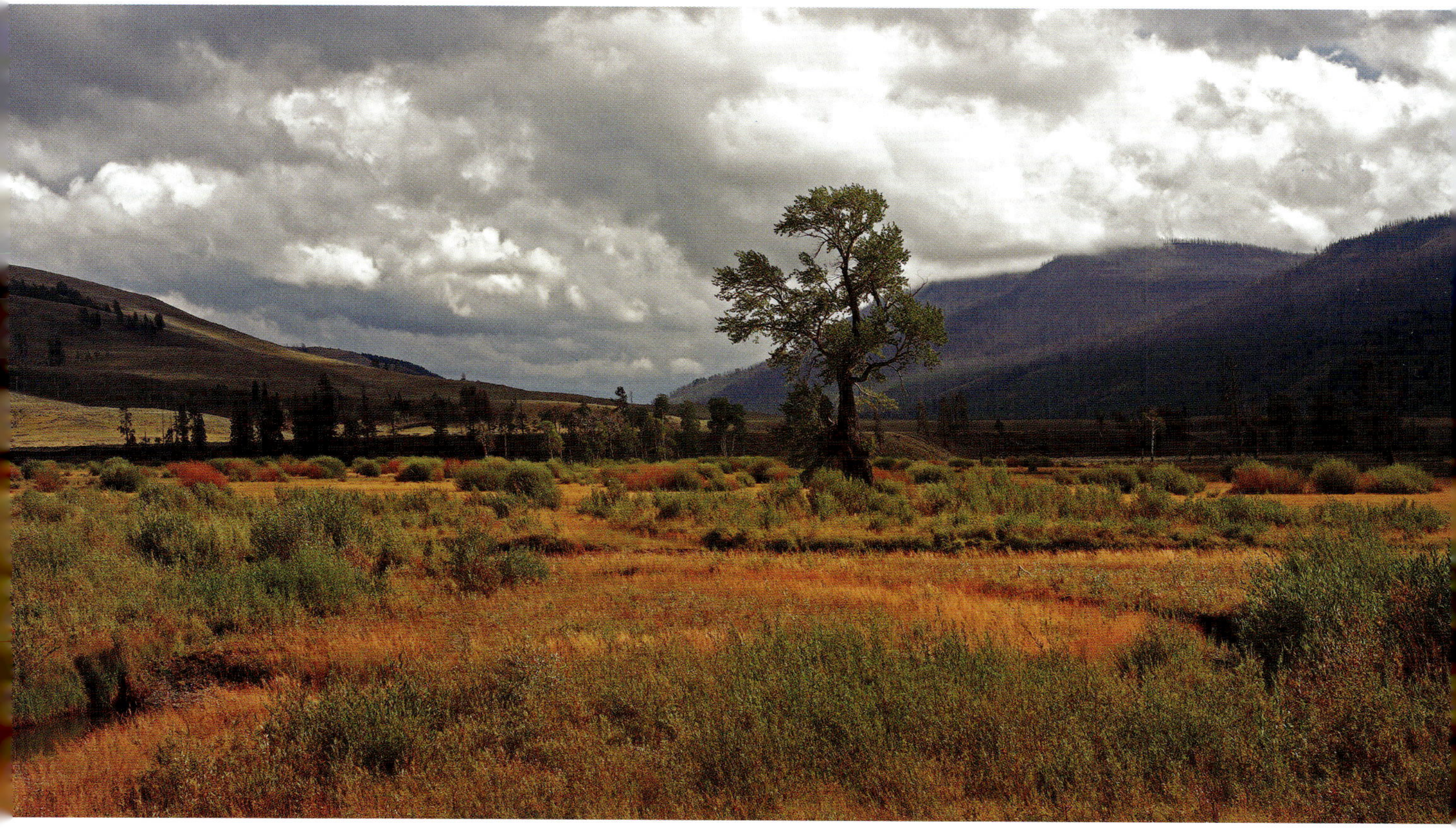

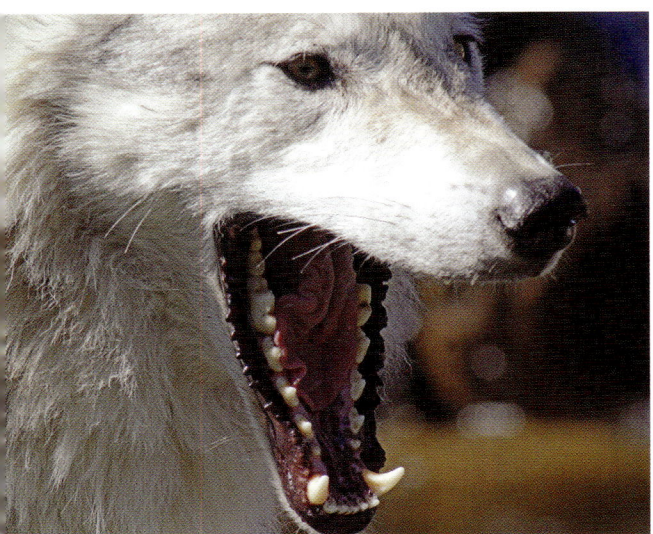

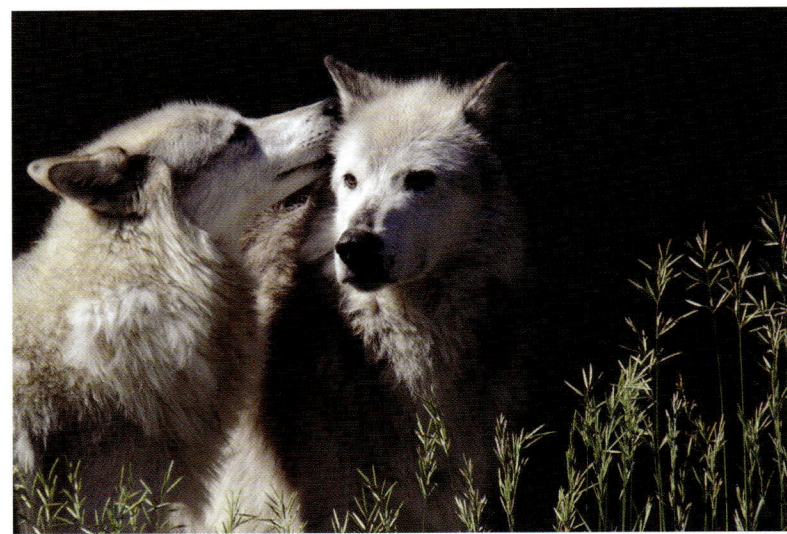

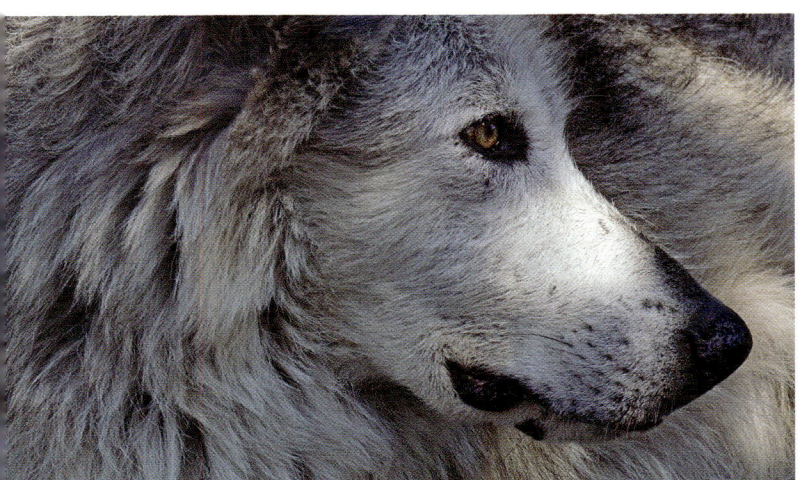

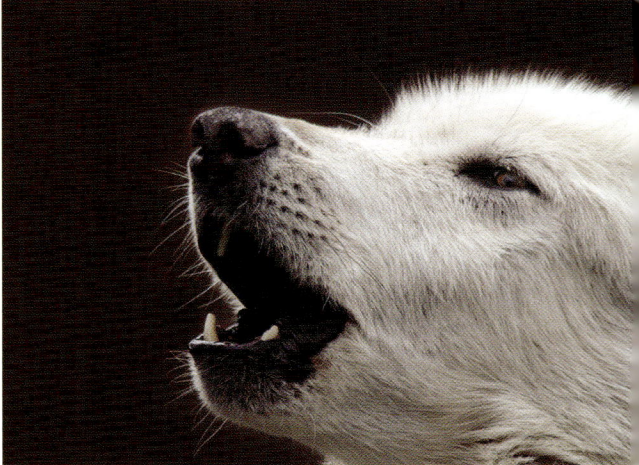

Gray wolves

Bison and calf

Grizzly bear

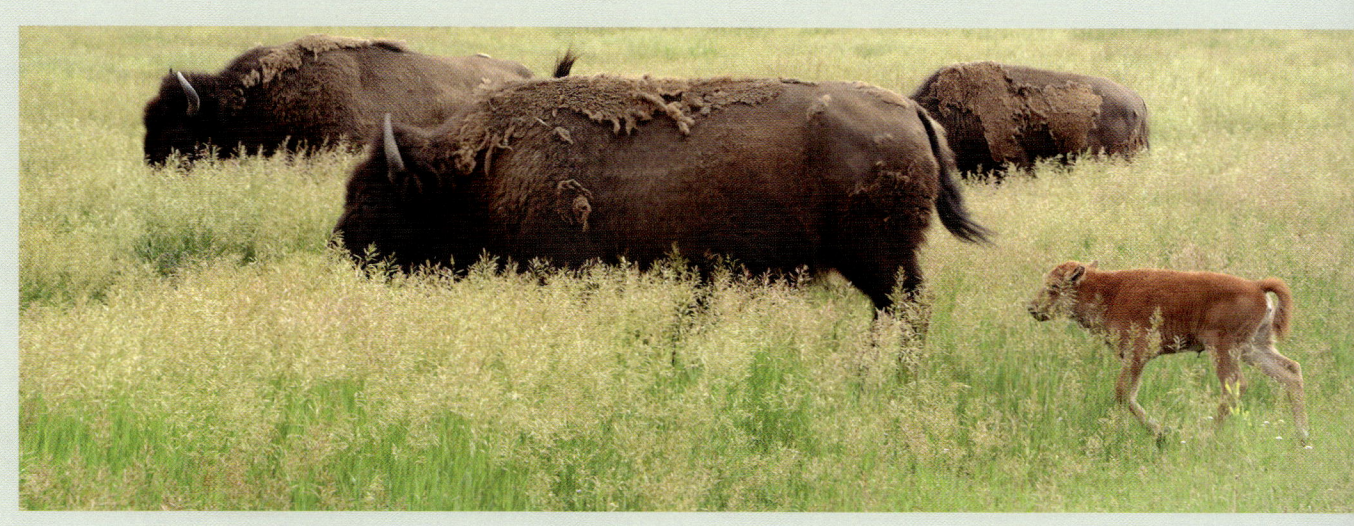

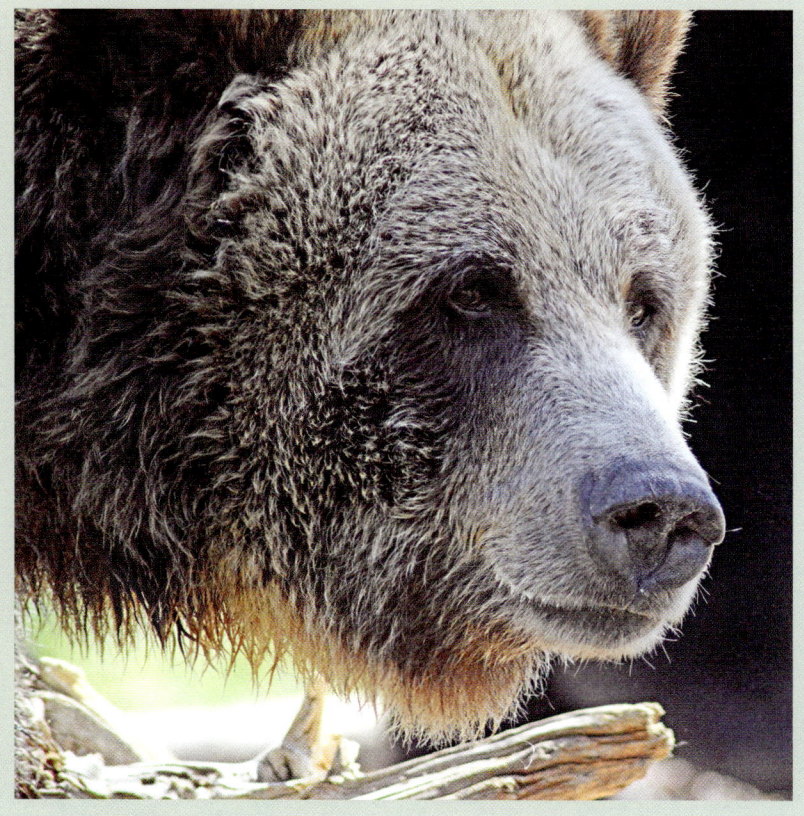

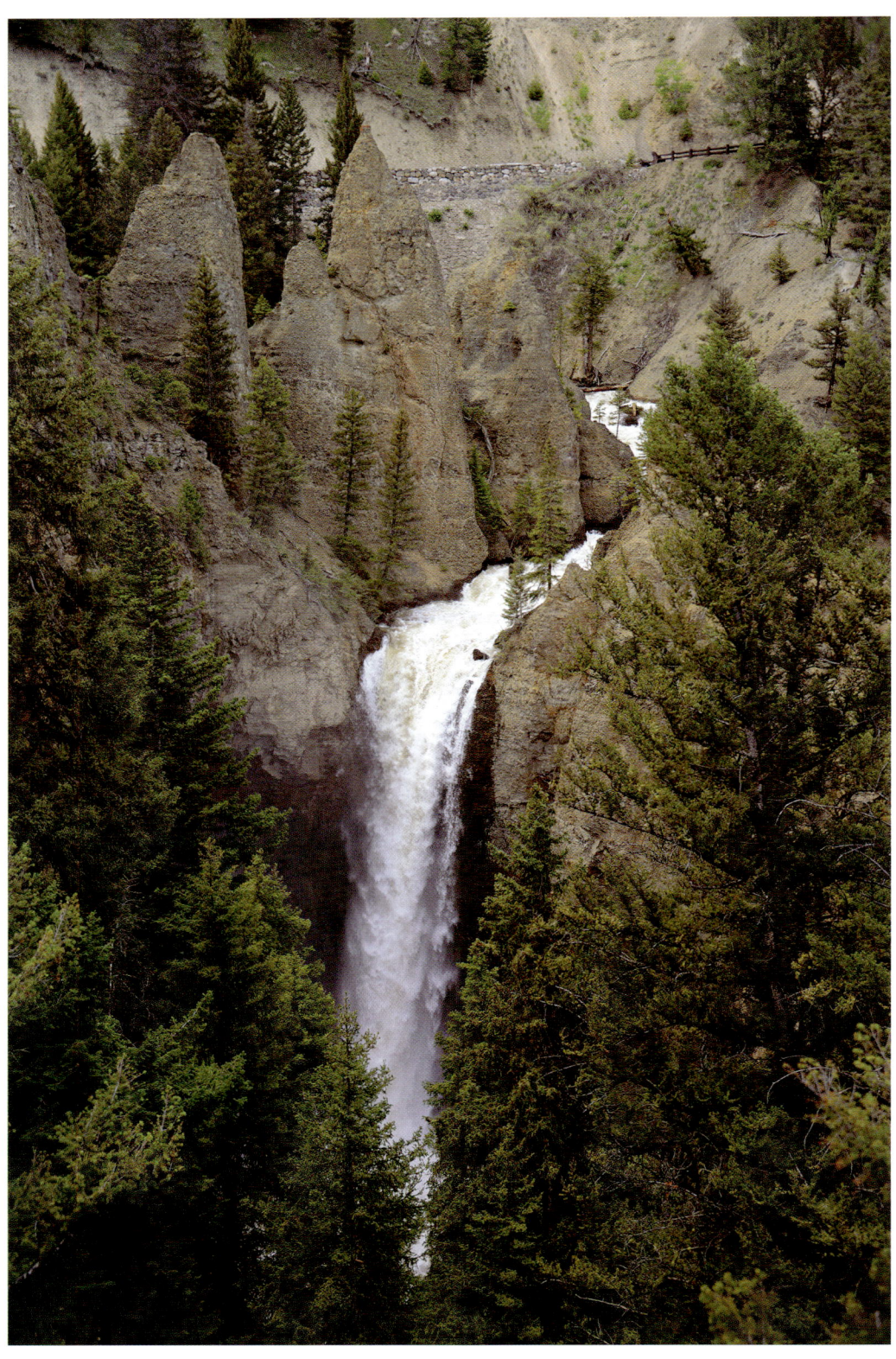

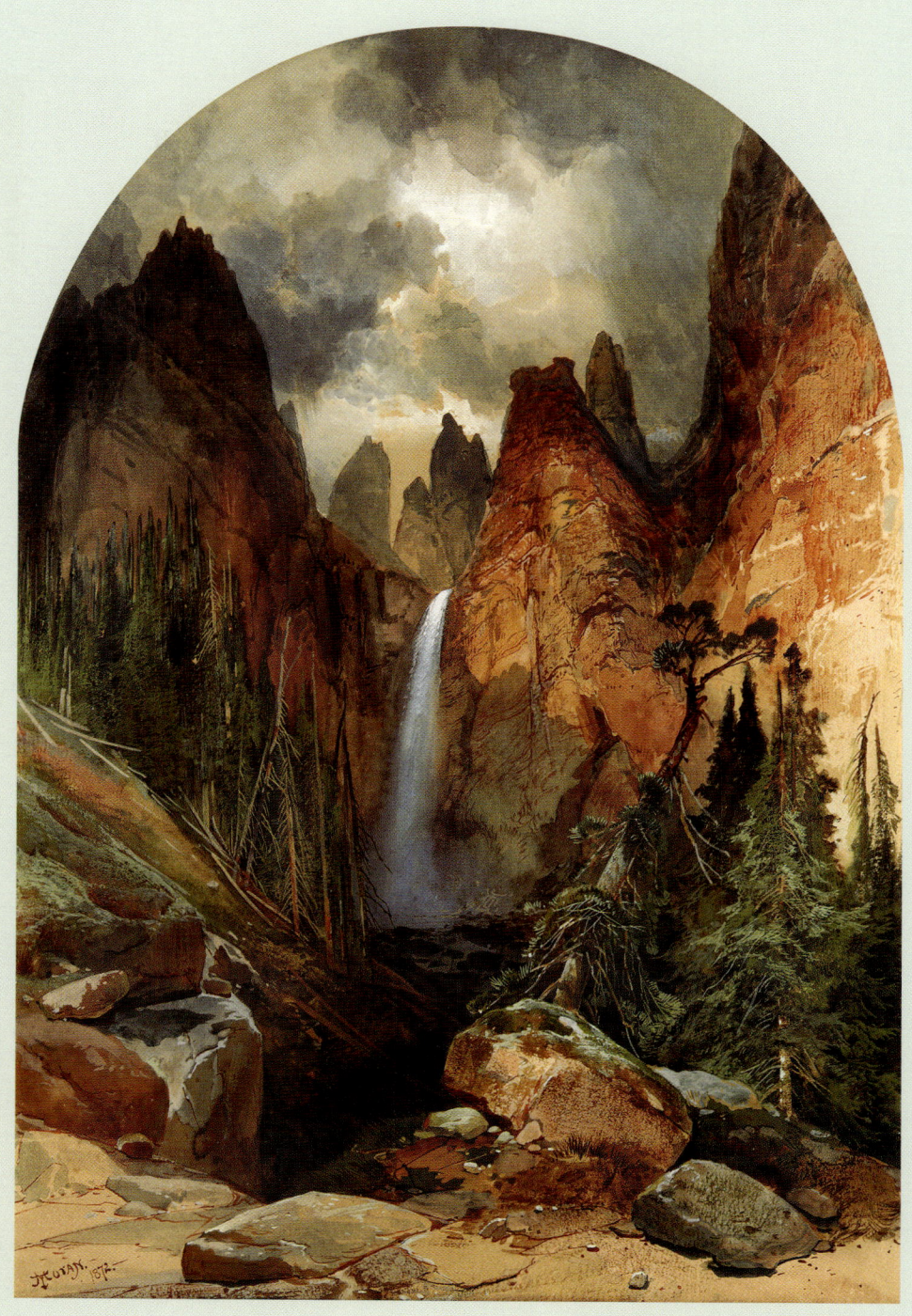

Tower Falls
Thomas Moran, 1872
Gilcrease Museum, Tulsa, OK
0226.1457

‹

Tower Fall

"The stream [Tower Creek], in its descent to the brink of the fall, is separated into half a dozen distorted channels which have zigzagged their passage through the cement formation, working it into spires, pinnacles, towers and many other capricious objects. Many of these are of faultless symmetry, resembling the minaret of a mosque; others are so grotesque as to provoke merriment as well as wonder. One of this latter character we named 'The Devil's Hoof,' from its supposed similarity to the proverbial foot of his Satanic majesty. The height of this rock from its base is about fifty feet.

"The friable rock forming the spires and towers and pinnacles crumbles away under a slight pressure. I climbed one of these tall spires on the brink of the chasm overlooking the fall, and from the top had a beautiful view, though it was one not unmixed with terror. Directly beneath my feet, but probably about one hundred feet below me, was the verge of the fall, and still below that the deep gorge through which the creek went bounding and roaring over the boulders to its union with the Yellowstone.

"I went around and almost under the fall, or as far as the rocks gave a foothold, the rising spray thoroughly wetting and nearly blinding me. Some two hundred yards below the fall is a huge granite boulder about thirty feet in diameter. Where did it come from?

"In camp today several names were proposed for the creek and fall, and after much discussion the name 'Minaret' was selected. Later, this evening, this decision has been reconsidered, and we have decided to substitute the name 'Tower' for 'Minaret,' and call it 'Tower Fall.'"

NATHANIEL PITT LANGFORD
The Discovery of Yellowstone Park: Journal of the Washburn Expedition to the Yellowstone and Firehole Rivers in the Year 1870, 1905

"Looking from the canyon below, it appears like some old castle with its turrets dismantled but still standing. From between two of these turrets the stream makes its final leap of one hundred ten measured feet, and then, as if satisfied with itself, flows peacefully into the Yellowstone.... You felt none of the shrinking back so common at the Great Fall, but rather, as you stood below and gazed upon its waters broken into white spray, you felt as though you wanted to dash into it and catch it as it fell. By a vote of the majority of the party this fall was called Tower Fall."

GENERAL HENRY D. WASHBURN
Explorations in a New and Wonderful Country, 1870

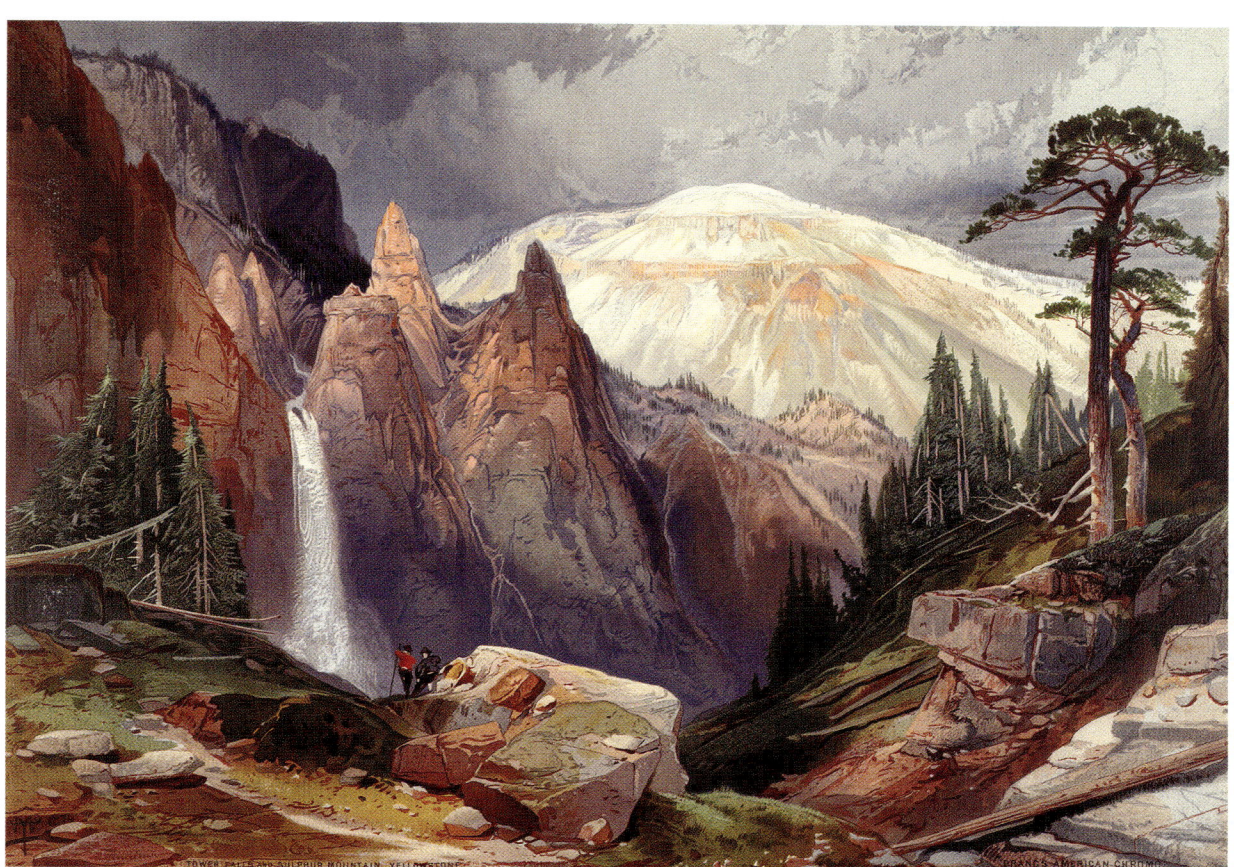

Tower Falls and Sulphur Mountain,
Yellowstone
Thomas Moran, 1874
Gilcrease Museum, Tulsa, OK
2426.47.6

"Nothing can be more chastely beautiful than this lovely cascade, hidden away in the dim light of overshadowing rocks and woods, its very voice hushed to a low murmur unheard at the distance of a few hundred yards. Thousands might pass by within a half-mile and not dream of its existence, but once seen, it passes to the list of most pleasant memories."

LIEUTENANT GUSTAVUS C. DOANE
Yellowstone Expedition of 1870

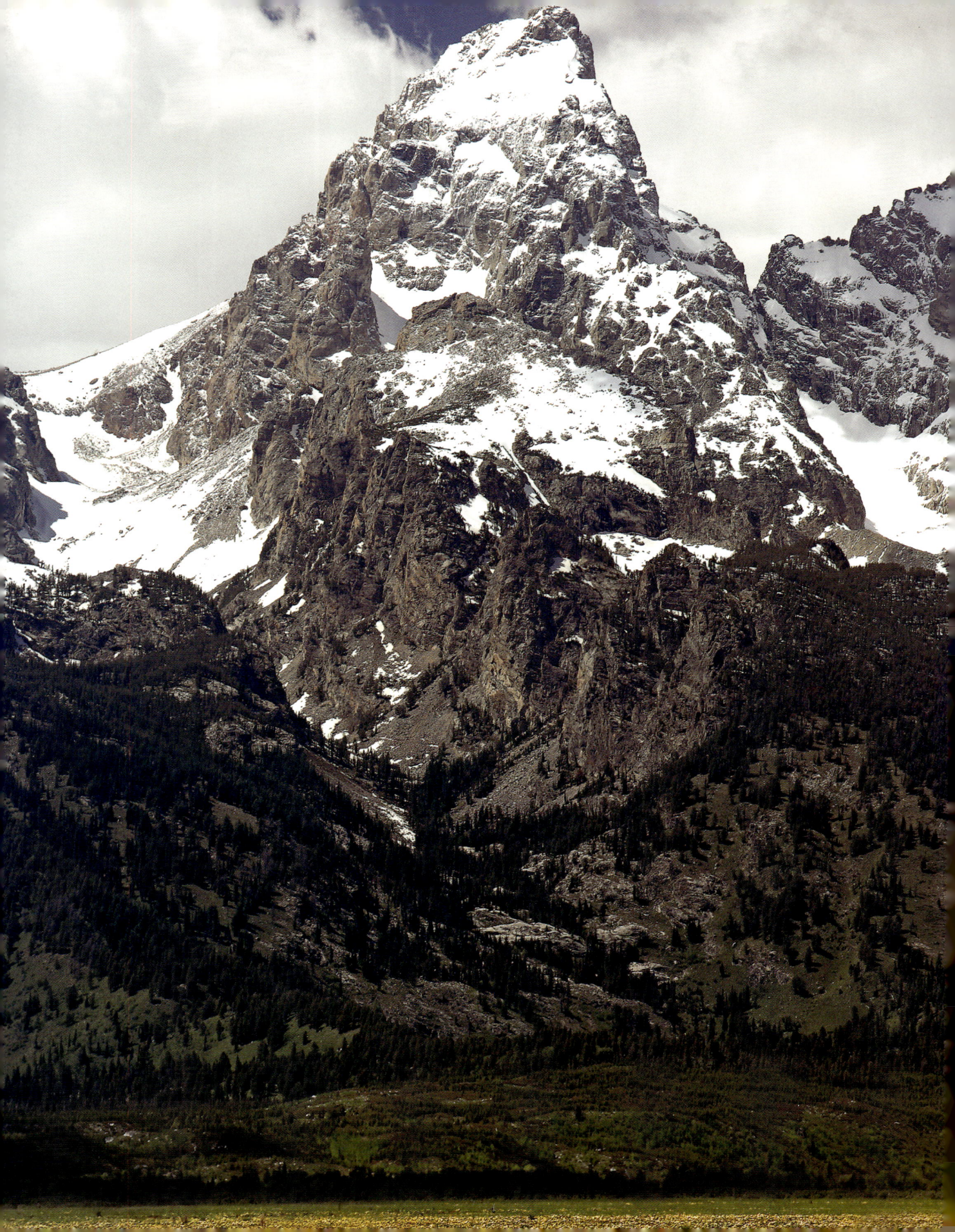

GRAND TETON NATIONAL PARK

GLACIER VIEW

JOHN D. ROCKEFELLER, JR. MEMORIAL PARKWAY

MORMON ROW

MOUNT MORAN AT OXBOW BEND

NATIONAL ELK REFUGE
> FLAT CREEK

SNAKE RIVER OVERLOOK

WILLOW FLATS

Grand Teton

GLACIER VIEW

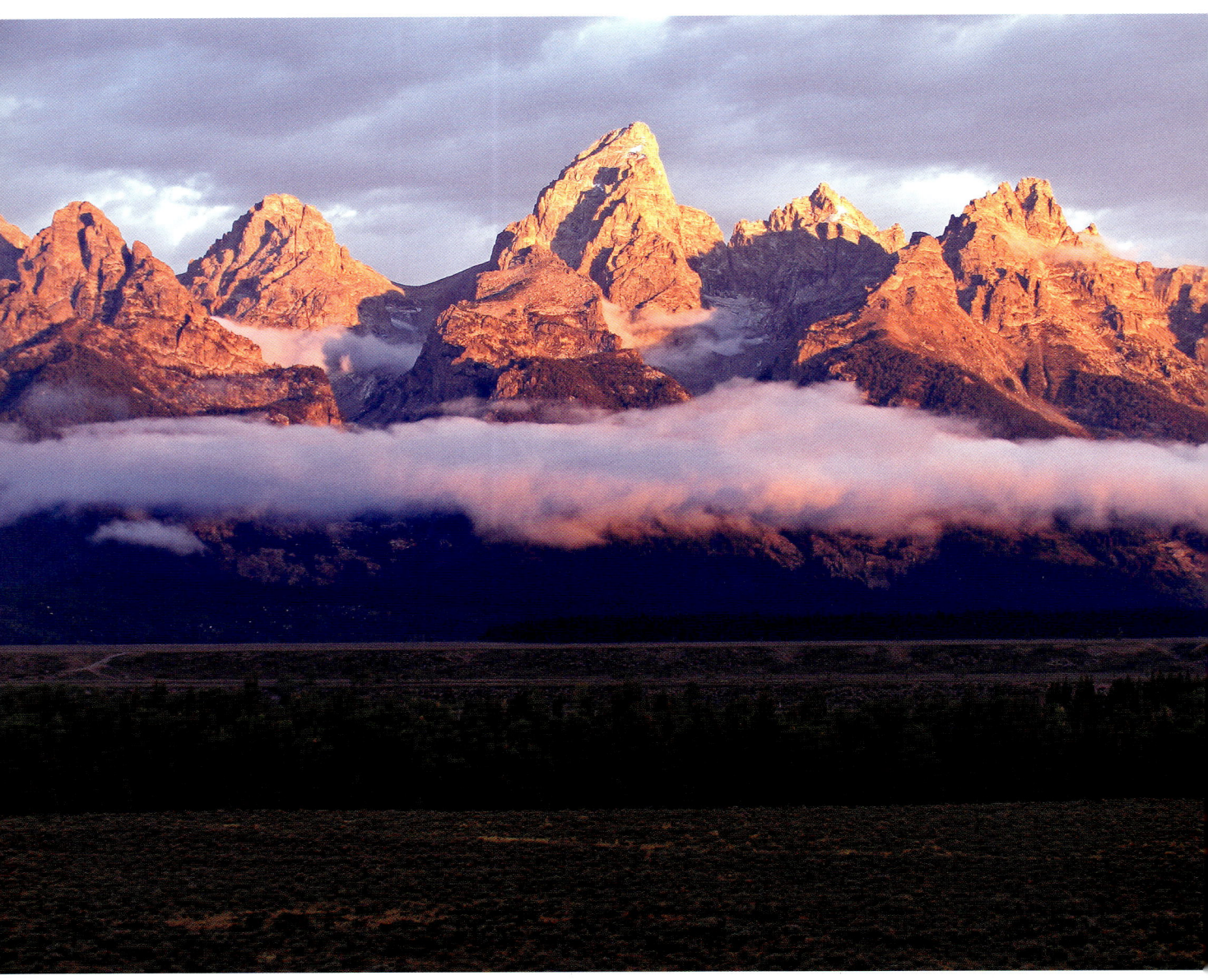

JOHN D. ROCKEFELLER, JR.
MEMORIAL PARKWAY

<

Morning light on the Tetons at Glacier View

John D. Rockefeller, Jr. Memorial Parkway

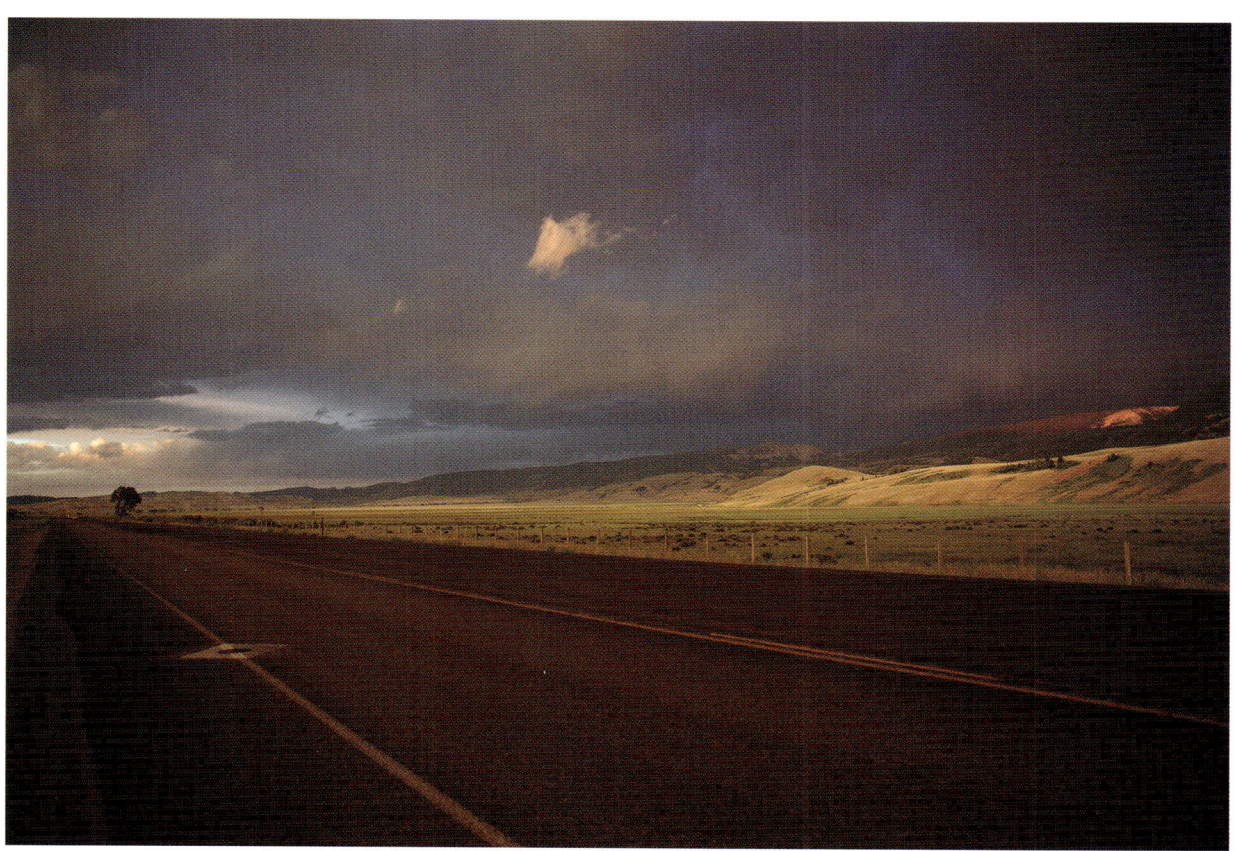

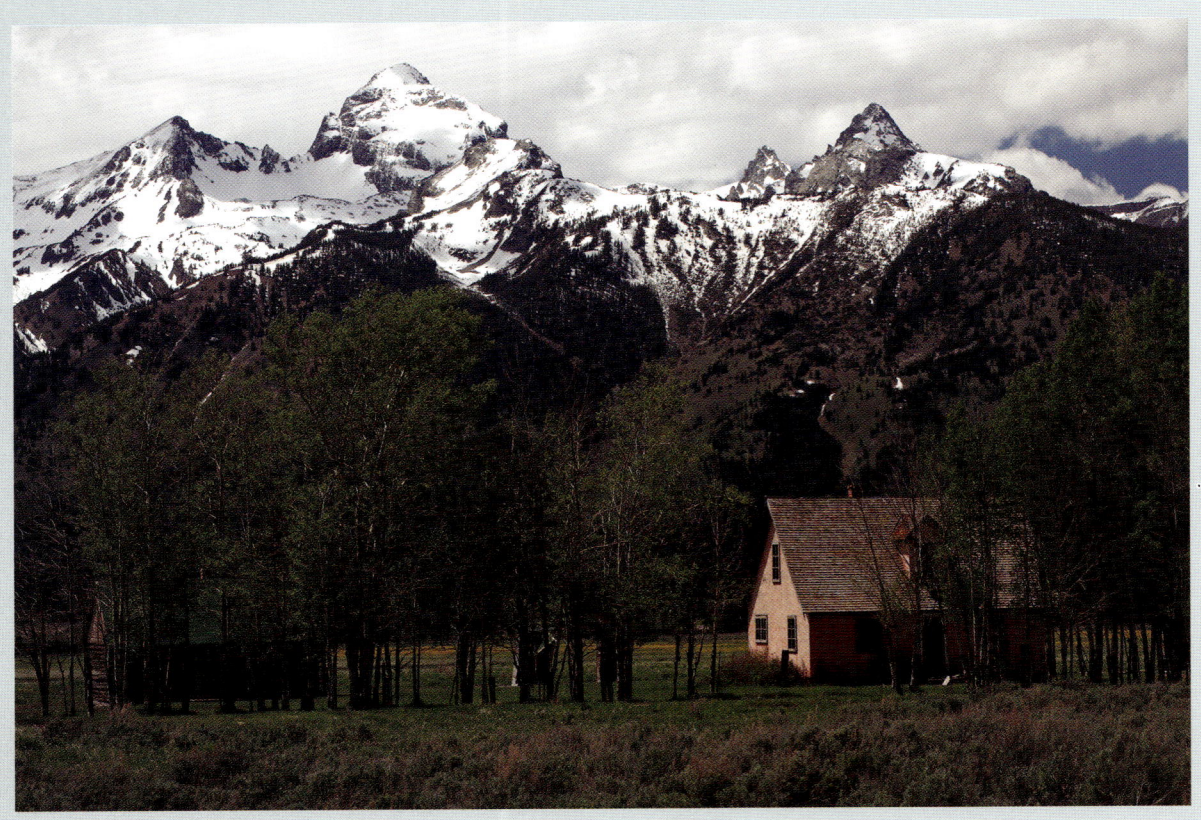

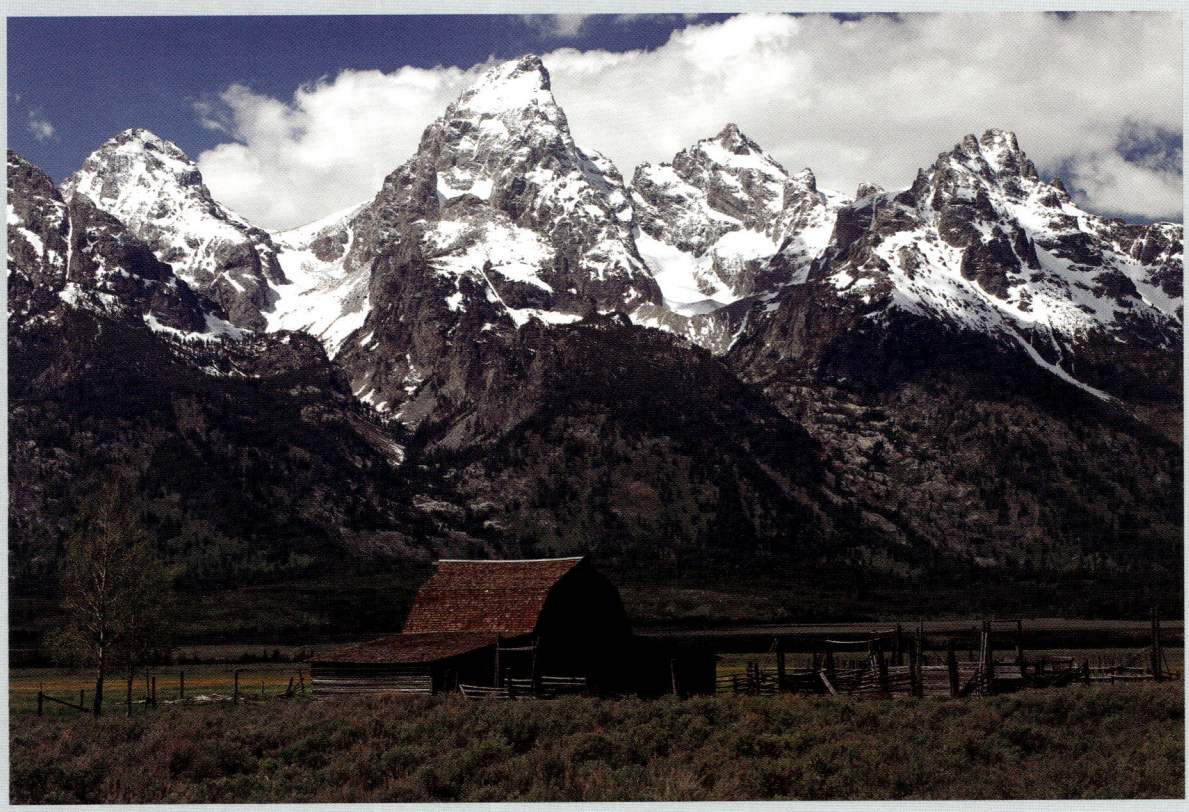

MORMON ROW

<
 Mormon Row (top)

<
John Moulton barn on Mormon Row (bottom)

T.A. Moulton barn on Mormon Row

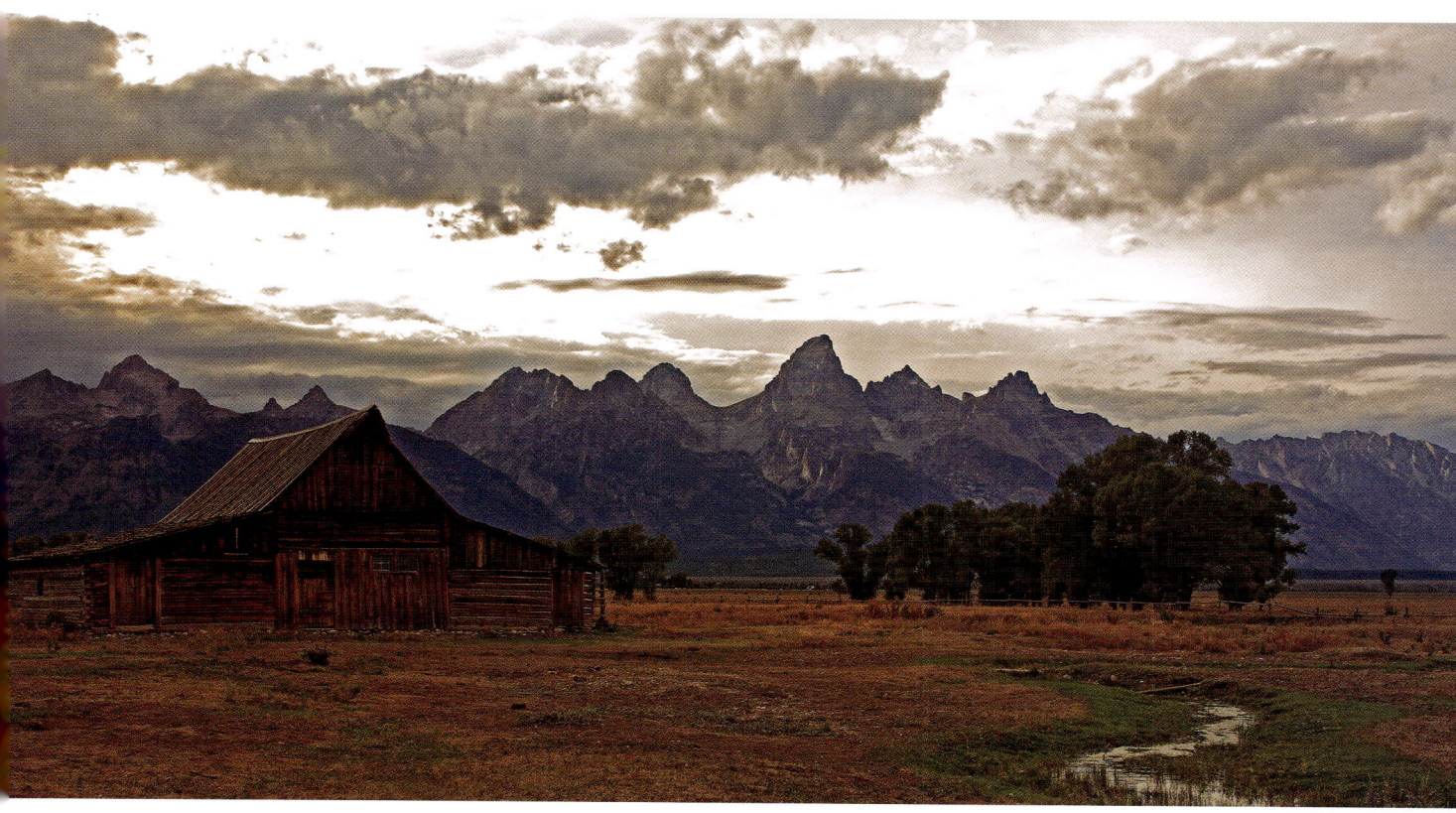

MOUNT MORAN AT
OXBOW BEND

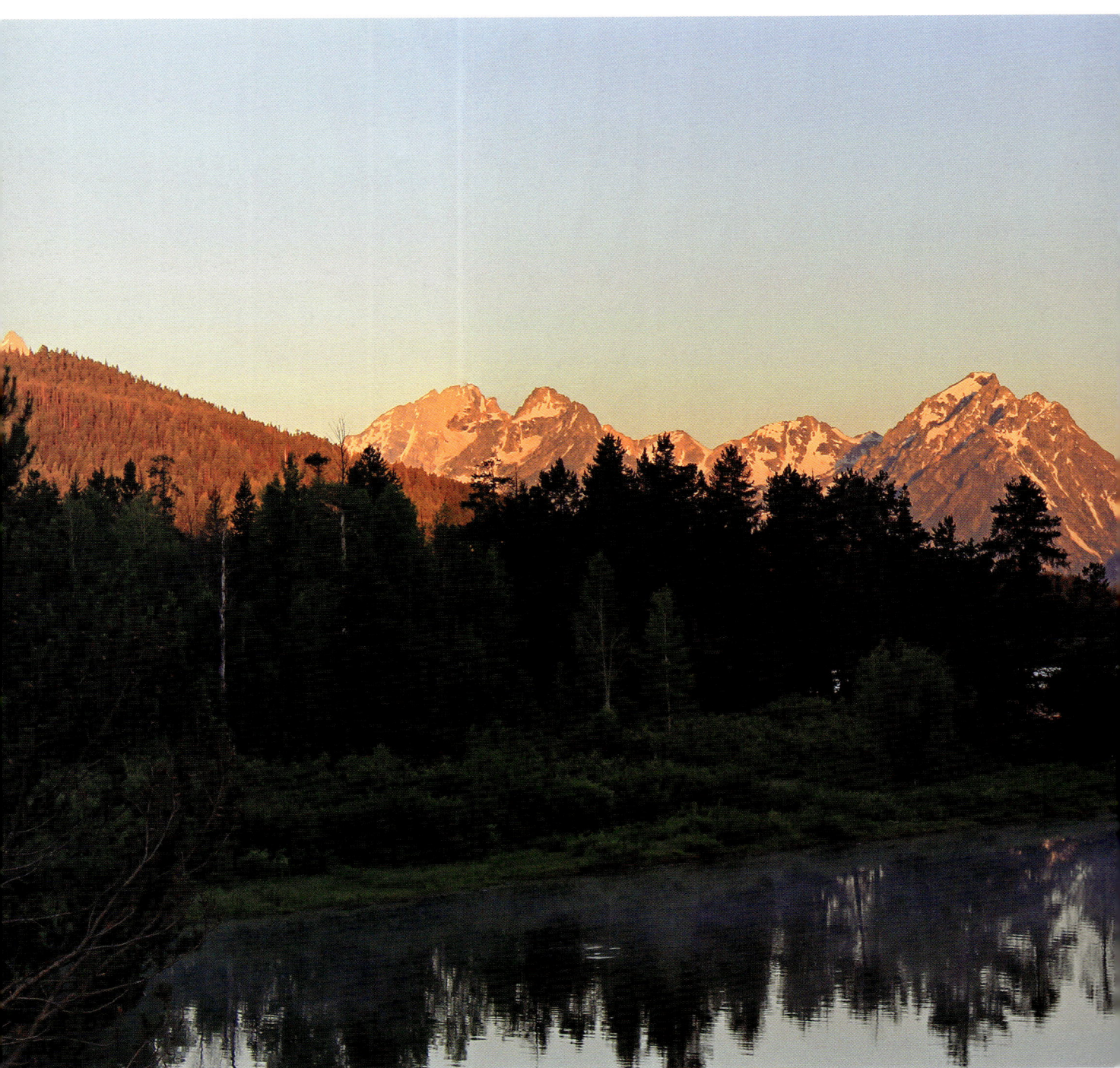

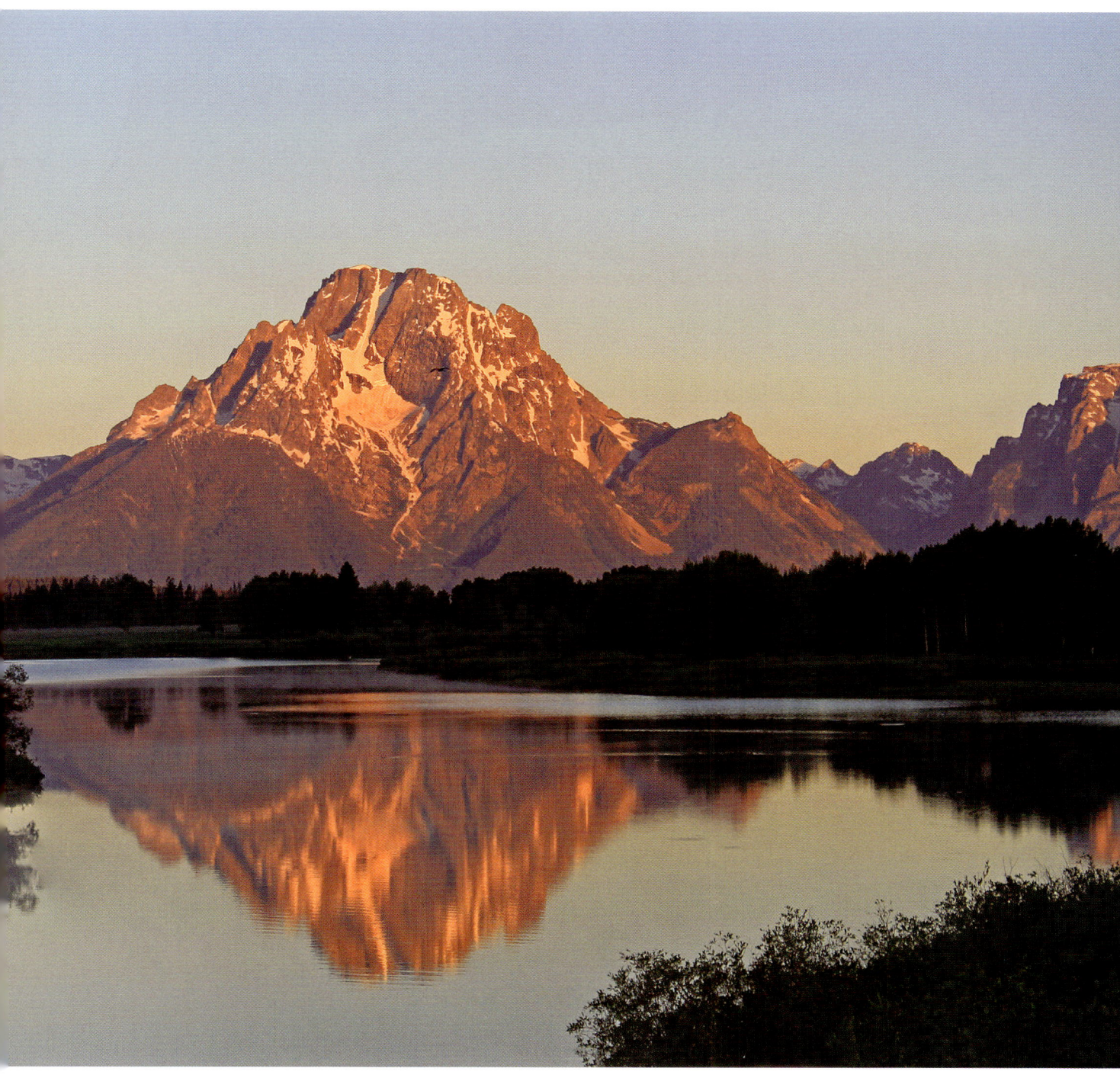

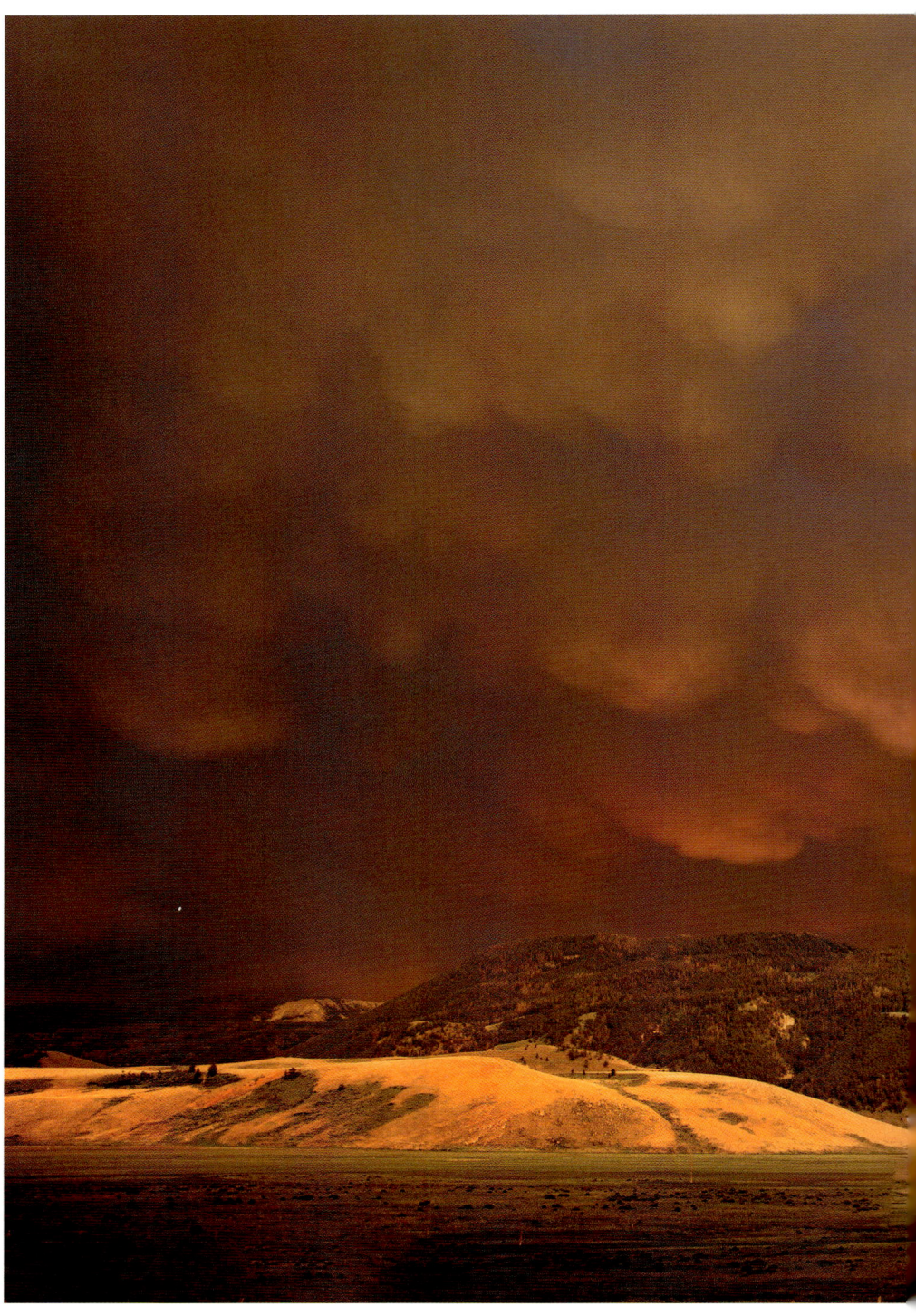

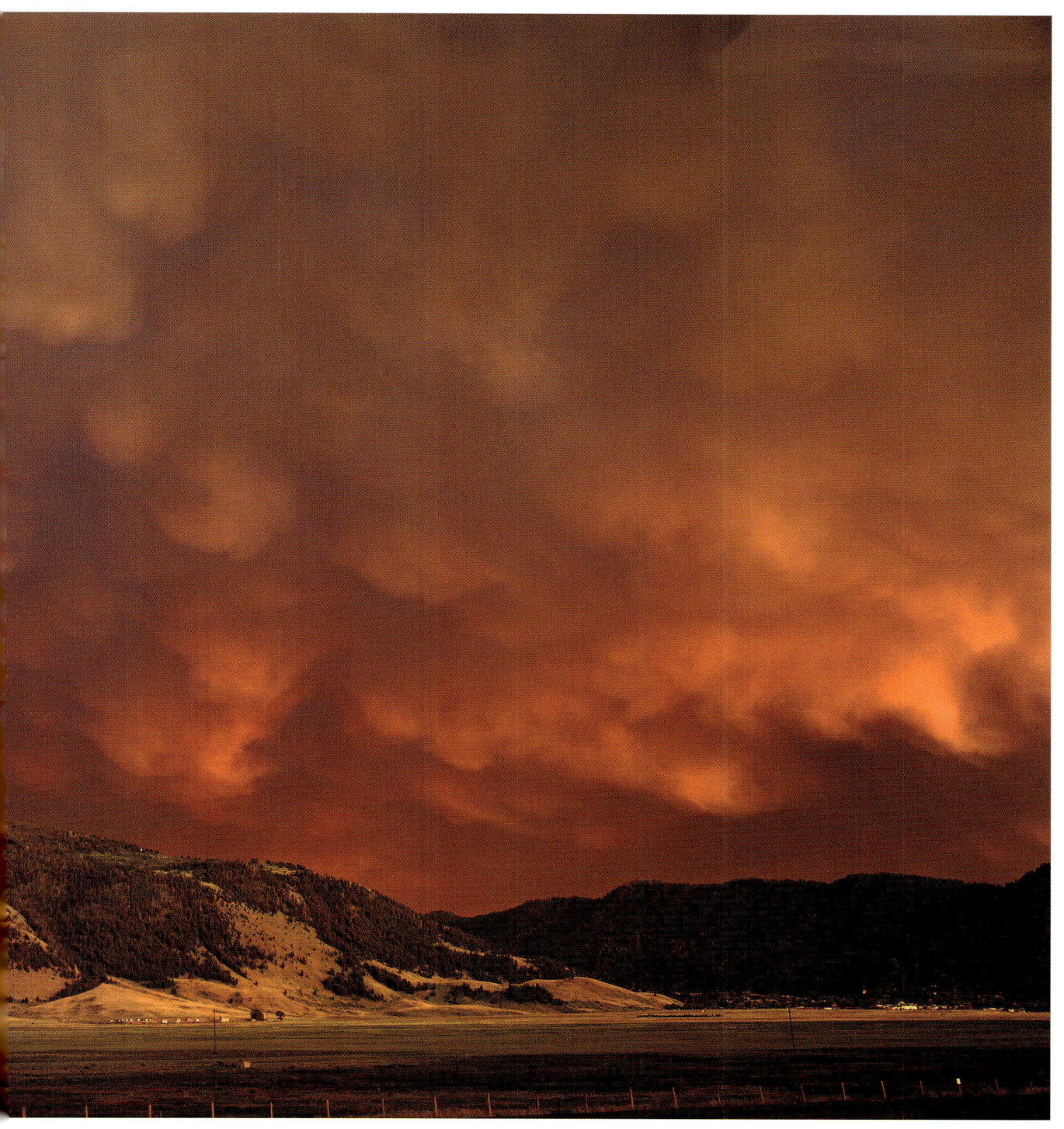

Last light of the day, National Elk Refuge

Flat Creek

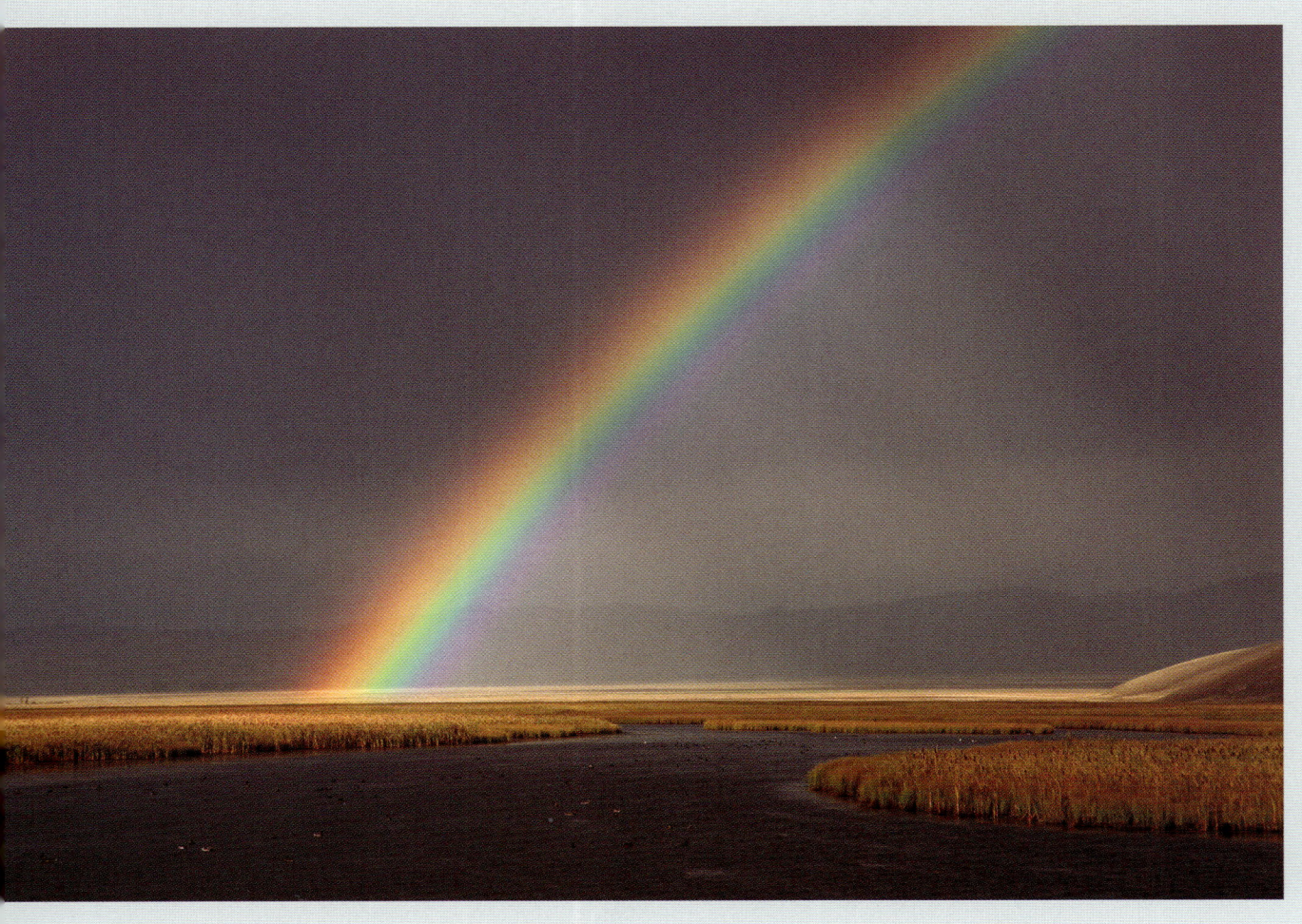

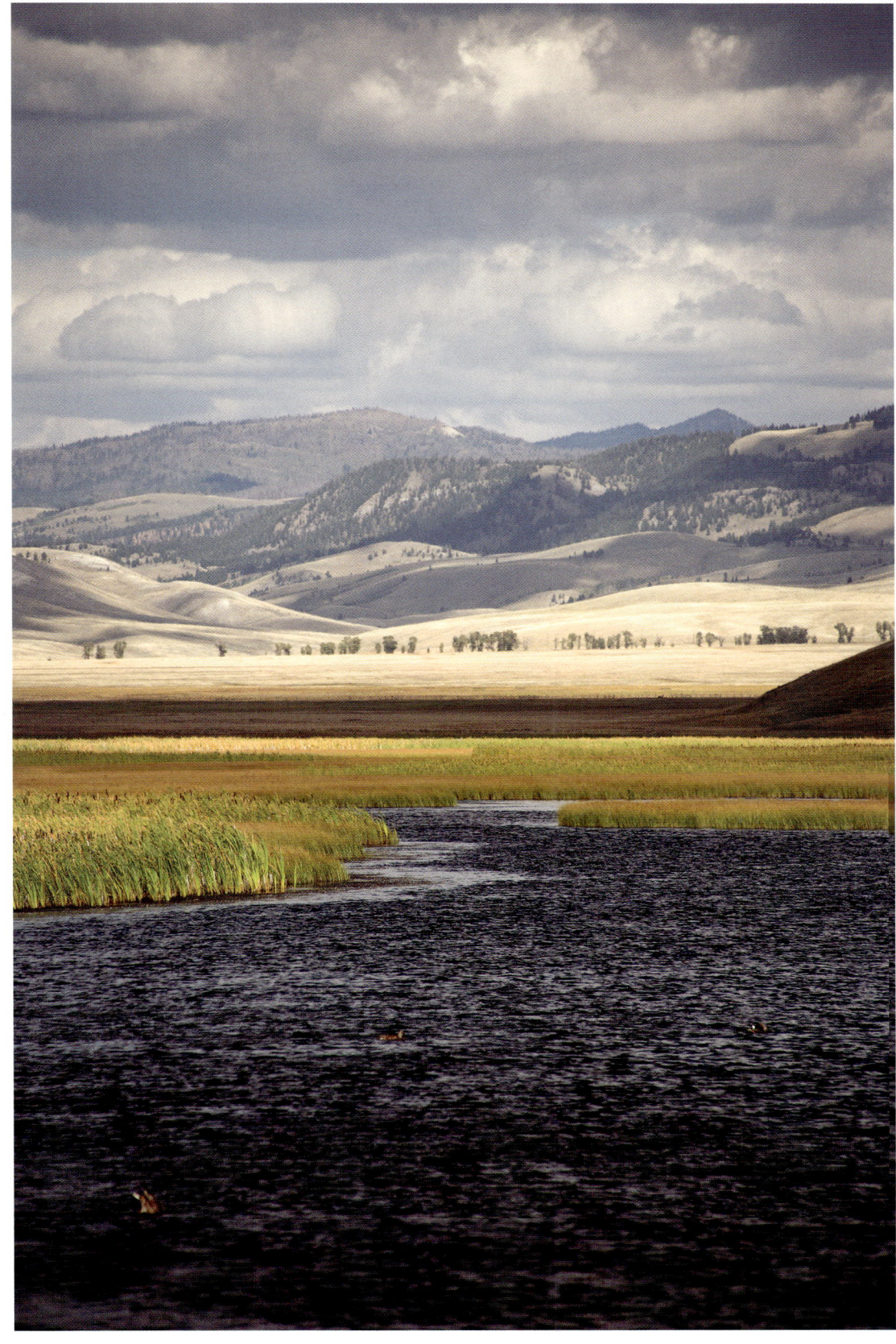

The Three Tetons
Thomas Moran, 1895
The White House Historical Association
966.591.1

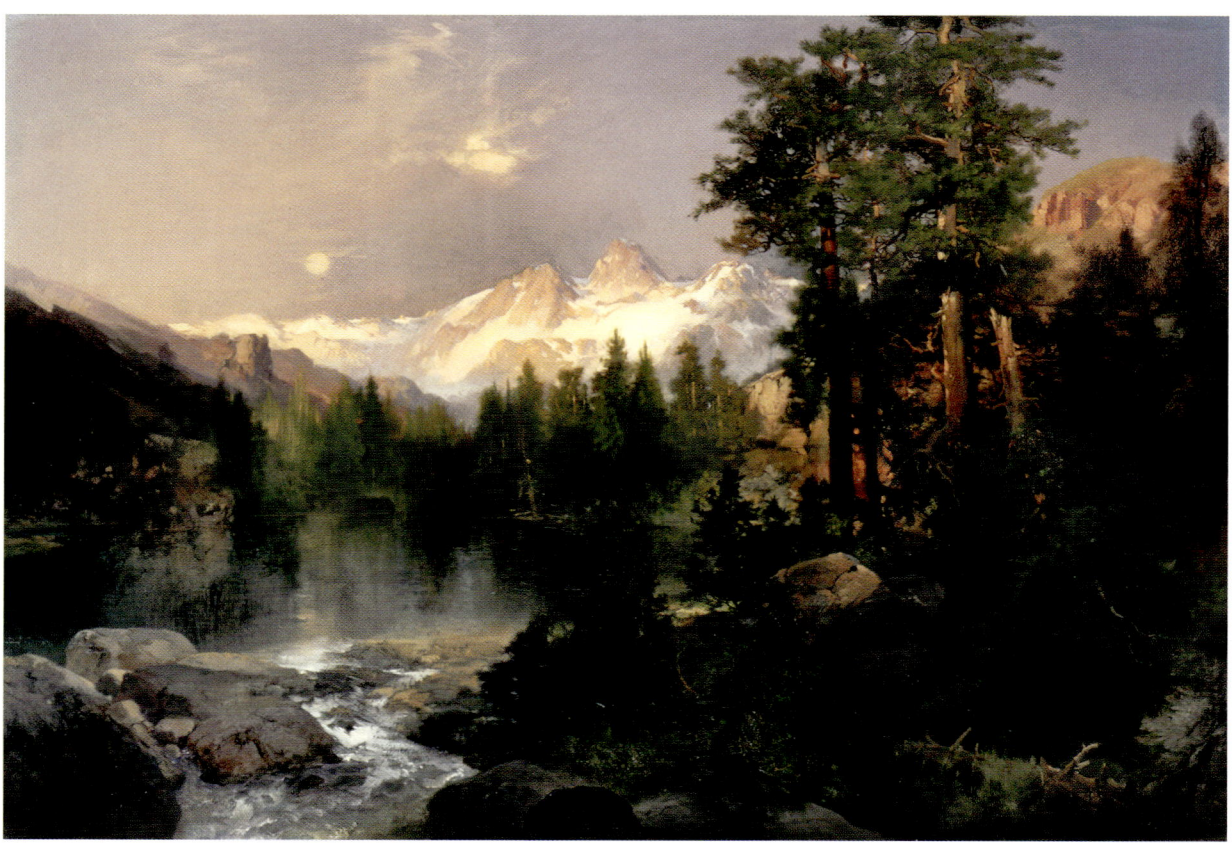

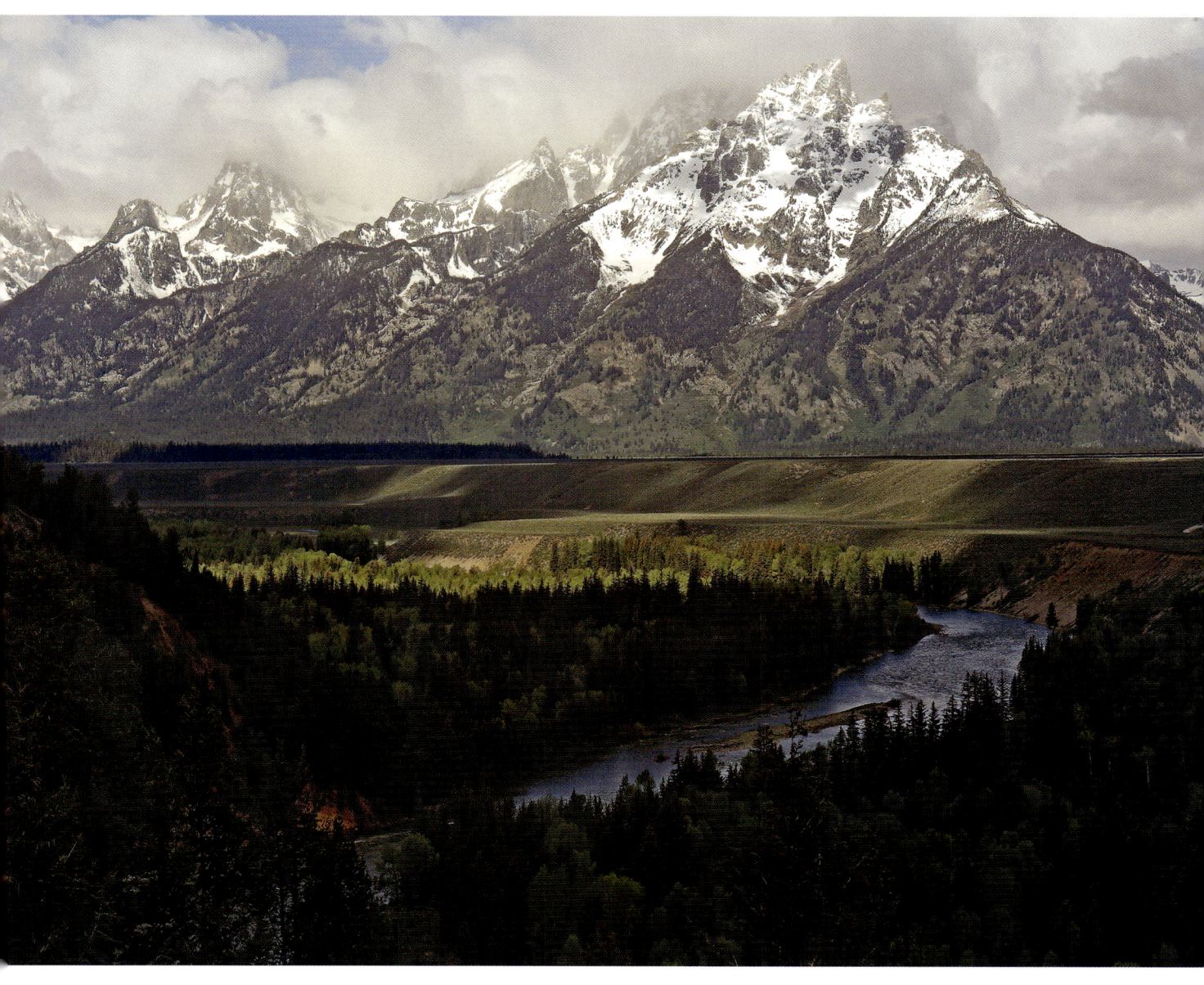

The Tetons–Snake River
Ansel Adams, 1942

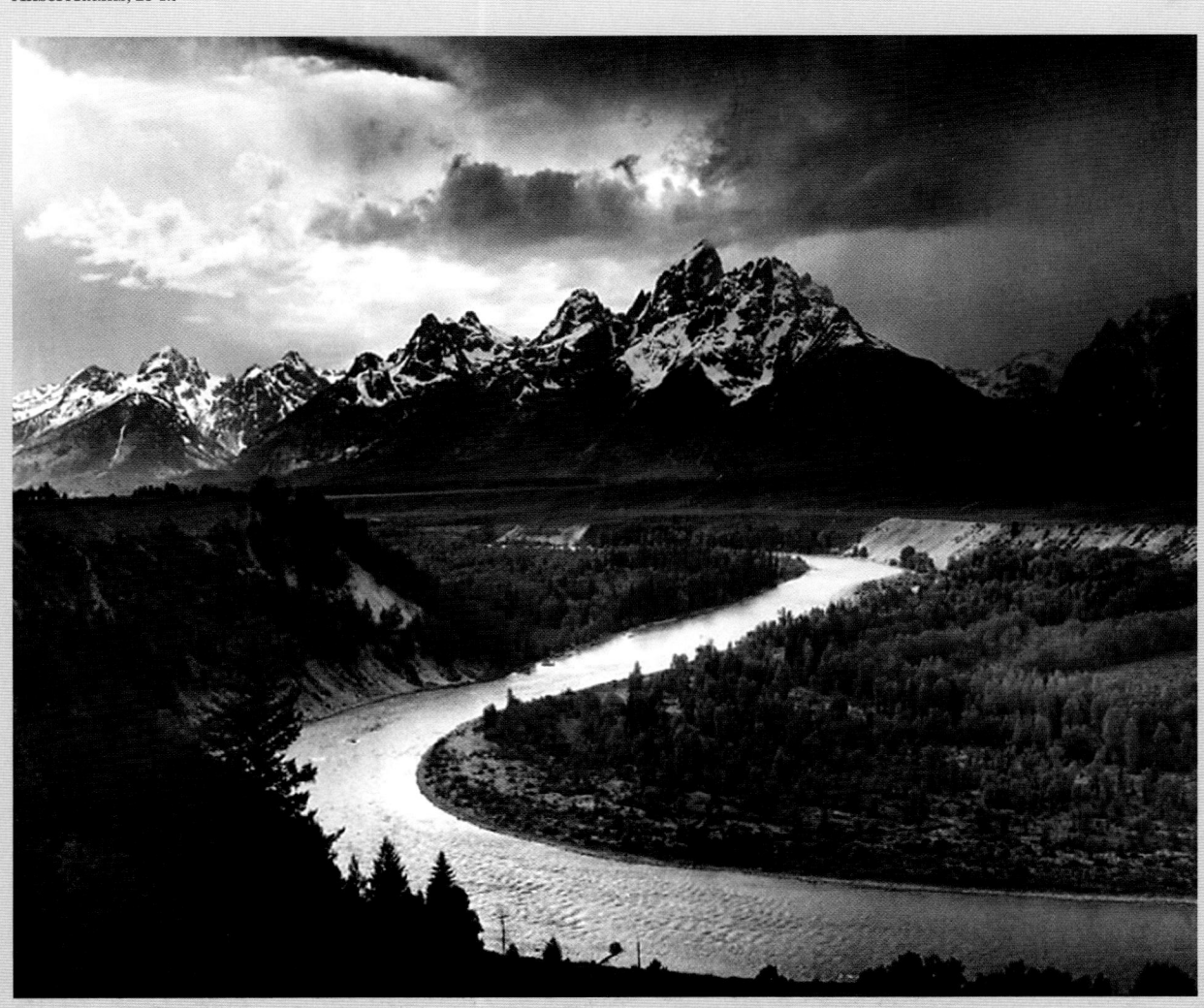

WILLOW FLATS

"A glorious night. Moon in the full, but empty stomachs. We are now far enough away from the lakes to be clear of the clouds of vapor and local snowstorms. Our camp is about at a central point with reference to obtaining a view of the Tetons, and at a distance of fifteen miles from the nearest part of the range. The moonlight view was one of unspeakable grandeur. There are twenty-two summits in the line, all of them mighty mountains, with the gleaming spire of Mount Hayden [Grand Teton] rising in a pinnacle above all.

"There are no foothills to the Tetons. They rise suddenly in rugged majesty from the rock-strewn plain. Masses of heavy forests appear on the glacial debris and in parks behind the curves of the lower slopes, but the general field of vision is glittering glaciated rock. The soft light floods the great expanse of the valley, the winding silvery river and the resplendent deeply carved mountain walls."

LIEUTENANT GUSTAVUS C. DOANE
Expedition of 1876-1877

Twilight on the Tetons and Jackson Lake
at Willow Flats

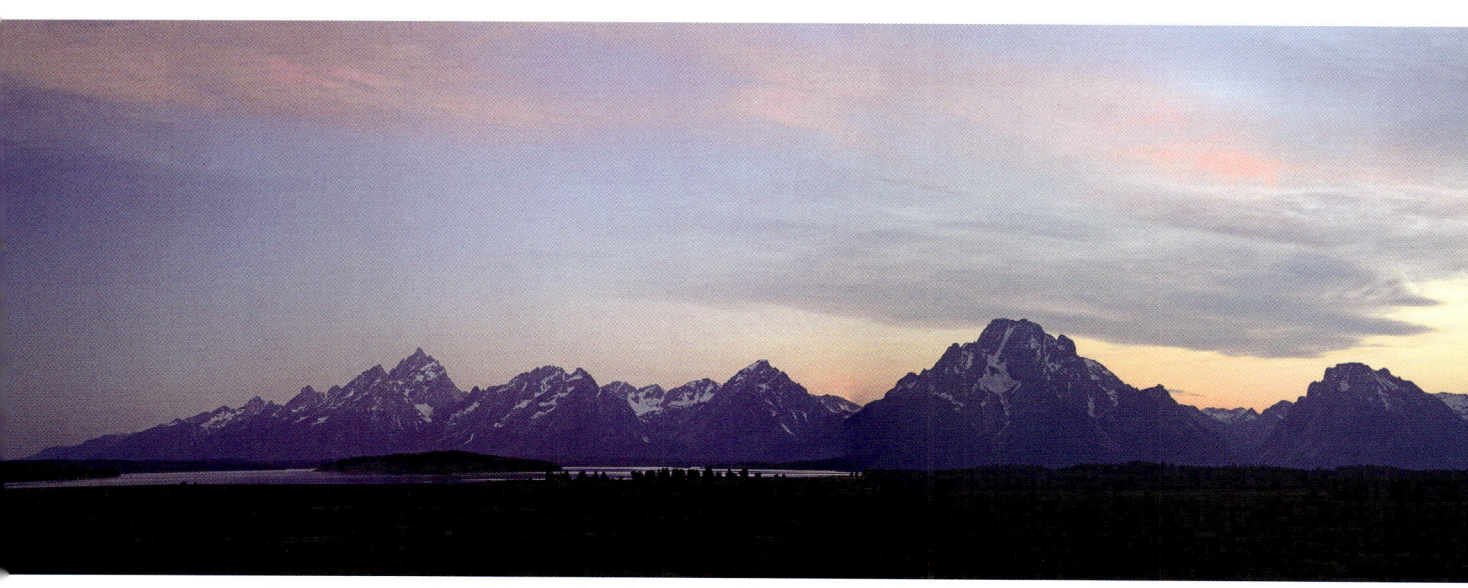

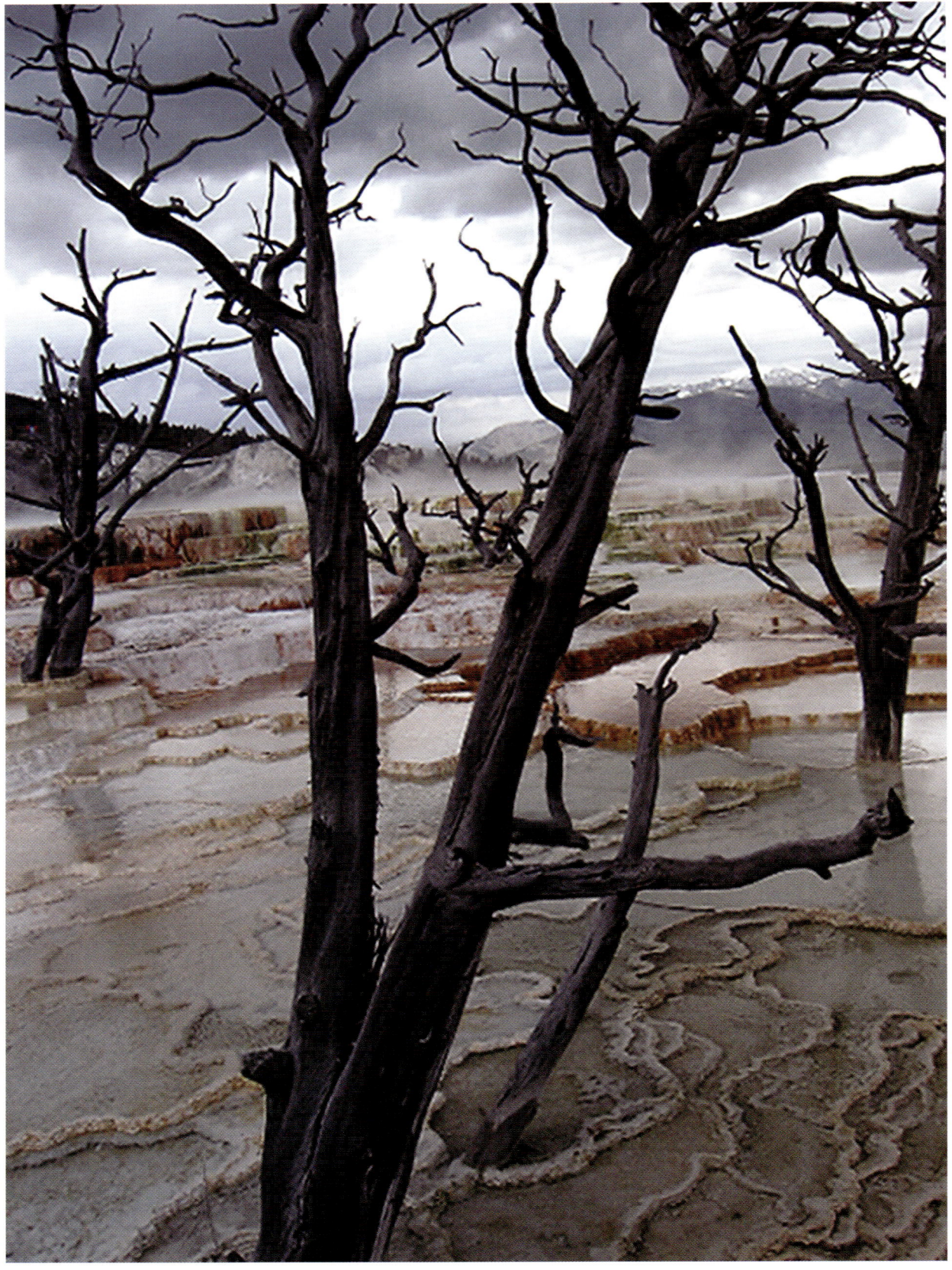

"My narrations today have excited great wonder, and I cannot resist the conviction that many of my auditors believe that I have 'drawn a long bow' in my descriptions. I am perfectly free to acknowledge that this does not surprise me. It seems a most natural thing for them to do so; for, in the midst of my narrations, I find myself almost as ready to doubt the reality of the scenes I have attempted to describe as the most skeptical of my listeners. They pass along my memory like the faintly defined outlines of a dream. And when I dwell upon their strange peculiarities, their vastness, their variety, and the distinctive features of novelty which mark them all, so entirely out of the range of all objects that compose the natural scenery and wonders of this continent, I who have seen them can scarcely realize that in those far-off recesses of the mountains they have existed so long in impenetrable seclusion, and that hereafter they will stand foremost among the natural attractions of the world. Astonishment and wonder become so firmly impressed upon the mind in the presence of these objects, that belief stands appalled, and incredulity is dumb. You can see Niagara, comprehend its beauties, and carry from it a memory ever ready to summon before you all its grandeur. You can stand in the valley of the Yosemite, and look up its mile of vertical granite, and distinctly recall its minutest feature; but amid the canyon and falls, the boiling springs and sulphur mountain, and, above all, the mud volcano and the geysers of the Yellowstone, your memory becomes filled and clogged with objects new in experience, wonderful in extent, and possessing unlimited grandeur and beauty. It is a new phase in the natural world; a fresh exhibition of the handiwork of the Great Architect; and, while you see and wonder, you seem to need an additional sense, fully to comprehend and believe."

NATHANIEL PITT LANGFORD
The Discovery of Yellowstone Park: Journal of the Washburn Expedition to the Yellowstone and Firehole Rivers in the Year 1870, 1905

Mammoth Hot Springs

SOURCES

Clawson, Calvin, journalist, 1871

Colter, John, explorer

Doane, Lieutenant Gustavus C., *Yellowstone Expedition of 1870*

Doane, Lieutenant Gustavus C., *Expedition of 1876-1877*

Folsom, David of the Folsom-Cook-Peterson Expedition, 1869

Folsom-Cook-Peterson Expedition, 1869

Hague, Arnold, geologist and assistant to Walter Weed, 1911

Hayden, Ferdinand Vandeveer, *Preliminary Reports*, 1871

Hayden, Ferdinand Vandeveer, *Preliminary Report of the United States Geological Survey of Montana and Portions of Adjacent Territories*, 1872

Hayden, Ferdinand Vandeveer, *The Yellowstone National Park, and the Mountain Regions of Portions of Idaho, Nevada, Colorado, and Utah*, 1876

Henderson, G.L., park interpreter, 1888

Holmes, William Henry, geologist with the F.V. Hayden survey, 1872

Hunter, Louis Richard, park visitor, 1888

Kipling, Rudyard, *American Notes*, 1891

Langford, Nathaniel Pitt, "Interesting Data of the Trip, from Notes Furnished by Hon. N. P. Langford," *Helena Daily Herald*, September 26, 1870

Langford, Nathaniel Pitt, *The Discovery of Yellowstone Park*, 1905

Lystrup, Herbert, naturalist, 1957

Moran, Thomas, painter

Muir, John, "The Yellowstone National Park," *The Atlantic Monthly*, April 1898

Norton, Harry J., *Wonderland Illustrated*, 1873

Parkinson, Edward S., *Wonderland; or, Twelve weeks in and out of the United States*, 1894

Peale, Albert Charles, geologist with the F.V. Hayden survey, 1872

Rollins, Alice Wellington, *The Three Tetons*, 1887

Roosevelt, President Theodore

Russell, Osborne, *Journal of a Trapper-Nine Years in the Rocky Mountains (1834-1843)*, 1921

Saltus, J. Sanford, *A Week in the Yellowstone*, 1895

Stoddard, Charles Warren, author

Strahorn, Robert Edmund, journalist, 1881

Trumball, Walter, *Overland Monthly*, June 1871

Washburn, General Henry D., *Explorations in a New and Wonderful Country*, 1870

Weed, Walter, *Notebook Volume III*, 1883

Wineman, Mode, author

Wingate, George Wood, *Through the Yellowstone Park on Horseback*, 1886

Winser, Henry J., *The Yellowstone National Park-A Manual for Tourists*, 1883

Wylie, W.W., *Yellowstone*, 1882

"Boiling," *The Brooklyn Daily Eagle*, August 15, 1883

"The Yellowstone Park: Wonders of the Mammoth Hot Springs Basin," *The New York Times*, July 22, 1883

INDEX